MASSACHUSETTS INSTITUTE OF TECHNOLOGY
Department of Architecture & Platform for a permanent modernity

MIT CAMBRIDGE USA

Archiprix INTERNATIONAL

HunterDouglas AWARDS

ARCHITECTURE + URBAN DESIGN + LANDSCAPE ARCHITECTURE

www.archiprix.org WORLDS BEST GRADUATION PROJECTS

2011

010 PUBLISHERS, ROTTERDAM 2011

TOW AWAY
ZONE

PREVIOUS WINNERS

ARCHIPRIX INTERNATIONAL MONTEVIDEO 2009

09_deeply rooted tree / *Pasqual Herrero Vicent, Spain*
Deviational Space / *Espen Folgerø, Norway*
MAJA TURG: a market for Tallinn / *Max Rink, Netherlands*
MArchitecture / *Ryo Kitazawa, Japan*
Markerpark / *Sander Lap, Netherlands*
Metropolitan Markets / *Matthew Murphy, Scotland*
Regional Museum of Mine Site: North of Chile / *Tomás García de la Huerta, Chile*
Tokyo Littoral Art Center / *Kazuaki Hattori, Japan*

ARCHIPRIX INTERNATIONAL SHANGHAI 2007

The Urban Design Of Xiagang District In Xiamen / *HongXiwen, Gao Junning, China*
Duo / *Hiroyuki Suga, Japan*
School_handmade in Bangladesh / *Anna Heringer, Austria*
Dredge Landscape Park / *Gerwin de Vries, Alexander Herrebout, Netherlands*
2 in 1 / *Karimullin Timur, Dmitry Kulikov, Russia*
GS0306 / *Michael Smith, Robert Garita, Costa Rica*
Agro-Industrial School of Rengo / *Alberto Fernandez, Chile*

ARCHIPRIX INTERNATIONAL GLASGOW 2005

Continuum Body of Urban memory / *Kiyoaki Takeda, Japan*
OsakaUrbanStation / *Jens Mehlan, Jörg Hugo, Austria*
A Prospective Vision of the Mouth of the Tammerkoski / *Paula Julin, Finland*
Micro-urbanism for Macrodensity. Beijing 700x800 for 35000 / *Marcella Campa, Stefano Avesani, Italy*
Silo-wet: a Laboratory for the Urban Body / *Emilie Bédard, Canada*
M SPA / *Martin Cobas, Federico Gastambide, Uruguay*

ARCHIPRIX INTERNATIONAL ISTANBUL 2003

Dealing with Vierhaven / *Harm Timmermans, Netherlands*
HK/WD2/WWhub / *Thomas Raynaud, France*
Postagriculture / *Achim Menges, England*
Wave Garden / *Yusuke Obuchi, United States*

ARCHIPRIX INTERNATIONAL ROTTERDAM 2001

Decommissioning and re-use of oil and gas platforms in the Adriatic Sea / *Danilo Romani and Daniela Brascugli, Italy*
Emerging of the Form: Ecotouristic Project in Mejallones / *Veronica Carvajal Cortes, Chile*
Floating City / *Jamie Bromley, England*
Hotel in the desert, Israel / *Alexandra Stage, Austria*
House for a fiction character, James Bond / *Jose Paulo Ferreira Rodrigues, Portugal*
IMAGEbuilding / *Jarrik Ouburg, Serge Schoemaker, the Netherlands*
Rotterdam Central Station / *Adam Collaitz Kurdahl, Denmark*
Transtation / *Atsuo Okishio, Japan*
Urban Pause - depth of air - / *Lars R van Es, USA*

Edited by: Henk van der Veen / *Text editing:* George Hall
Minutes of the jury meeting: Marina van Bergen / *Images of projects:* Designers of the projects
Photos: Henk van der Veen / *Design:* Antenna-Men, Rotterdam
Printed by: Die Keure, Bruges

This publication has been made possible through the support of: **Hunter Douglas**

Stichting Archiprix www.archiprix.org
010 Publishers, Rotterdam www.010.nl

ISBN 978-90-6450-754-0

CONTENTS

PROJECTS SECTION

CLYDEPORT
CASINO

Archiprix International in the USA

At university I learned that architects had the task of improving the world with their ideas and designs. After graduating, I also found out that, to do so, you have to understand the world to some extent. That is no simple chore. In the quest for understanding, contact with third parties plays a major role. Exchanges of ideas form the designer, whether it involves the type of city people want to live in or the degree of necessity of well-designed public space. The search for an answer as to why solutions in other countries and continents are sometimes so different, compared to the context in which we ourselves are engaged, sharpens the mind.

Archiprix International has proven to be an excellent stage for such an exchange of ideas. This is now the sixth edition of Archiprix International. The initiative was taken by Archiprix Nederland ten years ago. In 2001, Rotterdam was the Cultural Capital of Europe, which provided the impulse for the organization of the first Archiprix International. After Europe (Rotterdam in 2001, Istanbul in 2003, Glasgow in 2005), Asia (Shanghai in 2007) and South America (Montevideo in 2009), Archiprix International has now arrived in North America. As such, a long-cherished wish has been fulfilled. In conjunction with one of the most eminent universities in the US, the Massachusetts Institute of Technology (MIT), the current edition of Archiprix International now looks out on the world from a different base.

This splendid book is full of extraordinary and inspiring graduation plans. It focuses on the results of an enormous quantity of conceptual and designing work by a great many young architects, urban planners and landscape architects from all over the world. Archiprix International 2011 has received a record number of submitted projects coming from a growing amount of participating universities and architectural programs. In addition, the number of participants in the international workshop has again increased this time around.

During the workshop, organized in conjunction with the MIT, newly-graduated designers from all over the world will work together intensively for a week long; they will hold discussions, establish contacts, and forge international networks for life.

Archiprix and main sponsor Hunter Douglas have enabled this exceptional event, this inspirational week in which the exchange of knowledge and ideas is the key activity. It is also a moment that simultaneously provides a global view of the top of global architectural education. And after this week, when everyone has returned home, the discussions will continue – bilaterally between the participants, and also on the Archiprix International website, the stage on which ideas are exchanged, plans are examined, and on which universities can present themselves by means of their excellent graduates.

Madeleine Maaskant
Chairwoman of the Archiprix Foundation

85
86
88
110
84
114
106
105
115
116
120
103
124
104
102
98
126
90
92
100
127
97
128
89
96
129
75
82
78
74
76
70
53
65
56
54
72
73
64
58
68
67
66
59
62
60

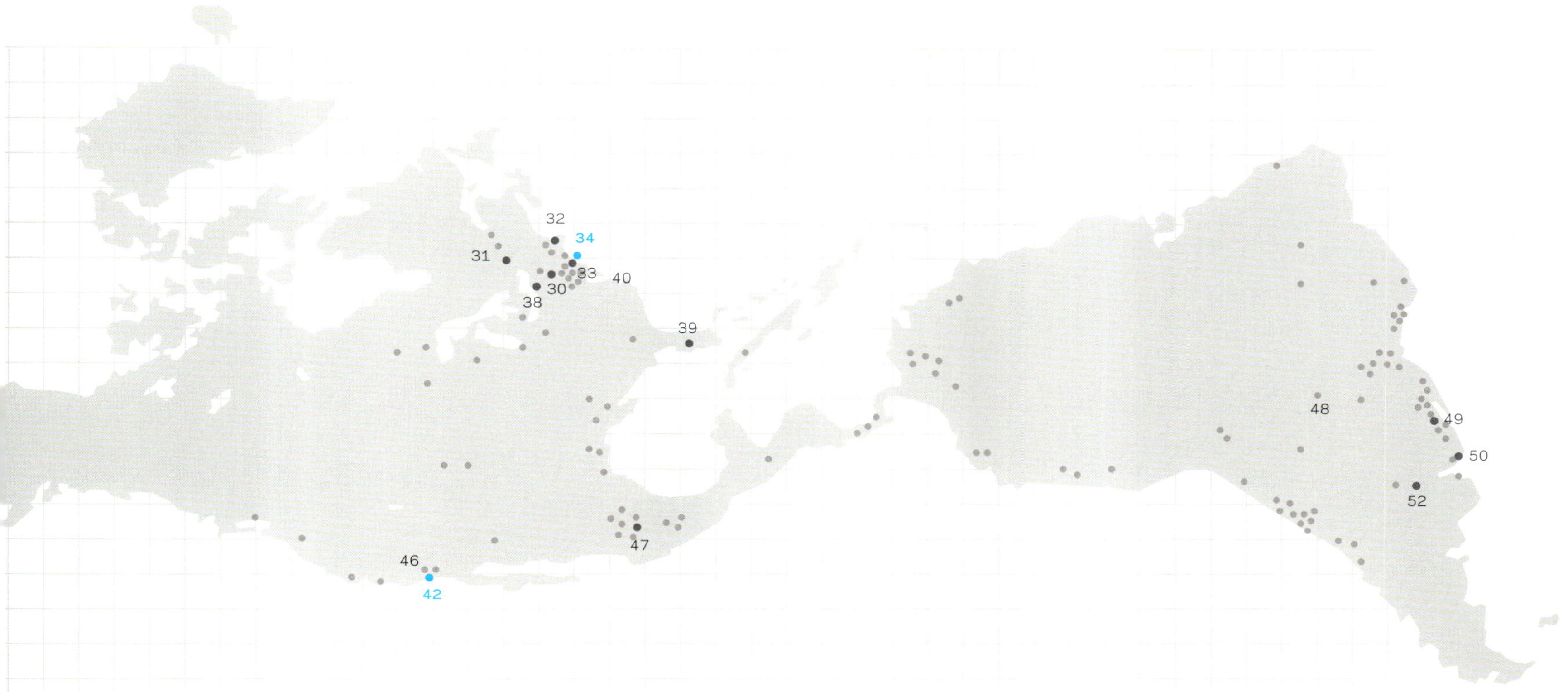
32
34
31
33
40
30
38
39
46
42
47
48
49
50
52

NORTH AMERICA

University of New Mexico, Albuquerque, United States
Iowa State University, Ames, United States
University of Massachusetts, Amherst, Amherst, United States
University of Michigan, Ann Arbor, Ann Arbor, United States*
University of Texas at Arlington, Arlington, United States
Georgia Institute of Technology, Atlanta, United States
Auburn University, Auburn, United States*
University of Texas at Austin, Austin, United States
Morgan State University, Baltimore, United States
Louisiana State University, Baton Rouge, United States*
Southern University and A & M College, Baton Rouge, United States
University of California, Berkeley, United States***
Andrews University, Berrien Springs, United States
Virginia Polytechnic Institute & State University, Blacksburg, United States
Boston Architectural College, Boston, United States
Massachusetts College of Art and Design Boston, United States*
Northeastern University, Boston, United States
Wentworth Institute of Technology, Boston, United States
Montana State University, Bozeman, United States
Roger williams University, Bristol, United States
Pratt Institute, Brooklyn, United States*
State University of New York at Buffalo, Buffalo, United States**
Woodbury University, Burbank, United States
Harvard University, Cambridge, United States**
Massachusetts Institute of Technology, Cambridge, United States**
University of Illinois at Urbana - Champaign, Champaign, United States**
University of North Carolina at Charlotte, Charlotte, United States
University of Virginia, Charlottesville, United States*
Illinois Institute of Technology, Chicago, United States
The School of the Art Institute of Chicago, Chicago, United States*
University of Illinois at Chicago, Chicago, United States
University of Cincinnati, Cincinnati, United States
Clemson University, Clemson, United States***
University of Maryland, College Park, United States
Texas A & M University, College Station, United States
The Ohio State University, Columbus, United States*
University of Miami, Coral Gables, United States
University of Colorado at Denver, Denver, United States**
University of Detroit Mercy, Detroit, United States*
University of Oregon, Eugene, United States*
North Dakota State University, Fargo, United States*
University of Arkansas, Fayetteville, United States*
Florida Atlantic University, Fort Lauderdale, United States
University of Florida, Gainesville, United States**
Hampton University, Hampton, United States
University of Hawaii at Manoa, Honolulu, United States
Rice University, Houston, United States*
University of Houston, Houston, United States*
Cornell University, Ithaca, United States*
Kent State University, Kent, United States
University of Tennessee, Knoxville, United States
University of Louisiana at Lafayette, Lafayette, United States*
University of Kansas, Lawrence, United States
University of Kentucky College of Architecture, Lexington, United States*
University of Nebraska Lincoln, Lincoln, United States
Southern California Institute of Architecture SCI-Arc, Los Angeles, United States*
University of California, Los Angeles, United States*
University of Southern California, Los Angeles, United States*
Texas Tech University, Lubbock, United States*
Kansas State University, Manhattan, United States
Southern Polytechnic State University, Marietta, United States*
The University of Memphis, Memphis, United States*
Florida International University, Miami, United States
University of Wisconsin-Milwaukee, Milwaukee, United States*
University of Minnesota, Minneapolis, United States*
Mississippi State University, Mississippi State, United States
University of Idaho, Moscow, United States
Ball State University, Muncie, United States
Yale University, New Haven, United States***
Tulane University, New Orleans, United States*
City College of the City University of N.Y., New York, United States
Columbia University, New York, United States**
New York Institute of Technology, New York, United States*
Parsons The New School for Design, New York, United States*
Pratt Institute, New York United States*
The Cooper Union, New York, United States**
New Jersey Institute of Technology, Newark, United States
Auburn University, Rural Studio, Newbern, Alabama, United States*
University of Oklahoma, Norman, United States
Norwich University, Northfield, United States
University of Notre Dame, Notre Dame, United States
California College of Arts & Crafts Architecture & Design, Oackland, United States
Miami University, Oxford, United States*
Drexel University, Philadelphia, United States
Philadelphia University, Philadelphia, United States*
Temple University, Philadelphia, United States
University of Pennsylvania, Philadelphia, United States*
University of Pennsylvania, Philadelphia, United States*
Carnegie Mellon University, Pittsburgh, Pennsylvania, United States*
California State Polytechnic University, Pomona, United States
Portland State University, Portland, United States
University of Oregon. Portland Program, Portland, United States*
Prairie View A & M University, Prairie View, United States
Princeton University, Princeton, United States**
Rhode Island School of Design, Providence, United States*
Washington State University, Pullman, United States
North Carolina State University, Raleigh, United States*
Louisiana Tech University, Ruston, United States**
University of Utah, Salt Lake City, United States
The University of Texas at San Antonio, San Antonio, United States*
NewSchool of Architecture and Design, San Diego, United States
California Polytechnic State University, San Luis Obispo, United States*
Savannah College of Art and Design, Savannah, United States**
Frank Lloyd Wright School of Architecture Scottsdale, United States
University of Washington, Seattle, United States
Lawrence Technological Institute, Southfield, United States
Drury College, Springfield, United States
Washington University in St. Louis, St. Louis, United States**
Oklahoma State University, Stillwater, United States
University of Connecticut, Storrs, United States
Syracuse University, Syracuse, United States
Florida A & M University, Tallahassee, United States
University of South Florida, Tampa, United States
Arizona State University, Tempe, United States
Rensselaer Polytechnic Institute, Troy, United States
University of Arizona, Tucson, United States*****
Tuskegee University, Tuskegee, United States
The Pennsylvania State University, University Park, United States*
Catholic University of America, Washington D.C., United States
Howard University, Washington D.C., United States
University of Hartford, West Hartford, United States

SOUTH AMERICA

Universidad de Belgrano, Buenos Aires, Argentina
Universidad de Buenos Aires, Buenos Aires, Argentina
Universidad de Palermo, Buenos Aires, Argentina**
Universidad Nacional de General Sarmiento, Buenos Aires, Argentina
Universidad Torcuato Di Tella, Buenos Aires, Argentina
Universidad Nacional de General San Martín, Buenos Aires - San Martín, Argentina
Universidad Católica de Córdoba, UCC, Córdoba, Argentina*
Universidad Nacional de Cordoba, Córdoba, Argentina*
Universidad Nacional de La Plata, La Plata, Argentina
Univ. Nacional de la Rioja, La Rioja, Argentina
Universidad Nacional de Mar del Plata, Mar del Plata, Argentina
Universidad de Mendoza, Mendoza, Argentina
Universidad Nacional del Nordeste, Resistencia, Chaco., Argentina*
Universidad Nacional de Rosario, Rosario, Argentina*
Universidad Nacional de San Juan, San Juan, Argentina
Universidad Nacional de Tucumán, San Miguel de Tucumán, Argentina
Universidad Nacional del Litoral, Santa Fé, Argentina*
Universidad Nacional de Tucuman, Tucuman, Argentina
Universidad Mayor de San Simon, Cochabamba, Bolivia*
Universidad Privada del Valle, Cochabamba, Bolivia**
Universidad Nuestra Senora de La Paz, La Paz, Bolivia**
Univ. Autónoma Gabriel René Moreno, Santa Cruz de la Sierra, Bolivia
Universidad Privada de Santa Cruz, Santa Cruz de la Sierra, Bolivia***
Univ. Autónoma Juan Misael Saracho, Tarija, Bolivia*
Universidade de Alfenas, Alfenas, Brazil
Universidade da Região da Campanha-URCAMP, Bage, Brazil
Universidade do Vale do Itajaí, Balneário Camboriú, Brazil*
Faculdade de Arquitetura de Barra do Pirai, Barra Do Pirai, Brazil
Universidade Estadual Paulista - UNESP, Bauru, Brazil
União das Escolas Superiores, Belem, Brazil
Universidade Federal do Para-UFPA, Belem, Brazil
Centro Universitário Metodista Izabela Hendrix, Belo Horizonte, Brazil
Pontificia Universidade Catolica de Minas Gerais-PUC/M, Belo Horizonte, Brazil***
Universidade Federal de Minas Gerais - UFMG, Belo Horizonte, Brazil***
Universidade Regional de Blumenau - FURB, Blumenau, Brazil***
Universidade de Brasilia-UnB, Brasilia, Brazil**
Centro Universitário de Brasilia - UniCEUB, Brasilia-DF, Brazil*
Pontificia Universidade Catolica de Campinas-PUCCA, Campinas, Brazil
Universidade Estadual de Campinas, Campinas, Brazil
Centro de Ensino Superior Prof. Plinio M. dos santo, Campo Grande, Brazil
Universidade Federal de Mato Grosso do Sul, Campo Grande, Brazil*
Universidade Luterana do Brasil, Canoas, Brazil**
Pontifícia Universidade Católica do Paraná-PUCPR, Curitiba, Brazil**
Universidade Federal do Parana-UFPR, Curitiba, Brazil***
Universidade Positivo, Curitiba, Brazil**
Universidade Tuiuti do Paraná, Curitiba, Brazil*
Sistema Barddal de Ensino, Florianópolis, Brazil
Universidade Federal de Santa Catarina-UFSC, Florianopolis, Brazil***
Universidade Federal do Ceara-UFC, Fortaleza, Brazil*
União das Faculdades Francanas-UNIFRAN, Franca, Brazil
PUC GOIÁS - Pontifícia Universidade Católica de Goiás, Goiania, Brazil**
Universidade de Guarulhos-UNG, Guarulhos, Brazil
Universidade Federal da Paraiba-UFPb, Joao Pessoa, Brazil
Universidade Federal de Juiz de Fora, Juiz de Fora (MG), Brazil
Centro Universitário Univates, Lajeado, Brazil*
Centro de Estudos Superiores de Londrina, Londrina, Brazil
Universidade estadual de Londrina-UEL, Londrina, Brazil*
Universidade Federal de Alagoas -UFAL, Maceio, Brazil
Universidade de Marilia-UNIMAR, Marilia, Brazil
Universidade Estadual de Maringá, Maringá, Brazil*
Universidade Braz Cubas-UBC, Mogi Das Cruzes, Brazil**
Universidade de Mogi das Cruzes, Mogi Das Cruzes, Brazil
Universidade Federal do Rio Grande do Norte-UFRN, Natal, Brazil
Universidade Federal Fluminense-UFF, Niteroi, Brazil*
Universidade Feevale, Novo Hamburgo, Brazil*
Universidade Catolica de Pelotas-UCPEL, Pelotas, Brazil
Universidade Federal de Pelotas-UFPEL, Pelotas, Brazil*
Centro Universitário Metodista - IPA, Porto Alegre, Brazil
Centro Universitário Ritter dos Reis, Porto Alegre, Brazil**
Pontifícia Universidade Católica do Rio Grande do Sul - PUCRS, Porto Alegre, Brazil*
Universidade Federal do Rio Grande do Sul-UFRGS, Porto Alegre, Brazil***
Universidade Católica de Pernambuco - UNICAP, Recife, Brazil*
Universidade Federal de Pernambuco-UFPE, Recife, Brazil****
Centro Universitário Moura Lacerda, Ribeirao Preto, Brazil
Unidades Escolares da Instituição Moura Lacerda-IML, Ribeirao Preto, Brazil*
Centro Universitário Metodista Bennett, Rio De Janeiro, Brazil*
Faculdade s Integradas Silva e Souza, Rio De Janeiro, Brazil
Pontifícia Universidade Católica do Rio de Janeiro, PUC-Rio, Rio de Janeiro, Brazil*
UniSUAM, Rio de Janeiro, Brazil
Universidade Federal do Rio de Janeiro, Rio De Janeiro, Brazil****
Universidade Gama Filho, Rio De Janeiro, Brazil
Universidade Santa Ursula, Rio De Janeiro, Brazil
Universidade Federal da Bahia-UFBA, Salvador, Brazil
Univ. Federal de Santa María, Santa María. Rs, Brazil
Universidade Catolica de Santos, Santos, Brazil
Centro Universitário Central Paulista - UNICEP, Sao Carlos, Brazil
Univ. De Sao Paulo, Sao Carlos, Brazil
Faculdades Integradas Dom Pedro II, São José do Rio Preto, Brazil
Univezrsidade do vale de Paraiba-UNIVAP, Sao Jose Dos Campos, Brazil
Universidade do Vale do Rio dos Sinos-UNISINOS, Sao Leopoldo, Brazil***
Escola da Cidade, Sao Paulo, Brazil
Faculdade de Belas Artes de São Paulo, Sao Paulo, Brazil
Fundação A. Penteado-FAAP, Sao Paulo, Brazil*
Universidade Anhembi Morumbi, Sao Paulo, Brazil*
Universidade de Sao Paulo - USP, Sao Paulo, Brazil******
Universidade Estadual Paulista "Julio Mesquita Filho"-UNESP, Sao Paulo, Brazil**
Universidade Mackenzie, Sao Paulo, Brazil
Universidade S. Judas Tadeu-USJT, Sao Paulo, Brazil*
Universidade de Taubate-UNITAU, Taubate, Brazil
Universidade de Uberaba-UNIUBE, Uberaba, Brazil
Universidade Federal de Viçosa-UFV, Viçosa, Brazil*
Universidade Federal do Espirito Santo-UFES, Vitoria, Brazil
Universidad Católica del Norte, Antofagasta, Chile****
Universidad Concepción, Concepcion, Chile
Universidad del Bio-bio, Concepcion, Chile***
Universidad del Desarollo, Concepcion, Chile*
Universidad de La Serena, La Serena, Chile**
Universidad los Lagos, Osorno, Chile
Pontificia Universidad Católica de Chile PUCC, Santiago, Chile****
Universidad Arcis, Santiago, Chile
Universidad Central, Santiago, Chile**
Universidad Ciencias de la Informatica, santiago, Chile
Universidad de Chile, Santiago, Chile**
Universidad de Chile, Santiago, Chile*
Universidad de la Républica, Santiago, Chile
Universidad de las Americas, Santiago, Chile
Universidad de Santiago, Santiago, Chile*
Universidad de Santiago de Chile, Santiago, Chile*
Universidad del Desarrollo, Santiago, Chile**
Universidad Diego Portales, Santiago, Chile*
Universidad Finia Terrae, Santiago, Chile*
Universidad Mayor, Santiago, Chile**
Universidad Nacional Andres Bello, Santiago, Chile
universidad tecnologica metropolitana, Santiago, Chile*
Universidad UNIACC, Santiago, Chile*
University of Talca, Talca, Chile**
Universidad Autonoma, Temuco, Chile
Universidad de Temuco, Temuco, Chile
Universidad del Valparaíso, Valparaiso, Chile
Universidad Tecnica Santa Maria, Valparaiso, Chile
Universidad Catolica de Valparaíso, Vina Del Mar, Chile
Universidad de las Americas, Viña del Mar, Chile**
Universidad de Vina del Mar, Vina Del Mar, Chile
Universidad Marítima de Chile, Vina Del Mar, Chile***
Corporacion Universitaira de la Costa, Barranquilla, Colombia
Universidad Autonoma del Caribe, Barranquilla, Colombia***
Universidad del Atlantico, Barranquilla, Colombia*
Pontificia Universidad Javeriana, Bogota, Colombia****
Universidad Antonio Narino, Bogota, Colombia**
Universidad Catolica de Colombia, Bogota, Colombia
Universidad de América, Bogota, Colombia
Universidad de la Gran Colombia, Bogota, Colombia
Universidad de La Salle, Bogota, Colombia****
Universidad de Los Andes, Bogota, Colombia***
Universidad Jorge Tadeo Lozano-Bogota, Bogota, Colombia******
Universidad Nacional de Colombia, Bogotá, Colombia*
Univeridad Piloto de Colombia, Bogota, Colombia***
Universidad Santo Tomas, Bucaramanga, Colombia*
Universidad del Valle. Facultad de Artes Integradas, Cali, Colombia*
Universidad San Buenaventura, Cali, Colombia***
Universidad Jorge Tadeo Lozano, Cartagena, Colombia*
Universidad Francisco de Paula Santander, Cúcuta, Colombia
Universidad Nacional de Colombia, Manizales, Colombia**
Santo Tomás Medellín, Colombia
Universidad Nacional de Colombia, Medellin, Colombia***
Universidad Pontificia Bolivariana, Medellin, Colombia****
Corporacíon Universitaria del Sinu, Monteria, Colombia
Fundacion Universitaria de Popayan, Popayan, Colombia**
universidad tecnologica del choco diego luis cordoba, Quibdó, Colombia*
Universidad de Cuenca, Cuenca, Ecuador
UEES, Universidad de Especialidades Espiritu Santo, Guayaquil, Ecuador**
Universidad Catolica Santiago de Guayaquil, Guayaquil, Ecuador*
Universidad Estatal de Guayaquil, Guayaquil, Ecuador*
Universidad Laica Vicente Rocafuerte de Guayaquil, Guayaquil, Ecuador
Universidad Particular de Loja, Loja, Ecuador*
Universidad Eloy Alfaro de Manabi, Manta, Ecuador
Pontificia Universidad Catolica del Ecuador, Quito, Ecuador****
Universidad Central del Ecuador, Quito, Ecuador**
Universidad Escuela Politecnica Javeriana del Ecuador, Quito, Ecuador
Universidad Internacional Sek, Quito, Ecuador
Universidad San Francisco de Quito, Quito, Ecuador***
Univ. Católica "Nuestra Señora de la Asunción", Asunción, Paraguay
Univ. Nacional de Asunción Facultad de Arquitectura, Asunción, Paraguay
Universidad Nacional San Agustin de Arequipa, Arequipa, Peru**
Universidad Particular de Chiclayo, Chiclayo, Peru*
Universidad San Pedro, Chimbote-Perù, Peru
Universidad Nacional de San Antonio Abad del Cusco, Cusco, Peru
Universidad Nacional del Centro del Perú, Huancayo, Peru
Universidad Nacional Pedro Ruiz Gallo, Lambayeque, Peru
Pontificia Universidad Católica del Perú, Lima, Peru**
Universidad Feminina del Sagrado Corazon, Lima, Peru*
Universidad Nacional de Ingenieria, Lima, Peru*
Universidad Nacional Federico Villarreal, Lima, Peru
Universidad Peruana de Ciencias Aplicadas, Lima, Peru***
Universidad Ricardo Palma, Lima, Peru****
Universidad Nacional de Piura, Piura, Peru
Universidad Nacional Jorge Basadre Grohmann, Tacna, Peru
Universidad Antenor Orrego Trujillo, Trujillo, Peru
Universidad Cesar Vallejo, Trujillo, Peru
Universidad Privada Antenor Orrego, Trujillo, Peru
Universidad de la Republica - Uruguay, Montevideo, Uruguay*****
Universidad ORT Uruguay, Montevideo, Uruguay*
Colegio de Ingenieros, Arquitectos y Afines, Caracas, Venezuela
Universidad Central de Venezuela, Caracas, Venezuela
Universidad Jose Maria Vargas, Caracas, Venezuela**
Universidad de Zulia, Maracaibo, Venezuela*
Universidad Rafael Urdaneta, Maracaibo, Venezuela
Universidad de los Andes, Merida, Venezuela*
Universidad Nacional Experimental del Tachira.UNET, San Cristobal, Venezuela**
Universidad Simón Bolívar, Sartenejas, Venezuela***

OCEANIA

Adelaide University, Adelaide, Australia*
University of South Australia, Adelaide, Australia
University of Canberra, Belconnen, Australia
Queensland University of Technology, Brisbane, Australia
University of Queensland, Brisbane, Australia
University of Technology Sydney, Broadway, Australia
The University of Newcastle, Callaghan, Australia*
The University of Western Australia, Crawley, Australia*
Deakin University, Geelong, Australia*
University of Tasmania, Launceston, Australia
F.D.U. (Faraday Deakin University), Melbourne, Australia
Oceanic Polytechnic, Melbourne, Australia
Royal Melbourne Institute of Technology, Melbourne, Australia
University of Melbourne, Melbourne, Australia****
University of Newcastle, Newcastle NSW, Australia*
Curtin University of Technology, Perth, Australia
University of New South Wales, Sydney, Australia****
University of Sydney, Sydney, Australia*
Monash University, Victoria, Australia
Unitec New Zealand, Auckland, New Zealand*
University of Auckland, Auckland, New Zealand***

Victoria University of Wellington, Wellington, New Zealand*
Papua New Guinea University of Technology, Lae, Papua New Guinea

ASIA

Erevan Architectural & Building Institute, Erevan, Armenia
Azerbaijan University of Architecture and Construction, Baku, Azerbaijan
University of Bahrain, Sakhir, Bahrain
Bangladesh University of Engineering & Technology, Dhaka, Bangladesh**
Brac University, Dhaka, Bangladesh*
North South University, Dhaka, Bangladesh*
University of Asia Pacific, Dhaka, Bangladesh
Baotou University of Iron and Steel Technology, Baotou, Inner Mongolia, China
Inner Mongolia University of Technology, Baotou, Inner Mongolia, China
Beijing Forestry University, Beijing, China
Beijing Institute of Civil Engineering and Architecture, Beijing, China**
Beijing Jiaotong University, Beijing, China*
Beijing University of Technology, Beijing, China*
China Central Academy of Fine Arts Beijing, China*
North China University of Technology, Beijing, China
Tsinghua University, Beijing, China*
Jilin Architectural and Civil Engineering Institute, Changchun, Jilin, China
Sichuan University, Chengdu, Sichuan, China*
Southwest Jiaotong Universities, Chengdu, Sichuan, China
Chongqing University, Chongqing, China*
Logistical engineering university of PLA, Chongqing, China
Dalian University, Dalian, China
Liaoning Technical University, Fuxin, Liaoning, China
Fuzhou universities, Fuzhou, Fujian, China*
Guangzhou University, Guangzhou, China
South China University of Technology, Guangzhou, China*
Guizhou University of Architecture & Industry, Guiyang, Guiyang, China
Hebei university of engineering, Handan, China
China Academy of Art, Hangzhou, Zhejiang, China
Zhejiang University, Hangzhou, Zhejiang, China*
Zhejiang University of Technology, Hangzhou, Zhejiang, China
Harbin Institute of Technology, Harbin, Heilongjiang, China
Harbin Institute of Technology, Harbin, Heilongjiang, China*
Harbin University of Civil Engineering and Architecture, Harbin, Heilongjiang, China
Shijiazhuang railway institute, Hebei, China*
Anhui University of Architecture & Industry, Hefei, Anhui, China
Hefei University of Technology, Hefei, Anhui, China
Chinese University of Hong Kong, Hong Kong, China***
city universities of Hong Kong, Hong Kong, China
the universities of Hong Kong, Hong Kong, China
Inner Mongolia University of Technology, Huhe HaoteInner Mongolia, China
Centra south universities railway campus, Hunan, Changsha, China
Hunan University, Hunan, Changsha, China*
Shandong universities, Iinan, Shandong, China
Yangzhou universities, Jiangsu, Jiangsu, China
Shandong Jianzhu University, Jinan, Shandong, China**
Shenyang Institute of Technology, Jingzhou, Hubei, China
Yangtze universities, Jingzhou, Hubei, China*
Henan university, Kaifeng, Henan, China
Kunming University of Science and Technology, Kunming, Yunnan, China*
Yunnan Gongye Daxue, Kunming, Yunnan, China
Lanzhou University of Technology, Lanzhou,Gansu, China
Dalian University of Technology, Liaoning, China
East China Jiaotong University, Nanchang, Jianx, China
Nanchang universities, Nanchang, Jianx, China
Nanjing University, Nanjing, Jiangsu, China*
Nanjing University of Technology, Nanjing, Jiangsu, China
PLA University of Science and Technology, Nanjing, Jiangsu, China
Southeast University, Nanjing, Jiangsu, China
Guangxi universities, Nanning, Guangxi, China*
Qingdao technology universities, Qingdao, Shandong, China
Huaqiao University, Quanzhou, China
Shanghai Jiao Tong University, Shanghai, China
Shanghai Jiaotong University, Shanghai, China
Shanghai University, Shanghai, China*
Tongji University, Shanghai, China*
Shenyang Jianzhu University, Shenyang, China
Shenyang Jianzhu University, Shenyang, China
Shenyang University, Shenyang, China
Shenzhen University, Shenzhen, Guangzhou, China**
Hebei University of Science & Technology, Shijiazhuang, China
Suzhou universities of science & technology Suzhou, China**
Taiyuan University of Technology, Taiyuan, China
Hunan University of science & technology, Tanxiang, China
Hebei University of Technology, Tianjin, China
Tianjin University, Tianjin, China
Tianjin Urban Construction Institute, Tianjin, China
Huazhong University of Science and Technology, Wuhan, Hubei, China**
Hubei University of Technology, Wuhan, Hubei, China
Wuhan University, Wuhan, Hubei, China
WuHan University of Technology, Wuhan, Hubei, China
Xinjiang University, Wulumuqi, China
Chang'an University, Xi'an, Shanxi, China
Xi'an Jiaotong University, Xi'an, Shanxi, China
Xian University of Architecture and Technology, Xi'an, Shanxi, China**
Xiamen University, Xiamen, Fujian, China***
Northwestern Polytechnical university, Xi'an, Shanxi, China*
China University of Mining technology, Xuzhou, Jiangsu, China
Yantai University, Yantai, Shandong, China
Hebei Institute of Architecture and civil Engineering, Zhangjiakou, China
Henan universities of technology, Zhengzhou, Henan, China
North China University of Water Conservancy and Electric Power, Zhengzhou, Henan, China
Zhengzhou University, Zhengzhou, Henan, China
Georgian Technical University, Tbilisi, Georgia***
Tbilisi State Academy of Fine Arts, Tbilisi, Georgia****
University of Hong Kong, Hong Kong, Hong Kong**
Centre for Environmental Planning & Technology CEPT University, Ahmedabad, India****
College of Engg. of Technology, Akola, India
G.S. Mandal's Marathwada Institute of Technology, Aurangabad, India
Jawaharlal Nehru Engg. College, Aurangabad, India*
Bangalore Institute of Technology, Bangalore, India
Bms College of Engineering, Bangalore, India
Dayananda Sagar College of Engg., Bangalore, India
Ms Ramaiah Institute of Tech., Bangalore, India
R.V. College Engineering, Bangalore, India
University Visvesvaraya College of Engineering, Bangalore, India
Sri RAm Murti Smarak College of Engineering & Technology, Bareilly, India
Giani Zail Singh College of Engg. & Technology, Bathinda, India*
Karnataka Law Society's Gogte Institute of Technology, Belgaum, India***
Vishweshwaraiah Technological university, Belgaum, India
Malik Sandal Institute of Art & Architecture, Bijapur, India
Anna University, Chennai, India**
Bharat Institute of Science & Technology, Chennai, India
Dr. M.G.R.Engg.College, Chennai, India
Hindustan University of Technology, Chennai, India
MEASI Academy of Architecture, Chennai, India*
S.R.M Engineering College, Chennai, India*
Sathyabhama Engineering College, Chennai, India
Pravara Rural College of Architecture, district Ahmednagar, India
Goa College of Architecture, Goa, India
Apeejay Institute of Technology, Greater Noida [U.P.], India
Malnad College of Engineering, Hassan, India
Pradesh School of Planning & Architecture, Hyderabad, India
Sri Venkateswara College of Architecture, Hyderabad, India
IPS Academy School of Architecture, Indore, India
Stapathya Kala Bhawab Society's School of Architecture, Indore, India
Indian Institute of Technology, Karagpur, India
D.Y.. Patil College of Engg. & Technology, Kolpahur, India
Shri Prince Shivaju Maratha Boarding, Kolpahur, India
Jayakrsnti Shikshn Prasarak Mandal's Shivaji Architecture Colleg, Latur, India
Faculty of Architecture, Lucknow, India
Manipal Institute of Technology, Manipal, India*
Academy of Architecture, Mumbai, India*
I.E. Society's College of Architecture, Mumbai, India
Kamala Raheja Vidyanidhi, Mumbai, India
L.S. Raheja School of Architecture, Mumbai, India
LBHSS Trust's College of Architecture, Mumbai, India
Mumbai University, Mumbai, India**
Mumbai University, Mumbai, India
Rizvi College of Architecture, Mumbai, India
Priyadarshini College of Engg. & Architecture, Nagpur, Nagpur, India*
Visvesvaraya National Institute of Technology, Nagpur, India
M.V.P'S College of architecture, Nashik, Nashik, India*
Bharati Vidyapeeth's College of Architecture, Navi Mumbai, India
Dr. D.Y. Patil College of Architecture, Navi Mumbai, India***
Pillai's College of Architecture, Navi Mumbai, India
Jamia Millia Islamia, New Delhi, India*
School of Planning & Architecture, New Delhi, India***
TVB School of Habitat Studies, New Delhi, India**
Vastu Kala Academy, New Delhi, India
Mahatma Education Society's, New Panvel, India
BKPS College of Architecture, Pune, India
Bharati Vidyapeeth's College of Architecture, Pune, India
M.C.E.Society's Allana College of Architecture Pune, India
Maharshi Krve Stree Shiksan Santha's Dr. Bhanuben Nanavati, Pune, India*
Maratwhada Mitra Mandal's College of Architecture, Pune, India*
STES, Sinhgad Technical Education Society, Pune, India
Vivekanand Institute of Technology's, Pune, India
Saurastra University, Rajkot, India*
Birla Institute of Technology, Ranchi, India
Shri V.B. Patil Trust's College of Architecture, Sangli, India
CSI Institute of Technology, Secunderabad, India
Shri Siddeshwar Shikshan Mandal's College of Architecture, Solapur, India
Veer Narmad South Gujarat University, Surat, India****
Periyar Maniammai College of Technology for Women, Thanjavur, India
National Institute Of technology,Tiruchchirappalli, Tiruchchirappalli, India
M.S. University of Baroda, Vadodara, India
Arvindbhai Patel Institute of Environmental Design, Vallabh Vidya Nagar, India***
Sardar Vallabh Bhai Patel Institute of Technology, Vasad, India
Andhra University, Vishakapatnam, India
Institut Teknologi Bandung, Bandung, Indonesia
Parahyangan Catholic University, Bandung, Indonesia*
University of Indonesia, Depok, Indonesia*
Bina Nusantara, Jakarta, Indonesia*
Trisakti University, Jakarta, Indonesia*
Gadjah Mada, Jogyakarta, Indonesia
Brawijaya University, Malang, Indonesia
Diponegoro University, Semarang, Indonesia*
Petra Christian University, Surabaya, Indonesia**
Universitas Kristen Duta Wacana, Yogyakarta, Indonesia
Islamic Azad University of Khorasgan, Isfahan, Iran*
Shiraz Azad University, Shiraz, Iran
IUST, Tehran, Iran
Shahid Beheshti University, Tehran, Iran
Tehran university, Tehran, Iran**
Mosul, Mosul, Iraq*
Technion - Israel Institute of technology, Haifa, Israel**
The Neri Bloomfield School of Design (WIZO haifa), Haifa, Israel****
Bezalel Academy of Art and Design, Jerusalem, Israel**
Tel Aviv University, Tel Aviv, Israel*
Aichi Sangyo University, Aichi, Japan
Chubu University, Aichi, Japan*
Konan Women's Junior College, Aichi, Japan
Nagoya University of Arts, Aichi, Japan
Toyohashi University of Technology, Aichi, Japan
Toyota National College of Technology, Aichi, Japan
Akita Polytechnic College, Akita, Japan
Hachinohe Institute of Technology, Aomori, Japan
Chiba Institute of Technology, Chiba, Japan*
Chiba Institute of Technology, Chiba, Japan
Chiba Polytechnic College, Chiba, Japan
Chiba University, Chiba, Japan
Chiba University, Chiba, Japan*
Nihon University, Chiba, Japan*
Nihon University, Chiba, Japan
Nihon University, Chiba, Japan
Nihon University, Chiba, Japan
Science University of Tokyo, Chiba, Japan
Science University of Tokyo, Chiba, Japan
Fukui University, Fukui, Japan
Fukui University of Technology, Fukui, Japan
Ariake National College of Technology, Fukuoka, Japan
Fukuoka University, Fukuoka, Japan
Kinki University, Fukuoka, Japan
kinki University, Fukuoka, Japan
Kinki University, Fukuoka, Japan
Kurume Institute of Technology, Fukuoka, Japan
Kyushu Institute of Design, Fukuoka, Japan
Kyushu Sangyo University, Fukuoka, Japan
Kyushu University, Fukuoka, Japan
Kyushu University, Fukuoka, Japan*
Nishinippon Institute of Technology, Fukuoka, Japan
Towa University, Fukuoka, Japan
Koriyama Women's University, Fukushima, Japan
Nihon University, Fusushima, Japan
Gifu National College of Technology, Gifu, Japan
Gifu Women's University, Gifu, Japan
Maebashi City College of Technology, Gunma, Japan
Fukuyama Polytechnic College, Hiroshima, Japan
Fukuyama University, Hiroshima, Japan
Hiroshima Institute of Technology, Hiroshima, Japan
Hiroshima Institute of Technology, Hiroshima, Japan
Hiroshima University, Hiroshima, Japan
Kinki University, Hiroshima, Japan
Kure National College of Technology, Hiroshima, Japan
Dohoto University Junior College Division, Hokkaido, Japan
Dohto University, Hokkaido, Japan
Dohto University, Hokkaido, Japan
Hokkaido Polytechnic College, Hokkaido, Japan
Hokkaido Tokai University, Hokkaido, Japan
Kushiro National College of Technology, Hokkaido, Japan
Muroran Institute of Technology, Hokkaido, Japan
Akashi College of Technology, Hyogo, Japan
Tsukuba College of Technology, Ibaraki, Japan
University of Tsukuba Ibaraki, Japan
University of Tsukuba Ibaraki, Japan*
University of Tsukuba, Ibaraki, Japan
Ishikawa National College of Technology, Ishikawa, Japan***
Kanazawa Institute of Technology, Ishikawa, Japan
Kanazawa Institute of Technology, Ishikawa, Japan
Kanazawa University, Ishikawa, Japan
Kanazawa University, Ishikawa, Japan
Kagawa Polytechnic College, Kagawa, Japan
Daiichi University, Kagoshima, Japan
Kagoshima University, Kagoshima, Japan
Keio University, Kanagawa, Japan
Nihon University, Kanagawa, Japan
Nihon University, Kanagawa, Japan
Polytechnic University, Kanagawa, Japan
Tokai University, Kanagawa, Japan*****
Tokyo Institute of Polytechnics, Kanagawa, Japan*
Meij University, Kawasaki, Japan
Kyushu Kyoritsu University, Kitakyushu, Japan
Kobe Design University, Kobe, Japan*
Kobe University, Kobe, Japan
Kumamoto Institute of Technology, Kumamoto, Japan
Kumamoto Institute of Technology, Kumamoto, Japan
Kumamoto University, Kumamoto, Japan
Kyushu Tokai University, Kumamoto, Japan
Yatsushiro National College of Technology, Kumamoto, Japan
Kyoto Institute of Technology, Kyoto, Japan***
Kyoto Prefectural University, Kyoto, Japan
Kyoto Seika University, Kyoto, Japan*
Kyoto University, Kyoto, Japan*
Kyoto University, Kyoto, Japan
Kyoto University, Kyoto, Japan
Kyoto University, Kyoto, Japan
Kyoto University, Kyoto, Japan
Kyoto University, Kyoto, Japan
Mie University, Mie, Japan
Mie University, Mie, Japan
Miyagi National College of Technology, Miyagi, Japan
Miyagi Polytechnic College, Miyagi, Japan
Miyakonojo National College of Technology Miyazaki, Japan
Shinshu University, Nagano, Japan
Nagasaki Institute of Applied Science, Nagasaki, Japan
Nagasaki University, Nagasaki, Japan
Daido Institute of Technology, Nagoya, Japan
Meijo University, Nagoya, Japan
Nagoya City University, Nagoya, Japan
Nagoya Feminine Culture Junior College, Nagoya, Japan
Nagoya Institute of Technology, Nagoya, Japan
Nagoya University, Nagoya, Japan****
Sugiyama Jogakuen University, Nagoya, Japan*
Nara Women's University, Nara, Japan
Nagaoka University of Technology, Niigata, Japan
Niigata Institute of Technology, Niigata, Japan
University of Niigata Niigata, Japan
Nippon Bunri University, Oita, Japan
Oita University, Oita, Japan
Sanyo Gakuen College, Okayama, Japan
Okinawa Prefectural University of Arts, Okinawa, Japan
University of Ryukyus, Okinawa, Japan*
Heian Jogakuin University, Osaka, Japan
Kansai University, Osaka, Japan
Kinki University, Osaka, Japan*
Osaka City University, Osaka, Japan
Osaka City University, Osaka, Japan
Osaka Institute of Technology, Osaka, Japan
Osaka Institute of Technology Junior College, Osaka, Japan**
Osaka Sangyo University, Osaka, Japan
Osaka University, Osaka, Japan
Osaka University, Osaka, Japan
Osaka University of Arts, Osaka, Japan
Osaka University of Arts, Osaka, Japan
Setsunan University, Osaka, Japan
Saga University, Saga, Japan
Kyoei Gakuen Junior College, Saitama, Japan
Nippon Institute of Technology, Saitama, Japan
Nippon Institute of Technology, Saitama, Japan
Shibaura Institute of Technology, Saitama, Japan
Toyo University, Saitama, Japan
Hokkai-Gakuen University, Sapporo, Japan
Hokkaido Institute of Technology, Sapporo, Japan
Hokkaido Tokai University, Sapporo, Japan
Hokkaido University, Sapporo, Japan
Hokkaido University, Sapporo, Japan
Sapporo School of the Arts, Sapporo, Japan
College of Science and Technology, Tohoku, Sendai, Japan
Tohoku Institute of Technology, Sendai, Japan
Tohoku Institute of Technology, Sendai, Japan
Tohoku University, Sendai, Japan***
Shiga Polytechnic College, Shiga, Japan
The University of Shiga Prefecture, Shiga, Japan
Ashikaga Institute of Technology, Tochigi, Japan
Oyama National College of Technology, Tochigi, Japan
Atomi Gakuen Junior College, Tokyo, Japan
Hosei University, Tokyo, Japan*
Japan Women's University, Tokyo, Japan
Kogakuin University, Tokyo, Japan**
Kogakuin University, Tokyo, Japan**
Kokushikan University, Tokyo, Japan
Kyoritsu Women's University, Tokyo, Japan
Musashi Institute of Technology, Tokyo, Japan
Musashino Art University, Tokyo, Japan
Nihon University, Tokyo, Japan
Nihon University, Tokyo, Japan
Ochanomizu University, Tokyo, Japan
Science University of Tokyo, Tokyo, Japan
Shibaura Institute of Technology, Tokyo, Japan
Shibaura Institute of Technology, Tokyo, Japan
Showa Women's University, Tokyo, Japan
Tama Art University, Tokyo, Japan
Tokyo Denki University, Tokyo, Japan
Tokyo Institute of Technology, Tokyo, Japan
Tokyo Institute of Technology, Tokyo, Japan
Tokyo Institute of Technology, Tokyo, Japan
Tokyo Kasei Gakuin University, Tokyo, Japan
Tokyo Metropolitan University, Tokyo, Japan
Tokyo Metropolitan University, Tokyo, Japan
Tokyo Polytechnic College, Tokyo, Japan
Tokyo University of Agriculture, Tokyo, Japan
Tokyo University of the Arts, Tokyo, Japan***
Tokyo Zokei University, Tokyo, Japan
University of Tokyo, Tokyo, Japan
University of Tokyo, Tokyo, Japan
University of Tokyo, Tokyo, Japan
University of Tokyo, Tokyo, Japan**
Waseda University, Tokyo, Japan
Waseda University, Tokyo, Japan
Yonago National College of Technology, Tottori, Japan**
Aichi Institute of Technology, Toyota, Japan
Utsunomiya University, Utsunomiya, Japan
Wakayama University, Wakayama, Japan
Tohoku University of Art and Design, Yamagata, Japan
Tokuyama College of Technology, Yamaguchi, Japan
Kanagawa University, Yokohama, Japan***
Kanto Gakuin University, Yokohama, Japan
Kanto Gakuin University, Yokohama, Japan
Kanto Gakuin University, Yokohama, Japan****
Tokyo Institute of Technology, Yokohama, Japan
Tokyo Institute of Technology, Yokohama, Japan
Tokyo Institute of Technology, Yokohama, Japan
Yokohama National University, Yokohama, Japan*

Al al-Bayt University, Al mafraq, Jordan
al balqa applied university, albalqa, Jordan
University of Jordan, Amman, Jordan[****]
Jordan University of Science and Technology, Irbid, Jordan
Université Agraire d'Akmola, Akmola, Kazakhstan
Kazakh Leading Academy of Architecture and Civil Engineering, Almaty, Kazakhstan[***]
Kazakh National Technical University named after K.I. Satpayev, Almaty, Kazakhstan[*]
D.Serikbaev East-Kazakhstan State Technical University, Oust Kamenogorsk, Kazakhstan[*]
Ajou University, Ajou, Korea, South
Chonbuk National University, Chonbuk, Korea, South
Chonbuk Sanup University, Chonbuk, Korea, South
Chongju University, Chongju, Korea, South
Chosun University, Chosun, Korea, South
Chungang University, Chungang, Korea, South
Chungbuk National University, Chungbuk, Korea, South
Chungnam National University, Chungnam, Korea, South
kei-myung University, dae-gu, Korea, South
PAI CHAI University, Daejeon, Korea, South
Dong-A University, Dong-A, Korea, South
Dongeui University, Dongeui, Korea, South
Chonnam National University, Gwangju, Korea, South
Gyeongsang National University, Gyeongsang, Korea, South
Honam University, Honam, Korea, South
Inha University, Inha, Korea, South
Kangwon National University, Kangwon, Korea, South
Keimyung University, Keimyung, Korea, South
inje university, Kimhae, Korea, South
Kwangju University, Kwangju, Korea, South
Kyunghee University, Kyunghee, Korea, South
Kyungil University, Kyungil, Korea, South
Kyungnam University, Kyungnam, Korea, South
Kyungpook National University, Kyungpook, Korea, South
Yeungnam University, Kyungsan-shi, KyungbuK, Korea, South[*]
Kyungwon University, Kyungwon, Korea, South[*]
Miryang National University, Miryang, Korea, South
Mokwon University, Mokwon, Korea, South
Wonkwang University, Myongji, Korea, South
Pukyong National University, Pukyong, Korea, South
Pusan National University, Pusan, Korea, South
Dankook University, Seoul, Korea, South
Hanyang University, Seoul, Korea, South[**]
Hanyang University, Seoul, Korea, South
Hongik University, Seoul, Korea, South[*]
konkuk University, Seoul, Korea, South
Kookmin Universty, Seoul, Korea, South
Korea University, Seoul, Korea, South[***]
Kwangwoon University, Seoul, Korea, South
Kyunggi University, Seoul, Korea, South
Kyunggi University, Seoul, Korea, South
Seoul National Polytechnic University, Seoul, Korea, South
Seoul National University, Seoul, Korea, South
University of Seoul, Seoul, Korea, South[*]
wonkwang UNIVERSITY, Seoul, Korea, South
Yonsei University, Seoul, Korea, South
Yonsei University, Seoul, Korea, South[**]
Sungkyunkwan University, Suwon, Korea, South[**]
Suwon University, Suwon, Korea, South
Taegu University, Taegu, Korea, South
Taejon National University of Technology, Taejon, Korea, South
Taejon University, Taejon, Korea, South
The University of Ulsan, Ulsan, Korea, South[*]
University of Ulsan, Ulsan, Korea, South[**]
Myongji University, Yongin, Korea, South[*]
Kuwait University, Kuwait, Kuwait[**]
Kirgizski Architectural & Building Institute, Bishkek, Kyrgyzstan[*]
Académie Libanaise des Beaux-Arts (ALBA), Beirut, Lebanon[*]
American University of Beirut, Beirut, Lebanon[*]
American University of Beirut, Beirut, Lebanon
Beirut Arab University, Beirut, Lebanon[****]
Lebanese University, Beirut, Lebanon
Lebanese American University formerly Beirut University, Byblos, Lebanon[***]
Saint Joseph University, El Mansourieh Mar Roukouz, Lebanon
Université Saint-Esprit - USEK, Kaslik - Jounieh, Lebanon[**]
Notre Dame University - Louaize, Zouk Mosbeh, Lebanon[**]
National University of Malaysia, Bangi Selangor, Malaysia[**]
Universiti Teknologi Malaysia, Johor, Malaysia
University of Malaya, Kuala Lumpur, Malaysia[*]
University of Technology Malaysia, Kuala Lumpur, Malaysia[*]
University of Science Malaysia, Pulau Pinang, Malaysia[***]
University Putra Malaysia, Serdang, Malaysia
Universiti Teknologi Mara, Shah Alam, Malaysia[**]
Sultan Qaboos University, Alkhoud123, Oman
Dawood College of Engineering and Technology, Karachi, Pakistan
national college of arts lahore, Pakistan
University of Engineering and Technology, Lahore, Pakistan
Birzeit University, Birzeit, Palestine
Islamic University of Gaza, Gaza, Palestine
An-Najah National University, Nablus, West Bank, Palestine
La Consolacion College, Bacolod City, Philippines
Don Honorio Ventura College of Arts & Trades,, Bacolor, Philippines
Baguio Colleges Foundation, Baguio City, Philippines
Saint Louis University, Baguio City, Philippines
Western Mindanao State University, Baliwasan, Philippines
Pamantasan NG Araullo, Bitas, Philippines
Saint Joseph Institute of Technology, Butuan City, Philippines
Cagayan de Oro College, Carmen, Philippines
Cebu Institute of Technology, Cebu City, Philippines
University of San Carlos Technological Center, Cebu City, Philippines[*]
University of the Visayas, Cebu City, Philippines
Luzon Colleges, Dagupan City, Philippines
University of Pangasinan, Dagupan City, Philippines
Adamson University, Ermita, Philippines
University of San Agustin, Iloilo City, Philippines
Mapua Institute of Science and Technology, Intramuros, Philippines
Pamantasan NG Lungsod NG Maynila, Intramuros, Philippines
Aquinas University, Legaspi City, Philippines
Bicol University, Legaspi City, Philippines
Manuel S. Enverga University Foundation, Lucena City, Philippines
Bulacan College of Arts & Trades, Malolos, Philippines
Rizal Technological Colleges, Mandaluyong City, Philippines
Far Eastern University, Manila, Philippines[***]
Far Eastern University, Manila, Philippines
Feati University, Manila, Philippines
Manuel L. Quezon University, Manila, Philippines
Technological University of the Philippines, Manila, Philippines
University of Santo Tomas, Manila, Philippines[*****]
Central Colleges of the Philippines, Quezon City, Philippines
Technological Institute of the Philippines - QC, Quezon City, Philippines
University of the Philippines, Quezon City, Philippines[*]
Technological Institute of the Philippines - MLA, Quiapo, Philippines
Eulogio "Amang" Rodriguez Institute of Science & Technology, Sampaloc, Philippines
National University, Sampaloc, Philippines
University of the Assumption, San Fernando, Philippines[*]
University of Northeastern Philippines, San Roque, Philippines
Polytechnic University of the Philippines, Sta MESA, Philippines
Leyte Institute of Technology, Tacloban City 65oo, Philippines
University of Bohol, Tagbilaran, Philippines
Tarlac State University, Tarlac, Philippines
St. Louis College of Tuguerao, Tuguegarao, Philippines
University of Northern Philippines, Vigan, Philippines
King Fahd University of Petroleum and Minerals, Dhahran, Saudi Arabia[*]
Umm Al-Qura, Makkah, Saudi Arabia[*]
King Saud University, Riyadh, Saudi Arabia[*]
Singapore Polytechnic, Singapore, Singapore[**]
The National University of Singapore, Singapore, Singapore[***]
University of Moratuwa, Moratuwa, Sri Lanka[**]
Aleppo University, Aleppo, Syria[*]
Arab Europe University, Damascus, Syria
Damascus University, Damascus, Syria
Al-baath University, Homs, Syria[*]
Tishreen University, Lattakia, Syria
Chung Yuan Christian University, Chung-Li, Taiwan[**]
Chung Hua University, Hsinchu, Taiwan
National Chiao Tung University, Hsinchu, Taiwan
National United University, Miaoli, Taiwan
Feng Jia universities, Taichung, Taiwan[**]
Tunghai University, Taichung, Taiwan[***]
National Cheng Kung University, Tainan, Taiwan[***]
Tainan National College of the Arts (TNCA), Tainan, Taiwan
National Taipei University of Technology, Taipei, Taiwan[*]
national Taiwan universities of science & technology, Taipei, Taiwan
national Taiwan university, Taipei, Taiwan
Tamkang University, Taipei, Taiwan[*]
Tamkang universities, Tamsui, Taiwan[**]
Taadjik Polytechnical Institute, Dushanbe, Tajikistan
Assumption University, Bangkok, Thailand
Chulalongkorn University, Bangkok, Thailand[*****]
Kasem Bundit University, Bangkok, Thailand
Kasetsart University, Bangkok, Thailand[****]
King Mongkut's Institute of Technology, Bangkok, Thailand
Silpakorn University, Bangkok, Thailand[*]
Sripatum University, Bangkok, Thailand
Chiangmai University, Chiangmai, Thailand
Khon Kaen University, Khonkaen, Thailand[*]
Vongchavalitkul University, Korat, Thailand
Rajmangala University of Technology Rattanakosin, Nakhompratom, Thailand
Rangsit University, Pathumthani, Thailand[****]
Rajamangala University of Technology, Thanyaburi., Pratumthani, Thailand[***]
Ajman University of Science and Technology, Al-Ain, United Arab Emirates
United Arab Emirates University, Al-Ain, United Arab Emirates[****]
American University of Sharjah, Sharjah, United Arab Emirates[****]
University of Sharjah, Sharjah, United Arab Emirates
Samarqand State Architectural and civil engineering Institute, Samarqand, Uzbekistan[****]
Architectural & Building Institute, Tashkent, Uzbekistan
Dong Do University of Science and Technology, Hanoi, Vietnam
Ha Noi - Viet Nam Architectural University, Hanoi, Vietnam
Hanoi Architectural University, Hanoi, Vietnam[***]
National University of Civil Engineering, Hanoi, Vietnam[*]
Phuong Dong University, Hanoi, Vietnam
Ecole d'Architecture de Ho Chi Minh Ville, Ho Chi Minh Ville, Vietnam[***]
Hue: College of Sciences, Hue Vietnam
University of Aden, Aden, Yemen

AFRICA

Algiers University, Algiers, Algeria[*]
Université Mentouri, Constantine, Algeria
University of Botswana, Gaborone, Botswana
Université Nationale de Côte d'Ivoire, Abidjan, Cote d Ivoire
Al-Menia University, Al-Menia, Egypt
Alexandria University, Alexandria, Egypt[*]
Alexandria University, Alexandria, Egypt[*]
Assuit University, Assuit, Egypt
high instite for architecture, Cairo, Egypt
misr university for science and technology, Cairo, Egypt
Modern academy for engineering and technology in Maadi, Cairo, Egypt[*]
Thebes Academy, Cairo, Egypt
Ain Shams University, Cairo-Abbasia, Egypt[*]
Al-Azhar University, Cairo-Nasr City, Egypt
Zagazig University, Cairo-Shoubra, Egypt[*]
Helwan University, Cairo-Zamalek, Egypt[*]
Tanta University, El-Gharbia, Egypt[*]
Cairo University, Giza, Egypt
Mataria-Helwan University, Giza, Egypt
MISR International University, Giza, Egypt[**]
October 6 University, Giza, Egypt[*]
Al-Shrouk Academy, Helwan, Egypt
Helwan University, Helwan, Egypt
Al-Mansoura University, Mansoura, Egypt[***]
Al-Menofia University, Menofia, Egypt[**]
Tanta University, Tanta, Egypt
Addis Ababa University, Addis Ababa, Ethiopia[*]
Kwame Nkrumah University of Science and Technology, Kumasi, Ghana
University of Science & Technology, Kumasi, Ghana[**]
Mombasa Polytechnic, Mombasa, Kenya
Jomo Kenyatta University of Agriculture and Technology, Nairobi, Kenya[**]
University of Nairobi, Nairobi, Kenya
University of Liberia, Monrovia, Liberia
Alfath University, Tripoli, Libya
Ecole Supérieure d'Architecture de Casablanca, Casablanca, Morocco
Ecole Nationale d'Architecture, Rabat Instituts, Morocco[*]
Universidade Eduardo Mondlane, Maputo, Mozambique
Rivers State University of Science & Technology, Port Harcourt, Nigeria
The University of the Free State, Bloemfontein, South Africa[**]
The University of Cape Town, Cape Town, South Africa[***]
University of Witwatersrand, Johannesburg, South Africa[*]
University of Port Elizabeth, Port Elizabeth, South Africa[*]
Tshwane University of Technology, Pretoria, South Africa
University of Pretoria, Pretoria, South Africa[*****]
Sudan University of Science and Technology, Khartoum, Sudan
University of Khartoum, Khartoum, Sudan
Swaziland College of Technology, Mbabane, Swaziland
ARDHI University, Dar es Salaam, Tanzania[*]
EAMAU Ecole Africaine des Métiers d'Architecture et d'Urbanisme, Lomé, Togo
Ecole Nationale d'Architecture et d'Urbanisme, Tunis, Tunisia
MAKARERE UNIVERISTY, Kampala, Uganda
The Copperbelt University, Kitwe, Zambia[*]
National University of Science and Technology, BULAWAYO, Zimbabwe[*]

EUROPE

UFO University, Tirana, Albania
University POLIS, Tirana, Albania
Technische Universität Graz, Graz, Austria[****]
Universität Innsbruck, Innsbruck, Austria[*]
Haus der Architektur, Klagenfurt, Austria
Universität für Kunstlerische & Industrielle Gestaltung, Linz, Austria[****]
Academy of Fine Arts Vienna, Vienna, Austria[***]
Technische Universität Wien, Vienna, Austria[**]
University for Applied Arts Vienna, Vienna, Austria[****]
Belarussian National Technical University, Minsk, Belarus[*]
Artesis University College of Antwerp - Henry van de Velde, Antwerp, Belgium[*****]
Hogeschool voor Wetenschap & Kunst, associatie KULeuven, Brussels, Belgium[****]
Institut Superieur d'Architecture La Cambre, Brussels, Belgium[*]
Institut Superieur d'Architecture Victor Horta, Brussels, Belgium
Institut Supérieur d'Architecture Saint Luc, Brussels, Belgium[*]
Vrije Universiteit Brussel (VUB), Brussels, Belgium[*****]
Provinciale Hogeschool Limburg, Diepenbeek, Belgium[***]
Hogeschool voor Wetenschap & Kunst, associatie KULeuven, Gent, Belgium[*****]
Universiteit Gent, Gent, Belgium[**]
Katholieke Universiteit te Leuven K.U.L., Heverlee, Belgium[**]
Institut Supérieur d'architecture Lambert Lombard, Liege, Belgium
Institut Supérieur d'Architecture Saint Luc de Wallonie, Liege, Belgium[**]
Université de Liège Faculté des Sciences Appliquée, Liege, Belgium
Université Catholique de Louvain U.C.L., Louvain-La-Neuve, Belgium
Faculté Polytechnique de Mons, Mons, Belgium[**]
Institut Supérieur d'Architecture de Mons, Mons, Belgium
Institut Superieur d'Architecture Saint-Luc de Wallonne, Ramegnies, Belgium
Akademija Likovnih Umjetnosti, Sarajevo, Bosnia and Herzegovina
internatonal university of sarajevo, sarajevo, Bosnia and Herzegovina
University of Sarajevo, Sarajevo, Bosnia and Herzegovina
Université d'Architecture, Génie Civil et Géodesie, Sofia, Bulgaria[*]
University of Forestry Sofia, Sofia, Bulgaria
Varna Free University "Chernorizets Hrabar", Varna, Bulgaria
University of Zagreb, Zagreb, Croatia
University of Zagreb, Zagreb, Croatia[*****]
Brno University of Technology, Brno, Czech Republic[***]
Technical University of Liberec, Liberec, Czech Republic[**]
Czech Technical University in Prague, Prague, Czech Republic[****]
The Academy of Arts, Architecture and Design, Prague 1, Czech Republic[****]
Academy of Fine Arts in Prague, Prague 7, Czech Republic[**]
Aarhus School of Architecture, Aarhus, Denmark[***]
Kunstakademiets Arkitektskole, Copenhagen, Denmark[**]
University of Bath, Bath, England
University of Central England in Birmingham, Birmingham, England
University of Brighton, Brighton, England
University of the West of England, Bristol, Bristol, England[*]
University of Cambridge, Cambridge, England
Kent Institute of Art & Design, Canterbury, England
Faculty of Architects and Surveyors, Chippenham, Wiltshire, England
The University of Huddersfield Polytechnic, Huddersfield, England
Kingston University, Kingston Upon Thames, England
Leeds Metropolitan University, Leeds, England
De Montfort University, Leicester, England[**]
University of Lincoln, Lincoln, England
Liverpool John Moores University, Liverpool, England[*]
University of Liverpool, Liverpool, England[*]
Architectural Association, London, England[****]
London Metropolitan University, London, England
Royal College of Art, London, England[***]
South Bank University, London, England[*]
The Prince's Foundation for the Built Environment, London, England
The University of Westminster, London, England[****]
University College London, London, England[*]
University of East London, London, England
University of Greenwich, London, England[*]
The University of Luton, Luton, England
The Manchester Metropolitan University, Manchester, England
University of Manchester, Manchester, England
University of Newcastle, Newcastle Upon Tyne, England
University of Northumbria, Newcastle Upon Tyne, England
University of Nottingham, Nottingham, England
Oxford Brookes University, Oxford, England[***]
University of Plymouth, Plymouth, England[***]
University of Portsmouth, Portsmouth, England
University of Sheffield, Sheffield, England
Estonian Academy of Arts, Tallinn, Estonia[***]
Åbo Akademi University, Åbo, Finland
Aalto University, School of Science and Technology, Espoo, Finland[******]
Aalto Unversity, School of Science and Technology, Espoo, Finland[*****]
Lappeenranta University of Technology, Lappeenranta, Finland
University of Oulu, Oulu 10, Finland[****]
Tampere University of Technology, Tampere, Finland[****]
Vaasa Institute of Technology, Vaasa, Finland
Institut d'Aménagement Regional, Aix En Provence, France
Institut national d'horticulture d'Angers (INH), Angers, France
Ecole nationale supérieure de la nature et du paysage de Blois, Blois, France
Ecole Nationale des Beaux-Arts de Bourges, Bourges, France
Ecole d'Architecture de Clermont-Ferrand, Clermont Ferrand, France
Ecole nationale supérieure d'architecture de Normandie, Darnetal, France
Ecole Nationale des Beaux Arts, Dijon, France
Ecole nationale supérieure d'architecture de Grenoble, Grenoble, France
Université Pierre Mendès France, Grenoble, France
Ecole nationale supérieure d'architecture de Marne-la-Vallée, Marne la Vallée, France
Ecole nationale supérieure d'architecture de Marseille, Marseille, France[*]
Ecole nationale supérieure d'architecture de Montpellier, Montpellier, France[*****]
Ecole Nat. des Beaux Arts et Arts Appliqués, Nancy, France
Ecole nationale supérieure d'architecture de Nancy, Nancy, France
Ecole d'Architecture Paris - La Defense, Nanterre, France
Ecole nationale supérieure d'architecture de Nantes, Nantes, France
Ecole Nationale d'Art, Nice Cedex 2, France
Ecole d'Architecture de Paris-Tolbiac, Paris, France
Ecole d'Architecture de Paris-Villemin, Paris, France
Ecole d'Architecture Paris-Val-De-Seine, Paris, France[**]
Ecole Nationale Supérieure d'Architecture Paris-Malaquais, Paris, France[**]
Ecole nationale supérieure d'architecture de Paris-Belleville, Paris, France[**]
Ecole Nationale Supérieure d'Architecture de Paris-La-Villette, Paris, France[*]
Ecole Spéciale d'Architecture - E.S.A., Paris, France[***]
Ecole supérieure d'architecture des jardins de Paris (ESAJ), Paris, France

Ecole d'Architecure de Bretagne, Rennes, France*
Ecole nationale supérieure d'architecture de Saint-Etienne, Saint Etienne, France
Ecole nationale supérieure d'architecture de Strasbourg, Strasbourg, France
Institut National des Sciences Appliquees, Strasbourg, France
Ecole nat. supérieure d'architecture et de paysage de Bordeau, Talence, France
Ecole nationale supérieure d'architecture de Toulouse, Toulouse, France
Ecole d'Architecture de Lyon, Vaulx-En-Velin, France
Ecole nationale supérieure du paysage de Versailles (ENSP), Versailles, France
Ecole nationale supérieure d'architecture de Versailles, Versailles, France*
Ecole nat. supérieure d'architecture et de paysage de Lille, Villeneuve D'asq, France*
Fachhochschule Aachen, Aachen, Germany
Rheinisch-Westfälische Technische Hochschule Aachen, Aachen, Germany***
Alanus Hochschule, Alfter / Bonn, Germany*
University of Applied Sciences Augsburg, Augsburg, Germany*
Beuth Hochschule für Technik Berlin, Berlin, Germany**
Deutsche Akademie für Städtebau u. Landesplanung, Berlin, Germany
Kunsthochschule Berlin-Weissensee (KHB), Berlin, Germany*
Technische Universität Berlin, Berlin, Germany***
Universität der Künste Berlin, Berlin, Germany*
Hochschule Anhalt (FH), Bernburg, Germany
Fachhochschule Biberach, Biberach, Germany*
Fachhochschule Bochum, Bochum, Germany**
Technische Universität Braunschweig, Braunschweig, Germany****
Hochschule Bremen (FH), Bremen, Germany
Hochschule für Technik, Bremen, Germany
Fachhochschule Nordost-Niedersachsen, Buxtehude, Germany*
Fachhochschule Coburg, Coburg, Germany*
Brandenburgische Technische Universität, Cottbus, Germany***
Fachhochschule Darmstadt, Darmstadt, Germany
Technische Universität Darmstadt, Darmstadt, Germany**
FH Anhalt, Dessau, Germany*
Hochschule Ostwestfalen-Lippe Detmold, Germany*
Fachhochschule Dortmund, Dortmund, Germany
Universität Dortmund, Dortmund, Germany
Hochschule für Technik und Wirtsschaft (FH), Dresden, Germany
Technische Universität Dresden, Dresden, Germany*
Technische Universität Dresden, Dresden, Germany**
Fachhochschule Düsseldorf, Düsseldorf, Germany**
FH Erfurt , Erfurt, Germany
Universität-Gesamthochschule Essen, Essen, Germany
Fachhochschule Frankfurt, Frankfurt am Main, Germany*
Städelschule, Staatliche Hochschule für Bildende Künste, Frankfurt am Main, Germany*
University of applied sciences, Geisenheim, Germany
HafenCity Universität Hamburg, Hamburg, Germany**
Technische Universität Hamburg-Harburg, Hamburg, Germany
Universität Hannover, Hannover, Germany
Universität Hannover, Hannover, Germany*
SRH Hochschule Heidelberg, Heidelberg, Germany
Fachhochschule Hildesheim/Holzminden, Hildesheim, Germany
Fachhochschule Hildesheim/Holzminden, Holzminden, Germany
Fachhochschule Lippe und Höxter (University of applied Sciences, Höxter, Germany
Fachhochschule Kaiserslautern, Kaiserslautern, Germany
Universität Kaiserslautern, Kaiserslautern, Germany
Hochschule fur Technik, Karlsruhe, Germany*
KIT Karlsruher Institut für Technologie, Karlsruhe, Germany****
Universität Kassel, Kassel, Germany*****
Muthesius-Hochschule, Kiel, Germany
Fachhochschule Koblenz, Koblenz, Germany
Fachhochschule Köln, Köln, Germany*
Fachhochschule Konstanz, Konstanz, Germany
Hochschule für Technik, Wirtschaft und Kultur Leipzig (FH), Leipzig, Germany**
Fachhochschule Lübeck, Lübeck, Germany
FH Magdeburg , Magdeburg, Germany
Fachhochschule Mainz, Mainz, Germany
Fachhochschule Bielefeld/ abteilung Minden, Minden, Germany
Akademie der Bildenden Künste München, München, Germany
Fachhochschule München, München, Germany*
Technische Universität München, München, Germany**
Fachhochschule Münster, Münster, Germany*
Westfälische Wilhelms Universität Münster, Münster, Germany
Fachhochschule Nürnberg, Nürnberg, Germany
Fachhochschule Oldenburg, Oldenburg, Germany
FH Potsdam, Potsdam, Germany
Fachhochschule Regensburg, Regensburg, Germany
Westsächsische Hochschule Zwickau (FH), Reichenbach, Germany**
Hochschule für Technik u. Wirtschaft, Saarbrücken, Germany
Universität-Gesamthochschule Siegen, Siegen, Germany**
Akademie der Bildenden Künste Stuttgart, Stuttgart, Germany**
Fachhochschule Stuttgart, Stuttgart, Germany
Universität Stuttgart, Stuttgart, Germany****
Fachhochschule des Landes Rheinland-Pfalz / Abteilung Trier, Trier, Germany*
Fachhochschule Trier, Trier, Germany
Bauhaus-Universität Weimar, Weimar, Germany*
Hochschule für Architektur und Bauwesen, Weimar, Germany*
Fachhochschule Wiesbaden, Wiesbaden, Germany
Hochschule Wismar (FH), Wismar, Germany*
Bergische Universität, Wuppertal, Germany
Fachhochschule Würzburg-Schweinfurt-Aschaffenburg, Würzburg, Germany
Hochschule für Technik, Wirtschaft und Sozialwesen, Zittau, Germany
National Technical University, Athens, Greece*
Aristotle University of Thessaloniki, Thessaloniki, Greece*****
Univeristy of Thessaly, Volos, Greece*
Budapest University of Technology and Economics, Budapest, Hungary****
Corvinus University, Budapest, Hungary
Moholy-Nagy University of Art and Design Budapest, Budapest, Hungary***
Szenti István University, Budapest, Hungary*
University of Debrecen, Debrecen, Hungary
Széchenyi István University, Gyor, Hungary**
University of Pécs, Pecs, Hungary***
University of West Hungary, Sopron, Hungary*
ISARK - íslenski arkitettaskólinn, Reykjavík, Iceland
Queen's University of Belfast, Belfast, Ireland
The Queen's University of Belfast, Belfast, Ireland
College of Technology, Dublin, Ireland
University College Dublin, Dublin, Ireland
university of SASSARI, Alghero, Italy*
Università Politecnica delle Marche, Ancona, Italy**
Universita di Camerino, Ascoli Piceno, Italy*
Università di Napoli II, Aversa (Napoli), Italy**
Politécnico di Bari, Bari, Italy*
Politecnico di Bari, Bari Italy*
University of Cagliari, Cagliari, Italy
Università di Catania, Catania, Italy
Università degli Studi di Ferrara, Ferrara, Italy***
Università di Firenze, Florence, Italy****
Università di Genova, Genova, Italy****
Politecnico di Milano, Milan, Italy*****
Politecnico di Milano, Milan, Italy**
Università di Napoli, Napoli, Italy
Università di Napoli Federico II, Napoli, Italy
University of Padova, padova, Italy*
Università di Palermo, Palermo, Italy*
Università degli studi di Parma, Parma, Italy
Universita di Chieti, Pescara, Italy**
Un. Degli Studi di Reggio Calabria, Reggio Calabria, Italy
Università di Reggio Calabria, Reggio Calabria, Italy
American Academy in Rome, Rome, Italy
Terza Universita di Roma, Rome, Italy***
Università di Roma, Rome, Italy
Universita di Roma La Sapienza, Rome, Italy**
Università di Roma La Sapienza, Rome, Italy***
Università di Roma "La Sapienza", Rome, Italy
University of Catania, Siracusa, Italy
Politecnico di Torino, Torino, Italy****
Università degli Studi di Trieste, Trieste, Italy*
Studio Valle Architetti Associati, Udine, Italy
University IUAV of Venice, Venice, Italy****
University IUAV of Venice, Venice, Italy*
Centro Internaz. di Studi di Architettura A. Palladio, Vicenza, Italy
AAB RIINVEST, Prishtina, Kosovo*
University of Business and Technology, Prishtina, Kosovo
University of Prishtina, Prishtine, Kosovo*
Riga Technical University, Riga, Latvia***
Hochschule Liechtenstein, Vaduz, Liechtenstein*
Kaunas Technology University, Kaunas, Lithuania****
VDA Kaunas Art Institute, Kaunas, Lithuania****
Vilnius Academy of Arts, Vilnius, Lithuania*
Vilnius Gedimino Technical University, Vilnius, Lithuania**
University SS. Kiril and Metodij, Skopje, Macedonia***
The University of Malta, Msida - Msd06, Malta
Technical University of Moldova, Chisinau, Moldova***
Amsterdam School of the Arts, Amsterdam, Netherlands******
Academy of Architecture Arnhem, Arnhem, Netherlands*****
Delft University of Technology, Delft, Netherlands******
Eindhoven University of Technology, Eindhoven, Netherlands******
Hanzehogeschool, University of Applied Sciences, Groningen, Netherlands****
Maastricht academy of architecture, Maastricht, Netherlands******
Rotterdam Academy of Architecture and Urban Design, Rotterdam, Netherlands******
the Berlage Institute, Rotterdam, Netherlands
Fontys University of Applied Science, Tilburg, Netherlands******
Wageningen University, Wageningen, Netherlands*****
Bergen School of Architecture - BAS, Bergen, Norway****
Norwegian Architect's Academy, Oslo, Norway
Oslo School of Architecture, Oslo, Norway
The School of Architecture in Oslo-AHO, Oslo, Norway*
Norwegian University of Science, Trondheim, Norway**
Bialystok Technical University, Bialystok, Poland**
Polytechnika Czestochowska, Czestochowa, Poland
Politechniki Gdanskiej, Gdansk, Poland*
The Silesian University of Technology, Gliwice, Poland*****
Politechnika Krakowska, Krakow, Poland*
Lodz School of Art and Design, Lodz, Poland*
Politechniki Lodzkiej, Lodz, Poland
Academy of Fine Arts in Poznan, Poznan, Poland
Politechniki Poznanskiej, Poznan, Poland
Politechniki Szozecinskiej, Szczecin, Poland
Politechnika Warszawska, Warsaw, Poland****
Warsaw Agricultural University, Warsaw, Poland*
Wroclaw University of Technology, Wroclaw, Poland*****
Universidade de Coimbra - Faculdade de Ciências e Tecnologias, Coimbra, Portugal
Universidade de Évora, Évora, Portugal
Universidade de Évora, Escola de Ciências e Tecnologia, Évora, Portugal
Universidade do Minho, Guimarães, Portugal
ISCTE Instituto Superior de Ciências do Trabalho e da Empresa, Lisboa, Portugal
Universidade Autónoma de Lisboa, Lisboa, Portugal
Universidade Lusiada, Lisboa, Portugal**
Universidade Lusófona de Humanidades e Tecnologias, Lisboa, Portugal*
Universidade Técnica de Lisboa, Lisboa, Portugal
Universidade Técnica de Lisboa, Instituto Superior Técnico, Lisboa, Portugal*
Universidade Técnica de Lisboa, UTL, Lisboa, Portugal*
Escola de Arquitectura, Porto, Portugal
Escola Superior Artística do Porto, Porto, Portugal*
Faculdade de Arquitectura da Universidade do Porto, Porto, Portugal
Universidade do Porto, Porto, Portugal
Universidade Moderna Setubal, Setubal, Portugal
Escola de Arquitectura, Vila Nova De Famalicao, Portugal
Universidade Catolica Portuguesa - Viseu, Viseu, Portugal
Ion Mincu, University of Architecture and Urbanism, Bucarest, Romania
Spiru Haret, Bucarest, Romania
Universitatea Tehnica din Cluj, Cluj Napoca, Romania**
Universitatea Tehnica 'Gh. Asachi', Iasi, Romania*****
Universitatea Politehnica din Timisoara, Timisoara, Romania*
Altay State Technical University, Barnaoul, Russia*
Regional Design School, Bashkortostan, Russia
Belgorod State Technological Academy of Build Materials, Belgorod, Russia
Ural State Academy of Architecture and Arts, Ekaterinburg, Russia**
Irkutsk State Technical University, Irkoutsk, Russia*
Ivanovo Engineering-Construction Institute, Ivanovo, Russia
Kazan State University of Architecture and Engineering, Kazan, Russia***
Khabarosk State Technical University, Khabarovsk, Russia
Kostroma State Academy of Agriculture, Kostroma, Russia*
Kuban State University, Krasnodar, Russia
Krasnojersk Engineering Construction Academy, Krasnoyarsk, Russia**
Krasnoyarsk State Academy of Architecture and Civil Engineering, Krasnoyarsk, Russia
Magnitogorsk State Technical University, Magnitogorsk, Russia*
Académie de Restauration, Moscow, Russia
Moscou Architectural Institute - State Academy, Moscow, Russia****
State University on Land use, Moscow, Russia
Nizhegorodskaya Architectural Construction Academy, Nizhniy Nougorod, Russia
Nogorod State University, Nougorod, Russia
Novosibirsk Architectural Arts Academy, Novossibirsk, Russia**
Penza State University of Architecture and Construction, Penza, Russia
Rostov State Academy of Architecture & Arts, Rostov On Don, Russia**
Samara Architectural Construction Academy, Samara, Russia
Saratov State Technical University, Saratov, Russia*
Repin's Institute of Arts, Sculpture and Architecture, St. Petersburg, Russia
Saint-Petersbourg State University of Architecture & Civil Engen, St. Petersburg, Russia**
Université Technique de Tambov, Tambov, Russia
Southern Urals State University, Tchelyabinsk, Russia**
Tomsk Civil Architectural Construction Academy, Tomsk, Russia
Académie d'architecture et de construction de Tume, Tumene, Russia
Tyumen State Architectural-Building University, Tyumen, Russia
Ufa State Oil Technica University, Ufa, Russia
Ukhta State Technical University, Ukhta, Russia
Ulianovsk State Technical University, Ulianovsk, Russia*
North Caucasian State Technological University, Vladikavkaz, Russia****
Vladimirstate Technica University, Vladimir, Russia
Far Eastern State Technical University, Vladivostok, Russia
Volgograd State University of Architecture & Civil Engineering, Volgograd, Russia***
Vologda State Technical University, Vologda, Russia*
Voronej Architectural Construction Academy, Voronezh, Russia
Yaroslavl State Technical University, Yaroslavl, Russia*
Robert Gordon University, Aberdeen, Scotland
University of Dundee, Dundee, Scotland
Edinburgh College of Art, Edinburgh, Scotland***
University of Edinburgh, Edinburgh, Scotland**
University of Glasgow / The Glasgow School of Art, Glasgow, Scotland**
University of Strathclyde, Glasgow, Scotland*****
University of Belgrade, Belgrade, Serbia
University of Belgrade, Belgrade, Serbia**
University of Nis, Nis, Serbia*
Slovenska technicka univerzita, Bratislava, Slovakia******
Vysoka skola vytvarnych umeni, Academy of Fine arts and Design, Bratislava, Slovakia***
Technika univerzita, Kosice, Slovakia
University of Ljubljana, Ljubljana, Slovenia**
Universidad de Alicante, Alicante, Spain*
Universitat Politècnica de Catalunya, Barcelona - Catalonia, Spain*****
Escuela Técnica Superior de Arquitectura, Granada, Spain*
Escuela Técnica Superior de Arquitectura, La Coruna, Spain
Escuela Técnica Superior de Arquitectura, Las Palmas De Gran Canaria, Spain
Universidad Europea de Madrid, Madrid, Spain*
Universidad Politécnica de Madrid, Madrid, Spain*
[EPS.CEU] Escuela Politécnica Superior University CEU San Pablo, MADRID, Spain*
Universidad de Navarra, Pamplona, Spain***
Universitat Rovira i Virgili, Reus, Spain
Universidad del Pais Vasco, San Sebastian, Spain*
Universitat Politècnica de Catalunya, Sant Cugat del Vallès, Spain****
IE, Segovia, Spain
Universidad de Sevilla, Sevilla, Spain**
Universidad Politécnica de Valencia, Valencia, Spain**
Escuela Técnica Superior de Arquitectura, Valladolic, Spain
Chalmers Technical University, Goteborg, Sweden*
Lund Universitetet, Lund, Sweden*
Tekniska Högskolan i Lund, Lund, Sweden
Kungliga Tekniska Högskolan (KTH), Stockholm, Sweden
Ingenieurschule Bern HTL, Bern, Switzerland
Berner Fachhochschule, Biel, Switzerland
Berner Fachhochschule, Burgdorf, Switzerland**
HTW Chur, Chur, Switzerland
University of applied sciences Western Switzerland, Fribourg, Switzerland*
Ecole d'Ingénieurs de Genève, Geneve, Switzerland
Université de Genève (EAUG), Geneve, Switzerland
Hochschule Technik+Architektur Luzern, Horw, Switzerland
Ecole Polytechnique Fédérale de Lausanne (EPFL), Lausanne, Switzerland
Scuola Universitaria Professionale delle Svizzera Italiana, Lugano-Canobbio, Switzerland
Università della Svizzera italiana, Mendrisio, Switzerland***
Fachhochschule Nordwestschweiz, Muttenz, Switzerland*
HSR Hochschule für Technik Rapperswil, Rapperswil, Switzerland**
FHS St. Gallen, St. Gallen, Switzerland
Fachhochschule Aargau, Windisch, Switzerland
Fachhochschule Nordwestschweiz, Windisch, Switzerland
Zürcher Hochschule Winterthur, Winterthur, Switzerland
ETH Zürich (Swiss Federal Institute of Technology), Zurich, Switzerland*
Ingenieurschule Zürich HTL, Zurich, Switzerland
Cukurova University, Adana, Turkey
Bilkent University, Ankara, Turkey*
Gazi Universitesi, Ankara, Turkey*
Middle East Technical University, Ankara, Turkey******
Balikesir University, Balikesir, Turkey
Zonguldak Karaelmas, Bartin, Turkey
Uludag University, Bursa, Turkey**
Çanakkale Onsekiz Mart, Çanakkale, Turkey
Dicle University, Diyarbakir, Turkey
Trakya University, Edirne, Turkey
Firat University, Elazig, Turkey
Atatürk University, Erzurum, Turkey
Anadolu University, Eskisehir, Turkey
Osmangazi University, Eskisehir, Turkey
Suleyman Demirel University, Isparta, Turkey
Beykent University, Istanbul, Turkey*
Istanbul Kultur University, Istanbul, Turkey*****
Istanbul Technical University, Istanbul, Turkey*****
Mimar Sinan Fine Arts University, Istanbul, Turkey*
Yeditepe University, Istanbul, Turkey
Yildiz Technical University, Istanbul, Turkey*****
Dokuz Eylul University, Izmir, Turkey
Izmir Institute of Technology, Izmir, Turkey**
Erciyes University, Kayseri, Turkey*
Kocaeli University, Kocaeli, Turkey
Selcuk University, Konya, Turkey
Eastern Mediterranean University, Mersin 10, Turkey***
Girne American University, Mersin 10, Turkey*
International American University, Mersin 10, Turkey
International Cyprus University, Mersin 10, Turkey
Lefke European University, Mersin 10, Turkey
Middle East University, Mersin 10, Turkey
Namik Kemal University, Tekirdag, Turkey*
Karadeniz Technical University, Trabzon, Turkey*
Pridniprovska State Academy of Building and Architecture, Dnipropetrovsk, Ukraine
The Donbas National Academy of Civil Engineering & Architecture, Donetsk region, Makiyivka, Ukraine*
Kharkov State Municipal Academy of Town Planning and Development, Kharkov, Ukraine*
Kiev Academy of Arts, Kiev, Ukraine
Kiev State Technical University of Building and Architecture, Kiev, Ukraine***
Lviv Forestly Technical University, Lviv, Ukraine
National University 'Lvivska Politechnika', Lviv, Ukraine*
Odessa State Academy Building and Architecture, Odessa, Ukraine
Poltava State Technical University, Poltava, Ukraine
National Academy of Environment and Recreation Building, Simferopol, Ukraine**
Academy of Fine Art & Architecture, Voul, Ukraine*
Université Polytechnique d'Etat, Voul, Ukraine*
University of Wales - College of Cardiff, Cardiff, Wales

ARCHIPRIX INTERNATIONAL ROTTERDAM 2001, ISTANBUL 2003, GLASGOW 2005, SHANGHAI 2007, MONTEVIDEO 2009, **MIT CAMBRIDGE USA 2011**, MOSCOW 2013

CHANGING PARTNERS, STRUCTURAL NETWORK Since 2001 Archiprix International has been presenting the world's best graduation projects in the field of architecture, urban planning and landscape architecture. Each edition has been organized in conjunction with a partner somewhere in the world. Massachusetts Institute of Technology, MIT, School of Architecture + Planning, Department of Architecture, is the co-organizer of the 2011 edition. The partner receives the best graduation projects that have been submitted to the competition, and organizes the jury assessment, a large-scale exhibition of the plans, and the workshops in which the designers of the selected graduation projects can participate. By working with a consistently different partner, a dynamic synergy is created so that every edition acquires its own particular emphasis, the global character of the initiative is reinforced and the local network of the collaborating partner is activated. In this way, an international network of educational programs is created. Every edition witnesses a new challenge to incite the participation of educational programs in the region. However, the general strategy has turned out to be extremely successful. Originally, Archiprix International presented much work from European educational programs. In the Shanghai 2007 edition, the participation of Chinese programs soared. The same occurred in Latin America in 2009, and, in the current round, the number of participating programs in the US has increased fivefold in comparison to previous editions. This trend is clearly visible on the maps on pages 134 and 135, which show the number of participating programs per continent per edition. In the future, we shall continue this formula, which appears to inspire all, and we hope to reach more programs in regions that are still new to us. We shall begin this new quest in Eastern Europe and Northern and Central Asia with Archiprix International 2013 Moscow.

Archiprix International is based in Rotterdam, and it is from here that the Archiprix Foundation coordinates its activities. The Archiprix Foundation is a cooperative venture of advanced Dutch design programs in the domain of architecture, urban planning and landscape architecture: the Faculties of Architecture of Delft University of Technology and Eindhoven University of Technology, the academies of architecture in Amsterdam, Rotterdam, Tilburg, Arnhem, Maastricht and Groningen; Wageningen University: Department of Environmental Sciences, Landscape Architecture Group. The main sponsor is Hunter Douglas, who are a world market leader in window coverings and a major manufacturer of architectural products.

SIMPLE FORMULA WITH GREAT REACH The Archiprix International concept is a simple one: every two years, all higher education programs are invited to select and submit to us their best graduation projects. In conjunction with the cooperating partner, Archiprix International hands over the submitted plans to an international jury, and presents the plans to a broad public via the website www.archiprix.org, this book and exhibitions. It also puts the designers of the plans in contact with one another by means of workshops. Archiprix provides all institutions of higher education worldwide with the opportunity to present themselves by means of their best graduation plans. In the course of time, these educational institutions can build up a profile of themselves by consistently selecting a plan and submitting it to Archiprix. Archiprix continues to present all plans from all editions on its website. Equally important is the fact that Archiprix offers the youngest generation of talented designers worldwide a platform for their ideas, and brings them into contact with one another. Besides stimulating the professional development of commencing architects, urban planners and landscape architects, Archiprix International also has the aim of promoting the discussion on the quality of design education, of inspiring the professional community, and of drawing deserved attention to the world's best graduation plans. Everyone who takes the trouble to make an in-depth study of the plans will be seized by the wealth and lucidity of the work. The plans form a source of inspiration to professional colleagues and to students for whom the work defines a level of ambition they can aim at in their study. It gives us great pleasure to introduce, by means of this book, a new generation of designers who are ready to bring their talents into real-life practice.

Henk van der Veen
Director of Archiprix International

BEYOND EXPRESSION TRENDS FOR A GLOBAL STYLE AFTER THE ICON

The subversive power of Archiprix lies in its promise to organize an international conversation on the basis of architecture as a medium of a common culture across countries. The formal structure of a public building provides an ideogrammatic summary of an ideal about the collective, as envisioned by its author. As such, Archiprix projects could provide the basis for a powerful alternative to the conversation being held on the global architecture scene of late. Over the last decade, magazines and blogs, among other forms of expression, have constructed a mediatized scene in which the criteria of judgment for global architecture have become almost identical to the interests of the real estate industry, whose judgment on architectural value rests on the combination of iconic imagery with an otherwise conventional building product. The lack of critique has allowed a cunning move of signature icons, for instance, away from being a sales ploy aimed at adding value to otherwise generic developments, to dominating the disciplinary conversation of architecture with itself. While this has become accepted as 'the discourse of architecture', in fact it is simply a propaganda trick of real estate development. Furthermore, the economic crisis in the US, hosting this year's *prix*, has contributed to a sense that the field needs to move beyond its shapisms. Formalism should become, once more, a serious and independent exercise to find really communal formal abstractions, instead of hyping the hyper-subjectivized (signature). Developing a globalized culture about architecture not dominated by such 'bland architecture + icon shape' formulas, but instead searching for alternative definitions for architecture's formal structure, is, then, the great promise of Archiprix.

Already 50-something years ago, the International Style (late 1940s and 1950s) promised a unification through architecture with a single, polished, internationally modern, new kind of classicism articulating similarly universalist aspirations, beyond particular national or ethnic expressions. Hashim Sarkis delivered a speech at the 'Global Critical' conference at MIT in October 2010, sponsored by Archiprix, in which he argued for a 'city-world' where the aggregation of building into a global built form would be consciously recognized as a truly collective endeavor, worthy of being pursued and articulated as a common project. Sarkis explicitly referred to the International Style as a predecessor of that new global culture. However, by the late 1960s, the IS had lost its attractiveness as an overall global proposition. On the one hand, its universal character exacerbated anxieties about local identity (as in vernacular) under threat. On the other hand, the corporate recodification of everyday practices (ISO etc.) developed in these buildings around the same time and these control systems therefore became intuitively associated with the esthetics of the International Style. During post-decolonization 'international settlement studies', centers appeared within various Western universities, aiming to use local vernacular traditions for slum remedy and improvement, etc. This ended up banishing the issue from architecture proper, shifting it into adjacent fields of engineering, social policy and health policy. Today, modernization itself has become an indigenous process in almost every country, and denying other cultures the fruits of modernization and progress under the guise of an authenticity argument is hardly considered as an ethical argument any longer.

Has the harvest of this, largest ever, session of Archiprix shown us elements of an alternative global architecture culture? Are there shared intuitions amongst the spectrum of submitted projects displaying certain shared stylistic directions beyond the icon? Are there elements of a reinvigorated International Style, using architecture as a device for emancipation from historical and cultural bias? Yes, there is a striking evolution. The copies of starchitecture buildings are on the retreat. More importantly, several entries share an 'anti-expressive' attitude and, from that, instigate an inquiry into formal technique. My point is they are not rejecting formalism, but digging for formal means to avoid shapes. A new generation of architects use their authorial freedom not to generate more shapes, but actually to limit it. They consciously put an end to the entropy of shapes. This reductionist drive is more than just a hangover from the era of extreme expression. It is on the verge of becoming a formal project on its own terms, and is beginning to generate an entire apparatus of formal devices and design techniques. Amongst the winners, we see at least five such techniques: found objects; *cadavre exquis*; gutting; type; and objectified infrastructure.

The limitation of shapes finds its most apt articulation in the recuperation of existing ones. Like *objets trouvés*, or found objects, several projects choose to reuse existing forms. They inhabit existing shells, they take existing components and recombine them. The esthetic intuition at work here is one of rejection of the 'new shapes' as a vessel for vanguard ambitions. Rather, integrity towards the world can be found by a more thorough exploration of the almost endless, yet existent archive of surviving man-made shapes. These forms may be used out of scale or sideways; they display fossils of past modernity. The recuperation of this type of form is already a critique of its disposable consumer shape, for it returns as a ghost of the past, and therefore of ambitions failed or ideals stuck, yet imbued with new, even if sorry, life.

The *cadavre exquis* – or piece assembled by putting different fragments of texts by different authors into an apparent whole – appears in non-standard, yet non-smooth assemblies of nuts and bolts and off-the-shelf pieces. Again, strikingly, the designer interrogates the very notion that the object needs to look as if it has been designed as a strict composition. It takes real design talent to do this eloquently: for the cognitive shock resulting from the realization that what seemed like a smooth object is in fact a barely consistent stacking of off-the-shelf parts is the core of the esthetic experience.

Gutting is a third technique, achieved by taking a well-designed form and stripping it, slicing it and brutally violating its integrity. Gutting is a violent act leading to spectacular spatial and formal results. The interlacing of open and closed sections in one of the winning projects looks like the result of a beautiful shape shocked into a new kind of formal consistency after having been thrown through a shredder.

Fourth, type returns. Designing with type is like designing with the solution already discovered at the beginning of the design process. The inquiry, the research, begins with the examination of a solution. New in this edition of Archiprix is that type is no longer intertwined with historicizing esthetics: for the use of modernist types is now on the table. Yet, the use of the International Style as a default type has been proposed by one of the winning projects.

Finally, objectified infrastructure. The artefacts we all have in common are objects resulting from code, technocracy and engineering: roadways, Jersey barriers, etc. Yet these very objects and artefacts, sharing above all a quality of formal anonymity, are becoming a language *par excellence*. Like the architecture of the Ensamble office (Madrid), objectified infrastructure becomes a means to construct not roads but entire environments.

Archiprix 2011 promises a fresh generation of architectural form. Deliberately not new – for new is over. But full of brutality, distortion, reuse of trash, slicing and forcing. Not nihilist but rejectionist; perhaps we are about to see a generation of architectural, global *punk*.

Alexander D'Hooghe
Director, MIT
Platform for Permanent Modernity

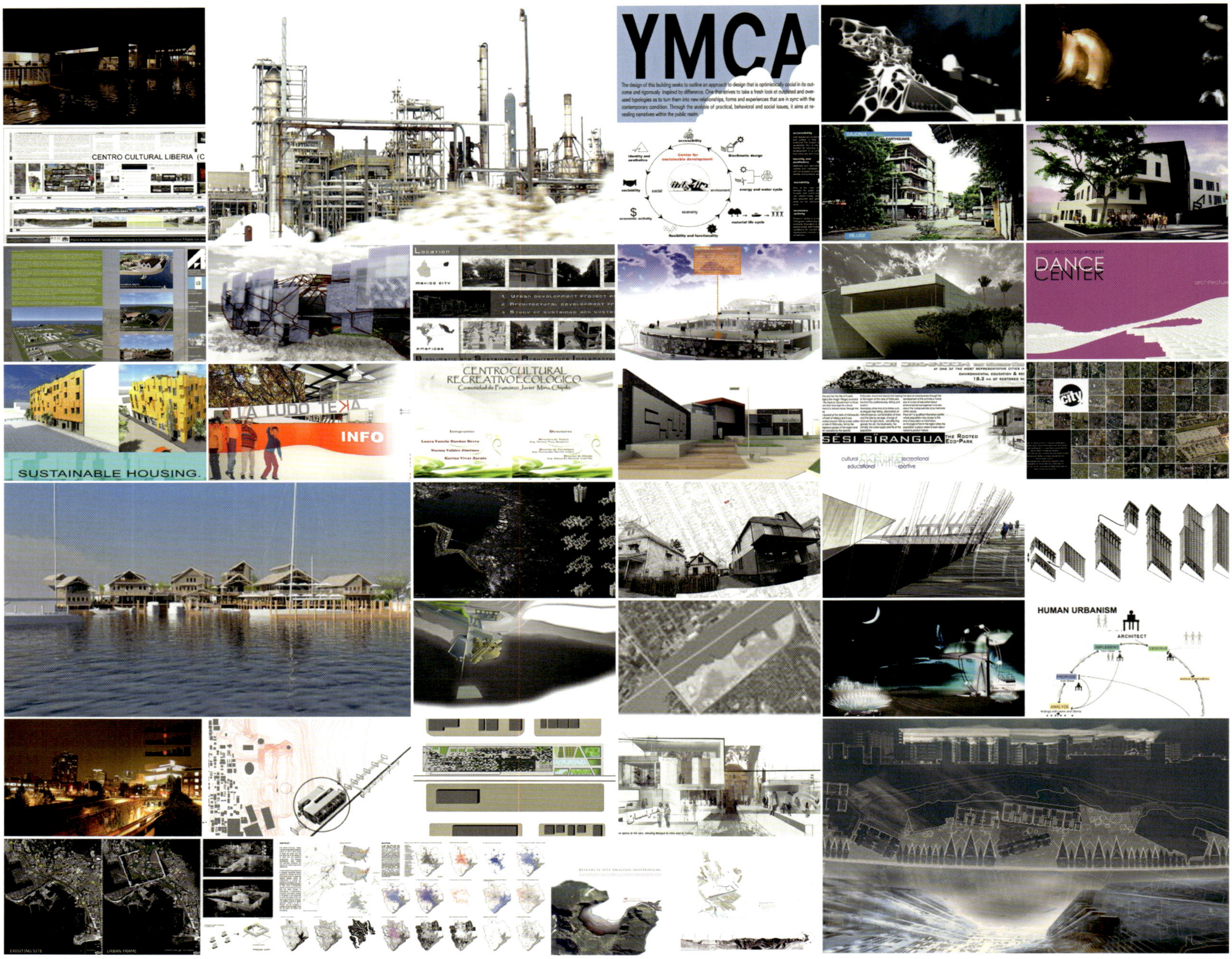

PARTICIPANTS NORTH AMERICA: ROW 1 - CANADA: **Community Harbor Revitalization**, Rachel Lacey, British Columbia Institute of Technology, Burnaby, Canada / **Escaping Rust**, Mirna Monla, McGill University, Montreal, Canada / **YMCA**, Alexandre Landry, Universite de Montreal, Montreal, Canada / **Écume Atmosphérique**, Samuel Bernier-Lavigne, Universite Laval, Quebec, Canada / **4 years old forever**, Colin Herperger, University of Manitoba, Winnipeg, Canada / **ROW 2** - **Liberia Cultural Center**, Carlos M. Mena Porras, Universidad del Diseño, Ciudad Colón, Costa Rica / **Holistic Strategies Tortuguero**, Esteban Zamora, Universidad de Costa Rica, San Jose, Costa Rica / **Sajonia**, Tamara Caldera Turcios, Universidad Veritas, San Jose, Costa Rica / **Conventions Center**, Luis Enrique Carrazana González, Universidad Central de las Villas, SANTA CLARA-Villaclara, Cuba / **ROW 3 - Reordenamiento y Proyeccion Urbano del Parque Industrial**, Luis Estuardo Flores Hernández , Univ. De San Carlos de Guatemala, Ciudad Guatemala, Guatemala / MEXICO: **Bioarchitecture. Biomimicry**, Luis Eduardo Guísar Benítez, Universidad de las Americas, Puebla, Cholula Puebla, Mexico / **Bioclimatic and Sustainable Architecture Implemented in Mexico** , Elizabeth López Romero, Centro Universitario Mexico (d.e.s.), Colonia del Mar, Mexico / **Centro de Rehabilitacion contra Adicciones**, Juan Carlos Castelo Mondragón, Fabiola Ivon Sequeira Moreno, Universidad Autonoma del Estado de Morelos, Cuernavaca, Mexico / **Hidro-Centro**, Domingo Delaroiere, Universidad Iberoamericana, Mexico, Mexico / **Classic and Contemporary Dance Center**, Dulce Adriana Luna Hernández, Universidad la Salle, Mexico, Mexico / **ROW 4 - Sustainable.housing.Talavera.CHCM**, Gabriel Lara García Rojas, Universidad Nacional Autonoma de Mexique, Mexico, Mexico / **Toy Library/ La Ludoteka**, Alejandra de la Rosa, Centro de Diseño Cine y Televisión, Mexico City, Mexico / **The Cultural Recreation Center for Ecological Community**, L. Y. Dueñas Berra, M. T. Vera Ramirez, N. Jiménez Valdez, K.Vivar Zarate, Benemerita Universidad Autonoma de Puebla , Puebla, Mexico / **Cultural Park and on site Pyramid's Museum in San Pedro Cholula**, Mauricio Manning Zerón, Universidad Iberoamericana Puebla, Puebla, Mexico / **Sési Sïrangua the Rooted Eco-Park**, Christian Garcia Arreguin, Universidad Popular Autonoma del Estado de Puebla, Puebla, Mexico / UNITED STATES: **Circuit City**, Lan Hu, Nayoung Kim, Woranol Sattayavinij, Gerrell Wilson, University of California, Berkeley, United States / **ROW 5 - Edgartown Harbor Landing**, Josh Gothard, Massachusetts College of Art and Design , Boston, United States / **Link City - Rinku** Andri Klausen, Pratt Institute, Brooklyn, United States / **QuadSpace**, Michael-John Bailie, Paul Dudkowski, Ernest Ng, Dan Stripp, State University of New York at Buffalo, Buffalo, United States / **Grounds for Architecture**, Katy Barkan, Harvard University, Cambridge, United States / **The End of the Times?**, Duncan McIlvaine, Massachusetts Institute of Technology, Cambridge, United States / **Making Them Really See**, Wilfredo Rodriguez, University of Illinois at Urbana - Champaign, Champaign, United States / **ROW 6 - Toledo Edison Acme Power Plant** , The School of the Art Institute of Chicago, Chicago, United States / **Thneed Dubai**, Michael Grieser, Ryan Whitby, The Ohio State University, Columbus, United States / **Human Urbanism**, Krista M. Wilson, University of Detroit Mercy, Detroit, United States / **ROW 7 - Portland Central Library/405 Cap**, Marc C Holt, University of Oregon, Eugene, United States / **Encompassing Spirituality : An Exercise in Formal Gathering**, Christopher J. Heidrich, North Dakota State University, Fargo, United States / **Rare Books Library and Cinema Art in Marfa, Texas**, Raquel Mayorga, University of Arkansas, Fayetteville, United States / **Architecture and Language**, Maya-Maria Joannides, University of Florida, Gainesville, United States / **Urban Frame**, Benson Gillespie, Rice University, Houston, United States / **Regional: City of Houston**, Jason Honeycutt, University of Houston, Houston, United States / **ROW 8 - Nebulous Space: Into and Out of the Cloud**, Stephen Clipp, Cornell University, Ithaca, United States / , **Machu Picchu: Reconnecting the landscape**, Sonia Carolina Sanchez, University of Louisiana at Lafayette, Lafayette, United States

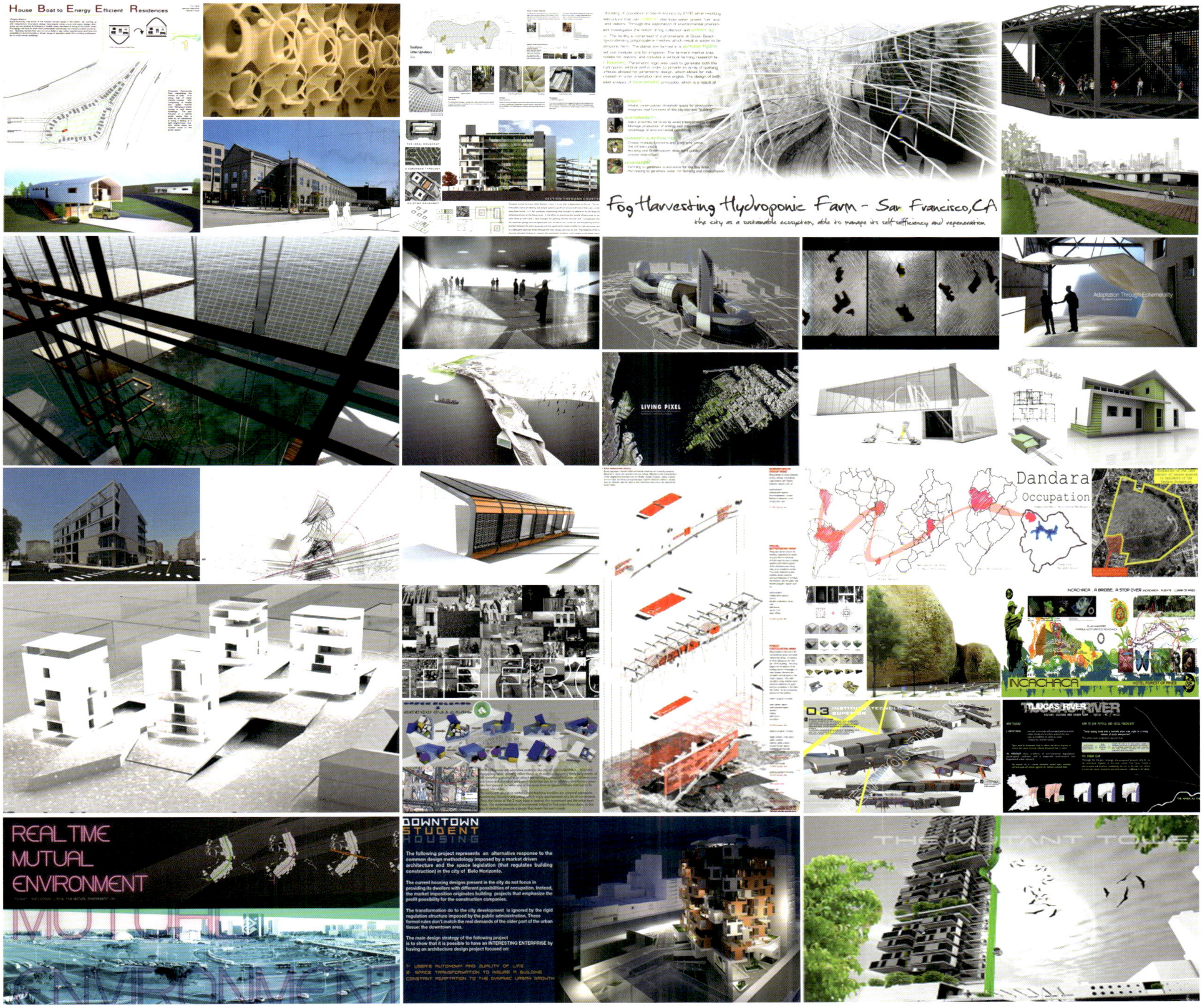

ROW 1 - House Boats to Energy Efficient Residences, Spencer L Dohrman, Martin L Franks, University of Kentucky College of Architecture, Lexington, United States / **Tendencies of Sensational Openings**, Yu Nong Khew, Southern California Institute of Architecture SCI-Arc, Los Angeles, United States / **Urban Upholstery**, Mira Henry, Molly Hunker, University of California, Los Angeles, United States / **Fog Harvesting Hydroponic Farm**, Michael K Leung, University of Southern California, Los Angeles, United States / **Participatory Democracy**, Dustin Willis, Southern Polytechnic State University, Marietta, United States / **ROW 2 - Formed Relationship**, Andrew Laufenberg, University of Wisconsin-Milwaukee, Milwaukee, United States / **Texas Doughnut Redux**, Emily Arden Wells, Yale University, New Haven, United States / **Dynamic Landforms**, Ana Cristina Jimenez, Tulane University, New Orleans, United States / **ROW 3 - Permeable Response**, Laura Charlton, Annie Kurtin, Columbia University, New York, United States / **Memorial + Museum for the Victims of the Political war in Peru**, José Vidalón, Parsons The New School for Design, New York, United States / **Fractal Boundaries**, Jun Pak, Cole Reynolds, Pratt Institute, New York , United States / **Play & Placement: Between Names and The Tunnels** , Yael Hameiri, The Cooper Union, New York, United States / **Adaptation Through Ephemerality**, David Cremer, Philadelphia University, Philadelphia, United States / **ROW 4 - The Rope**, Rebecca Fuchs, Adam Hostetler, University of Pennsylvania, Philadelphia, United States / **Living Pixel**, YoungJoon Choi, University of Pennsylvania, Philadelphia, United States / **The New 'Non-Standard'**, Jonathan Enns, Princeton University, Princeton, United States / **Habitech09**, Marcus Calhoun, Craig Jirak, Lance Mathews, Laura Thomas, Louisiana Tech University, Ruston, United States / **ROW 5 - Travis Park Center**, Ryan Schmidt, The University of Texas at San Antonio, San Antonio, United States / **Public Mass**, Michael Charters, California Polytechnic State University, San Luis Obispo, United States / **Plastics and Architectural Ecologies:**, Edward G. Hall, University of Arizona, Tucson, United States / **Harmonizing Humanitarian Efforts**, Adam John Longenbach, The Pennsylvania State University, University Park, United States / **PARTICIPANTS SOUTH AMERICA:** BRAZIL : **Dandara Occupation**, Tiago Castelo Branco Lourenço, Pontificia Universidade Catolica de Minas Gerais-PUC/M, Belo Horizonte, Brazil / **ROW 6 - cultural park hotel in Almagro**, Valeria Soledad Marquez, Simona Solorzano Gomez, Universidad de Palermo, Buenos Aires, Argentina / **TEFROPOLIS, City of ashes**, Nadia Barba, Emiliano Mitri, Milena Montersino, Universidad Nacional de Cordoba, Córdoba, Argentina / P11-1852, **Academy of Music, Dubai**, Manasseri Ezequiel, Vagni Federico, Universidad Nacional de Rosario, Rosario, Argentina / **Hotel Forest of Pines**, Richard Nelson Mamani Callisaya, Miguel Angel Quispe Mamani, Universidad Mayor de San Simon, Cochabamba, Bolivia / **ROW 7 - Scenic Arts Centre for the City of Cochabamba, Bolivia**, Daniel Eugenio Espinoza Ayo, Universidad Privada del Valle, Cochabamba, Bolivia / **Institut Tecnologico Superior**, Rory Felix, Univ. Autónoma Juan Misael Saracho, Tarija, Bolivia / **Tijucas River**, Hellen Morás de Andrade, Universidade do Vale do Itajaí, Balneário Camboriú, Brazil, South / **ROW 8 - Downtown Student Housing**, André C. B. Soares, Universidade Federal de Minas Gerais - UFMG, Belo Horizonte, Brazil / **Real Time Mutual Environment**, Ana Caroline Lecôncio Mota, Centro Universitário de Brasilia - UniCEUB, Brasilia-DF, Brazil / **The Mutant Tower**, Erick Capeleti Carbone, Universidade Federal de Mato Grosso do Sul, Campo Grande, Brazil

ROW 1 - **Flagship Store**, Rafael Kroth Paim, Universidade Luterana do Brasil, Canoas, Brazil / **Floating Cities - Cities of the Future**, Jonny Stica, Pontifícia Universidade Católica do Paraná-PUCPR, Curitiba, Brazil / **Capri Yacht Club: A New Proposal**, Pamela de Braga Pacheco Zardo, Universidade Federal do Parana-UFPR, Curitiba, Brazil / **Urbanization of Vila Bom Menino Settlement** Francisco Marquete, Universidade Positivo, Curitiba, Brazil **Performative Scenarios for the city**, Isis Soares Pereira do Nascimento, Universidade Federal de Santa Catarina-UFSC, Florianopolis, Brazil / **ROW 2** - **Museum of the Park**, Pedro Câmara, Universidade Federal do Ceara-UFC, Fortaleza, Brazil / **Body Experiences Complex**, Nilo Martins de Santana, PUC GOIÁS - Pontifícia Universidade Católica de Goiás, Goiania, Brazil / **Rehabilitation Center for Delinquent Adolescent**, César André Boehm, Centro Universitário Univates, Lajeado, Brazil / **Philosophising at the abyss**, Rafael Alcantara, Universidade estadual de Londrina-UEL, Londrina, Brazil / **ROW 3** - **Brazilian Embassy in Berlin**, Eduardo Verri Lopes, Universidade Estadual de Maringá, Maringá, Brazil / **Evolve**, Vanessa Cobianchi de Aguiar, Jaqueline Rodrigues Silva, Universidade Braz Cubas-UBC, Mogi Das Cruzes, Brazil / **Industry of Music**, Felipe Tenn-Pass, Universidade Feevale, Novo Hamburgo, Brazil / **Urban Station Park**, Gabriela Costa de Castro, Universidade Federal de Pelotas-UFPEL, Pelotas, Brazil / **System for Emergency Shelters**, Luiza Campana, Centro Universitário Ritter dos Reis, Porto Alegre, Brazil / **Interactive Place - Museum of Communication**, Fábio Maia Guzenski, Pontifícia Universidade Católica do Rio Grande do Sul – PUCRS, Porto Alegre, Brazil / **ROW 4** - **Islamic Center**, Rodrigo Mathias, Universidade Federal do Rio Grande do Sul-UFRGS, Porto Alegre, Brazil / **Antromangue Cultural Center - Manguebeat in poetry**, Rafael Campos Rangel, Universidade Católica de Pernambuco - UNICAP, Recife, Brazil / **Music Square**, Natalia Bartolomeo, André Zupekan, Centro Universitário Metodista Bennett, Rio De Janeiro, Brazil / **Changing the voids** , Caio Calafate, Pontifícia Universidade Católica do Rio de Janeiro, PUC-Rio, Rio de Janeiro, Brazil / **Fixed & Flows**, Fagner Marçal, Universidade Federal do Rio de Janeiro, Rio De Janeiro, Brazil / **ROW 5** - **Museum of Contemporary Art Rio Grande do Sul**, Fabiana Kieling da Costa, Universidade do Vale do Rio dos Sinos-UNISINOS, Sao Leopoldo, Brazil / **Social Condensers**, Luís Pompeo Martins, Universidade de Sao Paulo - USP, Sao Paulo, Brazil / **Itaquera Culture and Leisure Center**, Lucas Nobre, Universidade Estadual Paulista "Julio Mesquita Filho"-UNESP, Sao Paulo, Brazil / **Itinerant Thematic Mediatheque**, Marcelle Gabriolli Meneghini, Universidade S. Judas Tadeu-USJT, Sao Paulo, Brazil / **ROW 6** - CHILE: **Ritual Space Consolidation**, José A. Gallardo del Castillo, Universidad Católica del Norte, Antofagasta, Chile / **Ferry Terminal and Hotel for Panguipulli City: South of Chile**, María Josefina Escobar Díaz, Universidad del Desarollo, Concepcion, Chile / **Ship Terminal in Tjuvholmen, Oslo - Norway**, Gustavo 'LeSclamb' Vilches, Universidad de La Serena, La Serena, Chile / **Valdivia`s Foundation**, Juan Pablo Alcalde Dominguez, Pontificia Universidad Católica de Chile PUCC, Santiago, Chile / **The Foundry**, Daniel Iragüen, Universidad Central, Santiago, Chile / **ROW 7** - **Experimental Vertical Farm**, Claudio Palavecino Llanos, Universidad de Chile, Santiago, Chile / **Technical Industrial School**, Felipe Sepúlveda Rojas, Universidad del Desarrollo, Santiago, Chile / **High Security Penitentiary in Curimón Chile**, Daniel Dintrans Sanhueza, Universidad Diego Portales, Santiago, Chile / **Paseo Tajamares del Mapocho, Santiago, Chile.**, Paulo Plass Alvarez, Universidad Mayor, Santiago, Chile / **ROW 8** - **Navigable Pavilion and Pier in Dalcahue, Chiloe**, Andrés Salgado Henríquez, universidad tecnologica metropolitana, Santiago, Chile / **KIDS, cuerpos en movimiento.**, Nicol Müller, University of Talca, Talca, Chile / **Urban Membrane**, Andrè Geoffroy, Universidad de las Americas, Viña del Mar, Chile / COLOMBIA: **Cartagena de Indias, Home Port**, Alberto Andres Herrera Salas, Diana Carolina Rojas Galan, Pontificia Universidad Javeriana, Bogota, Colombia / **Link between urban sustainability and cultural landscape**, Jose Fernando Pérez Alcobé, Universidad de La Salle, Bogota, Colombia

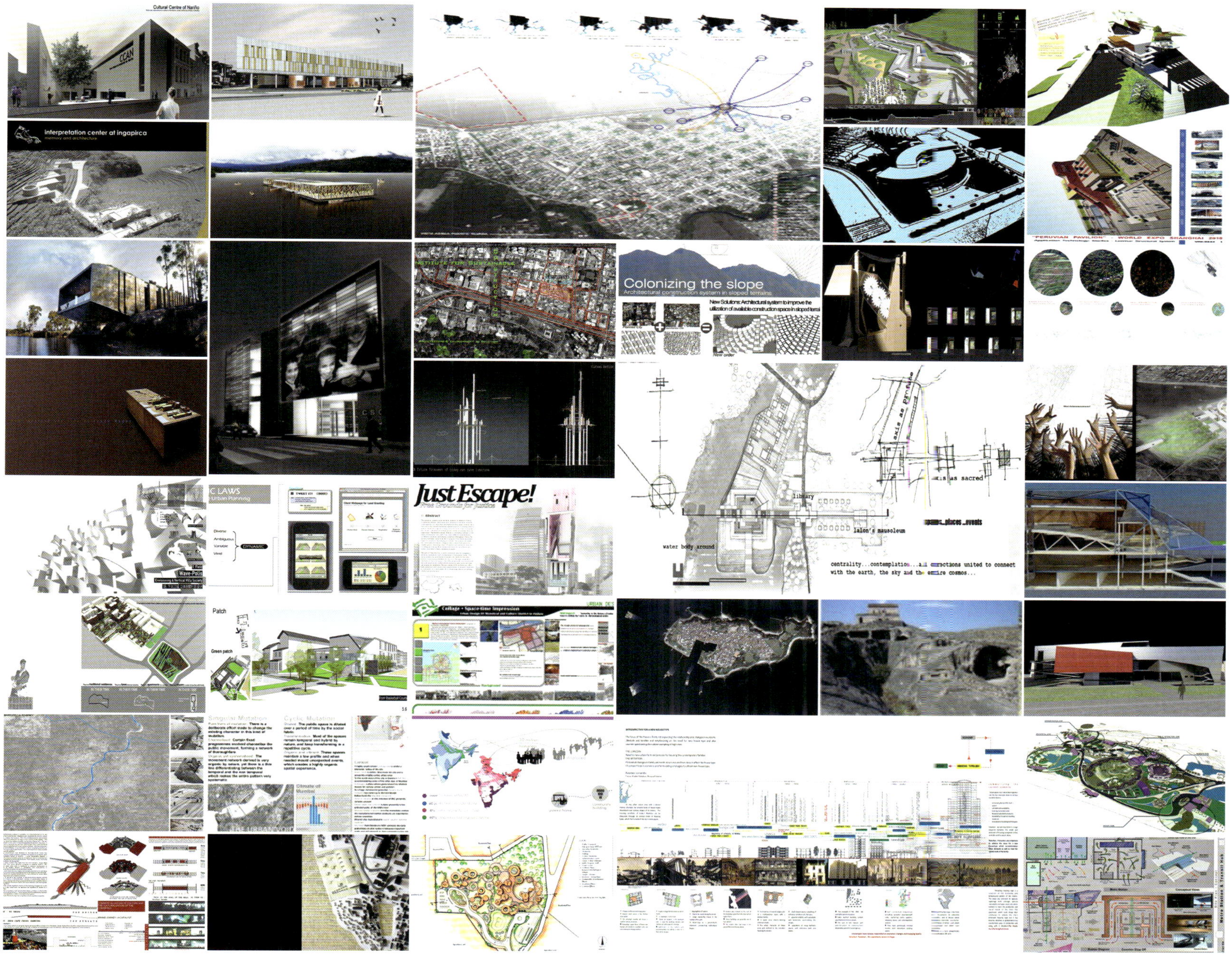

ROW 1 - Cultural Centre of Nariño. , Manuel Felipe Woodcock, Universidad de Los Andes, Bogota, Colombia / **Mandela Public Library**, Mauricio Mendez Wiesner, Universidad Jorge Tadeo Lozano-Bogota, Bogota, Colombia / **Self-sustainable housing prototypes, Puerto Tejada Cauca (Col)**, Mario Fernando Camargo Gómez, Universidad del Valle. Facultad de Artes Integradas, Cali, Colombia / **A new necropolis**, Hector Fabian Marin, Juan Carlos Sanchez, Universidad Nacional de Colombia, Manizales, Colombia / **Architectural Blog**, Karina Alexandra Rodriguez, Pontificia Universidad Catolica del Ecuador, Quito, Ecuador / **ROW 2 - Interpretation Center at Ingapirca**, Felipe Jose Palacios, Universidad San Francisco de Quito, Quito, Ecuador / **Lodging for Birdwatchers and Butterflywatchers** , Demostenez Mori Pelaez, Pontificia Universidad Católica del Perú, Lima, Peru / **Children's Cancer Hospital**, Maria Luisa Pineda, Universidad Peruana de Ciencias Aplicadas, Lima, Peru / **Peruvian Pavilion - Expo Shanghai 2010**, Roxana Garrido, Karen Matos, Universidad Ricardo Palma, Lima, Peru / **ROW 3 - Spa Ferrando**, Nicolás Newton, Gonzalo Parma, Universidad de la Republica - Uruguay, Montevideo, Uruguay / **CCS**, Heripsime Susana Moumdjian, Dahyana Posada, Universidad ORT Uruguay, Montevideo, Uruguay / **Institute for Sustainable Construction**, Daniella Molina, Universidad Jose Maria Vargas, Caracas, Venezuela / **Colonizing the slope**, Ricardo Bombín, Rafael Romero, Universidad Simón Bolívar, Sartenejas, Venezuela / **PARTICIPANTS OCEANIA Hawkesbury Ponds Fairgrounds**, Thomas Cole, University of New South Wales, Sydney, Australia, Oceania / **Interconnections of System Densities** , Sarosh Mulla, University of Auckland, Auckland, New Zealand, Oceania / **ROW 4 - PARTICIPANTS ASIA** - **Regenerating the Life of Panam Nagar**, Monon bin Yunus, Bangladesh University of Engineering & Technology, Dhaka, Bangladesh, Asia / **Global Warming, Sea Level Rise & Future City, 2100+, Bangladesh**, Shakil Ahmad Shimul, Brac University, Dhaka, Bangladesh, Asia / **Lalon Shah Memorial Complex**, Mehbuba Tune Uzra, North South University, Dhaka, Bangladesh, Asia / **White lie ---- the fifth illusion**, Tian Qiu, Beijing Jiaotong University, Beijing, China, Asia / **ROW 5 - Wave-Polis**, Yinghua Wen, China Central Academy of Fine Arts , Beijing, China, Asia / **Open Dynamic Laws**, Haonan LU, Chongqing University, Chongqing, China, Asia / **Just Escape**, Justin Law Chun Wai, Chinese University of Hong Kong, Hong Kong, China, Asia / **Music Garden**, Haosheng Zhang, Hunan University, Hunan, Changsha, China, Asia / **ROW 6 - In Their Time**, Ying Cai, Dizi Wu, Yangtze universities, Jingzhou, Hubei, China, Asia / **Suzhou High School Culture and Art Centre**, Ying Wang, Suzhou universities of science & technology , Suzhou, China, Asia / **Collage▪Space-time Impression** , Yiqiao Li, Chuchu Wei, Huazhong University of Science and Technology, Wuhan, Hubei, China, Asia / **Renewal Plan of Xiao'deng Island**, Qiu Chang, Sun Sheng, Huang Zhexuan, Xiamen University, Xiamen, Fujian China, Asia / **Museum of Contemporary Art**, Teimuraz Ninua, Georgian Technical University, Tbilisi, Georgia, Asia / **David Kakabadze Contemporary Museum of Art in Tbilisi, Georgia**, Nutsa Kandelaki, Tbilisi State Academy of Fine Arts, Tbilisi, Georgia, Asia / **ROW 7 - Re-Structuring the Development Along a Non-Perennial River**, Piyas Choudhuri, Centre for Environmental Planning & Technology CEPT University, Ahmedabad, India, Asia / **Mutating Culture in an urban milieu**, Shantesh Ramesh Kelvekar, Karnataka Law Society's Gogte Institute of Technology, Belgaum, India, Asia / **Emergency Habitats**, Noorain A Ahmed, Manipal Institute of Technology, Manipal, India, Asia / **Introspective for a new housetype**, Faiza Khan, Academy of Architecture, Mumbai, India, Asia / **International Exposition Promoting BioDiversity Conservation**, Anuj Vijay Kale, M.V.P'S College of architecture, Nashik, Nashik, India, Asia / **ROW 8 - Metreon - Mall and Library**, Kaustubh Kashelkar, Dr. D.Y. Patil College of Architecture, Navi Mumbai, India, Asia / **Liberation through Design : Crematorium**, Meenakshi Chauhan, School of Planning & Architecture, New Delhi, India, Asia / **Tribal Cultural &Heritage Center,Dahanu &HeritagePlaza,Kolhapur**, Maitreyi S Gulawani, Pranjali S. Shetty, Maharshi Krve Stree Shiksan Santha's Dr. Bhanuben Nanavati, Pune, India, Asia / **Metro Station at Shivajinagar, Pune**, Gautam N Attarde, Maratwhada Mitra Mandal's College of Architecture, Pune, India, Asia

ROW 1 - Indian Institute Of Management, Shillong, Anand Sonecha, Saurastra University, Rajkot, India, Asia / **Bhasha Bhavan' House Of Languages**, Dishant Jariwala, Veer Narmad South Gujarat University, Surat, India, Asia / **Spaceport at Ras-Ul-Khaimah, U.A.E.**, Priyank V Shah, Arvindbhai Patel Institute of Environmental Design, Vallabh Vidya Nagar, India, Asia / **Portable Kitchen for Disaster**, Andro Kaliandi, Berlinda Adi Puspita, University of Indonesia, Depok, Indonesia, Asia / **City Hotel at Kali Besar Timur Jakarta Old Town**, Stephanie Monieca, Bina Nusantara, Jakarta, Indonesia, Asia / **ROW 2 - School of Musical Art Design in Jakarta**, Indira Sari Asima Naibaho, Trisakti University, Jakarta, Indonesia, Asia / **Bamboo Education and Development Facility**, Wijaya Suryanegara Yapeter, Petra Christian University, Surabaya, Indonesia, Asia / **Designing of Nano technology Research Center**, Sahar Nivi, Tehran university, Tehran, Iran, Asia / **Health resort (SPA) in Hammam Al Alil**, Omar Arshad Al Hafith, Mosul, Mosul, Iraq, Asia / **ROW 3 - Open Wound | Museum for Human Rights in Israel**, Eyal Ivri, The Neri Bloomfield School of Design (WIZO haifa), Haifa, Israel, Asia / **Quilt city - Be'er sheva**, Haim Elfasy, Eyal Silis, Bezalel Academy of Art and Design, Jerusalem, Israel, Asia / **Stem - Biomimetic Tower**, tamir lavi, Tel Aviv University, Tel Aviv, Israel, Asia / **Architecture from Shade**, Kensuke OHTSUKA, Tokai University, Kanagawa, Japan, Asia / **Next To Each Other**, Aya Fujimoto, Kyoto Institute of Technology, Kyoto, Japan, Asia / **ROW 4 - Onomichi**, Miwako Kido, Tokyo University of the Arts, Tokyo, Japan, Asia / **Museum of Dune**, Yoshikazu Tanaka, Yonago National College of Technology, Tottori, Japan, Asia / **Between the star and the moon**, Kiyonori Sugiyama, Kanagawa University, Yokohama, Japan, Asia / **ROW 5 - Shatana Visionary Intervention**, Naser Al Hiasat, Rakan Ayyoub, Lina Odeh Saman, University of Jordan, Amman, Jordan, Asia / **The Wedding Palace**, Tatyana Khaissundinova, Kazakh Leading Academy of Architecture and Civil Engineering, Almaty, Kazakhstan, Asia / **Transformation: 'Kazakhfilm' - movie studio of tomorrow**, Alina Turekulova, Kazakh National Technical University named after K.I. Satpayev, Almaty, Kazakhstan, Asia / **Landscape in Movement**, Kim Jungmin, Yeungnam University, Kyungsan-shi, KyungbuK, Korea, South, Asia / **Mutual Heterogeneity**, Hyojin Kwon, Changyeob Lee, Jungwoo Lee, Hanyang University, Seoul, Korea, South, Asia / **Arts & Cultural Center - Gap of Office**, Doosan Baek, Korea University, Seoul, Korea, South, Asia / **ROW 6 - 3S+G=Regeneration**, Dongchoul Park, University of Seoul, Seoul, Korea, South, Asia / **shared community space for poor artists and residents**, Kang bok Wee, Sungkyunkwan University, Suwon, Korea, South, Asi / **Culture Island**, Jae-Ho Song, University of Ulsan, Ulsan, Korea, South, Asia / **Urban Permutation**, Nataly Abou Reslan, Lebanese American University formerly Beirut University, Byblos, Lebanon, Asia / **Tuneful Boulevard**, Rita Helayel, Notre Dame University - Louaize, Zouk Mosbeh, Lebanon, Asi / **ROW 7 - Architecture As Pedagogy : A School Without A School**, Ssi Cze Beh, National University of Malaysia, Bangi Selangor, Malaysia, Asia / **SPMM Community Complex and Nature Park**, Edgar Nonato Mr Cusi, Far Eastern University, Manila, Philippines, Asia / **Prince Salman Center for Disability Research**, Nahar B Abdulfattah, King Saud University, Riyadh, Saudi Arabia, Asia / **The Floating City**, Han Yang, The National University of Singapore, Singapore, Singapore, Asia / **Flood and Slum in Jakarta City**, Binvi Wannaya, Chung Yuan Christian University, Chung-Li, Taiwan, Asia / **ROW 8 - Dynamic Seascape**, , Yu Tung Hsing, Tunghai University, Taichung, Taiwan, Asia - **Pocket Shelter**, Charles Rudi, National Taipei University of Technology, Taipei, Taiwan, Asia / **Guide to Density**, Che-Wei Yeh, Tamkang University, Taipei, Taiwan, Asia / **Plastic (bag) Architecture**, Zhi-Sheng Chen, Tamkang universities, Tamsui, Taiwan, Asia / **The flow of water/The frozen music** , Autthawut Kruethongsri, Rajamangala University of Technology, Thanyaburi., Pratumthani, Thailand, Asia / **Su_Per_formQ** , Aezad Alam, American University of Sharjah, Sharjah, United Arab Emirates, Asia

ROW 1 - Sustainable Community Cultural Centre of Hanhi people , Loc Huu Pham, Hanoi Architectural University, Hanoi, Vietnam, Asia / **Saigon Passenger Ship Terminal**, Nguyen Bao Thang, Ecole d'Architecture de Ho Chi Minh Ville, Ho Chi Minh Ville, Vietnam, Asia / **AFRICA - El Alamien Performing Art Center**, Khaled M.ElAmer M.El-Ashry, Alexandria University, Alexandria, Egypt, Africa / **Vaduz Performing Arts Center**, Mohamed Fawzy Abdelkarim, MISR International University, Giza, Egypt, Africa / **ROW 2 - Pulse Of Sinai**, Aly Ahmed kamal Soliman, October 6 University, Giza, Egypt, Africa / **Alexandria Vertical Take-Off & Landing Air Harbor**, Ahmad M. Mahmoud, Al-Mansoura University, Mansoura, Egypt, Africa / **Herero Cultural Centre and Genocide Memorial**, Willem Steenkamp, The University of the Free State, Bloemfontein, South Africa, Africa / **Khayelitsha - a playground for change and exchange**, Danielle Reimers, The University of Cape Town, Cape Town, South Africa, Africa / **ROW 3 - A Public Bathhouse**, Ruann van der Westhuizen, University of Pretoria, Pretoria, South Africa, Africa / **Proposed Centre for Occupational Therapy**, Godchance Gamaliel, ARDHI University, Dar es Salaam, Tanzania, Africa / **EUROPE - Lagos - Emergent urbanism**, Gunnar Ploner, Universität Innsbruck, Innsbruck, Austria, Europe / **The East Mediterranean - Insight and Outlook**, Sigi Atteneder, Universität für Kunstlerische & Industrielle Gestaltung, Linz, Austria, Europe / **Sanatorium**, Christian Tonko, Academy of Fine Arts Vienna, Vienna, Austria, Europe / **A Place under the Sun for Everyone**, marlene wagner, Technische Universität Wien, Vienna, Austria, Europe / **ROW 4 - Superhuman Enticement**, Julia Koerner, University for Applied Arts Vienna, Vienna, Austria, Europe / **Museum for Contemporary Art Brussels**, Steven Schenk, Artesis University College of Antwerp - Henry van de Velde, Antwerp, Belgium, Europe / **Maashaven Harbour Bridge**, James Richardson, Vrije Universiteit Brussel (VUB), Brussels, Belgium, Europe / **Kindergarten Revised**, Tim De Messemaeker, Hogeschool voor Wetenschap & Kunst, associatie KU Leuven, Gent, Belgium, Europe / **Water Urbanisms** , Linde Van Reeth, Katholieke Universiteit te Leuven K.U.L., Heverlee, Belgium, Europe / **Shipyard for sailboats at the island Korcula**, Bosko Opalic, University of Zagreb, Zagreb, Croatia, Europe / **ROW 5 - The Shabby Quarter in the Heart of Liberec**, Jiří Žid, Technical University of Liberec, Liberec, Czech Republic, Europe / **The Inner Periphery of Prague**, Filip Tittl, Czech Technical University in Prague, Prague, Czech Republic, Europe / **Limits in Architecture**, Vit Svoboda, The Academy of Arts, Architecture and Design, Prague 1, Czech Republic, Europe / **London Centre for Urban Agriculture**, Tim Nørlund Jensen, Aarhus School of Architecture, Aarhus, Denmark, Europe / **Beyond the Prison Bars:**, Robert Burke, Sophie Hamilton-Grey, Justin Johnston, University of Liverpool, Liverpool, England, Europe / **ROW 6 - A Crime of Passion**, Rachel Harding, Royal College of Art, London, England, Europe / **A Defensive Architecture**, Nicholas Adam Szczepaniak, The University of Westminster, London, England, Europe / **(Re)Constructing Landscape:**, Patrick John Clark, University of Plymouth, Plymouth, England, Europe / **Fortress in the 21st Century**, Grete Soosalu, Estonian Academy of Arts, Tallinn, Estonia, Europe / **Luukku-House Design and Construction 2009-2010**, Ulla Prami, Aalto University, School of Science and Technology, Espoo, Finland, Europe / **Urban Agriculture for Vila Brandão - Salvador, Brazil**, Vilja Larjosto, Aalto Unversity, School of Science and Technology, Espoo, Finland, Europe / **ROW 7 - Methods for morphogenesis and ecology in architecture -**, Toni Österlund, University of Oulu, Oulu 10, Finland, Europe / **Limits and Scales**, Coll Swann, Ecole nationale supérieure d'architecture de Montpellier, Montpellier, France, Europe / **Level Rise City**, Raphaël Boursier, Ecole Nationale Supérieure d'Architecture Paris-Malaquais, Paris, France, Europe / **Le Rezervoir**, Damien ANTONI, Ecole nationale supérieure d'architecture de Paris-Belleville, Paris, France, Europe / **Connected Environments**, Timothee Boitouzet, Ecole nationale supérieure d'architecture de Versailles, Versailles, France, Europe / **ROW 8 - About the water's force**, Marie Luise Kister, Rheinisch-Westfälische Technische Hochschule Aachen, Aachen, Germany, Europe / **House of Arts and Culture, Beirut**, Jonas Greubel, Daniel Schilp, Alanus Hochschule, Alfter / Bonn, Germany, Europe / **Utilization Concepts for In-Between-Spaces in Berlin**, Tobias Donat, Beuth Hochschule für Technik Berlin, Berlin, Germany, Europe

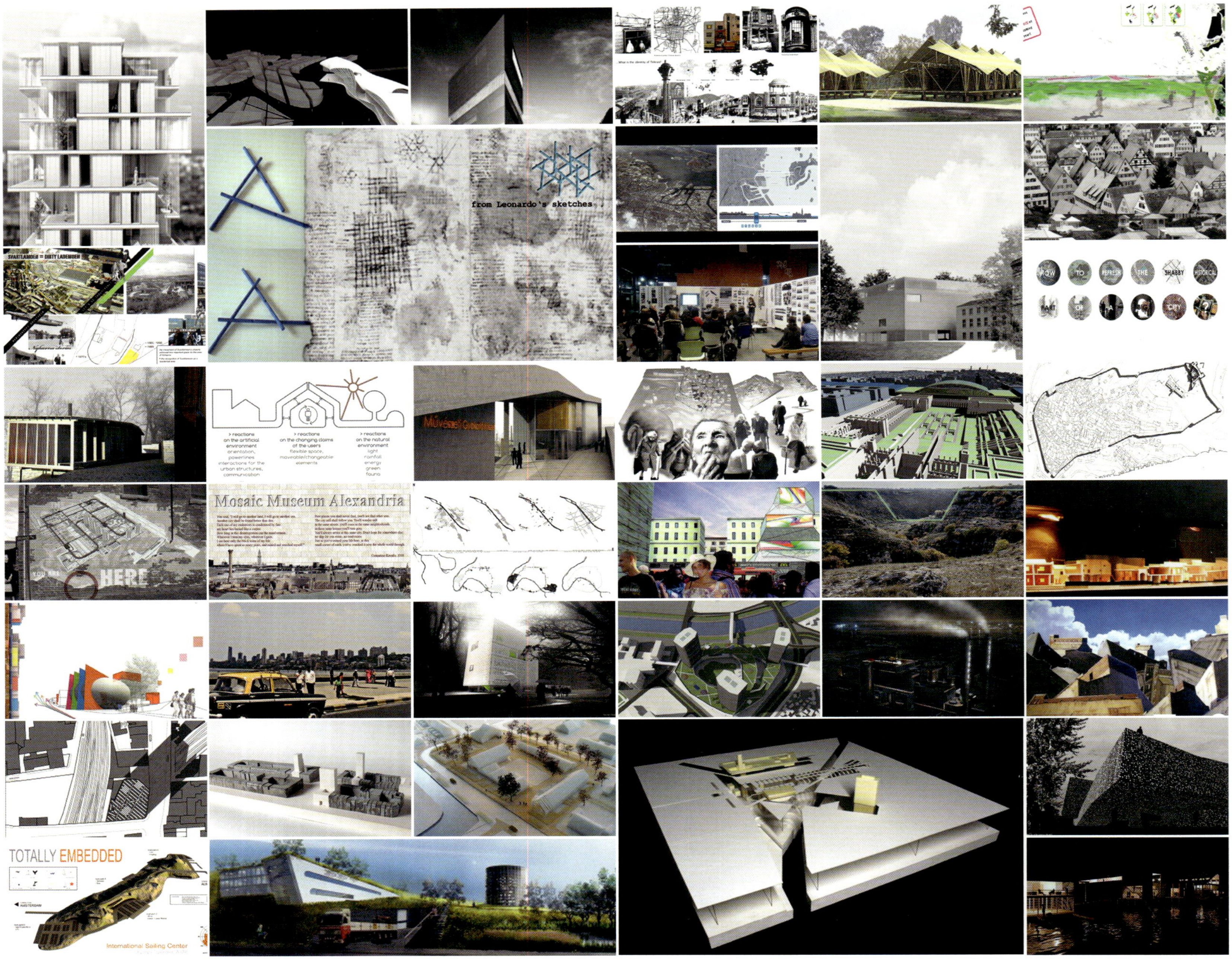

ROW 1 - Atmosphères, Timur Doğan, Technische Universität Darmstadt, Darmstadt, Germany, Europe / **Aperspectival space** , Deepak Srikumaran Jawahar, Städelschule, Staatliche Hochschule für Bildende Künste, Frankfurt am Main, Germany, Europe / **Intercultural Forum Istanbul**, Sebastian Lundelius, Universität Hannover, Hannover, Germany, Europe / **Tehran Yesterday Today Tomorrow**, Shahrzad Rahmani, KIT Karlsruher Institut für Technologie, Karlsruhe, Germany, Europe / **The orangutan project**, Caroline Krawczyk, Sarah Wloka, Universität Kassel, Kassel, Germany, Europe / **Productive Landscapes - Algaegardens**, Melanie Hammer, Waschma Sahin, Technische Universität München, München, Germany, Europe / **ROW 2 - LERO-System**, Huy Quang Nguyen, Akademie der Bildenden Künste Stuttgart, Stuttgart, Germany, Europe / **Venice HUB**, Stefanie Hickl, Thomas Quisinsky, Universität Stuttgart, Stuttgart, Germany, Europe / **A New Bauhaus-Museum**, Norma Tollmann, Bauhaus-Universität Weimar, Weimar, Germany, Europe / **Dinkelsbühl - Seaside** , Hannes Schmidt, Hochschule für Architektur und Bauwesen, Weimar, Germany, Europe / **ROW 3 - An imaginary/-ies conflict**, Alkmini Petraki, Maria Vlagoidou, Aristotle University of Thessaloniki, Thessaloniki, Greece, Europe / **Under construction**, Anna Vasof, Univeristy of Thessaly, Volos, Greece, Europe / **Chocolate Manufacture**, Gergely Szacsvay, Budapest University of Technology and Economics, Budapest, Hungary, Europe / **ROW 4 - Hikers' Shelter**, Aron Vass-Eysen, Moholy-Nagy University of Art and Design Budapest, Budapest, Hungary, Europe / **Contemporary Architecture Centre**, Roland Lipusz, Széchenyi István University, Gyor, Hungary, Europe / **Art Institute** , Simon Zsolt, University of Pécs, Pecs, Hungary, Europe / **FRA-M-MENTI**, Giuliana Frau, university of SASSARI, Alghero, Italy, Europe / **Bari, the Railway Junction and the Ex "Rossani" Barracks Area.**, Lucio Riccobono, Politecnico di Bari, Bari , Italy, Europe / **Rehabilitation of Girifalco Fortress, Cortona**, Aura Gnerucci, Maria Teresa Idone, Dania Marzo, Università di Firenze, Florence, Italy, Europe / **ROW 5 - You are Here**, Maurizio Pizzocro, Veronica Rusca, Lorenzo Trompetto, Università di Genova, Genova, Italy, Europe / **MMA Mosaic Museum Alexandria**, Viola Bertini, Elena Ciapparelli, Chiara Taddei, Politecnico di Milano, Milan, Italy, Europe / **Le nouvel horizon**, Sara Impera, Politecnico di Milano, Milan, Italy, Europe / **Development of a reversible media-architecture**, Fabrizio Furiassi, Università di Roma La Sapienza, Rome, Italy, Europe / **Architecture as Geological Metaphor**, Angela Sicolo, Marisa Vitale, Universita di Roma La Sapienza, Rome, Italy, Europe / **New Transit Camp Social Club**, Alberto Bottero, Francesco Strocchio, Politecnico di Torino, Torino, Italy, Europe / **ROW 6 - Museum of art**, Medina Spahiu, AAB RIINVEST, Prishtina, Kosovo, Europe / **Mumbai - Maximum City Tower**, Remo Baumgartner, Hochschule Liechtenstein, Vaduz, Liechtenstein, Europe / **Green House for Culture**, Paulius Vaitiekunas, VDA Kaunas Art Institute, Kaunas, Lithuania, Europe / **Hybrid center**, Filip Dubrovski, University SS. Kiril and Metodij, Skopje, Macedonia, Europe / **Westpoort Thermae**, Jeroen Atteveld, Amsterdam School of the Arts, Amsterdam, Netherlands, Europe / **The Graintower**, Loe van de Ven, Academy of Architecture Arnhem, Arnhem, Netherlands, Europe / **ROW 7 - Spaces, Poetics and Voids**, Simone Pizzagalli, Delft University of Technology, Delft, Netherlands, Europe / **Amsterdam Alphabet**, Gijs Adriaansens, Eindhoven University of Technology, Eindhoven, Netherlands, Europe / **Dwelling with care**, Nelleke Karst, Hanzehogeschool, University of Applied Sciences, Groningen, Netherlands, Europe / **Le Bleu du Ciel**, Huub Donkers, Maastricht academy of architecture, Maastricht, Netherlands, Europe / **Archicoustics**, Paul Michielsen, Rotterdam Academy of Architecture and Urban Design, Rotterdam, Netherlands, Europe / **ROW 8 - Totally Embedded**, Ronald Bongers, Fontys University of Applied Science, Tilburg, Netherlands, Europe / **Biodiverse business areas**, Eric Bovekerk, Richard Hereijgers, Wageningen University, Wageningen, Netherlands, Europe / **RE:BEIRA**, Guro Alver, Bergen School of Architecture - BAS, Bergen, Norway, Europe

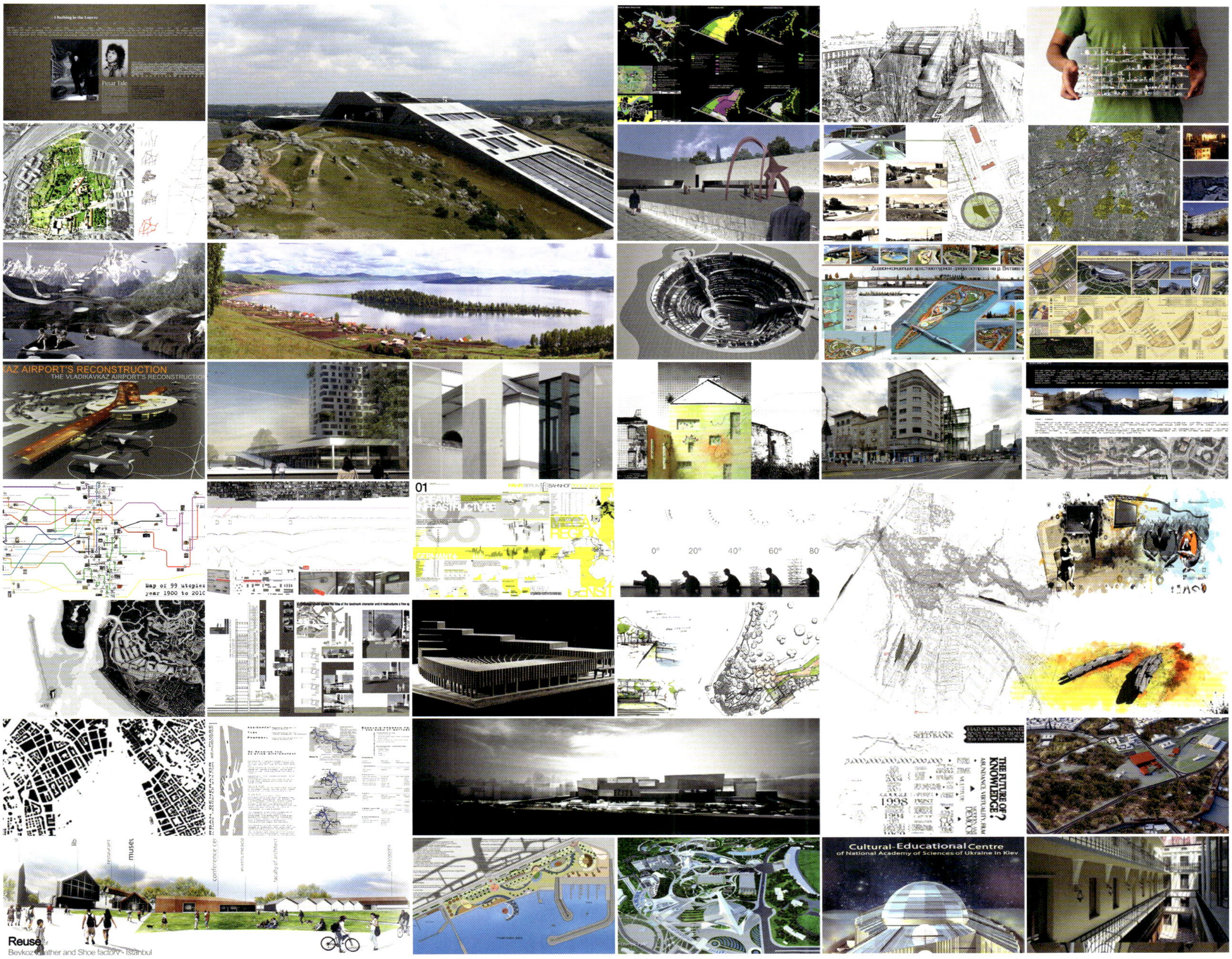

ROW 1 - Bathing in the Louvre, Kasia Heijerman, The School of Architecture in Oslo-AHO, Oslo, Norway, Europe / **On The Eagle Nests Track**, Mateusz Lesniak, Bialystok Technical University, Bialystok, Poland, Europe / **Project of ecology-recreation-education center in Olesnica**, Ada Kołodziejczyk, The Silesian University of Technology, Gliwice, Poland, Europe / **Library of Warsaw University of Technology**, Marcin Pajewski, Politechnika Warszawska, Warsaw, Poland, Europe / **XYZ Structure**, Maciej Siuda, Wroclaw University of Technology, Wroclaw, Poland, Europe / **ROW 2 - Topographic Skin**, Daniel Alexandre Gonsalves Silva, Universidade Lusófona de Humanidades e Tecnologias, Lisboa, Portugal, Europe / **(Re)Inhabiting the City - the New Lisbon Museum**, Gonçalo Silva Pereira, Universidade Técnica de Lisboa, UTL, Lisboa, Portugal, Europe / **Art Center**, Horia Tundrea, Universitatea Tehnica 'Gh.Asachi', Iasi, Romania, Europe / **Community Center**, Simionescu Oana Alexandra, Universitatea Politehnica din Timisoara, Timisoara, Romania, Europe / **ROW 3 - Fractal architecture.Conception of a habitation envelope 2110**, Anna Plekhanova, Kazan State University of Architecture and Engineering, Kazan, Russia, Europe / **Recreation-tourist system «Sky Lakes»** , Alena Vanshulina, Krasnojersk Engineering Construction Academy, Krasnoyarsk, Russia, Europe / **Penal (penitentiary) Institution**, Kristina Ishkhanova, Moscou Architectural Institute - State Academy, Moscow, Russia, Europe / **Landscape design of an Island in the Prague river**, Maria Yandulova, Southern Urals State University, Tchelyabinsk, Russia, Europe / **The reconstruction of the railway station "Ulianovsk-Central"**, Guzel Galimova, Ulianovsk State Technical University, Ulianovsk, Russia, Europe / **ROW 4 - The Vladikavkaz airport's reconstruction**, Bagriy Ksenia Ya, North Caucasian State Technological University, Vladikavkaz, Russia, Europe / **Cultural Center**, Alina Batishcheva, Volgograd State University of Architecture & Civil Engineering, Volgograd, Russia, Europe / **Innovational museum-laboratory**, Nikita Kolbovskiy, Yaroslavl State Technical University, Yaroslavl, Russia, Europe / **National Apiological Network : An Illustrated History**, Craig Johnston, University of Strathclyde, Glasgow, Scotland, Europe / **Hole in the Hole**, Milos Mirosavic, University of Belgrade, Belgrade, Serbia, Europe / **Information Centre**, Kristína Martoníková, Slovenska technicka univerzita, Bratislava, Slovakia, Europe / **ROW 5 - 100th Utopia [London 2100]**, Ángel Martínez García, Universidad de Alicante, Alicante, Spain, Europe / **The Plug Inn, Dorm in IIT**, Carles Sala Roig, Universitat Politècnica de Catalunya, Barcelona - Catalonia, Spain, Europe / **Berlin NEU-Bahnhof Zoologischer Garten**, Gonzalo del Val, Universidad Europea de Madrid, Madrid, Spain, Europe / **ZIPIZIP**, Rodrigo García González, Universidad Politécnica de Madrid, Madrid, Spain, Europe / **E-school**, Paula Ibarrondo, [EPS.CEU] Escuela Politécnica Superior University CEU San Pablo, MADRID, Spain, Europe / **ROW 6 - Sancti Petri**, Jimenez Fernandez-Palacios Luz, Universidad de Sevilla, Sevilla, Spain, Europe / **High-rise Mixed-use Building in Valencia**, Nuria Salvador Luján, Universidad Politécnica de Valencia, Valencia, Spain, Europe / **Varese Railway District**, Jessica Stuecklin, Università della Svizzera italiana, Mendrisio, Switzerland, Europe / **Campus Hotel Residence Hertenstein** , Carolin Ammann, HSR Hochschule für Technik Rapperswil, Rapperswil, Switzerland, Europe / **ROW 7 - A new building for the succulent plant collection of Zurich**, Derk Thijs, ETH Zürich (Swiss Federal Institute of Technology), Zurich, Switzerland, Europe / **Urban Generator - Culture Transfer Station**, Ezgi Balkanay, Middle East Technical University, Ankara, Turkey, Europe / **DCC**, Caner Bilgin, Istanbul Kultur University, Istanbul, Turkey, Europe / **Great Time Capsule**, Ege Özgirin, Istanbul Technical University, Istanbul, Turkey, Europe / **Suhaneler / Waterhouses**, Ethem Ovunc Tar, Mimar Sinan Fine Arts University, Istanbul, Turkey, Europe / **ROW 8 - Reuse of Beykoz Leather and Shoe Factory**, Onur AKIN, Yildiz Technical University, Istanbul, Turkey, Europe / **The Landscape Design Project of Tekirdağ Shoreline**, Beste Karakaya, Namik Kemal University, Tekirdag, Turkey, Europe / **Green line**, Oleksii Gertsev, Pavel Svetlichniy, The Donbas National Academy of Civil Engineering & Architecture, Donetsk region, Makiyivka, Ukraine, Europe / **The Cultural-Educational Centre of NAS of Ukraine in Kiev**, Alissa Bankovskaya, Kiev State Technical University of Building and Architecture, Kiev, Ukraine, Europe / **Development of the passages system in the central part of Lviv**, Nazar V. Ratushynskyj, National University 'Lvivska Politechnika', Lviv, Ukraine, Europe

LET'S TAG IT! MINUTES OF THE JURY MEETING

During the summer of 2010, parcels from every continent in the world started to arrive at the MIT in Cambridge (MA). On the 23rd of September the jury flew in, coming from China, India en the United States to judge the graduation projects. The MIT selected the members of the jury: *Kapil Gupta from Serie Architects*, lives in India and has his office in Mumbai and London. *Ralph Nelson of LOOM*, studied architecture on the east coast. His teaching career took him from California to Minnesota, and from Kentucky to Detroit. *Xiangning Li from Shanghai, China*. He trained as an architect, and currently teaches at the Tongi University and is the director of the Museum of Architecture to be newly built in Shanghai. *Yung Ho Chang*, chairman of the Archiprix International jury. He runs his own office, *Atelier FJCZ in Beijing, China*, and is the former Head of the Architecture Department of the MIT.

The jury meetings took place at the MIT on Friday 24 September on the top floor of the MIT's Media Lab designed by Fumihiko Maki, and on Saturday 25 September at the architecture department in the grand old main building. The 6th edition of Archiprix International has again broken all records, this time with 305 entries. Unfortunately not all entries met the criteria: some arrived too late at the MIT, some were only submitted online. Nevertheless, the jury still had to review a staggering number of entries: 296 projects, coming from 72 countries, all completed after 1 July 2008 and nominated as the best graduation project of their school or university.

'Can we see them one more time to make sure we haven't missed anything?' As preparation for the meeting, the jury members were asked to study in detail more than 70 projects online, each taking his share of the total amount of entries. In the first round on the 24th, the jury looked at all 296 submitted projects, neatly laid out on tables. No fewer than 65 projects were allocated an 'OK' or 'Maybe' tag, and made it to the second round. The discussion on which projects ought to be nominated took all Saturday morning and early afternoon. Ultimately, 24 projects were nominated.

Overall, the jury members were pleased to see that the architects and schools have not abandoned the basic design values. The jury considers architecture, urban design and landscape architecture as ongoing professions with their DNA deeply rooted in history and convention. These are professions that must reinterpret themselves in a critical way over and over again, resisting trends like the contemporary obsession for the iconic. The jury saw intelligence and courage in many projects, or, as one of the members put it: 'All face reality, some dream about reality'. The jury even went as far as stating that it didn't make sense to talk about some projects: 'They should just be built and we will go there to see it'! There seems to be a shift in interest, the jury noticed. Almost no parametric design projects were submitted, most of the projects refer directly to architecture and the discipline itself. They are projects where curiosity wins, and the designers are able to frame the times we live in and the challenges we face.

Although a large number of urban projects were submitted, the jury was disappointed with the quality of the work. The members looked for projects that address the city as well as architecture, and although it was clear that many designers are interested in the engagement of architecture and the city, they did not seem to know how to establish the link. There was a great deal of mapping, but very little strategic thinking about how to deal with multiple forces acting simultaneously for example. There still seems to be a strong division between architecture and the city. Again, there should not be too much emphasis on iconic buildings; architecture should be returned to its natural context, which is the city, in order to enrich both architecture and the city, according to the jury.

But, at an architectural level, it is a different story. Many of the submitted architectural projects connect seamlessly with the local conditions, and are even typical of their region.

Despite their international experience and their open-mindedness, some projects made the jury aware that they were perhaps not quite as familiar with all design societies as they might wish to be. As one jury member stated: 'There is a possibility of a black cat, an excellent project that we did not recognize as such because of the fact that it originates from a non-standard culture.' Some projects were reviewed again critically after the jury agreed that they would not enter into a cultural or geographic conversation, and that origin was not a part of the discussion.

'Can we leave for 10 minutes before we say, these are the ones?'
In the final round, the jury selected eight projects for an award. Although the winning projects are related to the DNA of recognizable architects or architectural styles, they are another evolutionary step beyond that DNA, and stand out because of the authentic voice of the individual designers and the clear positions they take. They are all very powerful projects and go beyond style. What they have in common is poetics. The eight award-winning projects are:

- ***Amsterdam Alphabet - Gijs Adriaansens***
  EINDHOVEN UNIVERSITY OF TECHNOLOGY, FACULTY OF ARCHITECTURE, BUILDING AND PLANNING, EINDHOVEN (THE NETHERLANDS).
  A catalogue of new, dense building types based on the typical Dutch 19th-century building block to regenerate the 19th-century urban tissue of Amsterdam.

Comments: A traditional project that develops a relevant, beautiful strategy and thus proves that the power of the avant-garde can be an illusion. It is not a strategy for reconstruction but offers a new vocabulary based on traditional values. The strategy could be operational in many cities. The position is interesting, the design proposals are unfortunately 'another icon'.

- ***A Defensive Architecture - Nicholas Adam Szczepaniak***
  THE UNIVERSITY OF WESTMINSTER, SCHOOL OF ARCHITECTURE AND THE BUILT ENVIRONMENT, LONDON (UNITED KINGDOM).
  The towers located in the sea are alive, dramatizing shifts in environmental conditions: breathing, creaking, groaning, sweating and crying when stressed. Internally, the towers serve as a vast repository for mankind's most valuable asset: knowledge.

Comment: A project that is beautifully expressed and fires the imagination. Beyond the intriguing images is architecture.

- ***National Apiological Network : An Illustrated Historie - Craig Johnston*** UNIVERSITY OF STRATHCLYDE, DEPARTMENT OF ARCHITECTURE, GLASGOW (UNITED KINGDOM).
  In 2008, beekeepers in the UK and USA reported that one third of honeybee colonies had not survived the winter. This project presents a fictional urban history recounting the relationship between humans, honeybees and flowers.

Comment: A unique, powerful proposal. It organizes the spatial circumstances for the bee on several scales, from architecture to urban design and landscape. The designer is a storyteller and curates the city by creating a track, a system, an infrastructure.

- ***The New 'Non-Standard' - Jonathan Enns***
  PRINCETON UNIVERSITY, SCHOOL OF ARCHITECTURE, PRINCETON (UNITED STATES).
  The project attempts to offer a test case for the potential of including non-standard inputs in the architectural design process, such as site-found geometries like trees.

Comment: The project is innovative, formal and specific at the same time. It shows a disciplined approach and a complex critique. The New Non-Standard transforms a system of columns into a poetic bearing system.

- ***A Public Bathhouse - Ruann van der Westhuizen***
  UNIVERSITY OF PRETORIA, FACULTY OF ENGINEERING, BUILT ENVIRONMENT AND INFORMATION TECHNOLOGY, PRETORIA (SOUTH AFRICA).
  A bathhouse, set in a South African urban context, integrated into an existing public transport interchange and thereby providing a basic service to commuters from informal and rural settings that are known to have poor services.

Comment: The designer cares for the place and found his own inspiration. It is an original project with a beautiful and personal presentation. The jury looked for the core values of architecture and finds them here.

- ***Spaces, Poetics and Voids - Simone Pizzagalli***
  DELFT UNIVERSITY OF TECHNOLOGY, FACULTY OF ARCHITECTURE, DELFT (THE NETHERLANDS).
  The prison designed on an empty plot in London is a formal interpretation of the language of the metropolis, a place where lives and stories unfold and are reconstructed into something new and different.

Comment: A brilliant project with beautiful images. It is a profound proposition that responds to the city, a Kafkaesque reading of the city. The project is innovative, remarkable, and shows a unique vision.

- ***Urban Upholstery - Mira Henry, Molly Hunker***
  UNIVERSITY OF CALIFORNIA, DEPARTMENT OF ARCHITECTURE AND URBAN DESIGN, LOS ANGELES (UNITED STATES).
  Urban Upholstery concentrates on the development of landscape strategies by coupling the infrastructural necessity of soil retention to a programmatic impulse toward physical comfort and tactile intimacy on a human scale.

Comment: It is an intelligent proposition, a very clear idea. The project uses a realistic technique and is crazy at the same time. It dovetails very well into the local context.

- ***You are Here - Maurizio Pizzocaro, Veronica Rusca, Lorenzo Trompetto***
  UNIVERSITÀ DI GENOVA, FACOLTÀ DI ARCHITETTURA, GENOA (ITALY).
  What does it mean to design a new city now that architecture has replaced this physical setting with a media context? You are Here is a critical analysis of the 20th-century city.

Comment: A sophisticated project with many layers. An up-to-date study and discussion of infrastructure, which comments in an intelligent way on the global theme of consumption. The strongest statement is that it does not call for an object but shows a love of infrastructure. It even romanticizes it in a fascinating way, it shows post-iconic infrastructure.

E SOLOMC

N R GUGGENHEIM MUSEUM

Alexandre Landry **NORTH AMERICA - CANADA - MONTREAL**

YMCA

DISCIPLINE(S): ARCHITECTURE / TUTOR: JEAN-PIERRE CHUPIN / **UNIVERSITE DE MONTREAL, SCHOOL OF ARCHITECTURE**

The design of this building seeks to outline an approach to design that is optimistically social in its outcome and rigorous in its process, one that strives to take a fresh look at outdated and overused typologies in order to turn them into new relationships, forms and experiences in sync with the contemporary condition. Through the analysis of practical, behavioral and social issues, it aims at revealing narratives within the public realm.

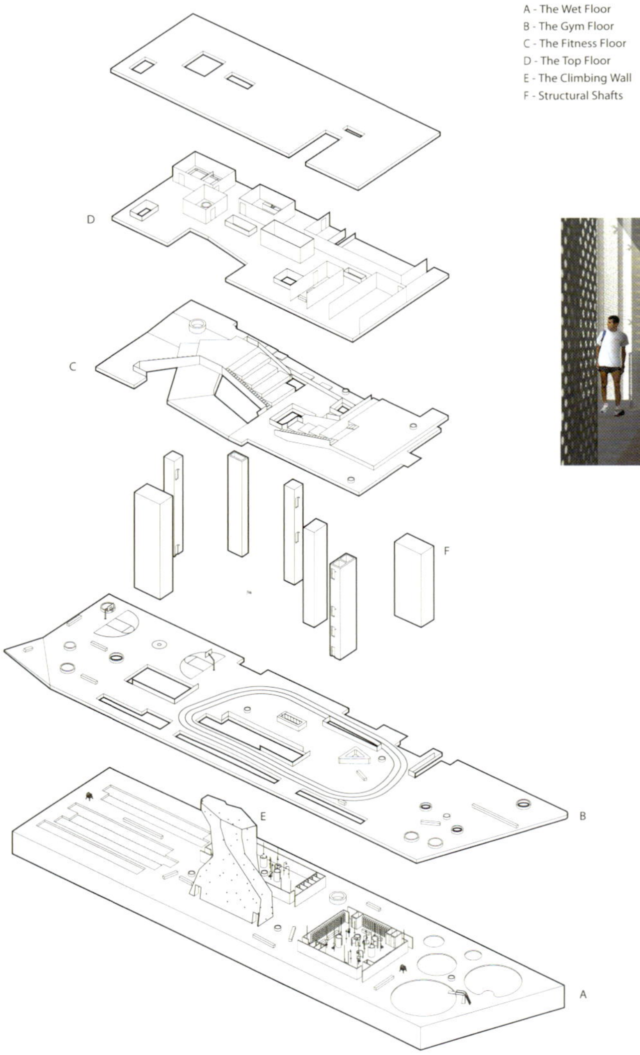

Structure and envelope

The Fitness Floor

The Gym Floor

The Climbing Wall

The Wet Floor

Samuel Bernier-Lavigne NORTH AMERICA - CANADA - QUEBEC

Écume Atmosphérique

ATMOSPHERIC HOTEL IN QUEBEC CITY

DISCIPLINE(S): ARCHITECTURE / TUTORS: PROJECT: MYRIAM BLAIS, THEORY: GEORGES TEYSSOT / **UNIVERSITE LAVAL, ECOLE D'ARCHITECTURE**

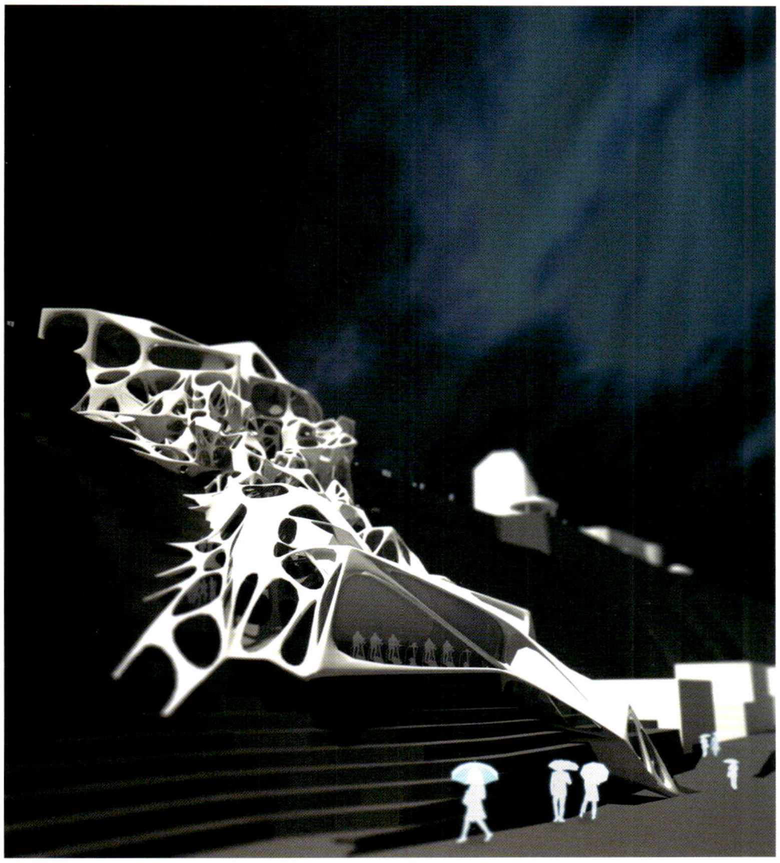

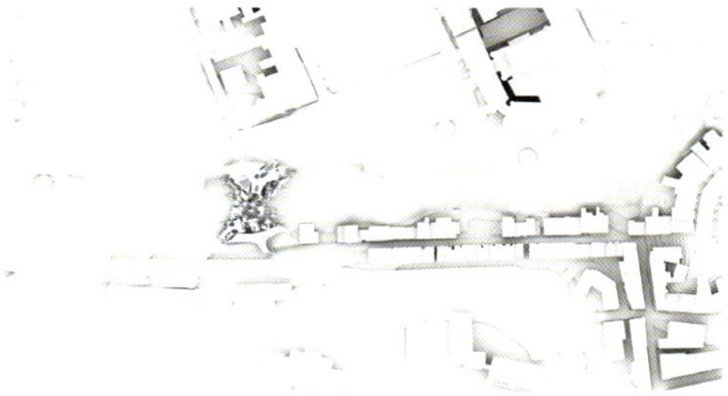

The old part of Quebec City

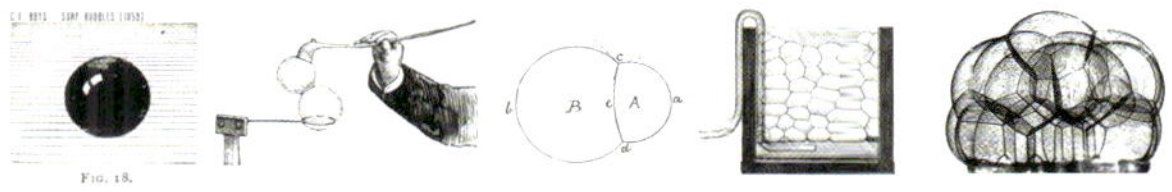

Form finding process: from bubble to foam (écume).

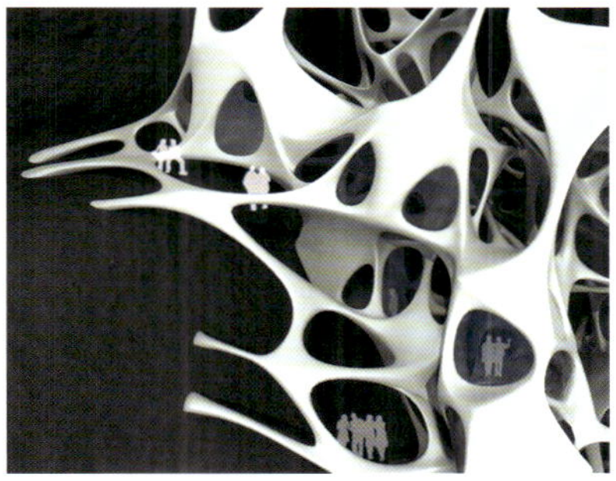

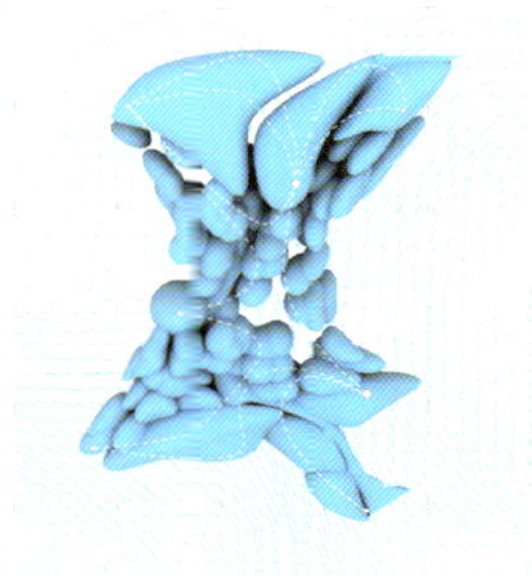

An atmospheric hotel in the old part of Quebec City / Dynamical forces of the site acting on the formation of space and matter.

Écume Atmosphérique is a project based on theoretical research into the natural organization of matter and its emergent structures. This project tends to exploit these critical notions by integrating them into a digital process of architectural design. The thesis explored in this process is the creation of specific atmospheres by the deployment of spatial foam (écume), a network with internal spaces, able to adapt itself to contextual forces. The materialization of the project emerges from the intersection of the bubble space, resulting in a cellular solid structure. In order to understand the physical stress in the whole structure and to adjust the densification locally, the material organization has to be analyzed by the Finite Element Method, which is usually used by engineers. Once the structure is efficient, the project can be physically constructed using digital robotic fabrication. This process results in an atmospheric hotel in Old Quebec City. As it is located in the famous cliff near the Château Frontenac and facing the Saint Lawrence River, it takes advantage of the city's tourist appeal. It establishes a new strong symbol in this part of the city which seems to be fixed in time. The hotel offers a multitude of rooms, each with a specific atmosphere resulting directly from its process of design. Each one of them has a bodyscape, based on the anthropometric positions of the body, in order to immerse the occupant in the atmospheric effect of the room at various moments of the day. The atmospheric possibilities are filtered by four types of skins, designed according to the forces that act directly on the inhabited space. Finally, due to its complex process of design, this heterogeneous architecture allows the individual to experiment with a specific atmospherical spectrum and thus creating a symbiosis between humans, space, matter and context.

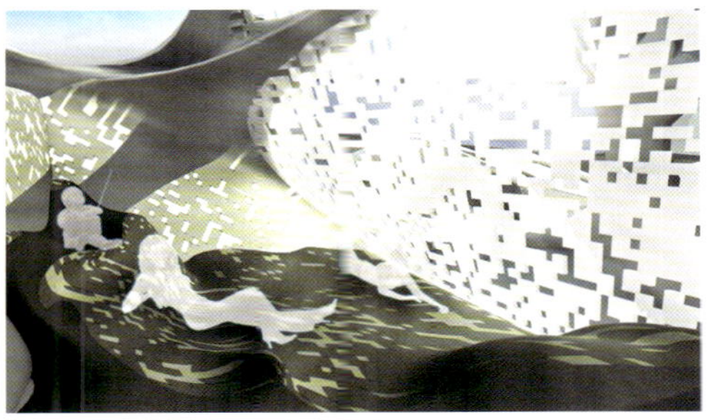

Spatial porosity in the main hall of the hotel / Moiré atmosphere between the speed of the road and the calm of the room

Duncan McIlvaine NORTH AMERICA - UNITED STATES - CAMBRIDGE

The End of the Times?

A PROPOSITION FOR JOURNALISTIC ARCHITECTURE

DISCIPLINE(S): ARCHITECTURE / TUTORS: PROFESSOR J MEEJIN YOON, MAUD, ADVISOR, PROFESSOR RAHUL MEHROTRA, MAUD, READER, PROFESSOR ANA MILJACKI, MARCH, PHD, READER / **MASSACHUSETTS INSTITUTE OF TECHNOLOGY, DEPARTMENT OF ARCHITECTURE**

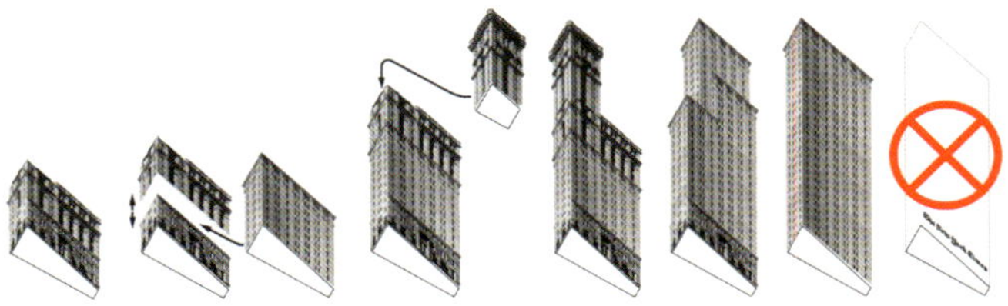

The rise and fall of the newspaper headquarters type.

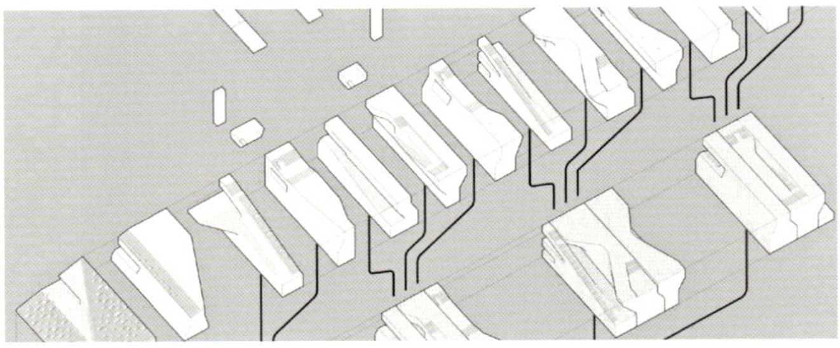

A new architecture for print media: archival infrastructure.

This architectural thesis formulates a conjectural building type to replace an obsolescent type: the corporate newspaper headquarters building. It postulates a scenario in which the primary function of the newspaper is to produce an enduring physical archive. In the epoch of "participatory journalism", the architecture of print media is no longer compelled to project "objective" authority. Instead, architecture performs as informational infrastructure. Inquiry into the evolution of the newspaper-headquarters building type led to the enabling narratives that were utilized as bases for architectural conjecture: 1. Reconsolidation of space for journalism: Spaces for journalism were privatized, fragmented and suburbanized during the golden age of corporate print media (1945-95). With demand now driven by an expanding population of media producer/consumers, space for journalism may be reconsolidated in a new civic building type. 2. Civic reconfiguration of the hyper-rational site type: The hyper-rational site type, optimized for efficient material flow, requires adaptation to emerging patterns of high-volume informational – rather than physical – throughput. Rectilinear, large-footprint sites can be repopulated with a new civic architecture within the urban/suburban typological estuary. 3. Journalism in the archive: Collapsing demand for print media does not invalidate the newspaper as an archival record, but could signal a potential change in the role of the professional journalist: from disseminator to curator. Demand for archival capacity, rather than production capacity, could come to dominate the architectural brief. The architectural proposition investigates the tectonic and spatial possibilities of these three narratives. The bulk of the building is an ultra-dense archive for media preservation, utilizing robotic (stacker crane) storage-and-retrieval technology borrowed from the manufacturing sector. Seams and fissures between the incrementally-constructed, interlocking archival volumes generate a new civic landscape at the city's periphery. Beyond making architecture for journalism, this thesis asks: when culturally significant building types approach obsolescence, how might architects invent new types to replace them?

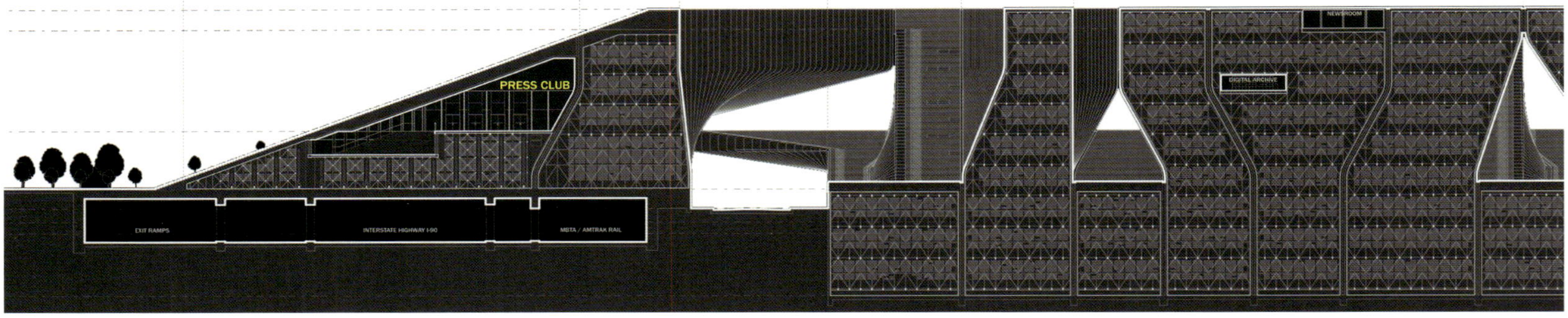

Reconsolidating space for journalism: the massive automated archive.

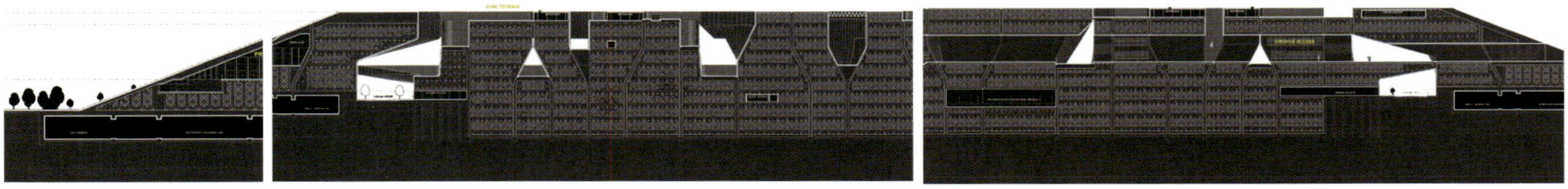

Adaptation of the hyper-rational site to civic use: layered terrains. Program driven by curation: middle terrain provides access to the archive.

Press club (refuge) occupies a void within the robotically-serviced archive / The upper terrain is an occupiable architectural surface, hosting newsrooms / Automated access points are sheltered within the archival mass.

(PF) Andri Klausen NORTH AMERICA - UNITED STATES - BROOKLYN

Link City - Rinku リンク

DISCIPLINE(S): ARCHITECTURE, URBAN DESIGN / TUTOR: NANAKO UMEMOTO / **PRATT INSTITUTE SCHOOL OF ARCHITECTURE**
PARTICIPANTS FAVORITE: 11 VOTES

View over Tokyo Bay

The LINK creates a multilayered transportation system connecting the rural Chiba Prefecture with the dense urban Tokyo City, whilst creating a new and exciting way of living on the water in Tokyo Bay. The city becomes a hub for transportation in the greater Tokyo area, creating a closed loop around the bay by expanding the existing monorail system and presenting a new seaport and a new international airport to compete with the world's largest airports [ATL, PEK, LHR] while solving Tokyo's airport expansion issues. A parallel programmatic scalar and characteristic shift is proposed, as opposed to a nodal system with a definite city centre. This shortens travel spans between residence, work and play, creating close community networks and a healthier way of living. Due to the geographical nature of the location - in a windy bay with strong ocean currents - a clean and stable energy system is created by the use of water and wind turbines, powering the city's whole public transportation network. A parallel programmatic scalar and characteristic shift is proposed as opposed to a nodal system with a definite city centre. This shortens travel spans between live, work and play, creating close community networks and a healthier way of living. Due to the geographic nature of the location, in a windy bay with strong ocean currents, a clean and stable energy system is created by the use of water and wind turbines - powering the cities whole public transportation network resulting in a clean and healthy city.

Wind Turbines

Underwater Turbines

WINNER PRINCETON UNIVERSITY **NORTH AMERICA, UNITED STATES, PRINCETO**

HE NEW 'NON-STANDARD' DESIGNED BY JONATHAN ENNS

WORLD'S BEST GRADUATION PROJECTS · ARCHITECTURE · URBAN DESIGN · LANDSCAPE ARCHITECTURE
2011
CAMBRIDGE USA
Archiprix
INTERNATIONAL www.archiprix.org
THE NEW 'NON-STANDARD'
Jonathan Enns
PRINCETON
UNIVERSITY
USA

HunterDouglas AWARD
WINNER
AWARDED JUNE 9TH 2011
GUGGENHEIM - NEW YORK
WORLD'S BEST GRADUATION PROJECTS · ARCHITECTURE · URBAN DESIGN · LANDSCAPE ARCHITECTURE

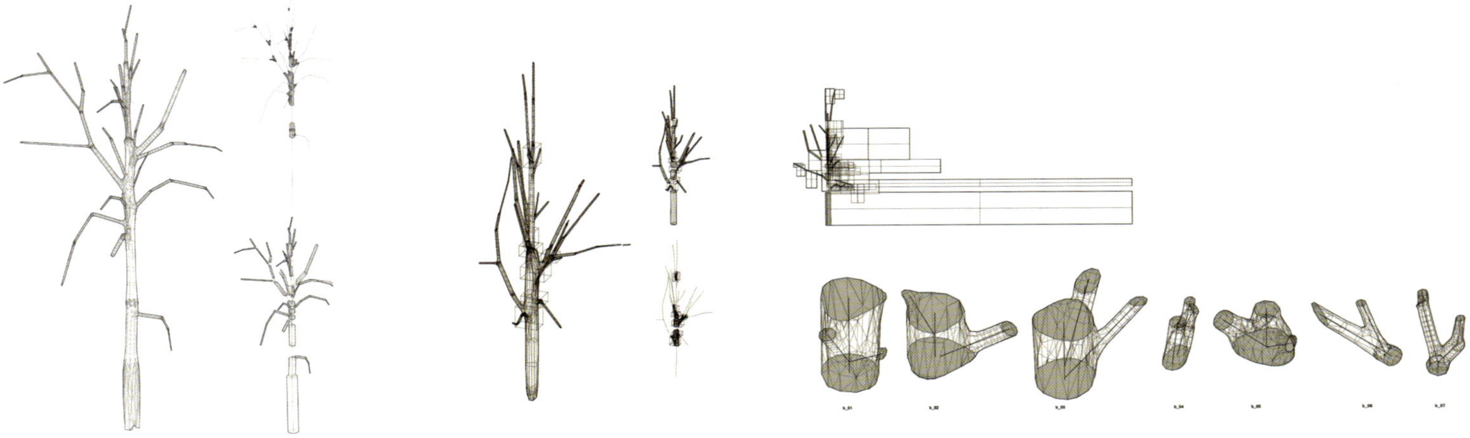

Geometry catalog from base instantiations

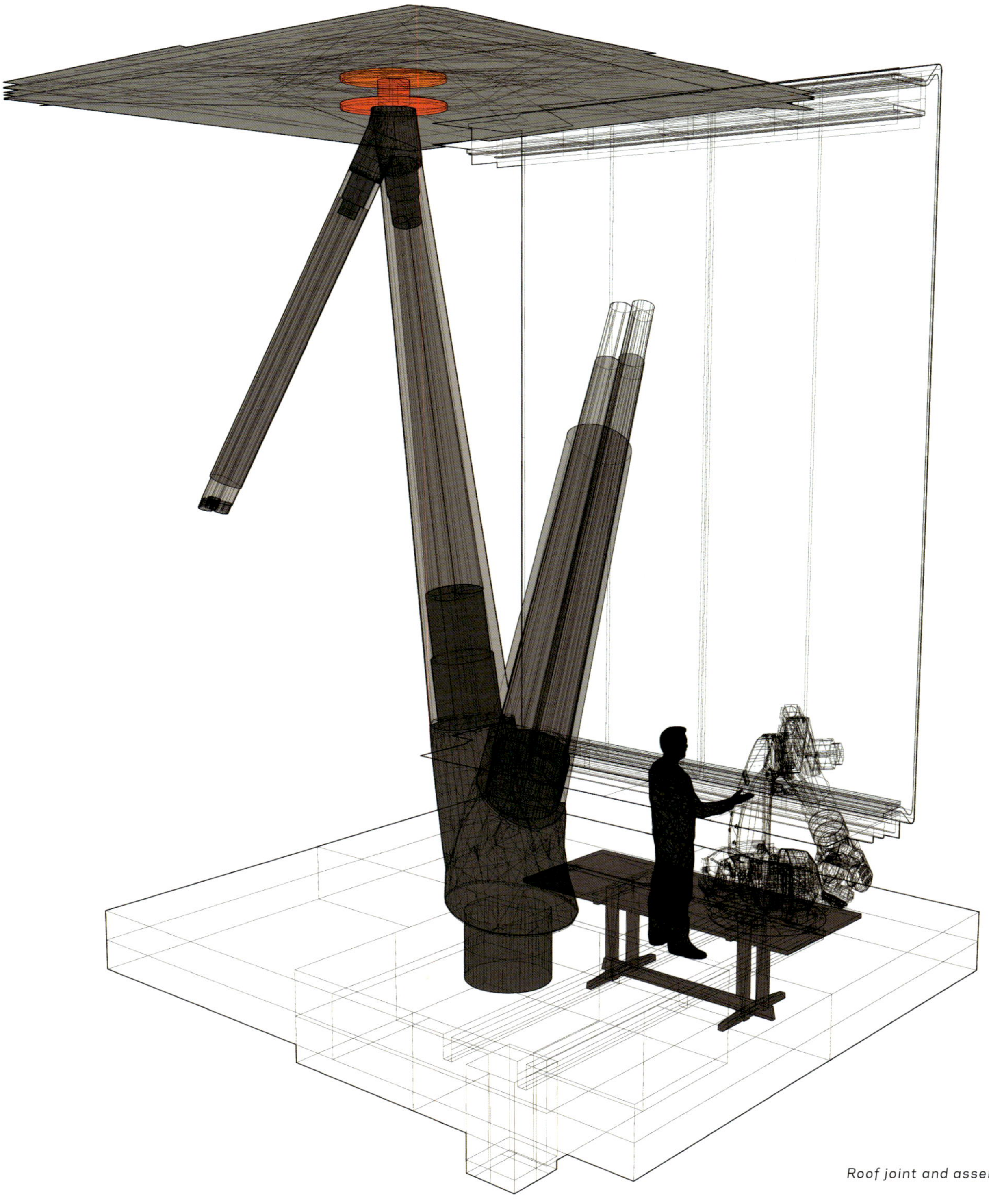

Roof joint and assembly detail

Jonathan Enns NORTH AMERICA - UNITED STATES - PRINCETON

The New **'Non-Standard'**

THE ANALYSIS AND MANIPULATION OF FOUND GEOMETRY AS A PRIMARY DESIGN DETERMINANT

DISCIPLINE(S): ARCHITECTURE / TUTOR: AXEL KILIAN / **PRINCETON UNIVERSITY, SCHOOL OF ARCHITECTURE - WINNER**

This project attempts to offer a test case for the potential of including non-standard inputs in the architectural design process. Until now the non-standard has been celebrated as a liberating alternative to the homogenizing formal tendencies of mass production. This type of production has continued, however, to require the use of standardized input material (the prototypical example being the ubiquitous stacked plywood CNC milling). Such practices constitute an unnecessarily inefficient production circuit that typically moves from non-standard input (such as a tree) to standardized material (such as plywood or dimensional lumber) and back to non-standard forms through digital fabrication. A more direct translation is proposed here, in the design of a workshop building for the fabrication and assembly of digitally designed furniture. Unlike more typical precedents, this simple enclosure - it is essentially a shed - is an experiment in analyzing, manipulating and utilizing site-found geometries - in this instance trees - rather than idealized or imposed ones. Such processes are not new, and are related ideologically to old techniques such as timber boat construction in which the form of the selected tree contributes to the final form of the boat. Common to these is a resistance to the absolute dominance of either the final conceptual image or a standardized material process. A preferred option is allowing the participation of irregular input material as a co-author in the determination of outward form. Now with the aid of digital design and manufacturing, this project attempts to offer a renewed look at alternatives to current practices both in terms of material efficiency, and in hopes of opening new potentials for formal exploration.

Exterior perspective

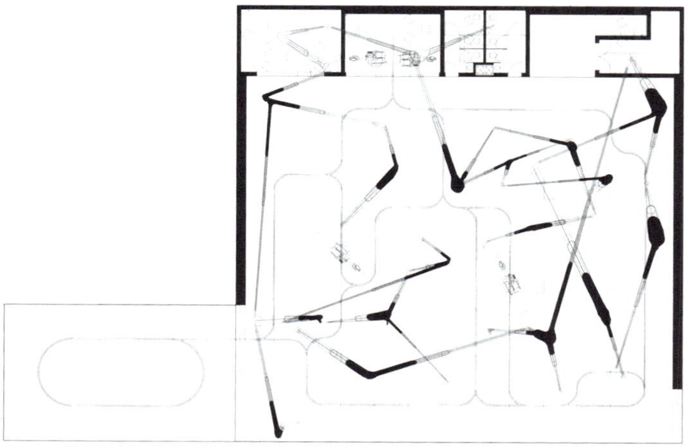

Building plan

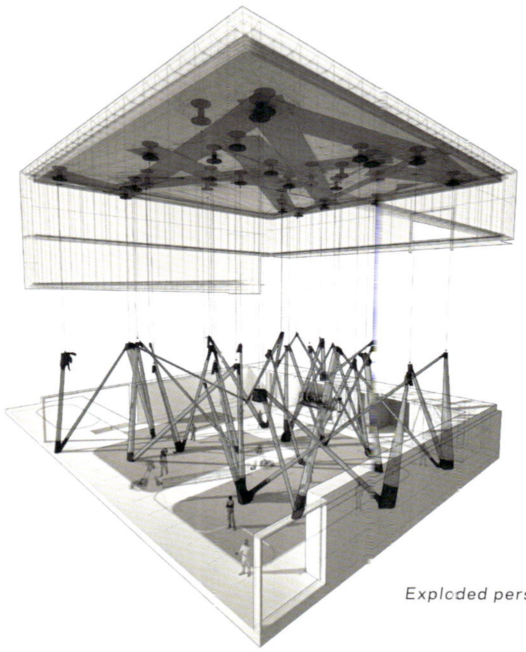

Exploded perspective

Ernest Ng, Michael-John Bailie, Paul Dudkowski, Dan Stripp **NORTH AMERICA - UNITED STATES - BUFFALO**

QuadSpace

DISCIPLINE(S): ARCHITECTURE / TUTORS: MEHRDAD HADIGHI, DR JEAN LAMARCHE, ANNETTE LECUYER, JOSE CHANG
STATE UNIVERSITY OF NEW YORK AT BUFFALO, SCHOOL OF ARCHITECTURE & PLANNING

The derelict urban landscape of post-industrial Buffalo, New York, is filled with vacant lots and houses which required extensive annual demolition work by the city of Buffalo. However, most of these abandoned infrastructures earmarked for demolition are still physically stable and suitable for alteration and adaption to new functions and uses. Many current urban revival visions, implemented at urban level to inject new life into streets and neighborhoods, are not effective in reviving individual infrastructures at an intimate level. QuadSpace operates on the potential of these abandoned houses within the urban landscape of the city and explores a synthesized strategy to manipulate and revive such derelict infrastructure into a choreographed inhabitable space for four individuals. The conception of this project within the city, self-motivated and independently funded by the students/ designers/ builders/ owners, attempts to create a sense of iconography and raise awareness for innovative attitudes towards the reconsidering the banal within this type of urban landscape. The thesis covers the insertion of an academic project as a full-scale construction exploration to manipulate and define, spatially and structurally, the division of four spaces within a 400 sq.ft. house. It seeks to re-evaluate the operations of architectural projects within academia and its role and relationship with the social, communal and economic environment within which it is based. The project critically investigates the effort and process of establishing an academic architectural research project as a full-scale construction inserted within the city of Buffalo, involving the physical manipulation and conversion of an existing derelict house into a habitable space.

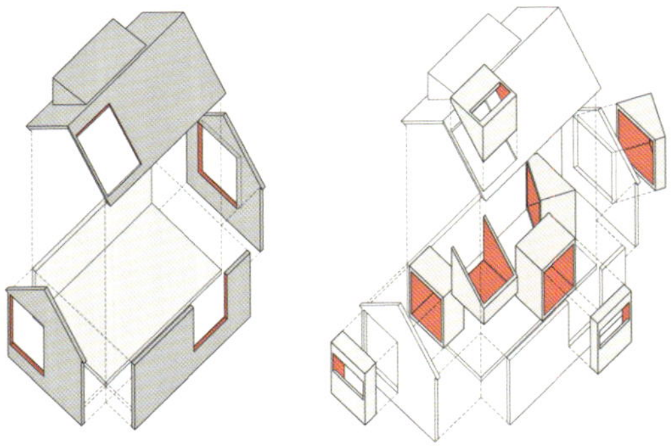

Blackrock neighborhood, Buffalo, New York

Front façade and back façade

Interiors

Maya-Maria Joannides NORTH AMERICA - UNITED STATES - GAINESVILLE

Architecture and **Language**

IMPOSITIONS ARE GENERATED FROM OLD TOWN, ITALIAN AND OTTOMAN MAPPINGS

DISCIPLINE(S): ARCHITECTURE / TUTORS: PROF. LEVENT KARA, PROF. HUI ZOU / **UNIVERSITY OF FLORIDA, SCHOOL OF ARCHITECTURE**

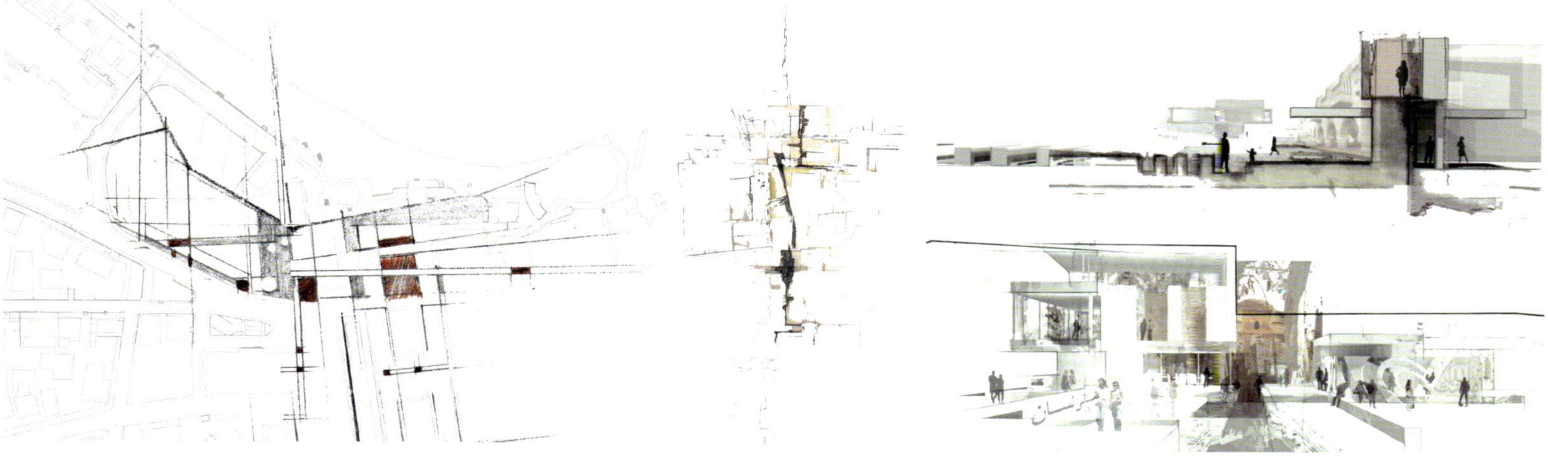

Initial collages evolve into mappings, then explored in three-dimensional models / Release: open center, allow Mosque to look eastward to Turkey

As language evolves, original meanings become blurred. Meaning and myth are buried in modern language. Though a meaning is tied to a word in modern language, it is instant and merely allows a distorted or minimal understanding of the origin of the word. It is the origin that yields a true understanding, and transforms the word into an experience. A two-dimensional understanding of meaning is slowly replacing the three-dimensional. As language is directly tied with concept formation and imagination, once language begins to flatten, imagination must do so too. Meaning in language affects thinking, and therefore must affect creating. As modern language becomes steadily detached from original meaning, modern architecture reflects this detachment in its deviation from ancient architectural symbols. The city of Rhodes, Greece, embraces primarily Italian, Ottoman and Greek history. Remnants of each period signify the passing of a time in which form was dictated by language and myth. The contrast of old versus new highlights not the remnants, but the survival of a language that once was the very basis of thought. Analytical mappings of Italian, Ottoman and Old Town architecture serve as methods of re-reading of the city of Rhodes, constructed from images representative of each period's architectural qualities. Embedded in each mapping is an understanding of each culture's presence in the city and understanding of form. The mappings act as generative devices in discovering architectural possibilities as interventions to be hosted by selected sites along the city's main avenue and harbor. The interventions offer a new reading of the city, one in which etymological interpretations of the city's first plan of public, private and sacred spaces influence both the abstract and physical qualities of each site, creating powerful moments of reflection and culminating in the arrival at a final intervention as a center for language and literature.

Approach and intersection: center for language and literature

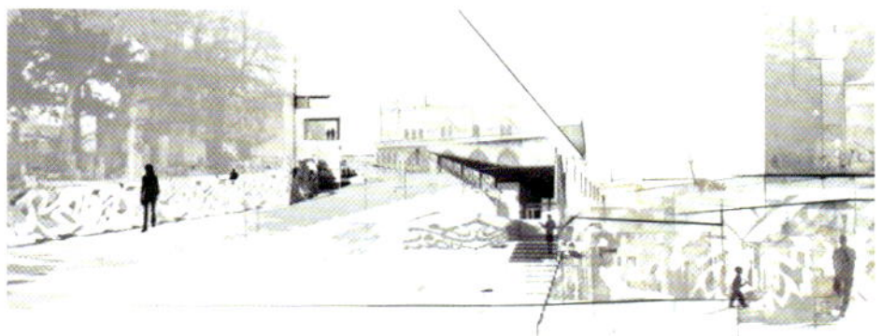

Approach: center for language and literature

Cradling of grounds: center for language and literature

Pixel esplanade & central aquasquare

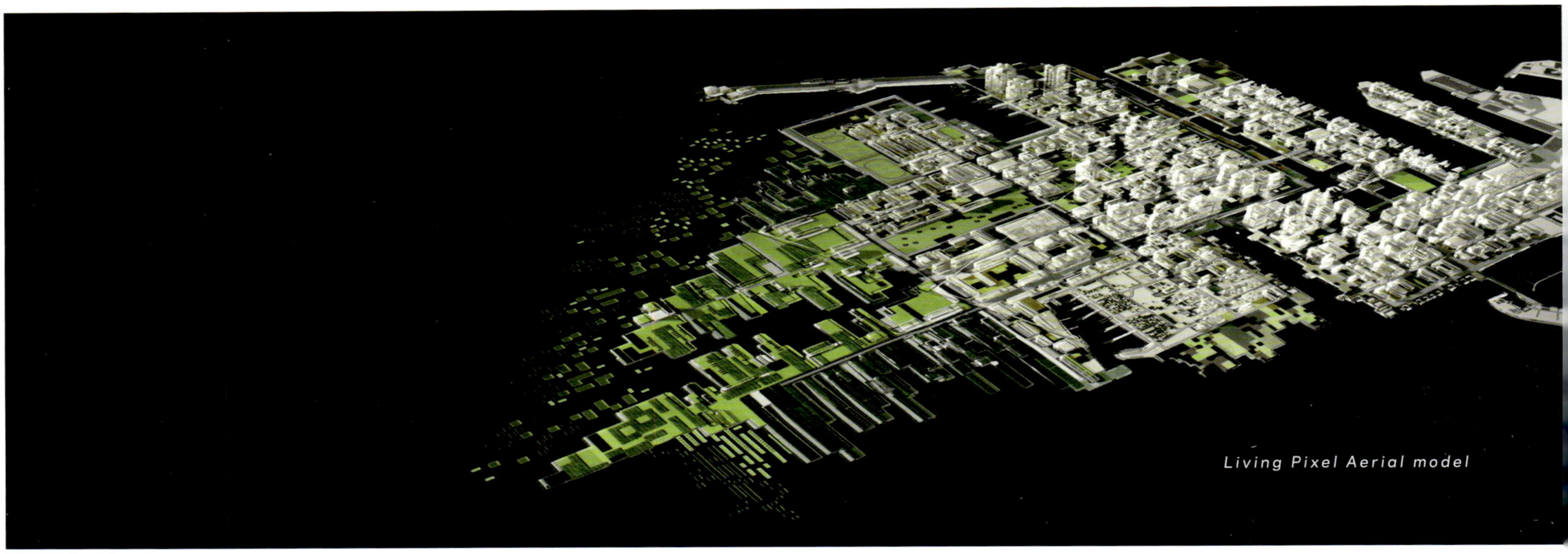

Living Pixel Aerial model

Swedish park

YoungJoon Choi NORTH AMERICA - UNITED STATES - PHILADELPHIA

Living **Pixel**

INFINITE LIFESTYLES FOR NEW DEVELOPMENT

DISCIPLINE(S): URBAN DESIGN, LANDSCAPE DESIGN / TUTORS: JAMES CORNER, RICHARD KENNEDY / **UNIVERSITY OF PENNSYLVANIA,** FACULTY OF LANDSCAPE ARCHITECTURE / **NOMINATED**

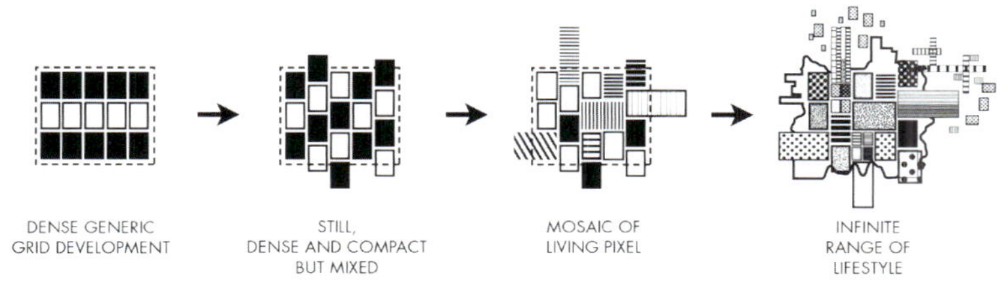

Pixelation Development strategy

LIVING PIXEL proposes a sustainable development on the basis of public open space. The idea of pixelation is the basis of an integrated relationship between open space and the built form, generating a wide range of lifestyles in a landscape symbolic of two adjacent countries. The symbolic landscape of a country involves cultural heritage in combination with urban and geographical patterns. Incorporating functional and aesthetic concerns, Living Pixel reinforces the specificity of the site and embodies the identity of the new city. The site is located at the tangent of Denmark and Sweden. Over 10,000 people commute between the two countries daily. The Living Pixel will form the junction of the two lifestyles - the place to experience their unique landscape and nature. Denmark has a significantly complex coastline and a democratic fabric of land use, which involve vibrant waterfront uses and coarse urban texture. Sweden has numerous islands here, where Swedish people like to enjoy their leisure. On the basis of a strong and clear circulation system, urban density, the transport hierarchy and building typologies are diversified to provide a multiple frontage of green and water. Along the perimeter of the site, a significant band of open spaces is created according to the context of each place. On the sea side facing Sweden, a Swedish park will form the largest open space for city, a nursery for further planting, and various recreation venues. Essentially, Living Pixel generates infinite lifestyles for Nordhavnen and responds to the social, economic and ecological fluctuations of the future with distinct characteristics and degree of flexibility.

Container cottage house

Sunset mosaic beach

WINNER UNIVERSITY OF CALIFORNIA **NORTH AMERICA, UNITED STATES, LOS ANGELES**

WORLD'S BEST GRADUATION PROJECTS · ARCHITECTURE · URBAN DESIGN · LANDSCAPE ARCHITECTURE
2011
CAMBRIDGE USA
Archiprix
INTERNATIONAL www.archiprix.org
URBAN UPHOLSTERY
Molly Hunker, Mira Henry
UNIVERSITY OF CALIFORNIA
USA

HunterDouglas AWARD
WINNER
AWARDED JUNE 9TH 2011
GUGGENHEIM - NEW YORK
WORLD'S BEST GRADUATION PROJECTS · ARCHITECTURE · URBAN DESIGN · LANDSCAPE ARCHITECTURE

RBAN UPHOLSTERY DESIGNED BY MOLLY HUNKER, MIRA HENRY

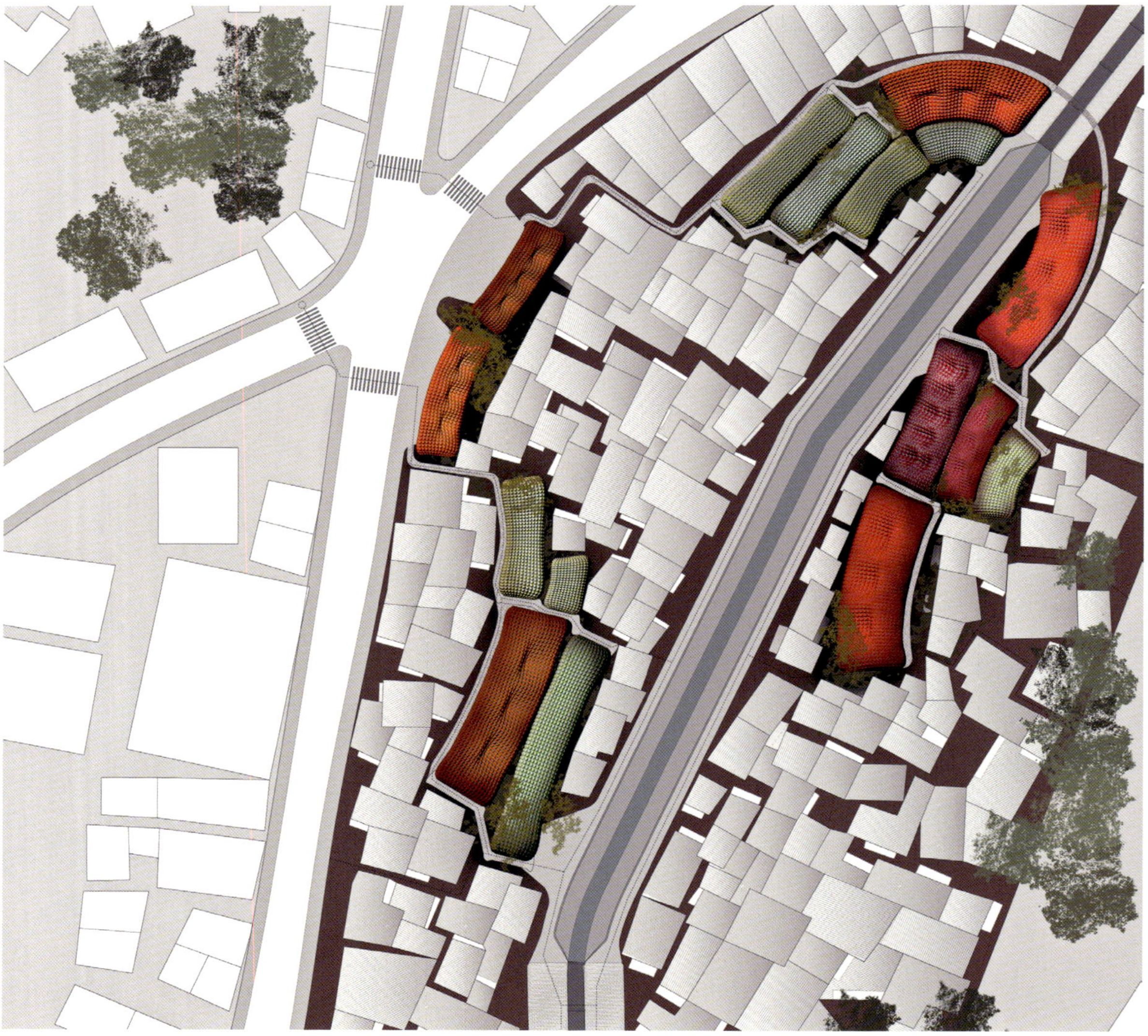

Blow-up plan

Molly Hunker, Mira Henry **NORTH AMERICA - UNITED STATES - LOS ANGELES**

Urban **Upholstery**

A CONCRETE CUSHION RECASTS THE FAVELA AS A PUBLIC LOUNGE, THE STRATEGY COUPLES SOIL RETENTION WITH A PROGRAMMATIC IMPULSE

DISCIPLINE(S): ARCHITECTURE / TUTOR: JASON PAYNE / **UNIVERSITY OF CALIFORNIA**
DEPARTMENT OF ARCHITECTURE AND URBAN DESIGN / **WINNER**

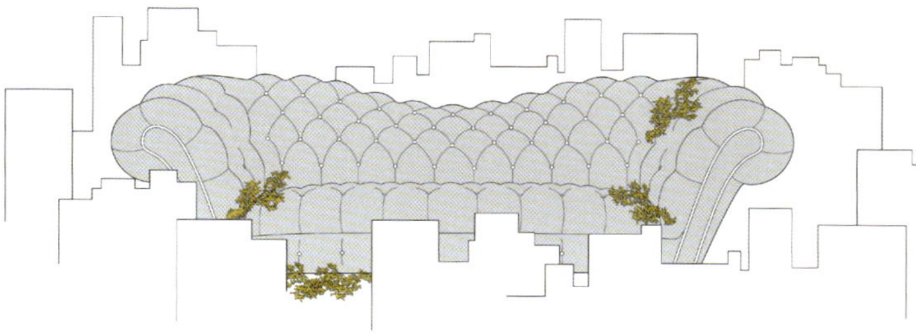

Color + pattern

This project grew from a year-long study of informal developments in Brazil. Our work incorporated traveling to Brazil on two occasions and working directly with the São Paulo Housing Authority (SEHAB) to participate in ongoing research on the topic. As the culmination of our research we chose to orient our design response to the specific favela called Eucaliptos. This is a small community organized along a riparian corridor outside the city of São Paulo, and is one that is currently under consideration for development by SEHAB. Our project, Urban Upholstery, concentrates on the development of novel landscape strategies by coupling the infrastructural necessity of soil retention to a programmatic impulse toward physical comfort and tactile intimacy on a human scale. Our efforts focus on the design of a concrete cushion which, while performing the structural job of retaining the soil, also assumes the visual language of a plush, over-stuffed couch. Ultimately, the formal associations of upholstery, with its own specific and familiar features and textures, recasts the Eucaliptos landscape as a public lounge. Derived from the logic of the SEHAB risk-zone map of this favela, our site analysis recalibrates the risk areas to be the highest zones of the topographic slope. Based on this, our proposed intervention is highly localized, limiting the need for the relocation of residents. Our approach has learned from the informal intelligence of organizational and construction techniques of the favela. By isolating and intensifying specific characteristics intrinsic to these techniques, our design recasts familiar elements as fantastical moments of delight. We thank the UCLA Department of Architecture and Urban Design's Cross-Cultural Initiative, the São Paulo Municipal Housing Secretariat, and SlumLab and for their collaboration and support.

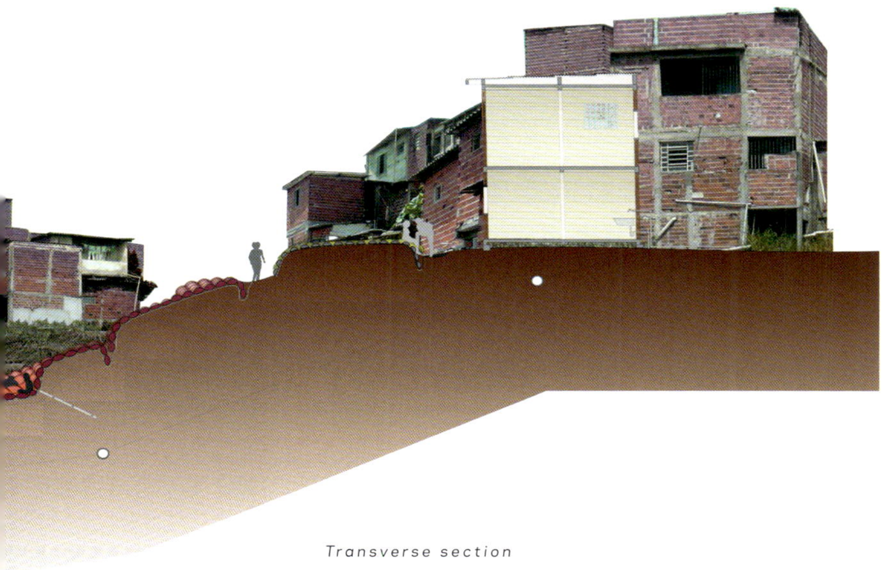

Transverse section

Yu Nong Khew NORTH AMERICA - UNITED STATES - LOS ANGELES

Tendencies of **Sensational Openings**

DISCIPLINE(S): ARCHITECTURE / TUTOR: ELENA MANFERDINI / **SOUTHERN CALIFORNIA INSTITUTE OF ARCHITECTURE SCI-ARC**

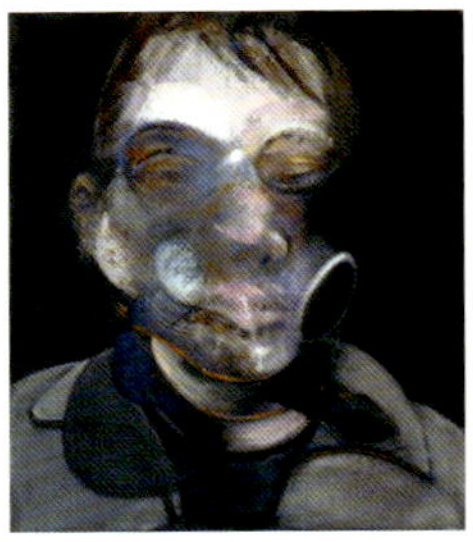
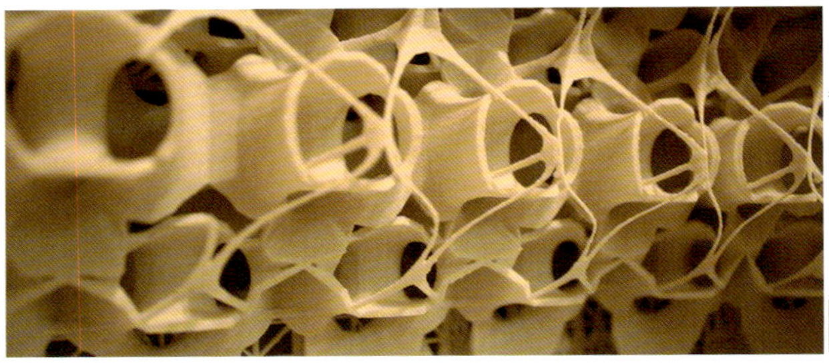
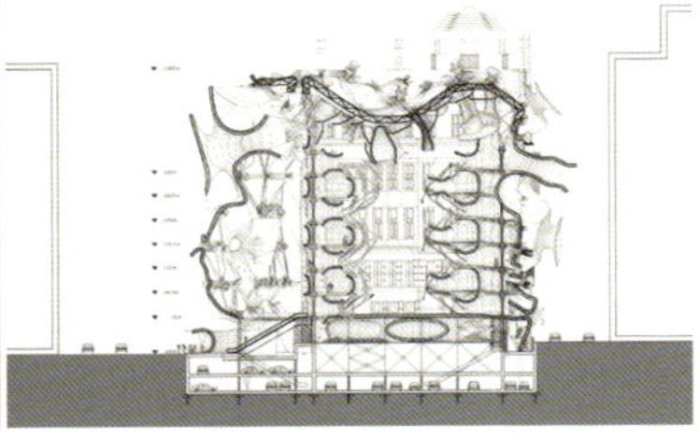

Francis Bacon paintings / Physical model / Cross section interior: balcony seating in the opera house

Drawing inspiration from Francis Bacon's paintings, it can be imagined that the openings on a façade are similar to the openings on a face. With the presence of the eyes, nose and mouth, we understand this composition as a face, and therefore we can estimate whether the body with the face is human or inhuman. Without these openings, a face is merely flesh and meat with no consciousness. Likewise, a façade without openings is architecture without soul, without consciousness and therefore not architecture. It is merely an object. "Significance is never without a white wall upon which it inscribes its signs and redundancies. Subjectification is never without a black hole in which it lodges its consciousness, passion, and redundancies. Since all semiotics are mixed and strata come at least in twos, it should come as no surprise that a very special mechanism is situated at their intersection. Oddly enough, it is a face: the white wall/black hole system...." (Deleuze-Guatarri, A Thousand Plateaus, 1987, p.176). Openings on façades are typically used as methods for environmental controls and as entry points. Beyond their functional value, in contemporary architecture, they are also used as a figurative method to build upon an image of a building. However, in my thesis, these openings form the soul of the building rather than the image of it. The building is not a space with a façade plastered on, but one with thresholds created by these openings on its façade, continuing throughout its entirety. These thresholds explore the connection between the outside and the inside, and present the idea of openings on façades as a three-dimensional element that begins at the façade and perpetuates itself throughout the entire building. Thus, façade becomes one that has depth and allowances. The openings on façades begin to take on roles they have never played before: the tendencies of sensational openings.

Rendering: front and back elevations

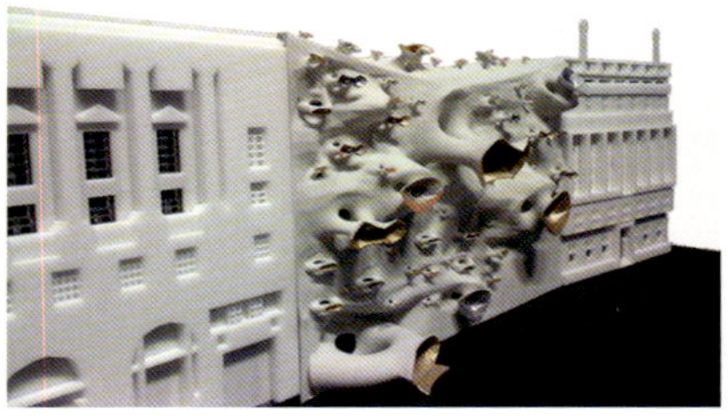

Site: central london

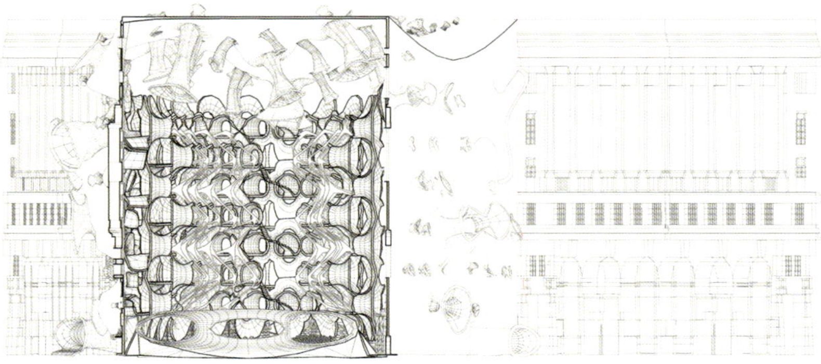

Short internal elevation

Interior: from balcony seats looking out with the city as the scene's backdrop

Domingo Delaroiere NORTH AMERICA - MEXICO - MEXICO

Hidro-Centro

A BUILDING: A TRIBUTE TO THE CULT OF WATER.

DISCIPLINE(S): ARCHITECTURE / TUTORS: JUAN PABLO SERRANO, LUIS BARRAGAN, JUAN PABLO CEPEDA
UNIVERSIDAD IBEROAMERICANA, DEPARTAMENTO DE DISENO

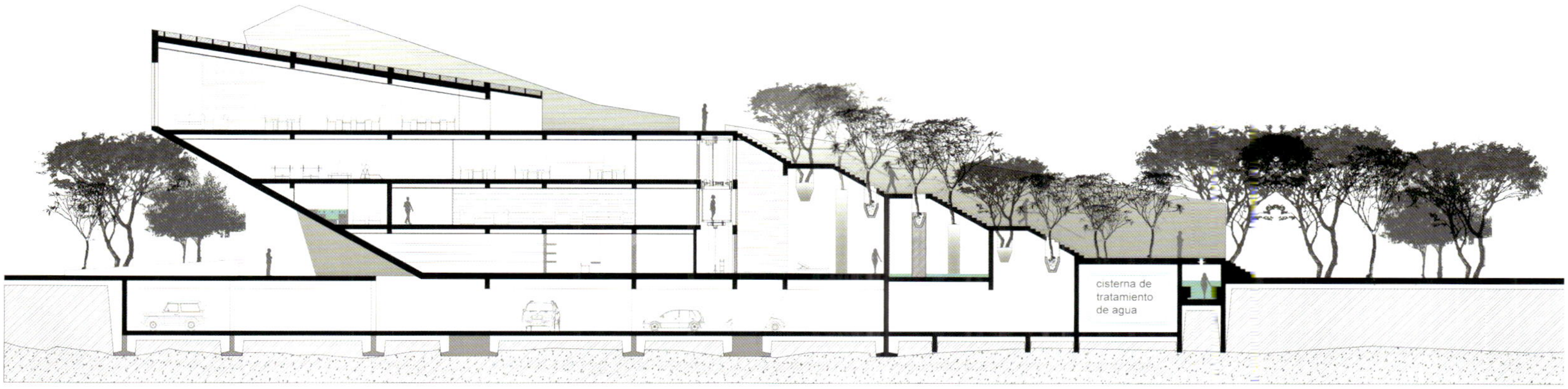

Live roof. The vegetation covers the building as the jungle covers the cenote

This building is as much a pyramid as a cenote, the portal of communication between two sacred worlds: the cosmos and the underworld. The shape is inspired by the pyramid, which forcefully interrupts the horizontality of the region and dominates the jungle, indicating a strategic point in its terrestrial and cosmic setting. The building proposes a return to Mayan shapes; thus making it a cultural center through the rite of water. It is a symbol of contemporary architecture and recognition of Mayan culture. A powerful symbol that is imposed on the city with the timelessness, mystery and the sensibility that we inherited from this culture. Today, buildings need to encourage social fabric and actively participate in shaping the city. Therefore, it is necessary to propose a variety of uses, in order to attract different users at different times. This hydro-center is comprised of bodies of water, a treatment center, a sports club, a café, restaurant and a public park.

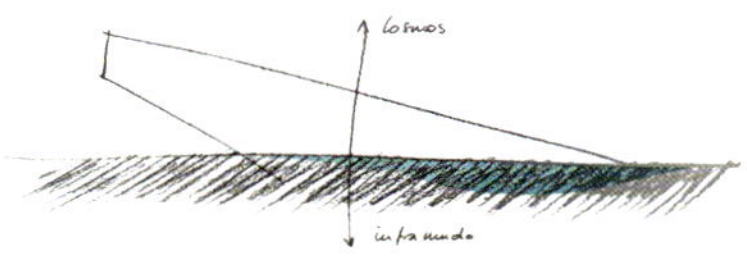

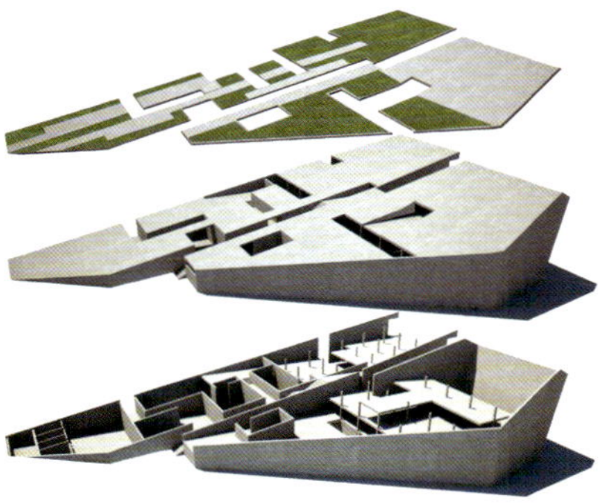

Erick Capeleti Carbone SOUTH AMERICA - BRAZIL - CAMPO GRANDE

The Mutant Tower

FLEXIBILITY AND ADAPTATION FOR VERTICAL HOUSING

DISCIPLINE(S): ARCHITECTURE, URBAN DESIGN, LANDSCAPE DESIGN / TUTOR: ANDREA NAGUISSA YUBA / **UNIVERSIDADE FEDERAL DE MATO GROSSO DO SUL** DEPARTAMENTO DE ESTRUTURAS E CONSTRUÇÃO CIVIL / **PARTICIPANTS FAVORITE: 10 VOTES**

The principle of housing originates from mankind's need for shelter, a place to develop and to carry out activities. The complexity of human beings, with all their particularities and personal beliefs that reinforce their individuality, gives rise to the idea that living space ought to be adapted to the activities of the people, not vice versa. It is a serious mistake that the design of accommodation for different household groups that cultivate different values and customs is nevertheless standardized. This contrasts with their habits. The dwelling is not just a cultural product, but part of the culture itself. It reflects and interferes directly in people's habits, which reinforces the need to conform to the values and behaviors that have grown contemporaneously. Besides the architectural issues, the disordered population growth in Brazil, coupled with the lack of city planning, has resulted in segregation, both spatial and social. Whereas the central areas have basic infrastructures such as sanitation, transportation and asphalt, the houses on the periphery, especially for low-income people, do not. These people have been driven away from the center by the over-valuation, which contributes to a marginalization process that converts into serious social problems.

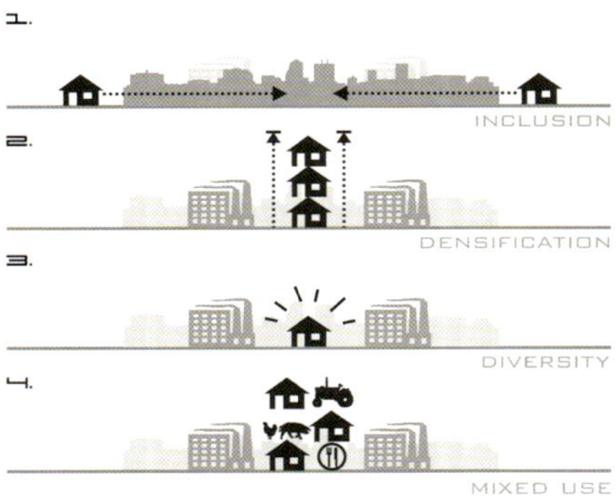

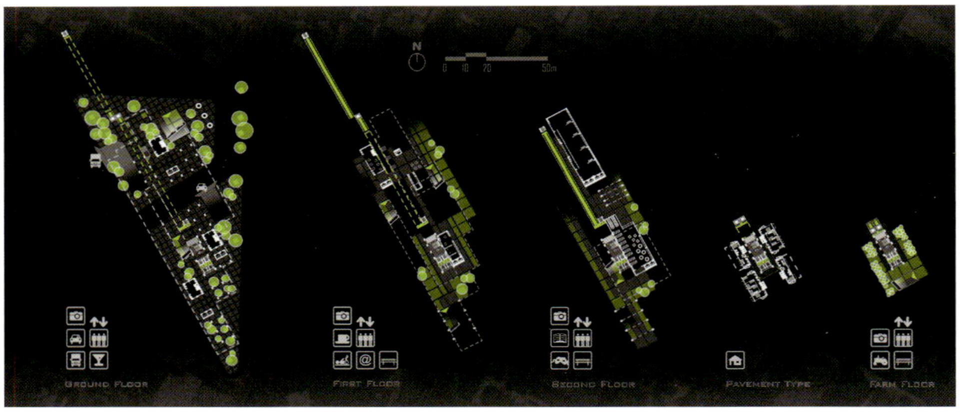

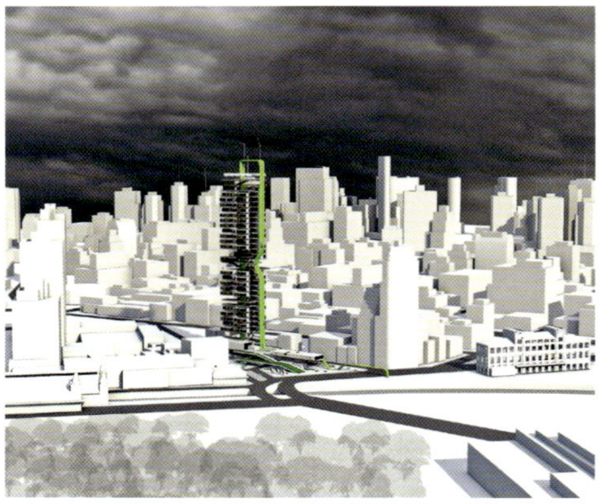

Isis Soares Pereira do Nascimento SOUTH AMERICA - BRAZIL - FLORIANOPOLIS

Performative Scenarios for the city

A BRIEF VISIT TO DANTE'S HELL

DISCIPLINE(S): URBAN DESIGN /TUTOR: LUIZ EDUARDO FONTOURA TEIXEIRA / **UNIVERSIDADE FEDERAL DE SANTA CATARINA-UFSC**
CURSO DE ARQUITECTURA E URBANISMO

Scenarios for CANTO I of Dante's Inferno

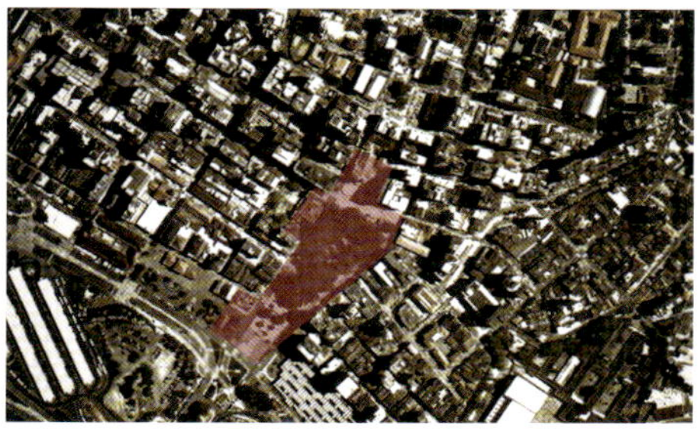

The contemporary city, bombarded with symbols and temporary myths, exists in unstable landscapes, preventing its users from capturing an impression without immediately deleting an old one. We live in a constant process of fragmentation, and we are witnessing the decline of the outside world experience, where space has become increasingly inefficient as the aseptic preparation of a "kinesthetic repertoire". In an attempt to reverse this situation, we decided to prepare a "scenographic project" using the city streets, specifically the historical center of Florianopolis, as theatrical space. The dramatic text chosen was the "Inferno" (Hell) part of the "Divine Comedy", written in the fourteenth century by Dante Alighieri. Marked by conflicts and questions of human existence in the Middle Ages, the "Divine Comedy" may be understood as a topical work, since it deals with contemporary human issues. The scenic design for "Dante's Inferno" relates the story of the main buildings of downtown Florianópolis to the conflicts experienced by Dante's character in the book. The main aim of the project is to trace the path of people who pass through "scenic interventions" which lead them to experimentation and reflection on the public spaces of their city. The buildings can be taken as evidence of interaction between actors, dancers and audiences, organizing an ambience of new situations and experiences of urban space during the night, when downtown is ignored and underused by its inhabitants. This project encourages the meeting of the citizen with his surroundings, someone who feels himself the owner of public spaces and not just a common user of a government property. It is a meeting of "self-sensory" humans, of people who open their feelings to note the sky, roofs, odors, textures and other people. It is a meeting in the broadest sense of the word.

Scenarios for CANTO II, II and IV of Dante's Inferno

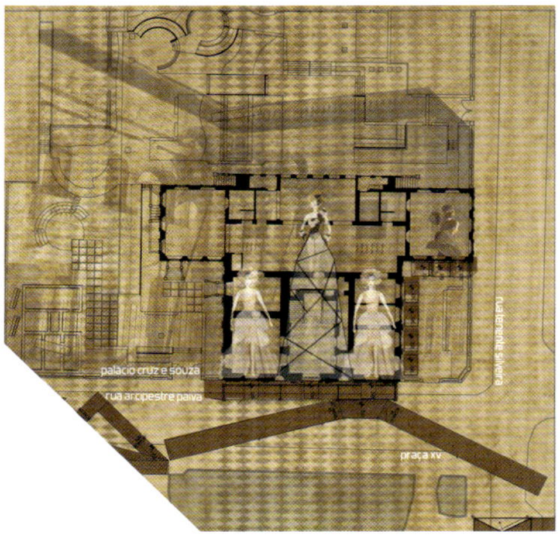

Scenarios for CANTO V of Dante's Inferno

Adjoining the water

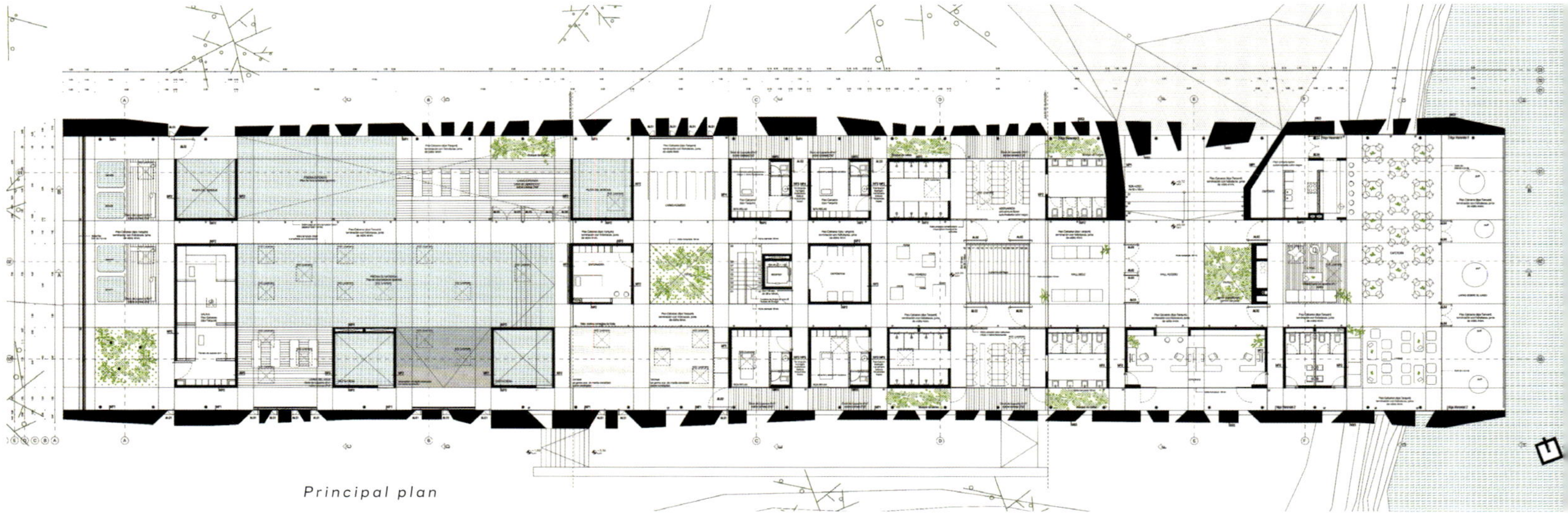

Principal plan

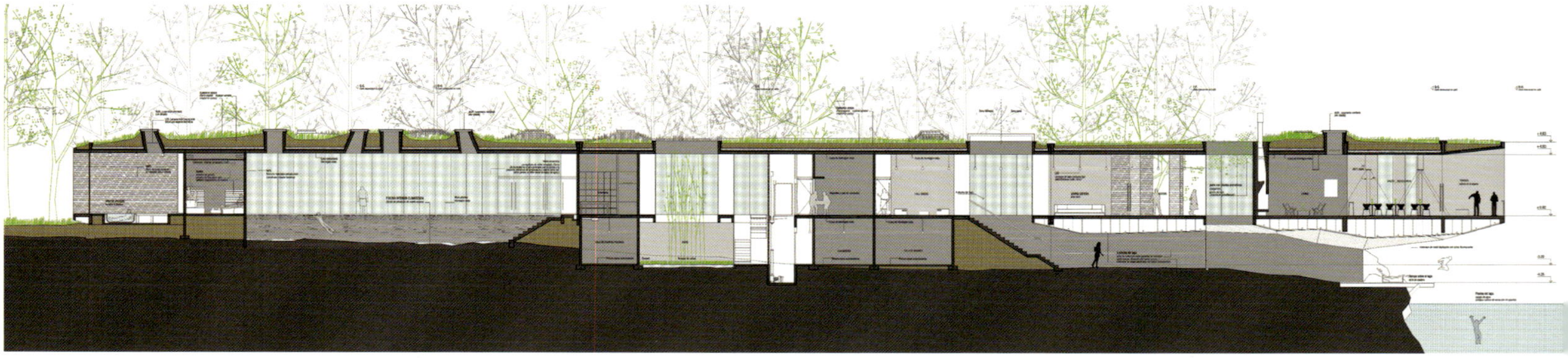

Longitudinal aspect

Cantera Ferrando - Colonia del Sacramento - Uruguay

Nicolás Newton, Gonzalo Parma **SOUTH AMERICA - URUGUAY - MONTEVIDEO**

Spa **Ferrando**

LEISURE AND HEALTH SPACE

DISCIPLINE(S): ARCHITECTURE / TUTORS: ARQ. HÉCTOR BERIO, ARQ. ESTEBAN DIESTE, ARQ. MARCELO BEDNARIK
UNIVERSIDAD DE LA REPUBLICA URUGUAY, FACULTAD DE ARQUITECTURA / **PARTICIPANTS FAVORITE: 12 VOTES + NOMINATED**

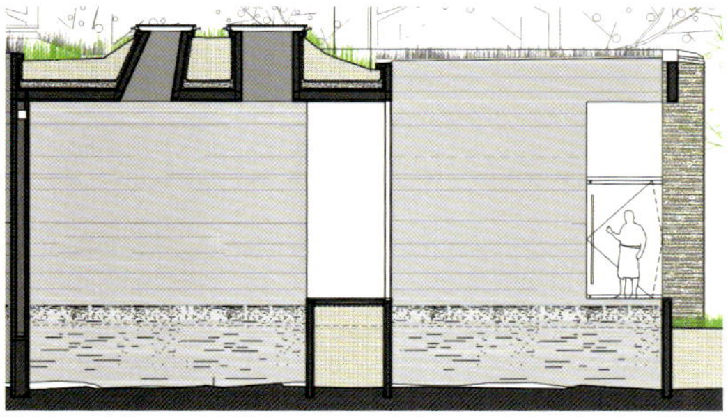

Cross section

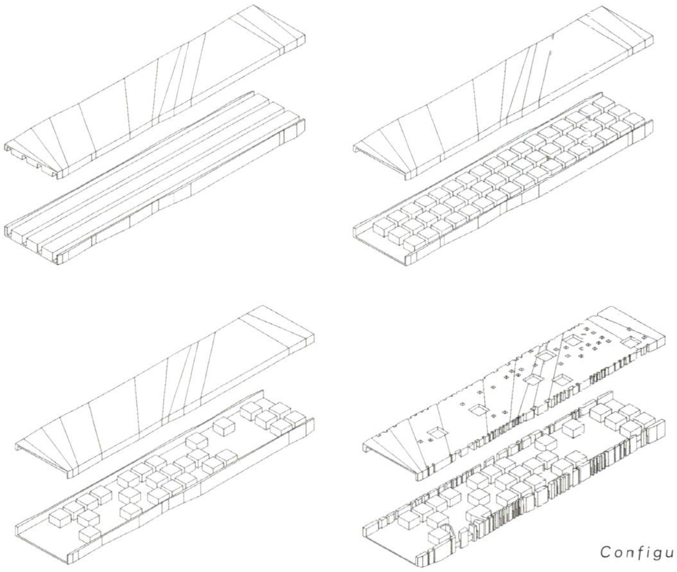

Configuration

For centuries, people have used thermal water resorts not only for pleasure but also for therapeutic reasons. This project involves a spa in a place where different treatments and therapies are provided, mainly with the use of water. Some presume that the name comes from the Belgian city of Spa, known for its baths as far back as the Roman era. Others speculate that the name is an acronym of the Latin phrase "salutem per aquam" (health through water). The location in a natural environment is part of the package of relaxation and decontextualization from urban civilization and daily routine, offering a possibility to regain natural balance. Bearing this in mind, the program exceeds the traditional definition of a spa as a leisure and health space, and creates an environment capable of providing wellness, peace and a relaxing atmosphere, where all the elements - air, sounds, colors, textures and forms - enhance the facility. The building has been conceived on the basis of its materiality, with construction determining design. It pursues a poetic balance with the natural surroundings. Nature is treated as one of the many materials. The reflections in the water, the breeze, the sound of the leaves moved by the wind, the clear views of the sky, are all elements of the composition. Material and formal austerity, and strong plastic expression are key elements in the search for intensity. Through its material condition, the building aims to promote different states of mind in the different spaces, with the use of light, textures, sounds, reflections, etc. Accordingly, it is no longer a building that accommodates a spa, but architecture that is part of the therapeutic treatment, with a tight relation to nature.

Interrelationships

Vagni Federico, Manasseri Ezequiel SOUTH AMERICA - ARGENTINA - ROSARIO

Academy of Music, Dubai

CONCERT HALL / MUSIC SCHOOL / LIBRARY

DISCIPLINE(S): ARCHITECTURE / TUTORS: PROFESSOR ANIBAL J. MOLINE, PROFESSOR GUILLERMO BANCHINI / **UNIVERSIDAD NACIONAL DE ROSARIO** FACULDAD DE ARQUITECTURA, PLANEAMIENTO Y DISENO / **PARTICIPANTS FAVORITE: 14 VOTES**

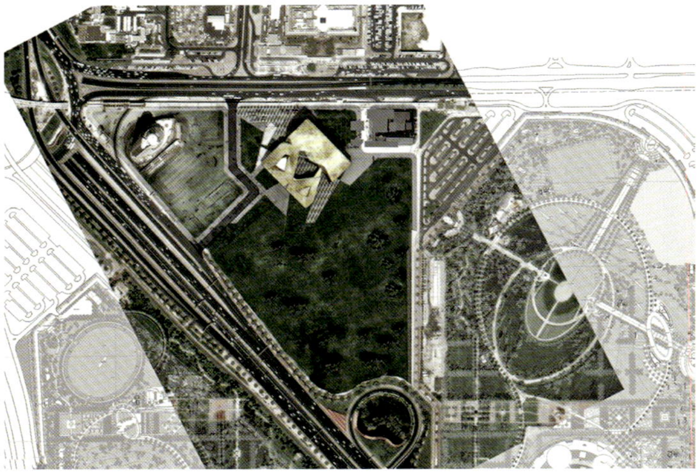

Implantation strategy

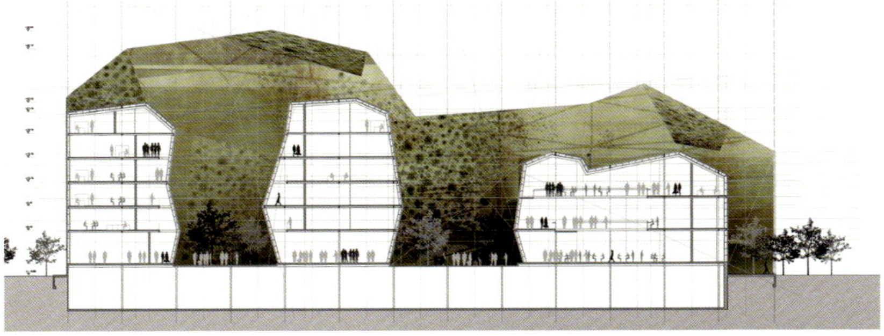

Crosss section

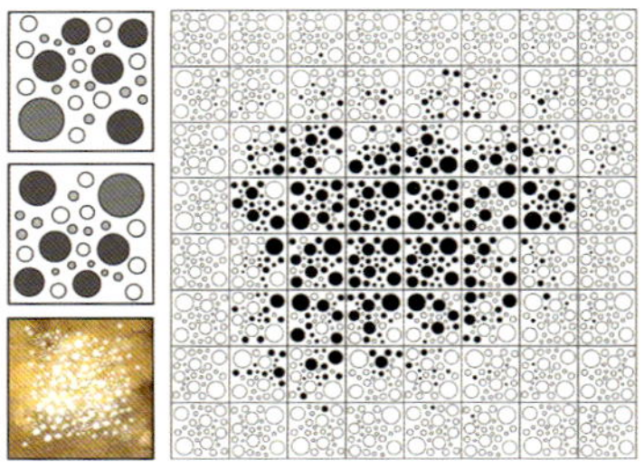

Skin

The starting points for the major strategies were: use of stone, as this is invariably part of the Dubai texture; Islamic architecture, characterized as a typology that has intermittent paths, visual obstruction, reaching a central courtyard that acts as a great receptor with different building entrances; a sieve, with a screened skin outside, allowing the filtration of sunlight. It also proposes green spaces with trees near bodies of water to provide fresh natural detail. The project is a great body, a stone hand primarily to protect the building and its internal and external routes from too much sun. In some sectors, this stone is partly intended to generate key areas from Islamic architecture, such as broken entrances giving on to the large patio. The screen uses double glazing to cushion the heat, in accordance with the sector to be protected (library, music rooms, school). This double skin has silk-screened panels in some areas, allowing different amounts of sunlight into different sectors. The school library resembles a cloister, a typology that has consistently worked throughout the history of architecture, allowing the units to function properly in terms of circulation and layout of rooms, courtyards and hallways, as well as a proper distribution of books, shelves and reading sections. The school sector is connected to the library, as is the case with the rehearsal rooms of the block containing the concert hall. Each block (library, school and concert halls) is meant for individual use in the event that the others are not in use.The concert halls and auditoriums are located at two corners of the stone, allowing a large hall with triple height and a set of stairs and ramps that allow a quick tour with excellent vistas. The central courtyard is designed as the hub of the entire program, opening views of various sectors of the city and the park, enabling pedestrian flow from many quarters. We propose a pedestrian-level bar under the shade of the trees, transforming the open space into a 'grand oasis'.

Atrium

Concert hall / Foyer

Interior images of library sector

Kiyonori Sugiyama ● **ASIA - JAPAN - YOKOHAMA**

Between the star and the moon

DISCIPLINE(S): ARCHITECTURE / TUTOR: MASASHI SOGABE / **KANAGAWA UNIVERSITY** DEPARTMENT OF ARCHITECTURE FACULTY OF ENGINEERING / **PARTICIPANTS FAVORITE: 11 VOTES**

I like stars. There is distance of several light-years between me and the stars. But I am related to a star when I think in terms of the big picture. The connection is based on what I can see. The star is connected to the moon and other stars, and to the sun in the morning. The cosmic structure enables us to experience the four seasons, clouds, rain, snow. We have a sense of distance in that things can seem to be long, while also seeming to be near.

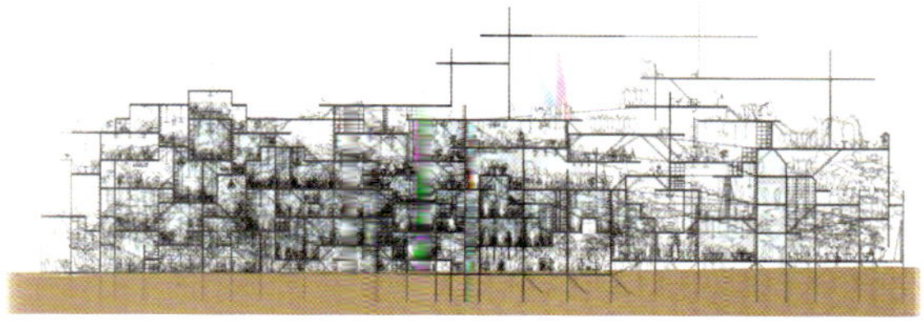

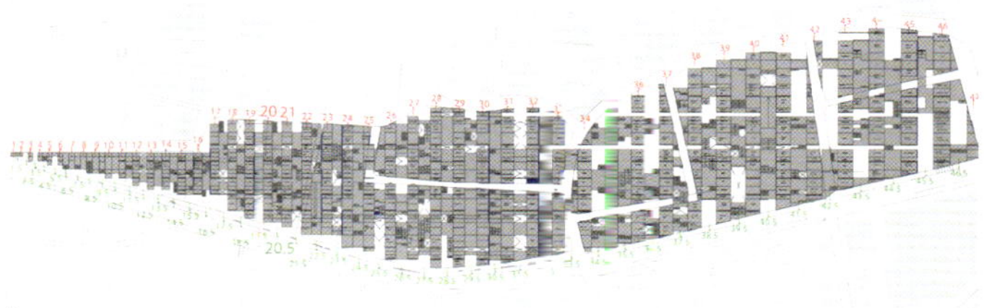

+5000 PLAN 1/1000

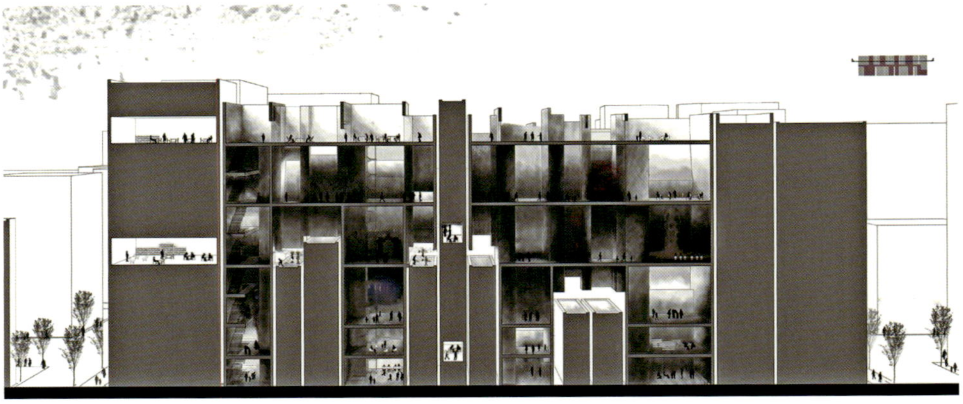

Existing buildings
Axis of Urban Shade
Rebuilt buildings

Kensuke Ohtsuka ASIA - JAPAN - KANAGAWA

Architecture from **Shade**

GINZA DARK MUSEUM OF ART WITHOUT PLAN

DISCIPLINE: ARCHITECTURE, URBAN DESIGN / TUTOR: HIDEKI YOSHIMATSU / **TOKAI UNIVERSITY**
DEPARTMENT OF ARCHITECTURE AND BUILDING ENGINEERING / **PARTICIPANTS FAVORITE: 14 VOTES + NOMINATED**

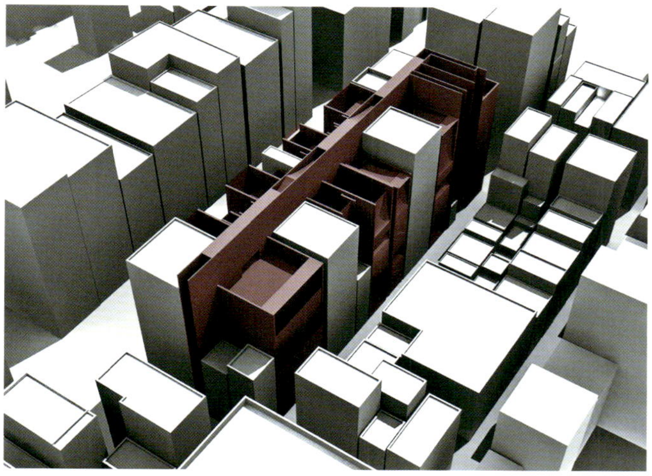

One of the main features of Japanese architecture is the sharp-angled long roof with eaves, which allows Japanese buildings to have shade by dividing the interior space by means of shoji (partitions of translucent paper on a wooden frame) and fusuma (vertical rectangular panels covered with paper which can slide sideways). Shades are created by darkening a space with light dark rather than by providing light in a dark space. Deep darkness between one less-dark space and another makes the space looks like 2 different spaces. We call this 'architecture without a plan', which means that different levels of darkness divide a space, rather than physical walls. Japanese cities are high-density. This environment has created a unique type of space in-between buildings, which is different from public spaces in Europe. For example, Ginza in Tokyo is full of tall buildings with spaces in-between. The rears of these buildings look like spines and function as frameworks. Such unique spaces in Ginza are hidden from the main streets. I would like to visualize these unique spaces in Ginza by allotting them an architectural function. Urban shade functions as a connector of buildings. Those tall thin buildings which create the unique spaces in Ginza should be kept as they are and buildings without this shape should be rebuilt. I propose constructing a Dark Museum with the space divided by shades. Those unique urban shades act as axes to make architecture of whole blocks in Ginza. The Dark Museum of Art is a sustainable urban project aimed at maintaining this unique structure of blocks in Ginza when the city is upgraded. The Dark Museum displays visually and intellectually appealing works such as those produced by Gary Hill, who made axes with shades in-between existing buildings, and Bill Viola, James Turrell and Olafur Eliasson.

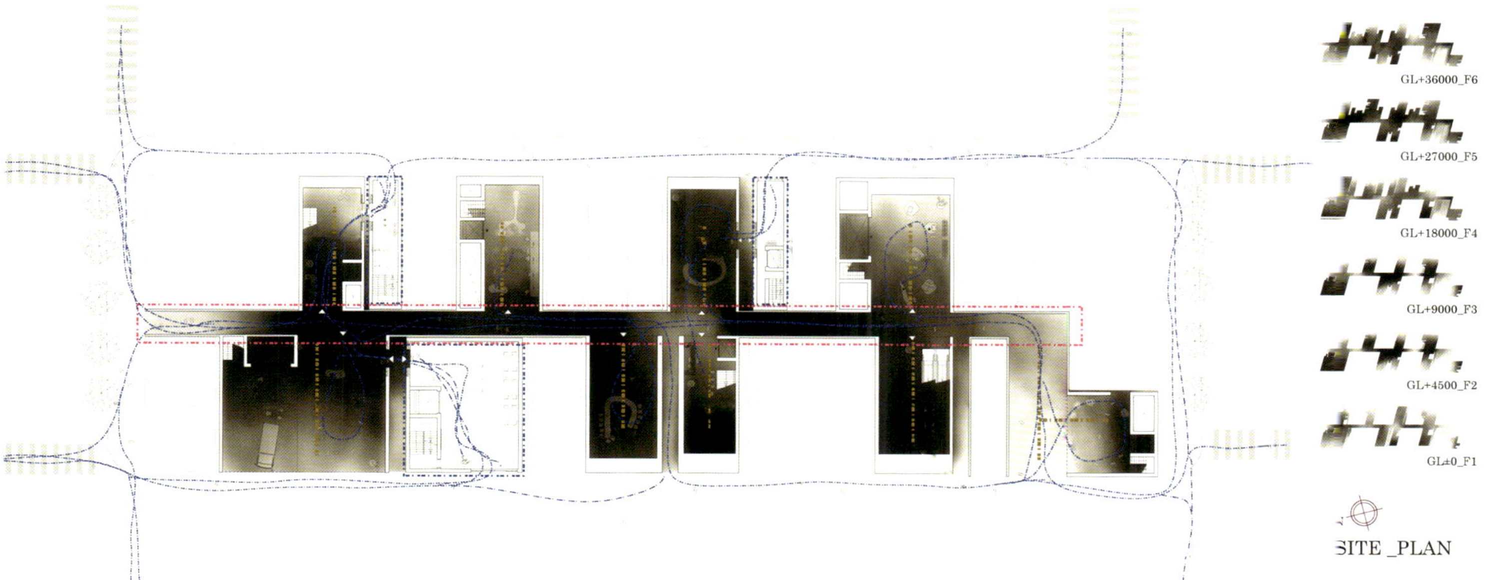

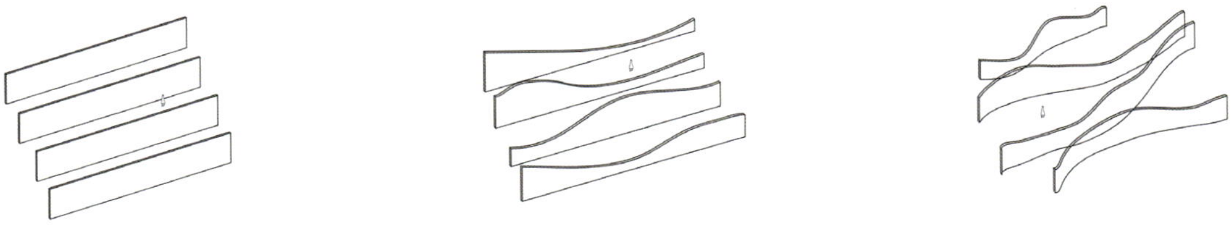

Concept

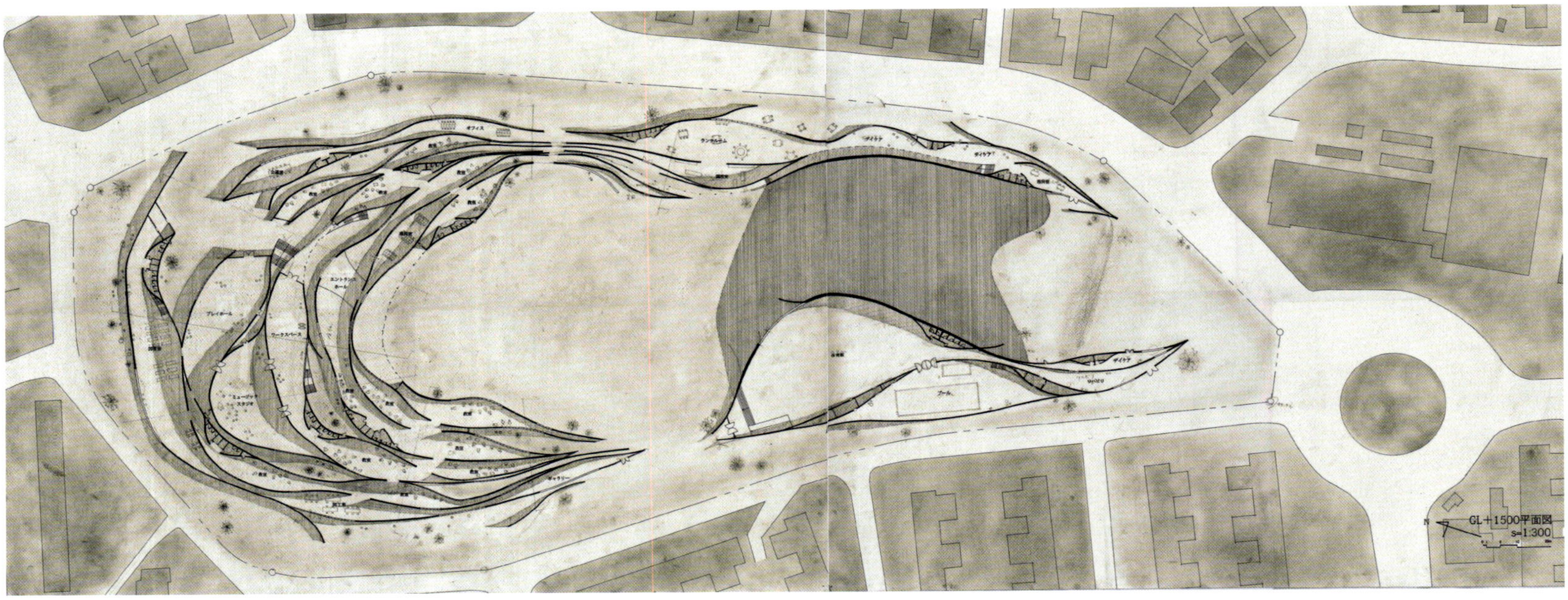

Plan

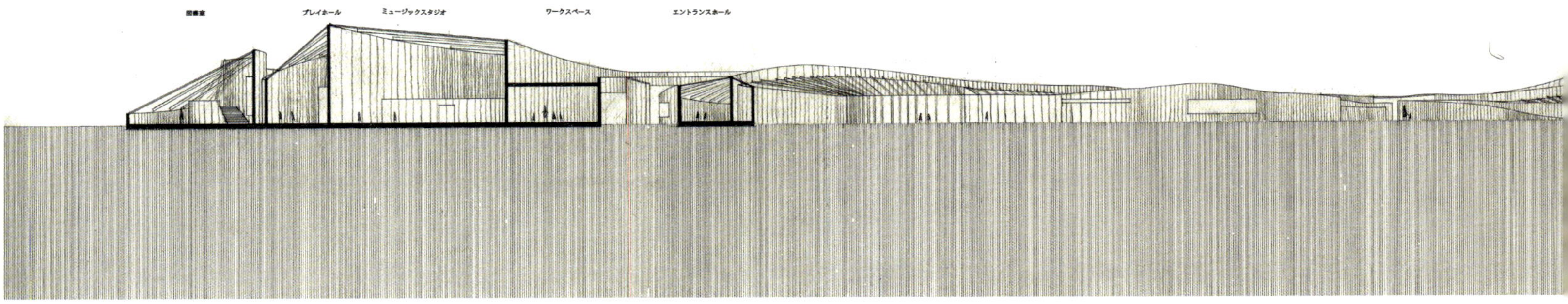

Section

Classroom 2

Aya Fujimoto ASIA - JAPAN - KYOTO

Next To Each Other

THINKING ABOUT HOW TO JUXTAPOSE ROOMS

DISCIPLINE: ARCHITECTURE / TUTOR: HIROAKI KIMURA / **KYOTO INSTITUTE OF TECHNOLOGY** DEPARTMENT OF ARCHITECTURE AND DESIGN
FACULTY OF ENGINEERING AND DESIGN / **NOMINATED**

What is next to you? Can you imagine that the room next to you is filled with candy, or with dinosaurs? People have abandoned their curiosity. This project is about an elementary school like a hillock. In this school, things change. Once you walk in, you feel the difference. The shadow dropping in the room, the vibration of a sound, the changes depend on time. A hall does not always remain a hall. "I noticed that the room next to a classroom changed into a library all of a sudden," the children say. They learn that there is no longer a classroom adjoining theirs. This school was planned with hope: hope that children could grow up with curiosity, children who can who can imagine the next room in eager anticipation.

Passage

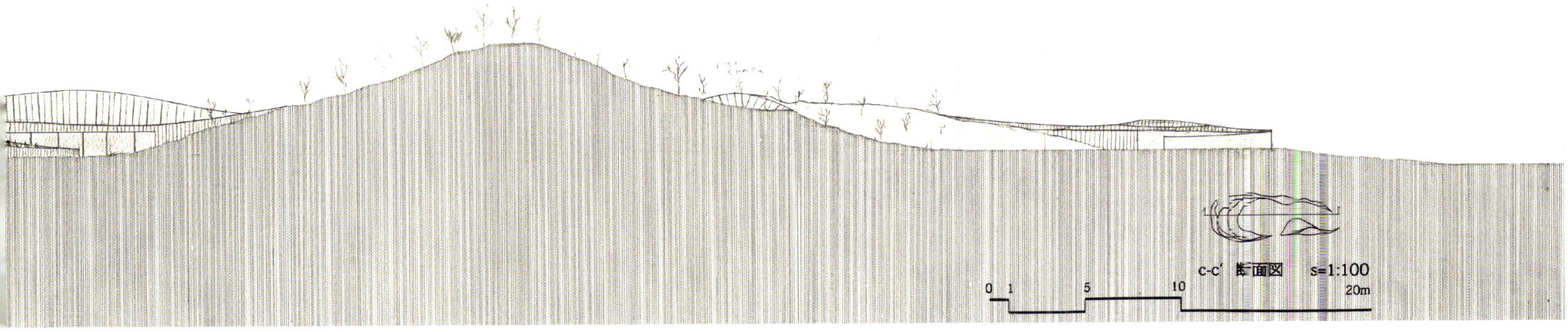

The whole

Loc Huu Pham ASIA - VIETNAM - HANOI

Sustainable Community **Cultural Centre**

A GUIDELINE FOR LOCAL HANHI PEOPLE TO IMPROVE THEIR QUALITY OF LIFE BY THEMSELVES

DISCIPLINE(S): ARCHITECTURE / TUTOR: PHD. ARCHITECT. LE QUAN / **HANOI ARCHITECTURAL UNIVERSITY**, FACULTY OF ARCHITECTURE

Main Façade / Concept / Model research / Bird's-eye view

As an agricultural country, Vietnam is considered to be highly susceptible to global climate change. Therefore, the importance of sustainable development in order to cope with climate change is always a concern. Living in the north-west mountainous areas of Vietnam, the Hanhi people have preserved their own culture and lifestyle, which reflect the unique character of Vietnamese people. They often use earth to build their homes, which are cool in the summer and warm in the winter. The villages of Hanhi look like many mushrooms rising on the mountain. Hanhi people have a unique national character but they lack a community center so that they can preserve and improve their culture. This idea is based on a green design to create a Sustainable Community Cultural Center for local people, and is oriented to sustainable economy, society and the environment. The notion of green is not only about the environment but also about the quality of life, including traditional values and the preservation and development of culture. By using local building materials such as earth, stone, wood, bamboo and straw, this building is designed to comply with the local people's possibilities and realistic conditions. The project also acts as a guideline for the residents to improve their quality of life all by themselves. The simple building circle is positioned directly in the middle of the village, making it convenient for everyone to approach. According to the ancient concept of the Hanhi people, they worship the Forest Angle, the Earth Angle, the Water Angle, the Harvest Angle - it is the Gods of Nature who shelter them from danger and give them a prosperous life in the mountainous areas. The Community Center has the image of 5 fingerprints in 1 circle on the mountain to symbolize harmony between humans and the gods. The fingerprints of gods and humans in one place expresses the desire of thousand generations of Hanhi people: a harmonious coexistence with nature.

Water-well area for community / Classrooms and Inner courtyard

Main entrance

Exterior

Interior

Edgar Nonato Mr Cusi ASIA - PHILIPPINES - MANILA

SPMM Community Complex and Nature Park

ENRICHING CULTURE THROUGH ARCHITECTURE

DISCIPLINE(S): ARCHITECTURE / TUTORS: ALFREDO LAPUEBLA, PAOLO MANALANSAN, LORELEI DEVIANA - DEAN OF FEU - IARFA
FAR EASTERN UNIVERSITY, INSTITUTE OF ARCHITECTURE & FINE ARTS

Preserving the culture of the Mangyans

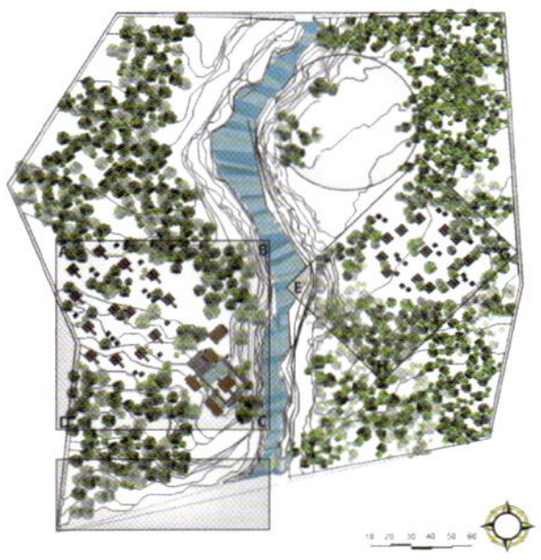

The Mangyans of Mindoro are often looked down upon and referred to as "Namamangmang" or "Namamangyan" (meaning "clueless"). The Mangyans are the native people of the island and are generally misunderstood as a result of the way in which they deal with non-Mangyans and, even more so, due to the way they approach life. This foreign mindset prevents many people from seeing how the Mangyans have beaten the harsh elements of rugged Mindoro Island with the simplest of solutions. The aim of this initiative is to help change this dismissive mindset by lending a supportive voice to the Mangyans' way of life and showcasing their unique culture and traditions, while highlighting the brilliant simplicity of their architectural knowledge. The Proposed Samahang Pangtribo ng mga Mangyan sa Mindoro (SPMM, i.e., Association for the Mangyan Tribes of Mindoro) is a Community Complex and Nature Park that will provide adequate shelter for the Mangyans, particularly the Irayas (sub-tribes). This community will elucidate their way of life, and share their cultural practices, thus helping to preserve the Mangyans' indigenous knowledge. We will also focus on the beauty of the flora and fauna of the island - creating a tourist destination to generate resources to help the locals. The project proposes an innovation that makes use of the way the Mangyan-Irayas construct their houses as a baseline for architectural design. This innovation will not just help the Mangyan-Irayas but also develop a potential design solution that conserves nature, preserves culture, and helps the people.

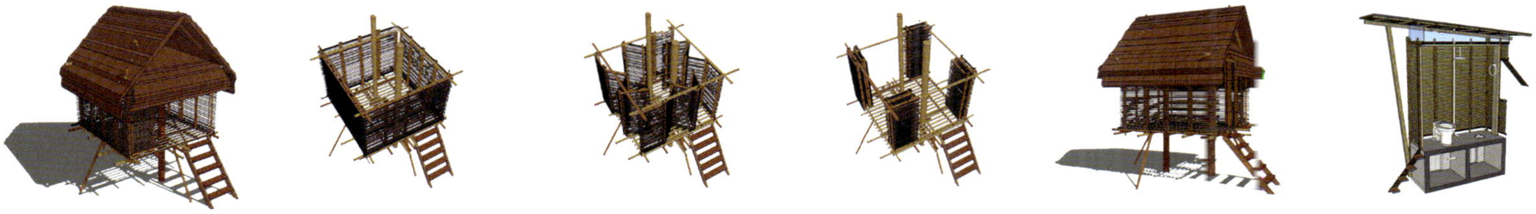

Architecture that's dynamic and flexible to nature and its forces

Balancing architecture with culture, the environment, and aesthetic value; resto, office, library and house

Designing with nature and culture to showcase the ingenuity of architecture / Integrating transformable architecture

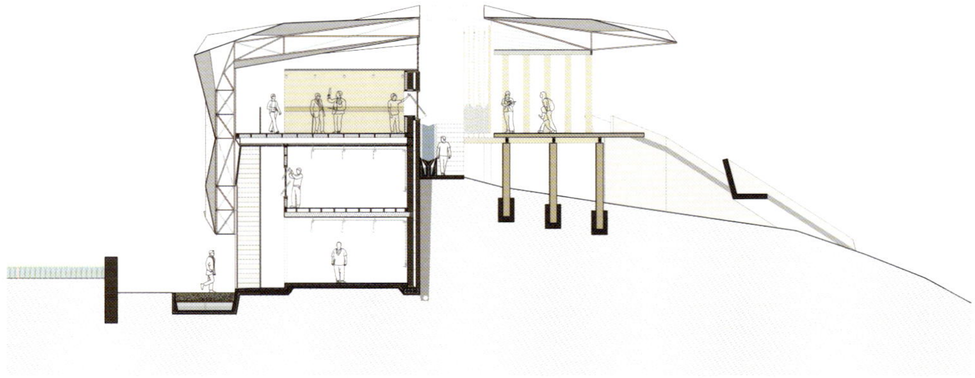

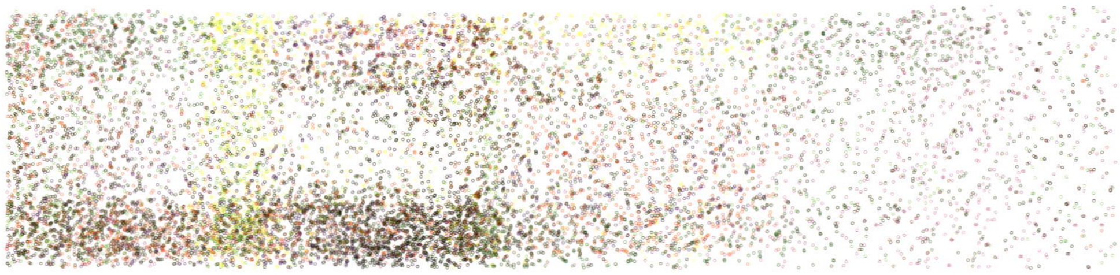

Providing accommodation for visiting doctors as well as treatment spaces

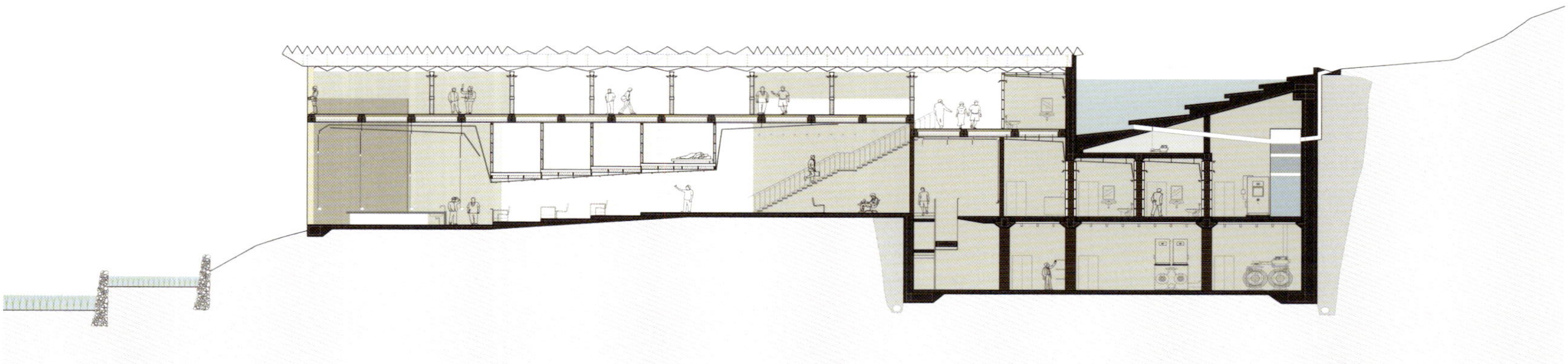

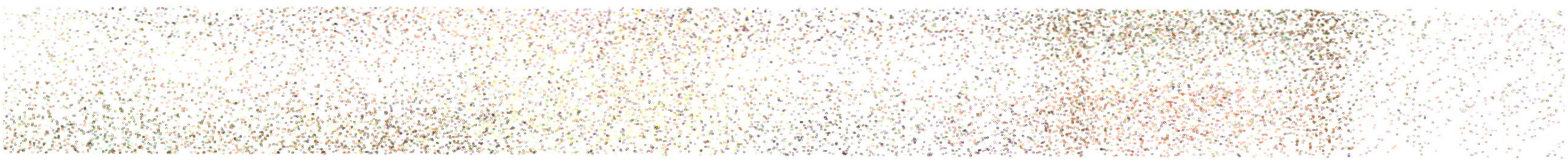

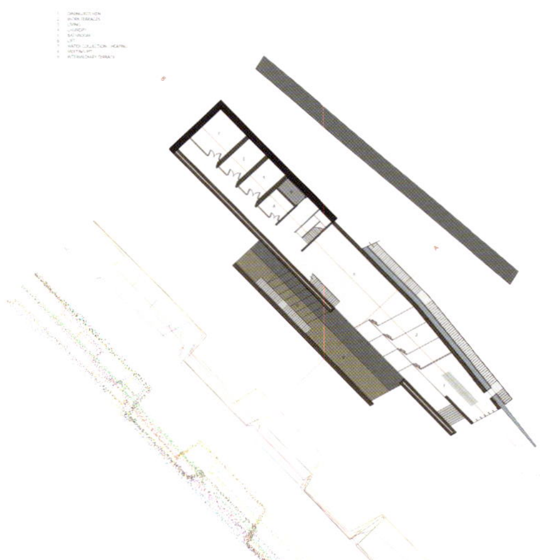

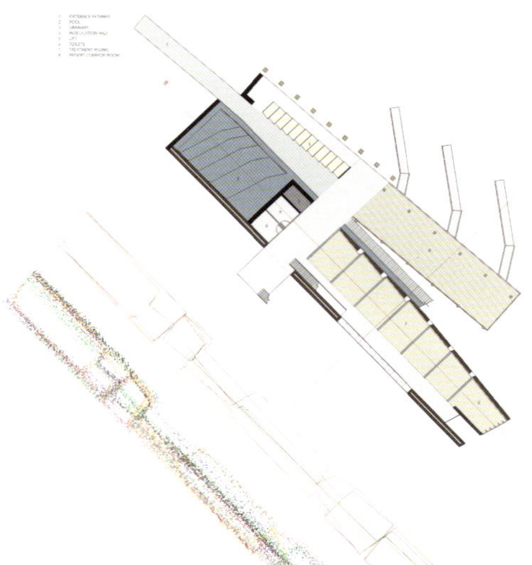

The terrace inhabitants need vital facilities for basic healthcare services

Sarosh Mulla OCEANIA - NEW ZEALAND - AUCKLAND

Interconnections of **System Densities**

ARCHITECTURE IN SYMBIOSIS WITH WORLD HERITAGE SITES

DISCIPLINE(S): ARCHITECTURE/ TUTORS: HARRIET COMPTON-RICHARDS, ROSS JENNER / **UNIVERSITY OF AUCKLAND**
FACULTY OF ARCHITECTURE, PROPERTY & PLANNING AND FINE ARTS / **NOMINATED**

The rice terraces of the Philippine Cordilleras are an endangered UNESCO World Heritage Site. They are in danger of degradation through a lack of labor, as the traditional inhabitants, the Ifugao, migrate to the cities in search of basic services. This has created a labor and knowledge shortage, leaving terrace walls in disrepair and nurseries unattended. These issues can be faced by instigating a revival of Baddang. This traditional custom of the Ifugao involves trading labor for food and shelter. This custom could be revived today to provide health services and basic labor for the rice terraces. The theory of collapsible space and time, translated from theoretical physics, has been used to understand and map the many interconnected systems at work. The density of these relationships provides insight into the existing situation and allows meaningful propositions to be developed. A series of healthcare clinics across the region, staffed by doctors on temporary visits, could vastly improve the health of the Ifugao, who have no access to health services such as basic vaccinations. In exchange for their labor, the doctors will be given an opportunity to experience a rich and diverse culture and location. They will be offered accommodation and tailored healthcare facilities within villages. For the Ifugao, access to these vital services will help to bridge the services gap between the villages and the lowland cities. The prototype healthcare building presented aims to demonstrate an experiential palimpsest of space, time and cultural values. As part of ongoing research into how to create sustainable communities, this project is looking for ways in which we can bring together our disparate skills and knowledge to find a balance between the spaces we inhabit and the way we inhabit them.

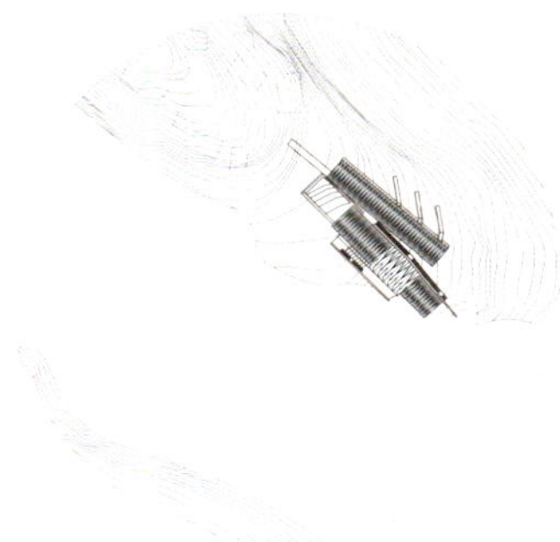

The endangered rice terraces of the Philippines

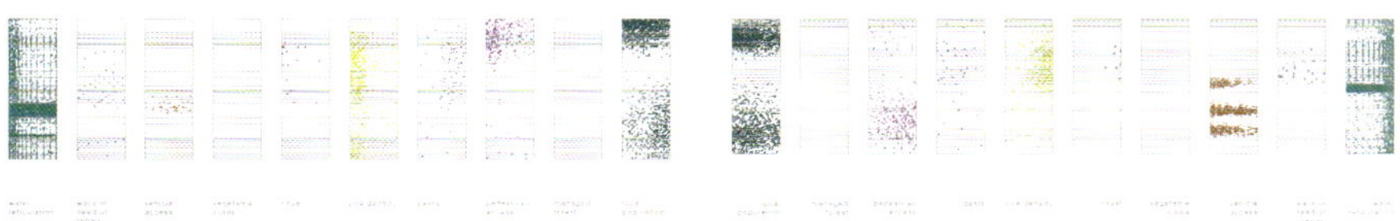

System densities give a holistic view of the many interconnected issues

Thomas Cole OCEANIA - AUSTRALIA - SYDNEY

Hawkesbury Ponds Fairgrounds

A LARGE PUBLIC SHOWGROUND AND A CREEK REGENERATION CENTRE IN THE SEMI-RURAL FRINGE OF SYDNEY

DISCIPLINE(S): ARCHITECTURE / TUTOR: OLIVIA HYDE / **UNIVERSITY OF NEW SOUTH WALES**
FACULTY OF THE BUILT ENVIRONMENT / **NOMINATED**

Hawkesbury Ponds Fairground lies in Sydney's semi-rural northwestern fringe. This project consists of two components: a large public showground and a creek regeneration centre. The surrounding area is a large low-density residential and light-industrial suburb with huge tracts of undeveloped land and no consolidated public space. It is situated on the Hawkesbury River floodplain and is consequently subject to sporadic bouts of destruction, which has led to many structures acquiring new programs: flood-damaged houses serve to facilitate drug use, while machinery sheds display evidence of parties and binge drinking. The Hawkesbury River floodplains are also under attack from another front: Sydney's sprawl is moving west and the zone has become a key interest area for significant residential development. It is only because of the waning natural environment that this growth has been officially condemned. A development report advises that the surrounding land should not be developed without the significant protection and restoration of the ponds, which contain endangered species of fish. The Hawkesbury Fairground and Creek Regeneration Centre is not only moving towards saving the endangered fish but also toward securing public space that will be of critical importance when the area is developed in the future. The Showground seeks events and activities whilst the Creek Regeneration Centre is an archeological attempt to reveal the vanishing quality of the site. This dual program also allows the continuation of the area's transient nature: twice a year the Creek Regeneration Centre is used to accommodate the local agriculture fair. The Creek Regeneration Centre is a external object penetrating the fouled water body, mass-producing native wildlife and pumping clean water through the sick creek. The showground displays agricultural produce within the same arena as the synthetic production of endangered species.

Kim Jungmin ASIA - KOREA, SOUTH - KYUNGSAN-SHI, KYUNGBUK

Landscape **in movement**

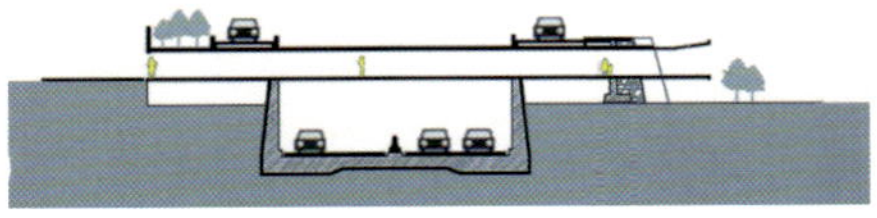

URBAN CAPILLARY, INFRASTRUCTURE

DISCIPLINE(S): ARCHITECTURE, LANDSCAPE DESIGN / TUTOR: KIM HYUN JIN / **YEUNGNAM UNIVERSITY** SCHOOL OF ARCHITECTURE

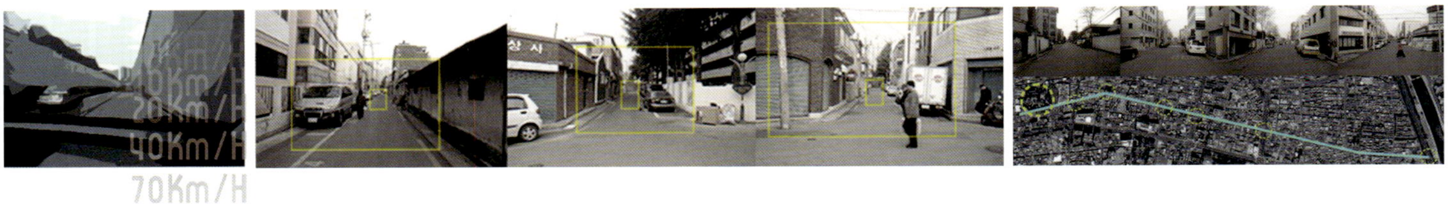

Existing urban infrastructural facilities perform their own functions, but when we review their relationship with the city, we occasionally find that they cause interruption or are isolated from human activity. Any event lets us tell the story of the place, and it should begin with discovering the possibilities of the space. Discovery is linked to reinterpretation, and we can focus on the place through the infrastructural construction. If the infrastructure enables flow, relationships and a serial landscape, then it has possibilities as space. Shinchon Expressway is the first high-speed way in Daegu. In 1990, it was proposed as a transport infrastructure to solve traffic congestion and allow distribution transportation. However, the connection between one spot and another creates another line that breaks the context of the city. Besides, the concrete-covered banks eliminate any connection with the waterfronts and have become standardized urban landscape. The landscape in the infrastructure is shown through the sequence that is experienced in the speed, and the sequence could be interpreted as serial landscape made by the united space. People (pedestrians and drivers) walk, see, hear and also feel and recognize the landscape. The Architectural Infrastructure might be interpreted through these two categories. Referring to speed and time, assuming uniform velocity without congestion, we can apply the formula S=VT. The road is regarded as an abstract space eliminating the view of pedestrians. On the road, drivers will experience changeover and movement. It takes about 20-30 seconds for drivers, and about 5 minutes for pedestrians to pass this 500m section. In each case, the difference experienced in the perception process will be an important element when we provide the inside and outside of the building. First, in the case of the lower structure associated with speed, it will be built by the design of a braking system including a numerical module (data result: 4 meters). In the case of the upper structure, the lines of each area will be made by a prototype analyzed by the quality of the horizontal lines. Ten horizontal lines will be classified, analyzed and designed individually by their characteristics. The landscape will be expressed by panoramas of historical narrative, a periscope bridging refracted horizontal lines, and floating parks seen as apartment housing. Built space makes the pedestrians' experience continuous by cooperating with the waterfront. Upper and lower structures of the expressway change its formation through various levels, and it will bring a great change to the drivers' primary perception. Existing transportation infrastructure itself is a moving exhibition of the city, and becoming a part of landscape means that pedestrians and drivers can be related.

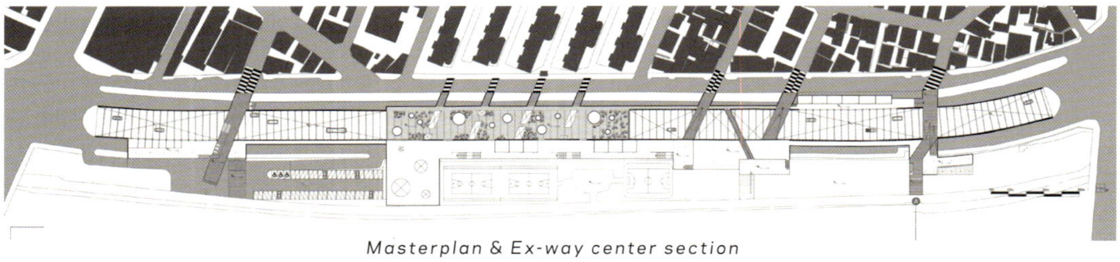

Masterplan & Ex-way center section

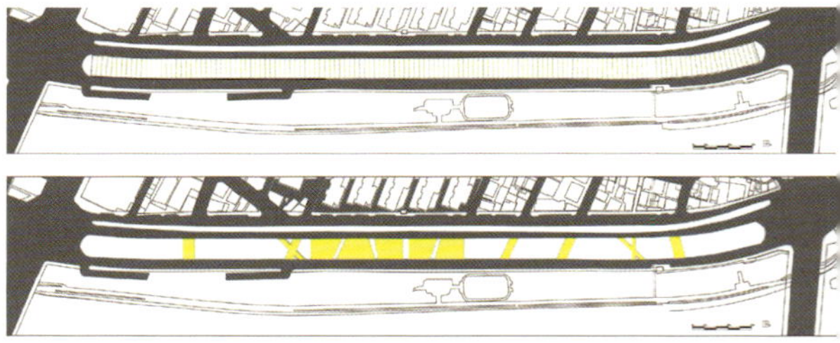

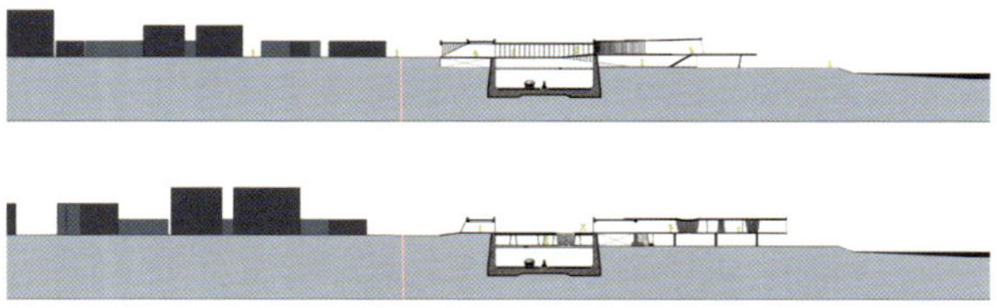

Apply to prototype section 1/2

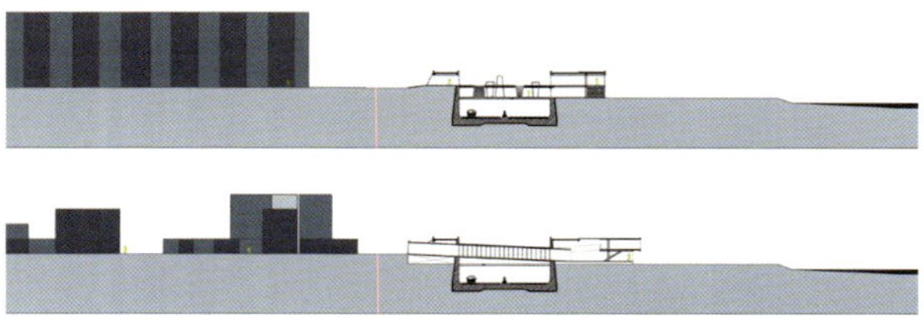

Apply to prototype section 1/2

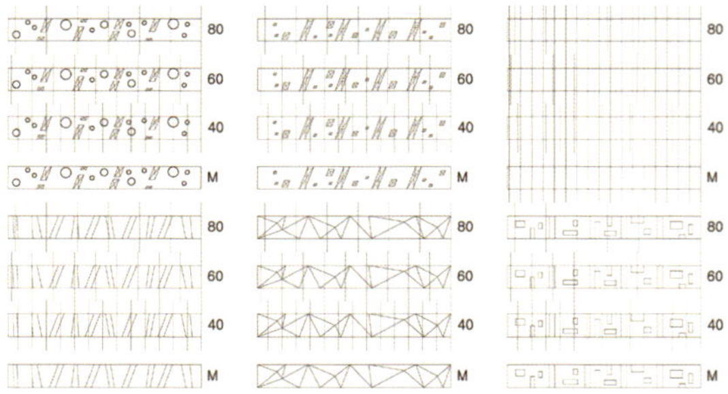

Data research

Dongchoul Park **ASIA - KOREA, SOUTH - SEOUL**

3S+G=Regeneration

SINGLE-PERSON HOUSE IN UNUSED SPACE IN MYUNG-DONG, SEOUL

DISCIPLINE(S): ARCHITECTURE / TUTOR: CHUNG KI, LEE / **UNIVERSITY OF SEOUL** COLLEGE OF URBAN SCIENCES - PROGRAM IN ARCHITECTURE / **PARTICIPANTS FAVORITE: 12 VOTES**

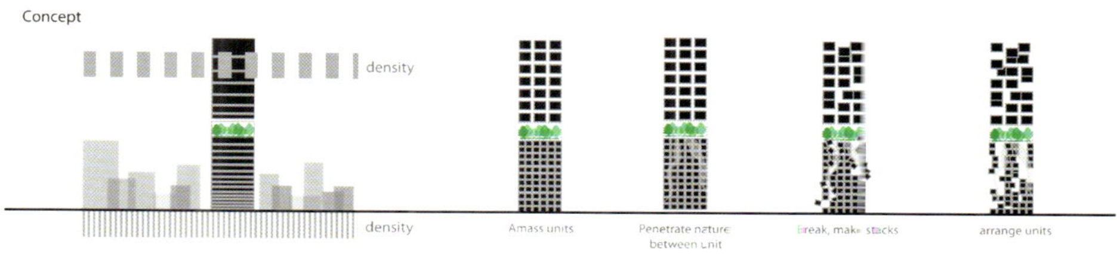

The continuing dissolution of the family and a large increase in single-person households present a new concept in society. Myung-dong Street in Seoul offers foreign-brand coffee shops, restaurants, boutiques, cinemas, and hairdressing salons. Although colorful, Myung-dong is expensive at more than $ 100,000 per square meter of ground. Myung-dong is Korea's primary regional tourism district, as well as its central business district. But it is a poor place in terms of residential environment, with many workers and disadvantaged people living here. This project provides a single-person house for them. It is possible to use the free interior space of a block. My goal is to regenerate unused space, improving the efficiency of the city as a whole. In the middle of the building, the Hanging Gardens form the air passages of the stack. It could be a communication space for residents of the building. The vertical flow of greenery offers a visual city park. In addition, the connection between buildings could be used as an emergency exit in case of fire, and could form an extension to the city park. My site is located in the middle of strip high-rise building. The concept of the building uses the density of Myung-dong with high density at low level, and low density at high level. This determines the size of the unit and the lighting. Because the buildings are surrounded on all sides, there ought to be public gardens, open on two sides.

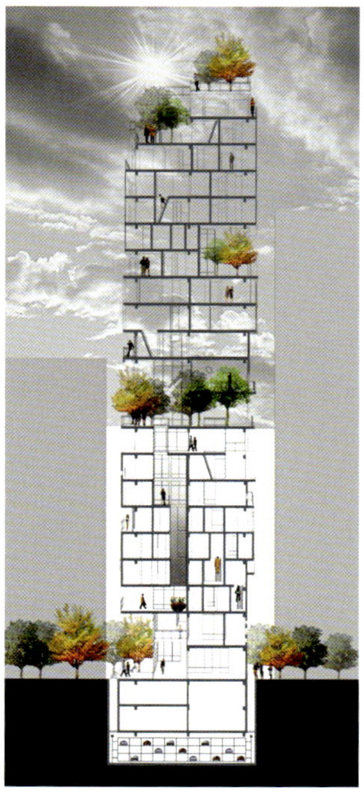

Unit Plan

Binvi Wannaya ASIA - TAIWAN - CHUNG-LI

Flood and Slum in Jakarta City

NEW SELF-BUILT SYSTEM

DISCIPLINE(S): ARCHITECTURE / TUTOR: GUANG-ZONG, ZENG / **CHUNG YUAN CHRISTIAN UNIVERSITY**
COLLEGE OF DESIGN, DEPARTMENT OF ARCHITECTURE

In recent years Jakarta city has consistently suffered from annual flooding and this has become a serious threat to common citizens. The flooding is caused by a complex of factors: garbage dumping, non-permeable land and the geographical situation of the city. To control the flooding, the Government chose to build the East Canal project, but the project yet has not been started due to budgetary and land-ownership problems. So the citizens have no choice other than to cope with the flooding themselves, in which case the people living in slum housing on Jakarta's river-bank area become direct victims of the flooding. During the high-water season, they move their belongings to the higher part of the house, but often they have no time for this, so that they suffer losses. And when the flood level rises above manageable level, they have to rely on emergency aid to take them to the nearest refugee camp. Their buildings are made of a mixture of brick, wood, bamboo and corrugated iron sheets. For economic reasons, they have developed their own self-built type of architecture, but these buildings are not sufficient to help them cope with this threat. This project is located in the Kampung Melayu Area in East Jakarta. This is a prototype of a new, self-built housing system and community. The project itself focuses on creating an opportunity for community and architecture, in order to deal with the flooding. There are two main ideas. The first: designing single self-built unit housing which consists of floating board structures, reducing people's need to move valuable goods, keeping their possessions safe from severe damage, and creating a single passage for possible group connection at 5-meter flood level. The second: creating a 5-meter passage network community simply by reproducing self-built unit housing and enabling the community to perform basic activities even during worst flooding season.

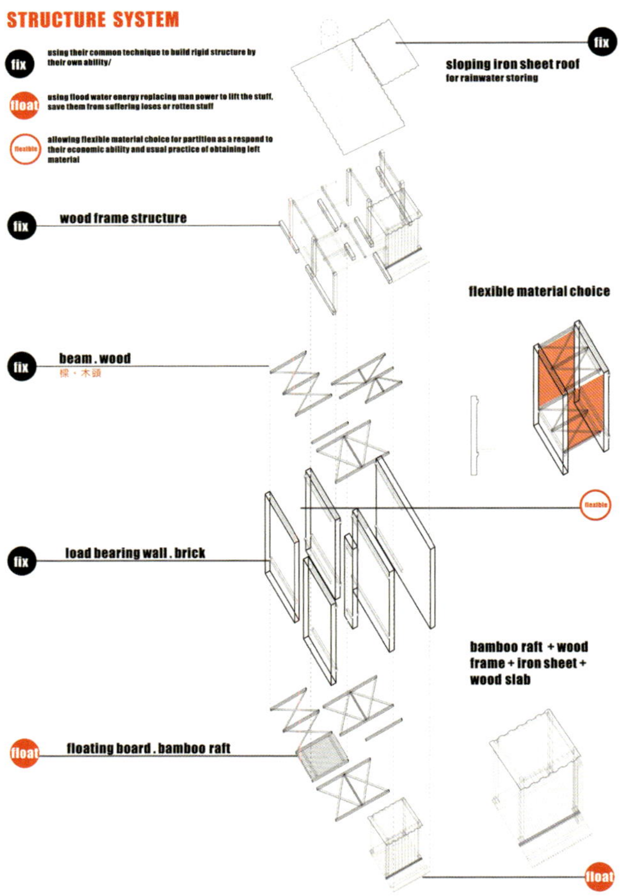

Zhi-Sheng Chen ASIA - TAIWAN - TAMSUI

Plastic (bag) **Architecture**

THE CONSTRUCTION OF KNOWLEDGE AND ARCHITECTURE SYSTEM

DISCIPLINE(S): ARCHITECTURE / TUTOR: KYLE C. YANG / **TAMKANG UNIVERSITIES** / COLLEGE OF ENGINEERING / **PARTICIPANTS FAVORITE: 15 VOTES**

The plastic bag is a readily available resource for people in Taiwan / below: The manual

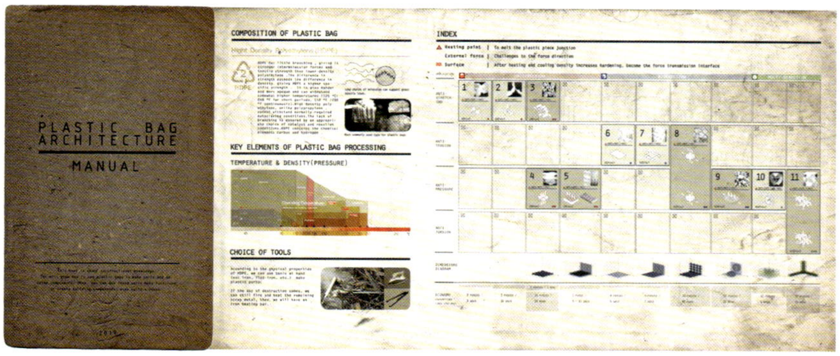

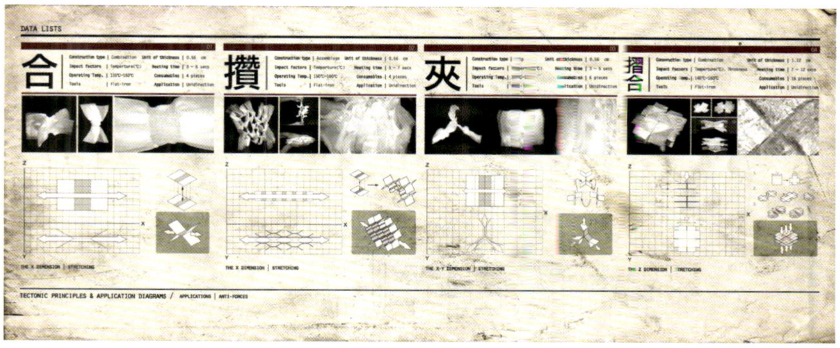

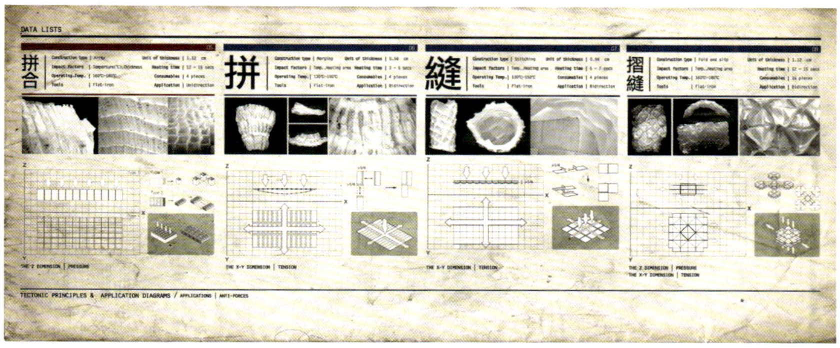

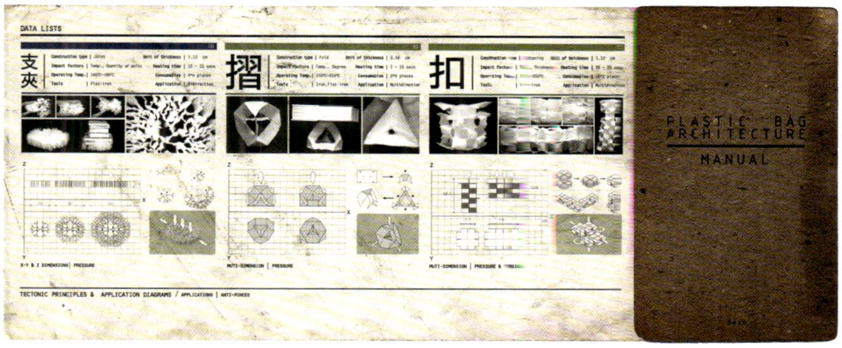

This project is about discovering the essence of architecture. The purpose is to gather knowledge and put it to use. When dealing with a new material, after conducting experiments, we can develop components according to their supply and constructional qualities. And we can also categorize them to form a set of organized knowledge. By applying this organized knowledge, we can respond to the basic need for survival and then try to realize another manifestation of architecture. What is architecture? Why construct? How should we construct? The essence of architecture has no single definition. The purpose of architecture is to satisfy mankind's needs. Constructional methods rely upon accumulating experiences. Tectonics forms the basis of architectural practice. Long ago, people used natural resources for building, and developed a set of building skills. Can we, as modern people living in modern cities, now utilize the resources at hand to amass a kind of constructional knowledge, allowing another possibility of architecture? According to statistics, people in Taiwan have used about 20 billion plastic bags in the past ten years. In Taiwan, all of us would use plastic bags every day. When buying breakfast in the morning, purchasing in traditional markets at noon, buying drinks in the afternoon, buying dinner at the cafeteria in the evening, or eating supper at night – because plastic bags are cheap and available. However, these plastic bags accumulate continually till that day ... If the day ever comes that all resources are depleted, we will still find the chance to survive. We will need buildings to protect us. We will have the basic needs for survival: a place to shelter us from bad weather, to warm us, keep us dry. What can we use to construct without wood, bricks and steel? The great amount of plastic bags at hand might be the answer.

The physical model 1:1

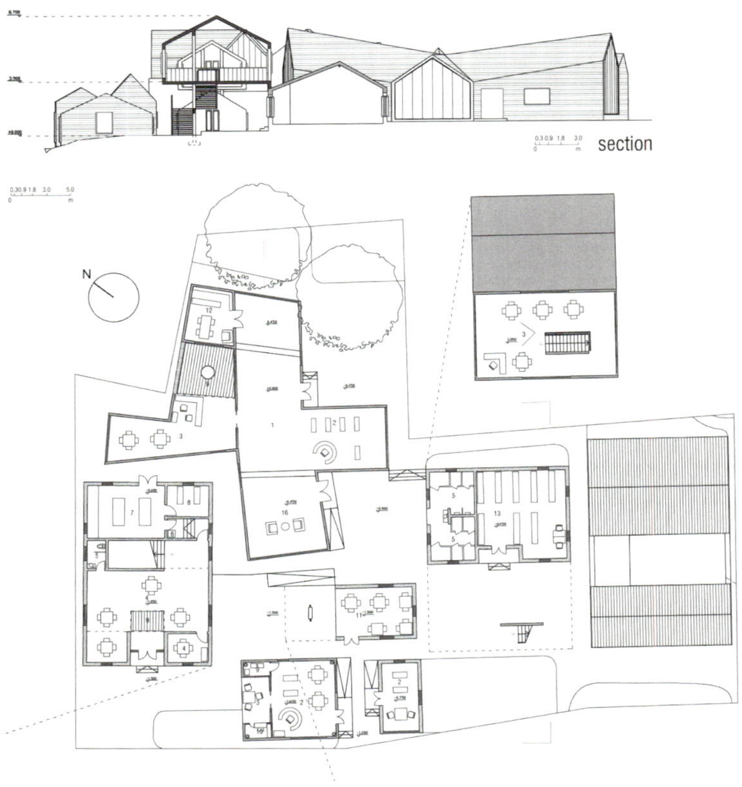

Commercial ship

Masterplan

Ships on tour

Qiu Chang, Huang Zhe Xuan, Sun Sheng ASIA - CHINA - XIAMEN, FUJIAN

Renewal Plan of Xiao'deng Island

SHIPS ON TOUR

DISCIPLINE: ARCHITECTURE, URBAN DESIGN / TUTOR: ZHANG YAN'LAI / **XIAMEN UNIVERSITY** SCHOOL OF ARCHITECTURE & CIVIL ENGINEERING / **NOMINATED**

In most cities, the urban area is well connected to the surrounding areas. With the city as a centre, the whole area can be a well-organized system. Strong connections with the city stimulates area development. However, our project is a tiny sea island in the region of the Taiwan Strait. As ships provide the only connection with the mainland, the island is rather isolated, making it extremely difficult to communicate with other areas in terms of culture, lifestyle and information. This being the case, the interaction system of Xiao'deng Island is poorly developed. This is a problem that faces most islands, and its possible solution is our primary target in this project. We are looking for methodologies that could help Xiao'deng Island present its regional culture, space, information and source to the world while, on the other hand, the world could offer Xiao'deng Island a different culture, other information, and so on. With this project we hope to generate a strong connection between Xiao'deng Island and the rest of the world. Having been isolated for a long time, Xiao'deng Island still contains a strong Minnan cultural character in the highly urbanized world. People on the island live in a way their ancestors did: they are still farming, fishing and worshiping their ancestors. They still believe what their forefathers believed, preserving old temples to celebrate ritual ceremonies in every regional festival. And the interesting Minnan buildings have also been partly retained, creating inviting street spaces. In addition, the island is covered with a large area of forest. Traditional entertainment such as the Taiwanese Opera and Pai Gow is still popular among local people. In all, we should focus on protecting the precious regionality of Xiao'deng Island and on presenting it to the world.

Routes of the tour

Concept of building ships

House reformation ship

Commercial ship

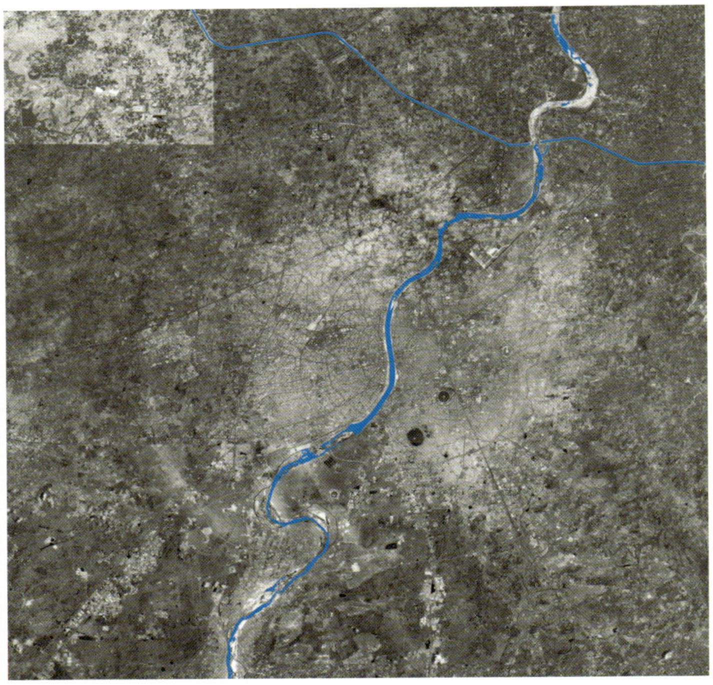

The journey of a non-perennial river through the city

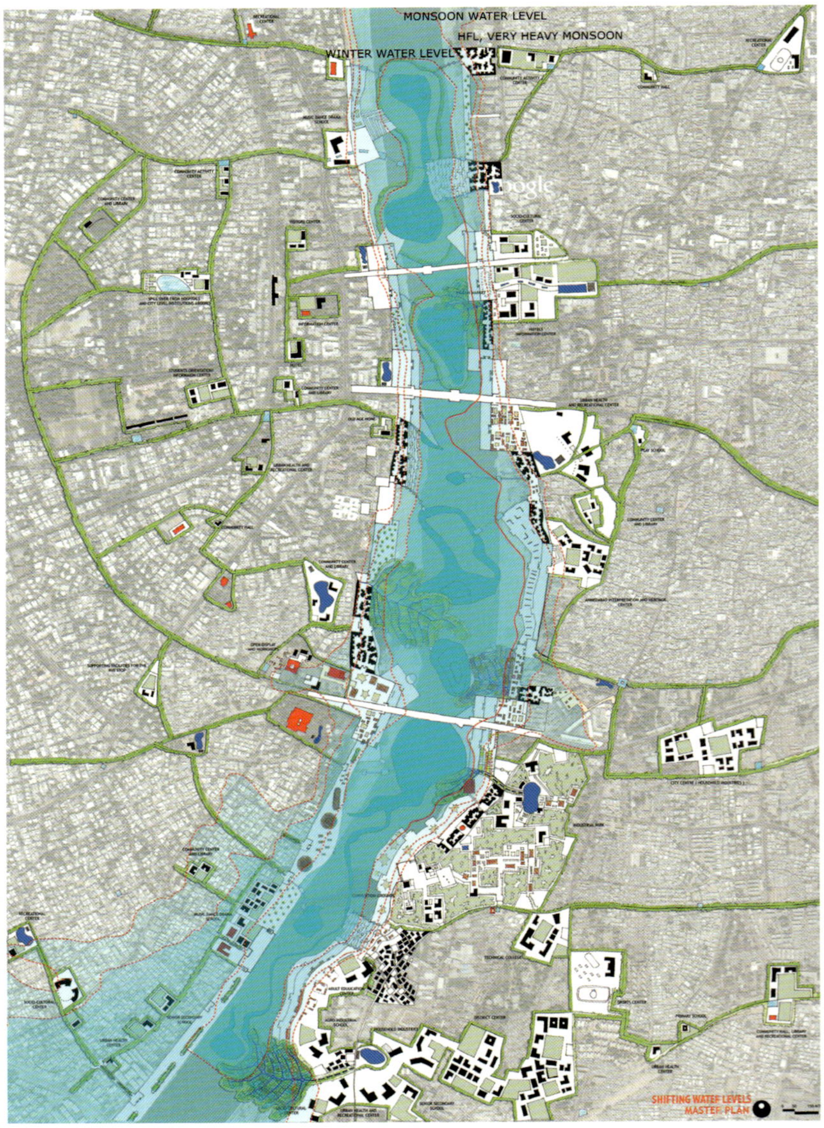

The Vision for the city presenting an ever-changing landscape

Piyas Choudhuri ASIA - INDIA - AHMEDABAD

Re-Structuring the Development
Along a Non-Perennial River

SABARMATI RIVER, AHMEDABAD

DISCIPLINE: ARCHITECTURE / TUTOR: PROF. RAJEEV KATHPALIA / **CENTRE FOR ENVIRONMENTAL PLANNING & TECHNOLOGY**
CEPT UNIVERSITY FACULTY OF ARCHITECTURE / **NOMINATED**

Understanding the relationship of the seasonal river with the city

The natural system of the river and its accompanying nature, which once defined urbanization, are falling into disuse. Current attitudes lean toward adopting mechanical rather than natural solutions, toward channeling and controlling rivers to make way for development, irrespective of their nature. The proposal looks at the issue of re-structuring development along a non-perennial river, specifically the Sabarmati River in Ahmedabad. The starting point of the project is the hypothesis that the river is still non-perennial and it has not been channeled, as is being done at present. Thus the maintenance of the nature of the river is of the utmost importance. The concern expressed is: how can this non-perennial river system be incorporated into the current milieu of functioning and growing urban systems? We seek to prevent further encroachment on the flood plain, to respect the river's dynamics and at the same time to make way for development. This vision looks at alternative water management techniques (both storm and waste) to reconnect the city to the water, to re-define the periphery, to establish accessibility mixed with utilities, and to bring about a dynamic landscape, a hard- and a softscape which at times would be flooded, thus allowing one to observe an ever-changing, dynamic phenomenon.

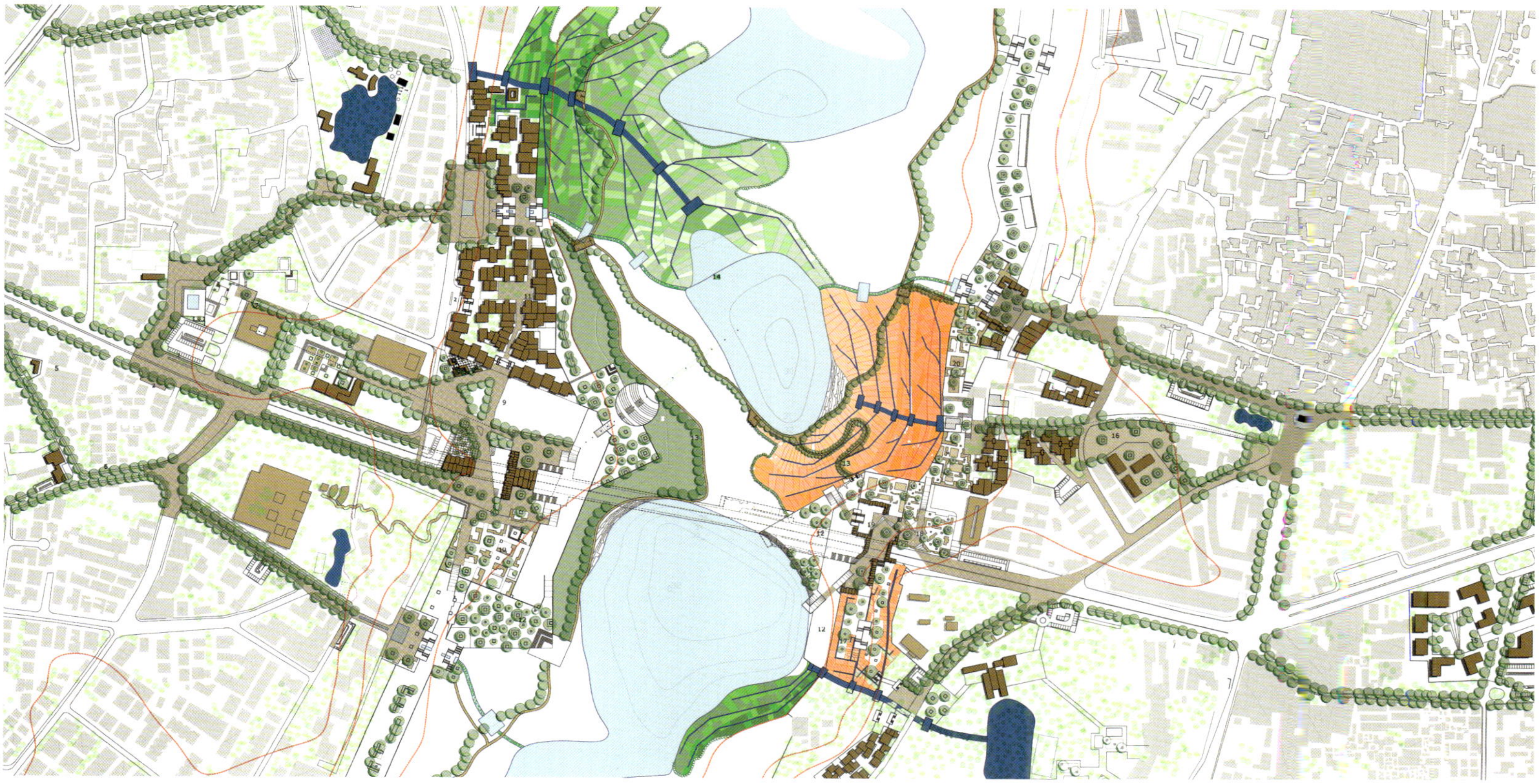

Design demonstration: institutions, slums, informal activities, water management

Monon bin Yunus ASIA - BANGLADESH - DHAKA

Regenerating **the Life of Panam Nagar**

THE FUTURE OF OUR PAST

DISCIPLINE(S): ARCHITECTURE / TUTORS: PROFESSOR DR M. SHAHIDUL AMEEN, PROFESSOR DR KHANDAKER SHABBIR AHMED, MD. RUHUL AMIN, DR ZAKIUL ISLAM, PATRICK ROZARIO, MD. MOHATAZ HOSSAIN / **BANGLADESH UNIVERSITY OF ENGINEERING & TECHNOLOGY**, DEPT. OF ARCHITECTURE, FACULTY OF ARCHITECTURE AND PLANNING

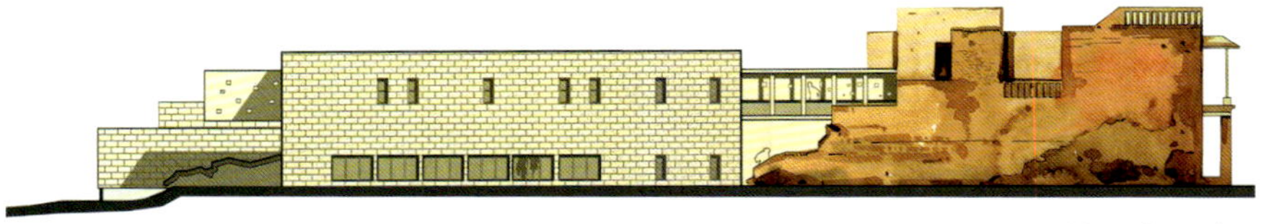

Library and conservation laboratory [a dialogue between old and new]

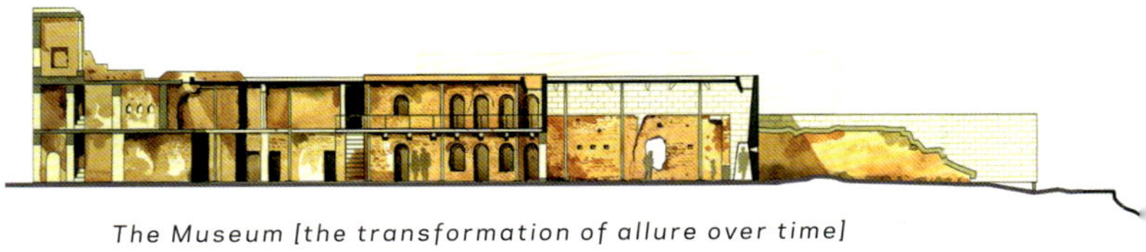

The Museum [the transformation of allure over time]

13 Weeks' Architecture deals with human experience and reaction to a space. There is a subtle aura of space in old and abandoned buildings. Each building has its own smell, feel and music. Panam Nagar is a unique example of early urban settlement in Bengal. The residences are close to each other with the central road being the major spine and the canals serving as secondary or service access. The architectural style of the buildings is English Renaissance, used throughout the cities of India in the 19th century. This is a coherent neighborhood of richly detailed buildings that tell us about the life and culture of our past. Its fortunate location in the tourist city of Sonargaon, surrounded by the ruins of the old capital, Mughal and pre-Mughal monuments, tombs and palaces, gives it an opportunity to be a successful educational and recreational center. Since the township has been designated by the Government of Bangladesh as a site of archeological significance and remains mostly unoccupied, renovating the structures to accommodate new functions appears to be necessary. The design has been developed to empathize with existing heritage, basically the insertion of new buildings on an old labyrinth to frame the past for the future. There is no distinct entrance or exit in any building. The new extensions have been placed at the back of the old buildings extending towards the canal, complementing the building pattern. In this way, the only guidance comes from the incidence of natural light, admitted in a controlled way to create focus and to make the visitors maneuver towards other spaces. Newly installed sculptures are framed by existing punches and holes in the old walls. Time was one of the most important factors in the design, with changes continually attempting to capture architectural expression. As the changes of light, weather and season affect both the allure and physical qualities of the structure, the "sedimentation of spaces' would grow with time. Contemporary structures are devoid of the ornamentation evident in historical buildings. In the new structures a sense of "Crafted Space" has been attempted, rather than imitating the ornamentation itself. The project is envisioned as an experiential architecture, rather than an iconic and expressive one.

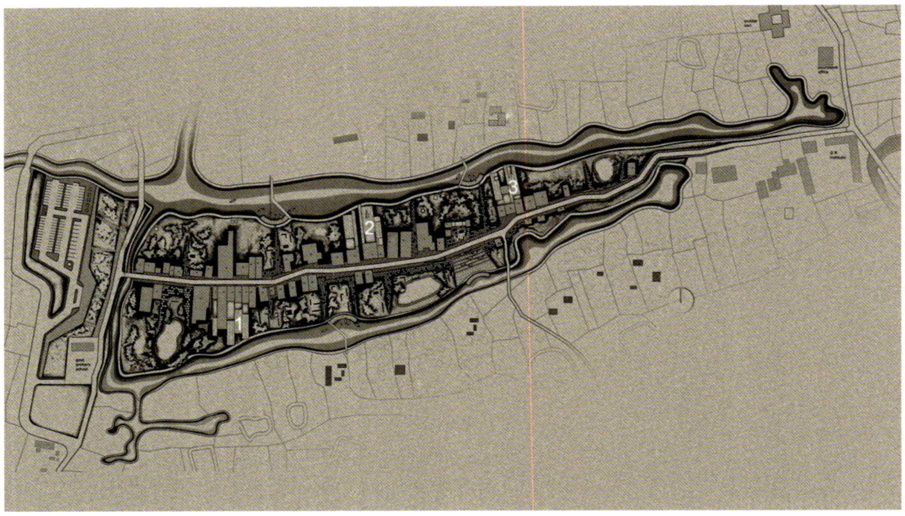

Proposed masterplan [inserting into the ruins]

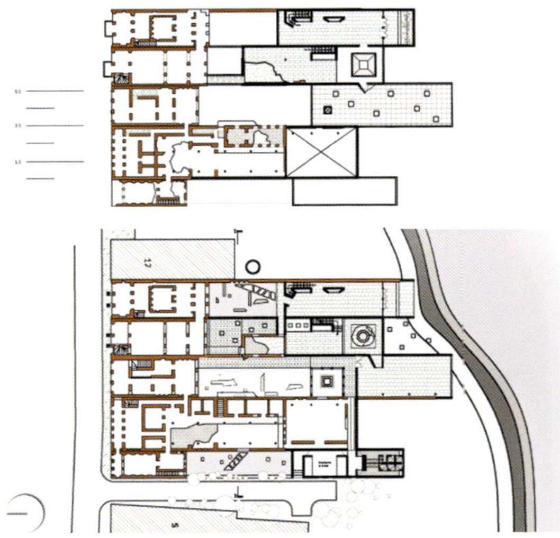

Anatomy of the ruins

The Cultural School [opening the edges]

The Museum [approach toward the light]

Shakil Ahmad Shimul ASIA - BANGLADESH - DHAKA

Future City 2100+ Bangladesh

GLOBAL WARMING, SEA LEVEL RISE

DISCIPLINE(S): ARCHITECTURE / TUTORS: DR.FUAD HASSAN MALLICK, ATIQUR RAHMAN, SAJID BIN DOZA, SHAJJAD HOSSAIN
BRAC UNIVERSITY DEPARTMENT OF ARCHITECTURE

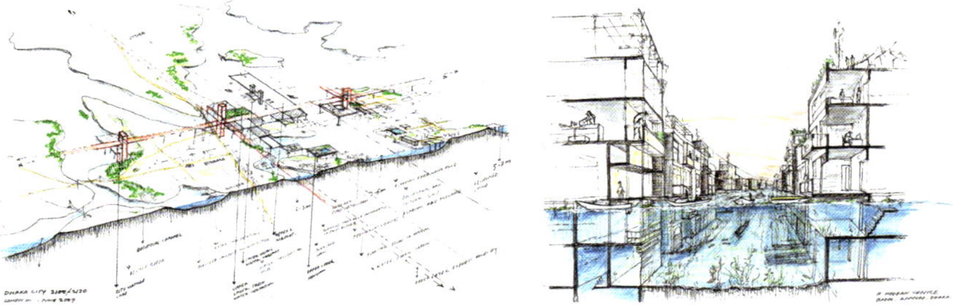

Sea-level rise in Bangladesh and in Dhaka / Design

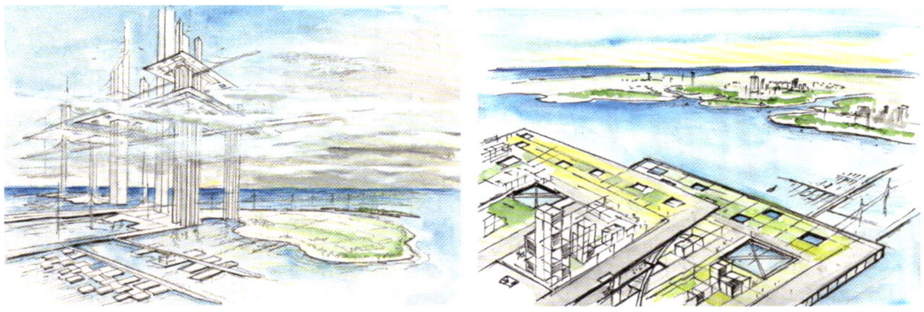

City views

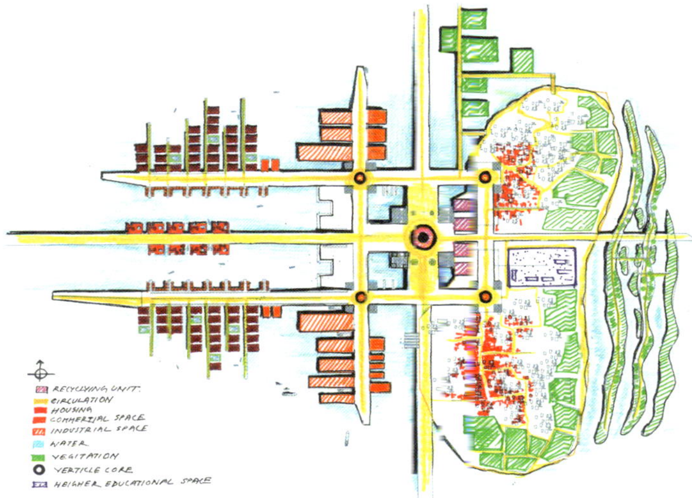

Land mass and floating mass

Down through the history of time, human civilization has changed and adapted in order to survive within nature and the body of natural laws. As time advanced, creation and innovation evolved. Architecture is the science of creation coupled to art. Subject to the laws of time, demand and technology, architecture has shaped itself accordingly, beginning with the 3-dimensional architecture of space. It has no single baseline concept, but rather several bases of space, water, air and, in the future, the whole of space. The intrusion of electro-mechanical and technological combinations enables more flexibility. The process starts at the very dawn of understanding the earth from its past, and ends with futuristic predictions and assumptions, including basic studies like geography and the demography of Bangladesh, hydrology and advanced technology, physics and aesthetics, and human psychology and physiology. Considering such basic parameters, I tried to design a city relying on the core of some proposals. It is not 'the only' solution. To me it is one of the solutions, but perhaps the basic parameters will be almost the same for all solutions. The process I have started is just a beginning for a new initiative. Maybe in the next, the person who is going to start working on it may be able to obtain some basic clues and directions for the work. My philosophy behind the work is: A future foreseen today can save tomorrow.

Model views

Tatyana Khaissundinova **ASIA - KAZAKHSTAN - ALMATY**

The Wedding **Palace**

WHERE TWO BECOME ONE

DISCIPLINE(S): ARCHITECTURE/ TUTOR: PRIEMETS OKSANA / **KAZAKH LEADING ACADEMY OF ARCHITECTURE AND CIVIL ENGINEERING** ARCHITECTURAL FACULTY

Analysis of the present situation / Inspiration; shaping sources

Kazakhstan gained its independence relatively recently, and we still feel the enormous influence of the Soviet period, particularly in architecture. I am referring to all these massive, dull grey buildings, faceless and indifferent. During the past ten years, the situation has begun to change for the better, especially in large cities such as Almaty and Astana. World-renowned architects like Kisho Kurokawa, Zaha Hadid, Norman Foster and others implement their great plans on the largest construction site in the Republic – Astana. But that is the capital city. What about the others? Attracting enormous investment and famous foreign architects seems to be impossible there. So, this is the time and opportunity for ambitious local architects to help our young developing country rise to a new level, creating a future that is organically interwoven with the architectural traditions of Kazakhstan. This project of the Wedding Palace for Shymkent City is my attempt to prove that it is possible to design a building that is modern, but at the same time demonstrates the national chic. People of multinational Kazakhstan celebrate weddings almost every day. That's why the theme of this work is very topical, especially for Southern Kazakhstan where there's no building at all of that type. It is necessary to mention that the project presented has great practical importance for providing high-quality service and the development of social infrastructure. The introduction of progressive technologies, the use of glass and steel frameworks, with a refined plasticity of façades, the interplay of texture and shades of color give the building a graceful and modern look.

Urban oasis / How the past can help in creating the future

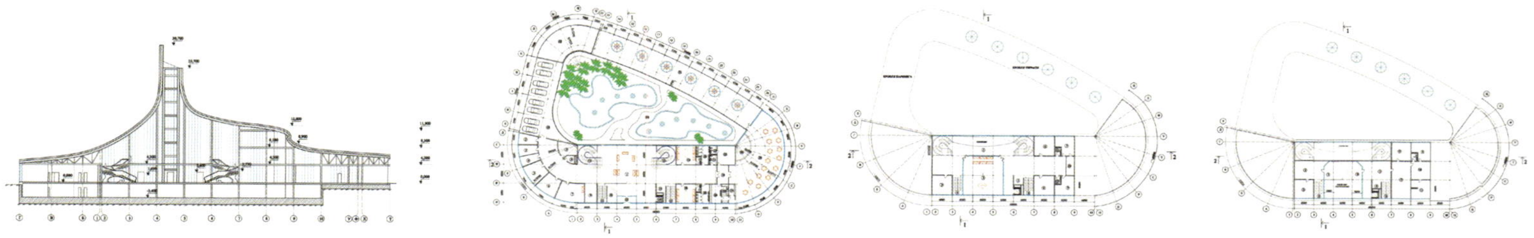

Lina Odeh Saman, Naser Al Hiasat, Rakan Ayyoub ASIA - JORDAN - AMMAN

Shatana Visionary Intervention

MORE TO A PLACE THAN ITS PHYSICAL DIMENSIONS

DISCIPLINE(S): ARCHITECTURE, URBAN DESIGN / TUTOR: PROF. SALEEM S. AL FAQIH / **UNIVERSITY OF JORDAN, ENGINEERING AND TECHNOLOGY** / DEPARTMENT OF ARCHITECTURE

Life in Shatana

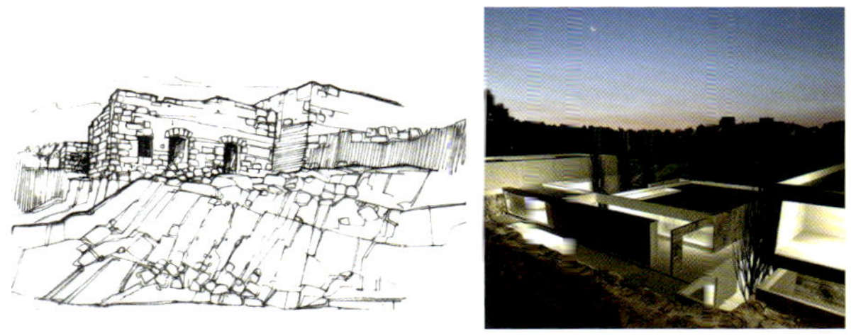

Analysis of old houses and the possibility of reusing them

How can one make a new beginning in the north of Jordan? Shatana, one of Irbid's most beautiful villages, is located in south Irbid, 70km from Amman. The village was named Shatana in the 16th century, and means "distant land". Nevertheless, the area is much older, as you would find Roman wells, Roman artifacts and formerly inhabited caves around the village. Astonishingly, an area as rich as Shatana in terms of culture, tradition and environment is being neglected. Its population has shrunk drastically in recent years, due to emigration to the city, and due to the lack of opportunities and facilities. Shatana Visionary Intervention articulates its history, as architecture confronts tradition and can reformulate memory in a way that points to the future: the goal is to present tradition's aesthetic quality in an entirely new and previously unforeseen way, disclosing the philosophy of time and place and world existence. The building is not an object to be viewed, it is formed merely by its relationship to everything that surrounds it, in a very physical and environmentally significant way. Old houses have been reused and regenerated in a modern way – into small B&B or exhibition components along the path leading to the main building, hence evoking feelings that when the old meets the past, a new perception will be generated and a new bond sensually formed. We aimed at allowing Shatana's visitors to pass through the entire village, which would bring great social and economical benefit to the village inhabitants, thus this was also imposed upon the main building architecture. Through the introduction of new spatial qualities one would be guided by light houses, silent walls and corridors. Everything is silent, spaces are empty on our site. Dispersed old houses are abandoned, retaining only some essential elements: ceilings, floors, slits of light, groves between old hewn stones. While moving through the village, an uneasy feeling is evoked: lives have taken place in those houses. So, in our intervention, a reflection of that spirit is realized in our building, as light changes the character of a place through a minimalistic approach to architecture, layered to be part of nature. This visionary intervention may increase land values, attract a global attention and investment in the village, thus decreasing the emigration to the city, and perhaps resulting in immigration where Shatanans would return to their homeland.

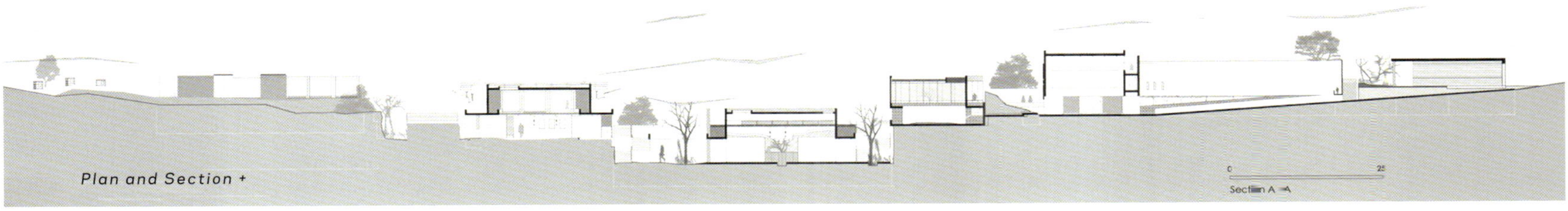

Plan and Section +

A building sunken in the earth, formed by the environment

Light through the building, reflecting its pattern in the village

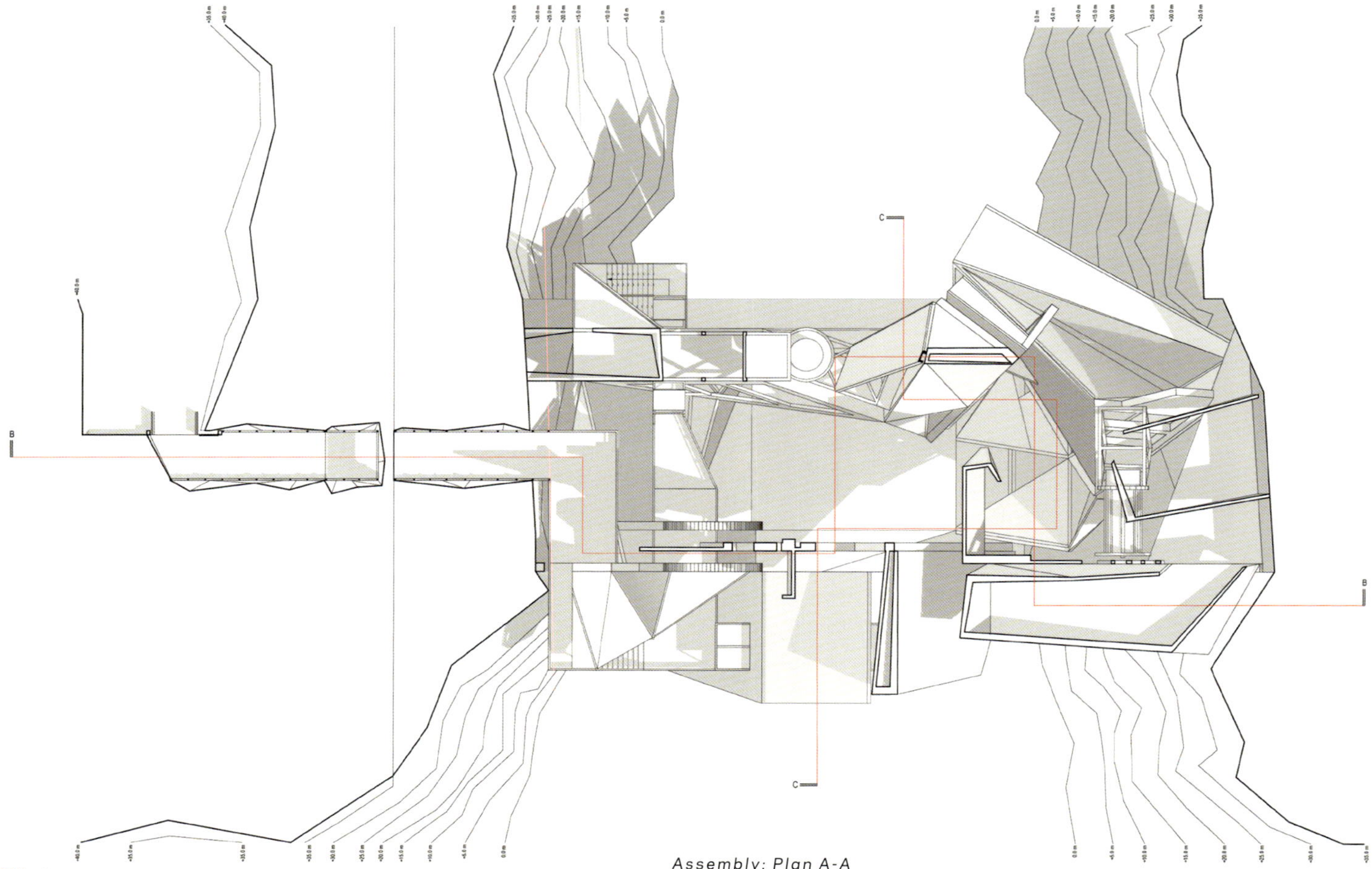

Assembly: Plan A-A

ASSEMBLY
PLAN A-A

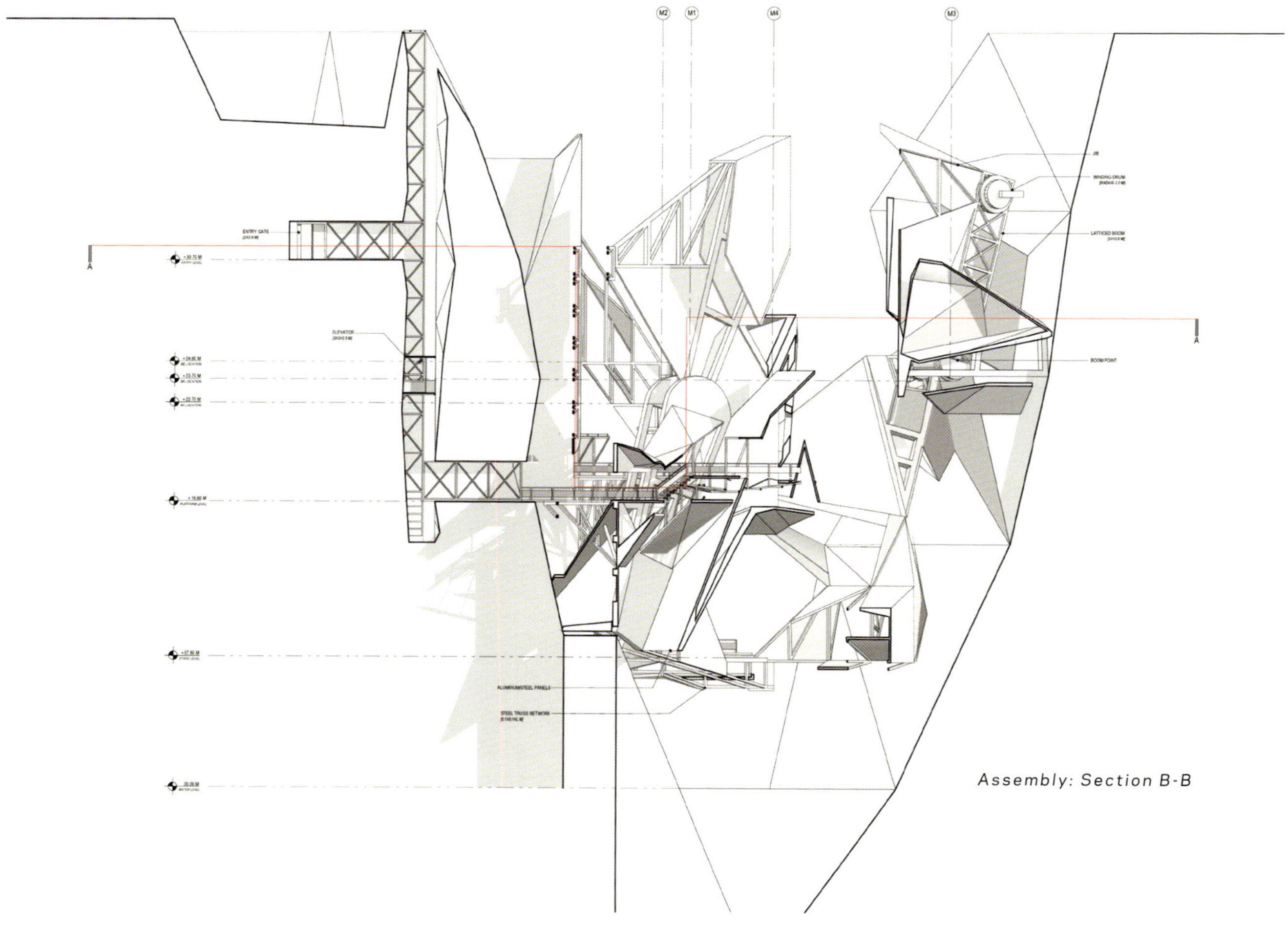

Assembly: Section B-B

ASSEMBLY
SECTION B-B

Aezad Alam ASIA - UNITED ARAB EMIRATES - SHARJAH

Su-Per-**form**®

A PROJECT ON THE COASTAL MOUNTAINS OF OMAN

DISCIPLINE(S): ARCHITECTURE / TUTOR: KYLE C. YANG / **TAMKANG UNIVERSITIES** COLLEGE OF ENGINEERING / **PARTICIPANTS FAVORITE: 15 VOTES**

The aim of this project was to explore the flexibility and transformation of space in relation to habitation and environmental changes at a remote site. Set in the mountains of the coastal region of Dibba, Oman, the project interacts specifically with the area's solar cycle and correspondingly transforms the structure to different configurations and ensuing different spaces. The rough terrain of Dibba offers an isolated and undisturbed landscape, where the potential of an adaptive theater can be expressed. The proposal evolved from analyzing and mapping the relationship between dependent and independent variables, through an event and performance device. Any change in the parameters of the independent variable inadvertently affects the nature of the dependent variable. The result of the interplay between the two variables generates distinct light and shadow compositions. The program of an open-air theater then germinates from the systematization of these variables, where the architectural form begins to imitate the dependent variable and the local environment condition: namely the sun's angle assuming the role of independent variable. The complexity of the ever-evolving form compliments the extreme vertical site of Dibba, as the theater projects from one cliff to another, creating a vertical shaft of molded sun light. Instigated by the solar cycle and the transfiguring structures, this drama of light and shadow is delineated by the progressive luminous patterns on the suspended stage. The design was derived from a rigorous fabrication process, and digital modeling was incorporated to accurately modulate the movement of multi-faceted planar structures in response to the moving light source. The consequence reveals two performances - the stage production and the spectacle of an active architectural form.

View from the sea

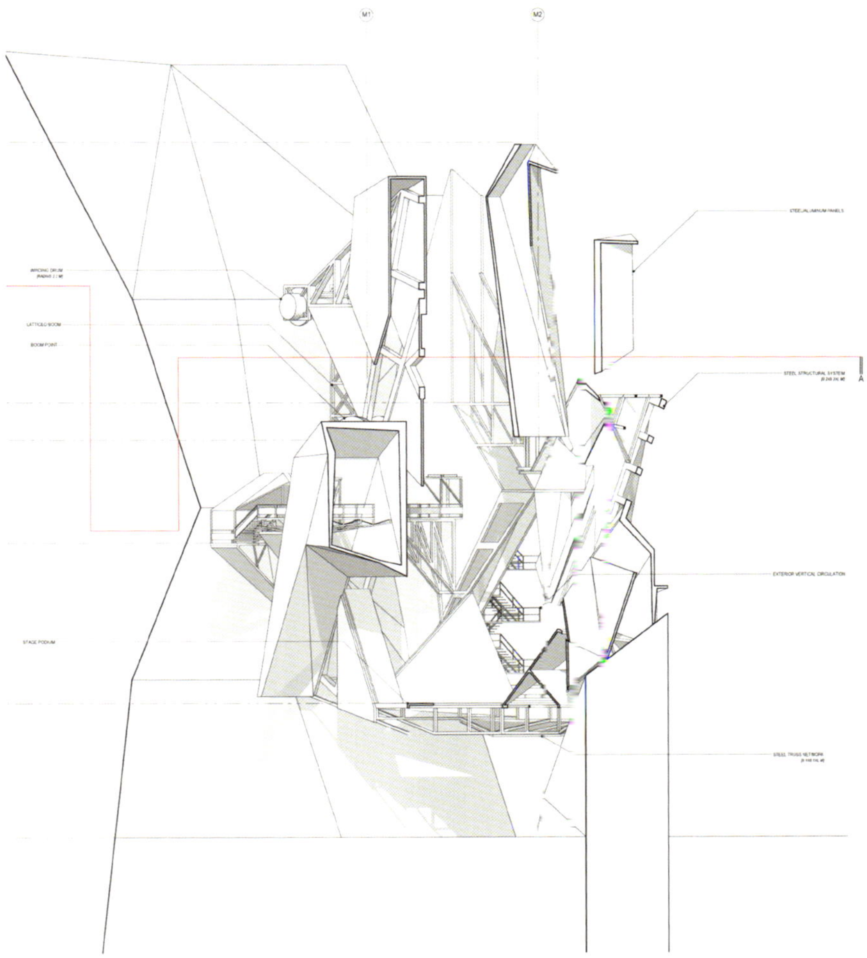

Assembly: Section C-C

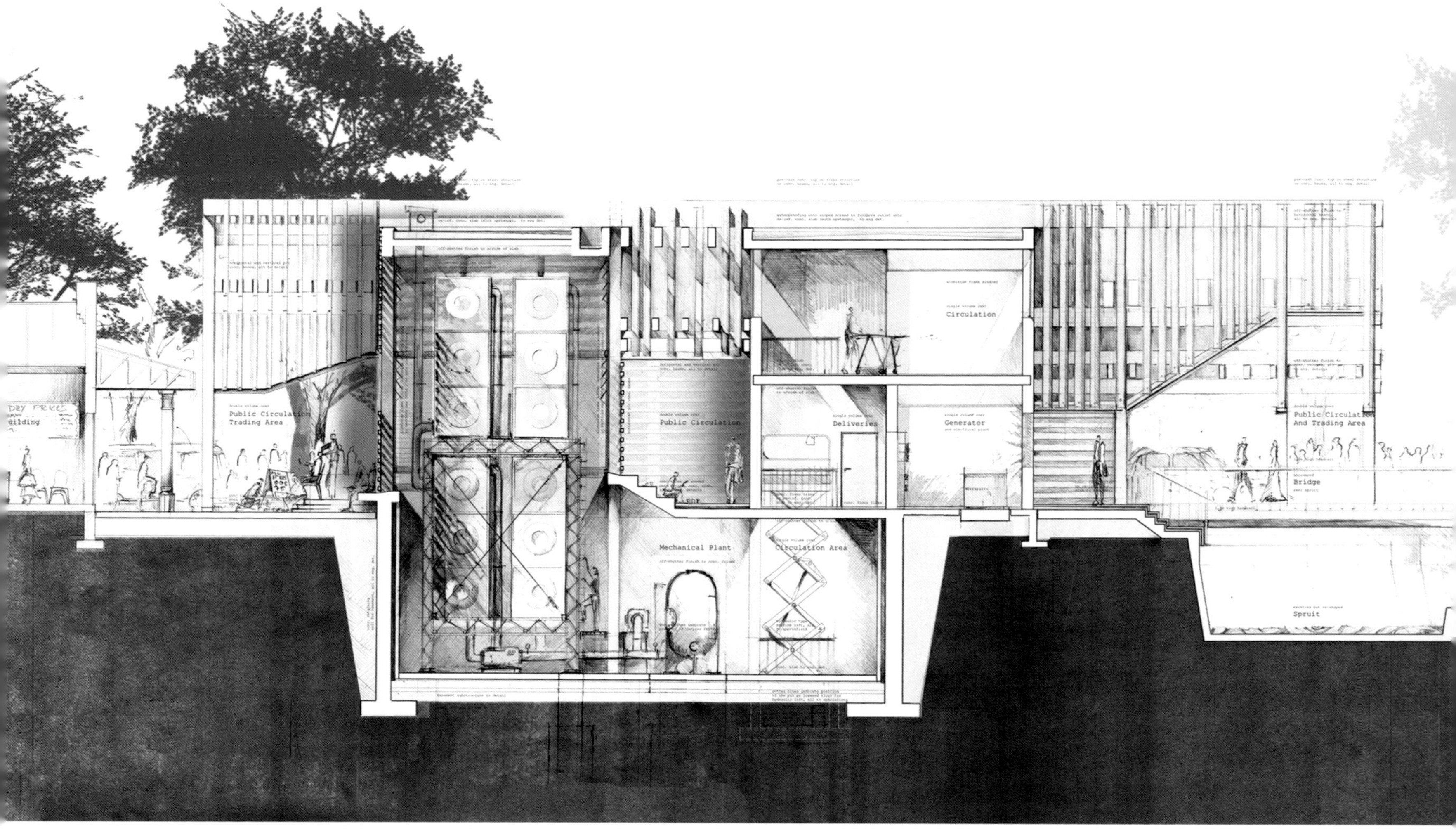

WINNER + PARTICIPANTS FAVORITE: 12 VOTES UNIVERSITY OF PRETORIA / **AFRICA, SOUTH AFRICA, PRETOR**

PUBLIC BATHHOUSE DESIGNED BY RUANN VAN DER WESTHUIZEN

WORLD'S BEST GRADUATION PROJECTS - ARCHITECTURE - URBAN DESIGN - LANDSCAPE ARCHITECTURE
2011
CAMBRIDGE USA
Archiprix
INTERNATIONAL www.archiprix.org
A PUBLIC BATHHOUSE
Ruann van der Westhuizen
UNIVERSITY OF PRETORIA
SOUTH AFRICA

LANDSCAPE ARCHITECTURE - URBAN DESIGN - ARCHITECTURE - WORLD'S BEST GRADUATION PROJECTS
HunterDouglas AWARD
WINNER
AWARDED JUNE 9TH 2011
GUGGENHEIM - NEW YORK

Interior perspective

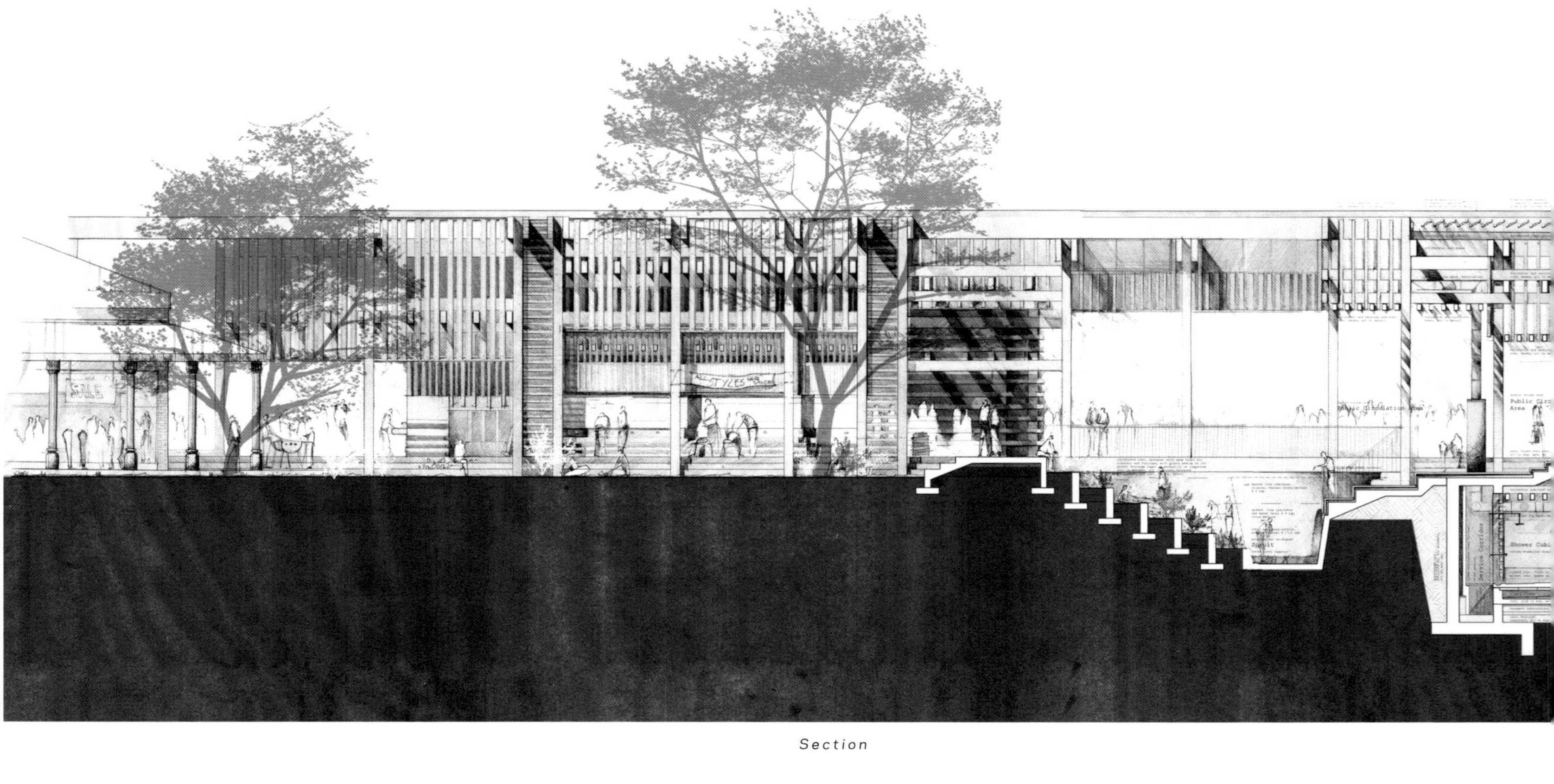

Section

Ruann van der Westhuizen **AFRICA - SOUTH AFRICA - PRETORIA**

A Public **Bathhouse**

INVESTIGATING RELEVANCE AND OPPORTUNITIES

DISCIPLINE: ARCHITECTURE / TUTORS: JACQUES LAUBSCHER, MARIANNE DE KLERK / **UNIVERSITY OF PRETORIA**, FACULTY OF ENGINEERING, BUILT ENVIRONMENT AND INFORMATION TECHNOLOGY / **PARTICIPANTS FAVORITE: 12 VOTES + WINNER**

This project consists of a public bathhouse in a South African urban context, realized as a building that introduces simple bathroom facilities into the ritual of commuting. It provides privacy without risking isolation, through the layering of the surface and the application of a permeable and appropriately robust shelter that welcomes public use. It makes an essential service available to those who do not have access to the most basic services, integrating a bathhouse into an existing public transport interchange and thereby providing a basic service to commuters from informal and rural settings that are known to have poor services. The manipulation and servicization of the urban surface capitalizes on the existing informal appropriation of public spaces. The surfaces act as a catalyst for unexpected and diverse forms of informal trade and activities crucial to providing a public presence and connection. The introduction of a sheltering mass, a singular matrix of precast concrete, is intended to act as a structure and shelter. The shelter is (1) placed (2) manipulated (3) integrated and appropriated informally, and (4) allows pedestrian movement and use to overlap. The goal is a building that seems to be at peace with itself in a similar way that certain objects, machines, tools or instruments are. Through a celebration of inherent properties, these objects are not mere vehicles for an artistic message, or channels for the implementation of technology: their presence is self-evident.

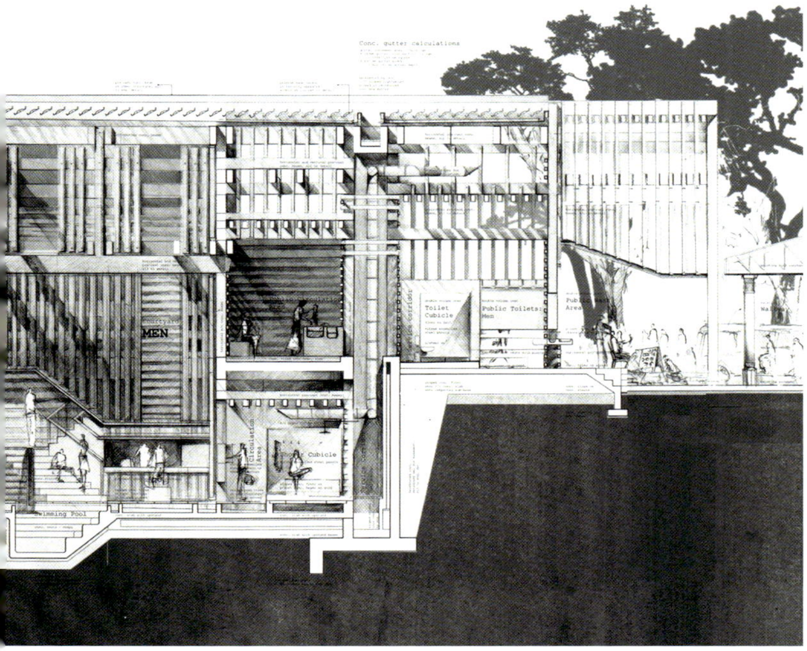

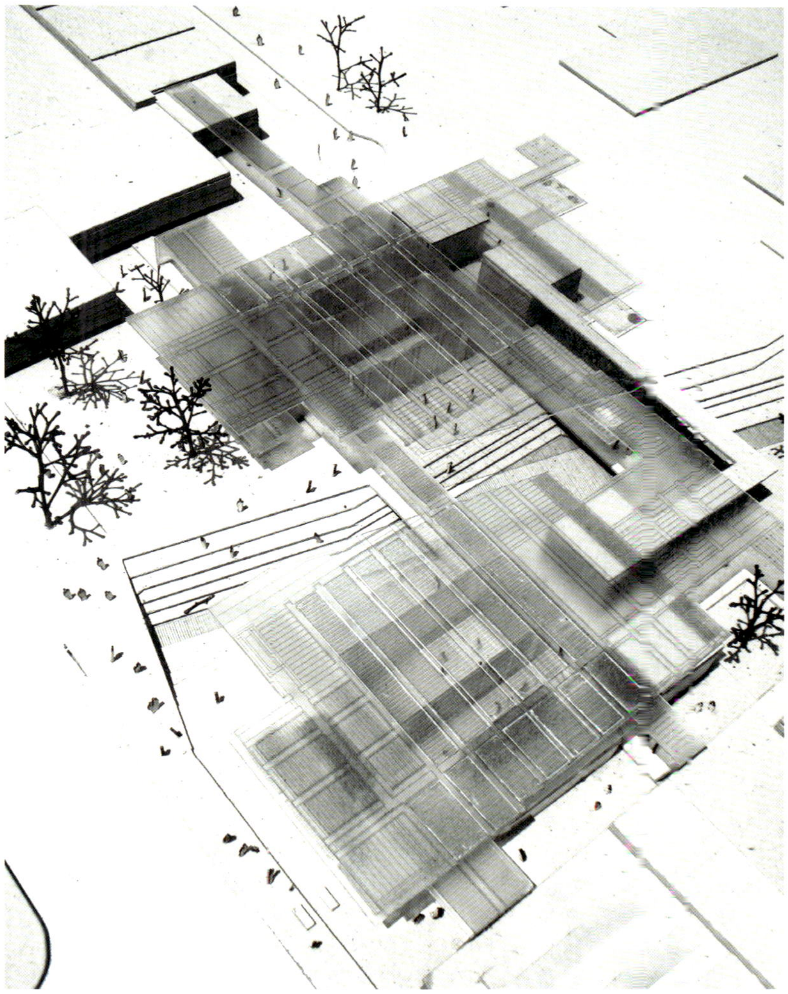

MOORDKOPPIE - OKAHANDJA

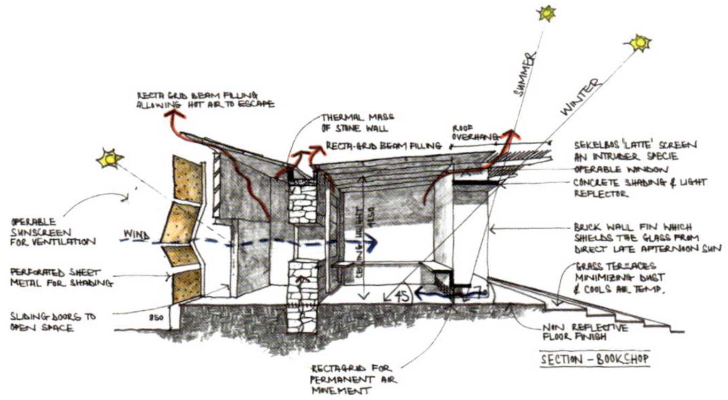
RECTA GRID BEAM FILLING ALLOWING HOT AIR TO ESCAPE
THERMAL MASS OF STONE WALL
ROOF OVERHANG
RECTA-GRID BEAM FILLING
SUMMER
WINTER
SEKELBOS 'LATTE' SCREEN AN INTRUDER SPECIE
OPERABLE WINDOW
CONCRETE SHADING & LIGHT REFLECTOR
OPERABLE SUNSCREEN FOR VENTILATION
WIND
BRICK WALL FIN WHICH SHIELDS THE GLASS FROM DIRECT LATE AFTERNOON SUN
PERFORATED SHEET METAL FOR SHADING
GRASS TERRACES MINIMIZING DUST & COOLS AIR TEMP.
SLIDING DOORS TO OPEN SPACE
850
45
NON REFLECTIVE FLOOR FINISH
SECTION - BOOKSHOP
RECTAGRID FOR PERMANENT AIR MOVEMENT

Willem Steenkamp **AFRICA - SOUTH AFRICA - BLOEMFONTEIN**

Herero Cultural Centre and Genocide Memorial

THE HERERO GATHER ANNUALLY AT GRAVE SITES IN NAMIBIA AND BOTSWANA

DISCIPLINE: ARCHITECTURE / TUTORS: PETRIA JOOSTE SMIT, JAN SMIT, JAN RAS / **THE UNIVERSITY OF THE FREE STATE** DEPARTMENT OF ARCHITECTURE / **NOMINATED**

The funeral of Samuel Maharero brought together the Namibian Herero and other Herero living in exile following the 1904 war and genocide. Their society was once again reunited, with the scattered historical groups coming together again to form a single Herero identity. The Herero have retained a strong cultural identity/heritage right down to the present day. They gather annually at different grave sites in Namibia and Botswana, using these annual pilgrimages to reaffirm their social unity. There is a need to remember those who died for freedom in the first genocide of the 20th century. In this way, the Herero can remember their forefathers and culture. The thesis focuses on the design of a Herero Genocide Memorial that can become a symbol of remembrance, reconciliation, etc., while simultaneously generating a self-sustaining income by being a functional cultural centre. An abstraction of the Herero culture, along with a memorial, is used to make a building that represents their culture, and responds to the specific site, parade of heroes and climate. By means of architecture, a building charged with symbolism, culture and history is created.

Carles Sala Roig **EUROPE - SPAIN - BARCELONA - CATALONIA**

The Plug Inn Dorm in IIT

RESIDENTIAL AREA IN THE IIT CAMPUS | CHICAGO | USA

DISCIPLINE(S): ARCHITECTURE, URBAN DESIGN, LANDSCAPE DESIGN / TUTOR: ALFONS SOLDEVILA BARBOSA / **UNIVERSITAT POLITÈCNICA DE CATALUNYA**, ESCOLA TÈCNICA SUPERIOR D'ARQUITECTURA DE BARCELONA

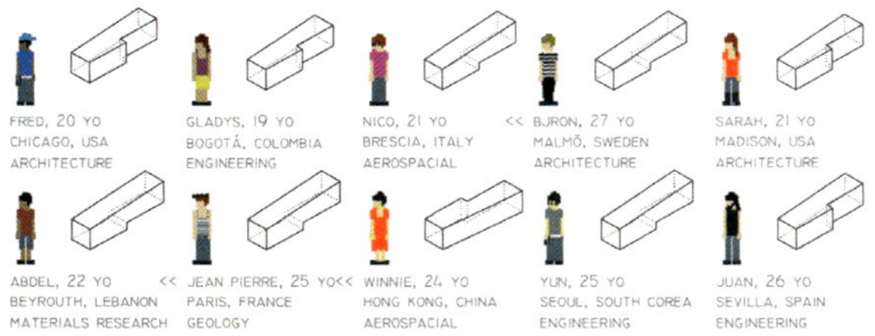

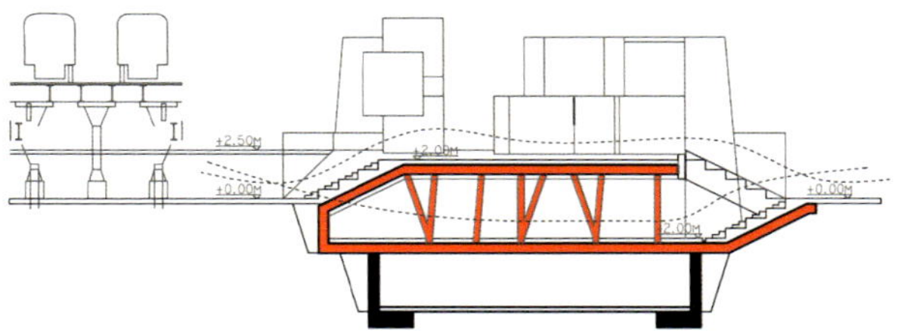

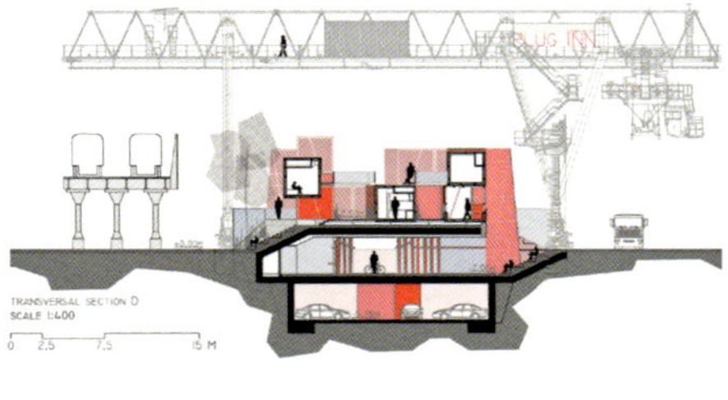

ON TIME! The Plug Inn responds to the time parameter / THE PLATE! The plate works as an infrastructural supplier

The Illinois Institute of Technology (IIT) campus, in Chicago, should stop considering the train line as a boundary between the dorm area and the faculties, and to link up connecting and supporting elements. The PLUG INN offers permeability through a double-plate system that gets a separate half-level up and down from the access point. The enveloped space (sandwich space) contains the permanent program to serve the campus and the building, thus becoming both a transition area and a meeting point. Conversely, the upper plate becomes a naked mutable landscape based on the work system, in contact with the train station. ON TIME is the work system on which this project has been based, as its relation to the train provides an obvious temporality. Moreover, it will be defined according to the tempos of the campus (a day, a week, a semester, a course, a degree). This residential habitat is developed through a system of capsules that are plugged into the upper plate, to the inputs and outputs of the structure and infrastructure (the PLUG INN). The caps are delivered as a standard GRP (Glassfibre Reinforced Plastic) structure by train or trailer, and are properly placed thanks to a mobile crane. The cap can rotate over itself to adapt its use into common spaces (kitchen, dining room, lounge, social shed, stairs, lift, etc.) located on layer N1, as well as private ones on layers N1 and N2 (dorm). These caps are customized according to the user's preferences, and must consider the ranked parameters (location, rotation, use, access) in relation to the whole, so as to settle in colonies of twelve dorms that share common caps and outdoor spaces (in-between), such as the wifi laundry or the vending area.

THE COLONY! Every 10 or 12 dorm caps share in-between spaces and common caps

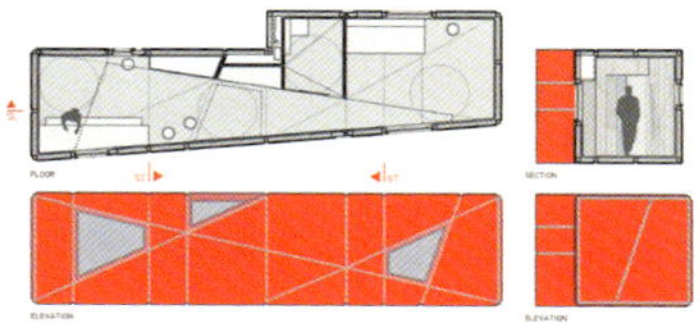

THE CAP! The capsules adopt different uses according to the acquired rotation

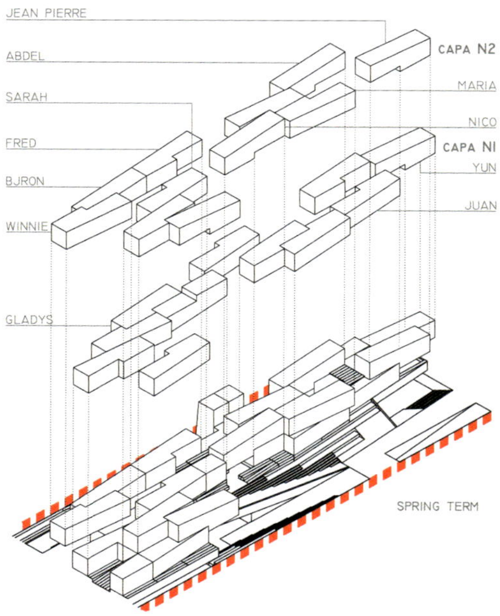

THE PLUG INN! The mutant system serves the changing colonies

Paula Ibarrondo EUROPE - SPAIN - MADRID

E-**school**

CAMPUS FOR DIGITAL TEACHING DEVELOPMENT

DISCIPLINE(S): ARCHITECTURE / TUTORS: JAVIER SAÉNZ GUERRA, MARIANO MOVINA INIESTA, BENITO JIMENEZ ALCALÁ, FERNANDO DE LAMA
ESCUELA POLITÉCNICA SUPERIOR UNIVERSITY CEU SAN PABLO, BELÉN HERMIDA, BILINGUAL PROGRAM COORDINATOR

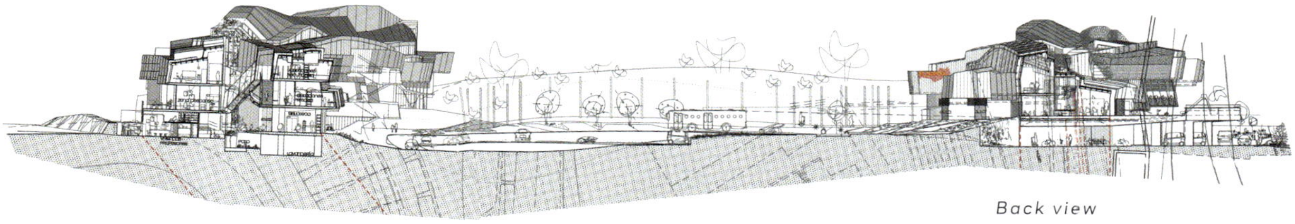

Back view

Education has not changed in centuries, either methodologically or architecturally. In the era of technology, the learning environment should be adapted to take full advantage of new discoveries. The target of this project is to create a pioneering center based on the use of the latest technology. The school would be the first target, but maybe later there would be a dwelling house, a university and perhaps something to draw the attention of companies, etc. The campus opens in a fan-shape to the antique village and to the castle. The project is a spiral path that traverses the buildings; this path is accompanied by vertical connections and transversal passages that shorten the distances. The materialization of this pedestrian path is supported by a wide and complex geometry, which should avoid monotony. A project with such characteristics should not be resolved with conventional construction systems. Solutions have been considered in order to maintain the structural integrity. The building covering is the most important part of the project and the geometry depends on the program developed under it. Its design has considered the hours of sunshine, orientation, wind, rain etc. It is divided into bands with different functions like skylights, second-skins, vacuum tubes, gutters, etc. The structural diagram is simple: there are two parts, one made of concrete that is related to the ground, rocky, formed by concrete structural walls and slabs. The other one is lightweight, independent and supports the covering, giving it an appearance of floating in mid-air; like two shellfish placed on the terrain. This steel structure is formed by huge concrete pillars that are dematerialized into steel tubes, which hold three dimensional steel beams of great solidity, from which the steel beams extend. These steel beams hold the covering of the building.

Plan (level +8,50m)

The learning environment should take full advantage of newer technologies

Back view

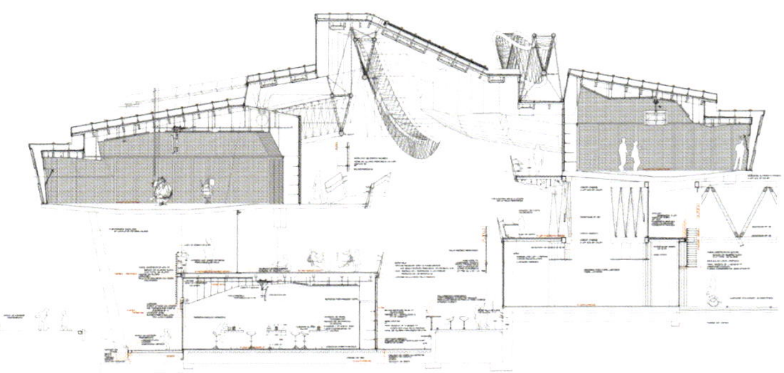

Native cross section

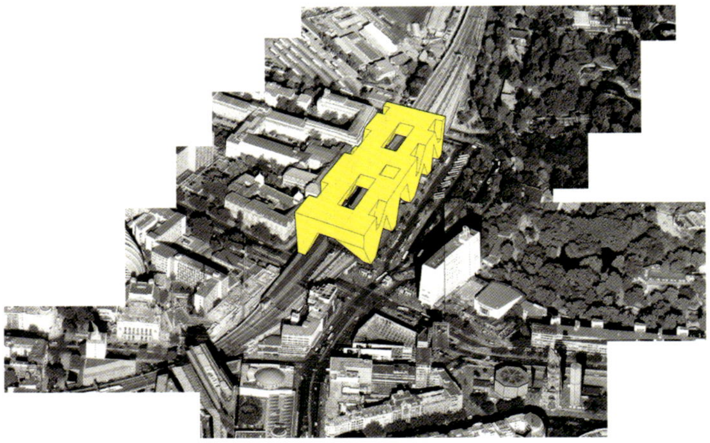

Location

Axonometric detail of model

View from the zoo

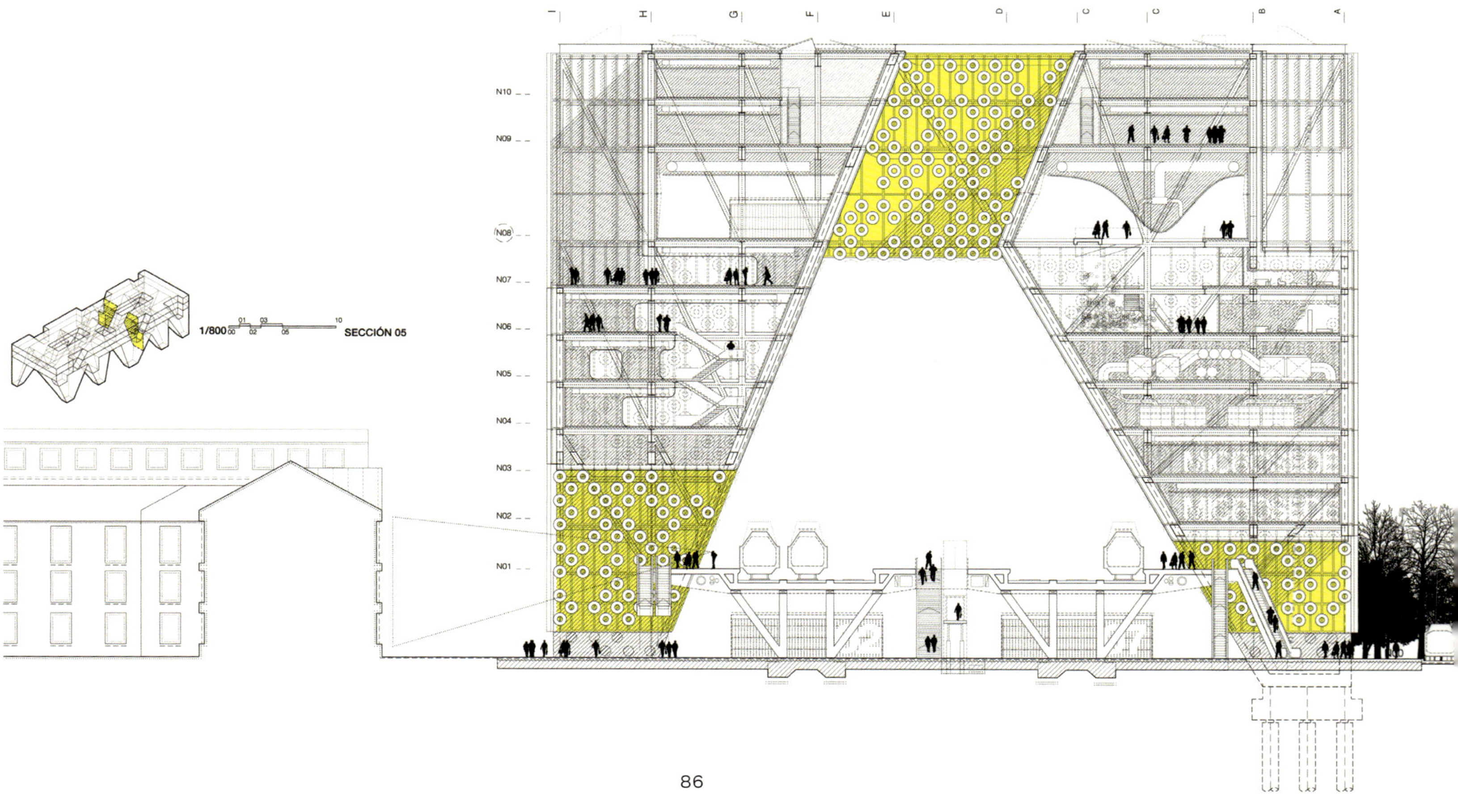

Gonzalo del Val EUROPE - SPAIN - MADRID

Berlin NEU-Bahnhof Zoologischer Garten

CREATIVE INFRASTRUCTURE

DISCIPLINE(S): ARCHITECTURE / TUTORS: VICTORIA ACEBO, ANGEL ALONSO / **UNIVERSIDAD EUROPEA DE MADRID**
ESCUELA DE ARQUITECTURA / **PARTICIPANTS FAVORITE: 14 VOTES + NOMINATED**

The economic need of big cities to remain at the forefront of the main international markets entails a constant reinvention task. Is it possible to generate a space capable of creating and exchanging innovation between companies and citizens? This project replaces the current railway station of Berlin Zoo with a great creative infrastructure. It is a private program capable of promoting knowledge culture though an open network and collaboration between private and public programs. The private program is composed by Google's head office in Europe and the technological innovation headquarters.
The public program is understood as a creative process divided into three "stages": information/education, creation and participation. All the programs are organized under a great interchange platform, a public hybrid space. This creative conglomerate envelops the new train station which is used to link the different urban scales. The structural model is composed of several transverse arcades. Three-legged trestles are organized in an alternative way. The structural system is a divided into modules for manufacture in workshops, reducing the cost of transport and assembly. Accordingly, the railway enables the transport of all material from the factories, avoiding inconvenience to the neighbors and reducing costs at the same time. To optimize the energy use, the facilities and the netserver room collaborate to use energy in the most efficient way. The heat emitted by the server room is recovered to climatize the rest of the complex, saving up to 50% of the energy that would otherwise be lost. The architectural skin should react to the environment.
Mixing working spaces with a train station produces two different languages in the façade. One displays an office character, which is depends on the various internal programs, and the other one is geared to the technical requirements of a station, such as the acoustic and lighting control. It aims to make architecture work as an engine of social intelligence.

Cross-section

Rodrigo García González EUROPE - SPAIN - MADRID

Zipi**zip**

DEPLOYABLE SYSTEM

DISCIPLINE(S): ARCHITECTURE / TUTORS: IGNACIO BORREGO, GÓMEZ-PALLETE / **UNIVERSIDAD POLITÉCNICA DE MADRID**
ESCUELA TÉCNICA SUPERIOR DE ARQUITECTURA / **PARTICIPANTS FAVORITE: 19 VOTES**

ZIPIZIP is a patent pending system (P200901789) to make high-rise buildings deployable. It is based on a transportable "scissors" structure that, when open, is supplemented by different elements to make it livable. The advantages of this construction is the speed with which it can be assembled and dismantled, so you can use the same building for different contexts. It is perfect for use during major events such as the Expo or the Olympics because it enables an increase in the density of a city or the temporary colonization of new land. It also enables the rent or exchange of infrastructures, mobilizing the actual static real estate market. ZIPIZIP is the result of research on deployable structures, and how they can be distributed not only horizontally but also vertically. After working with prototypes, the ZIPIZIP system has been applied to a real context: a building with offices, facilities and housing for a construction company that is drilling tunnels for the high-speed train in Spain. The building can be moved forward at the same time as the construction. The result is a tower consisting of 734 aluminum bars and 1167 junctions. There are only 6 different types of junctions and bars so it is easy to industrialize the product. The whole structure can be transported by a single truck and the total weight of the building is 147,325 kg. When erected it becomes an eleven-storey tower with a surface area of 210 m² per floor. When folded up, it is a package of only 5.46 x 8.12 x 4.82 m. This means a reduction of 78% in surface area and 97% in volume.

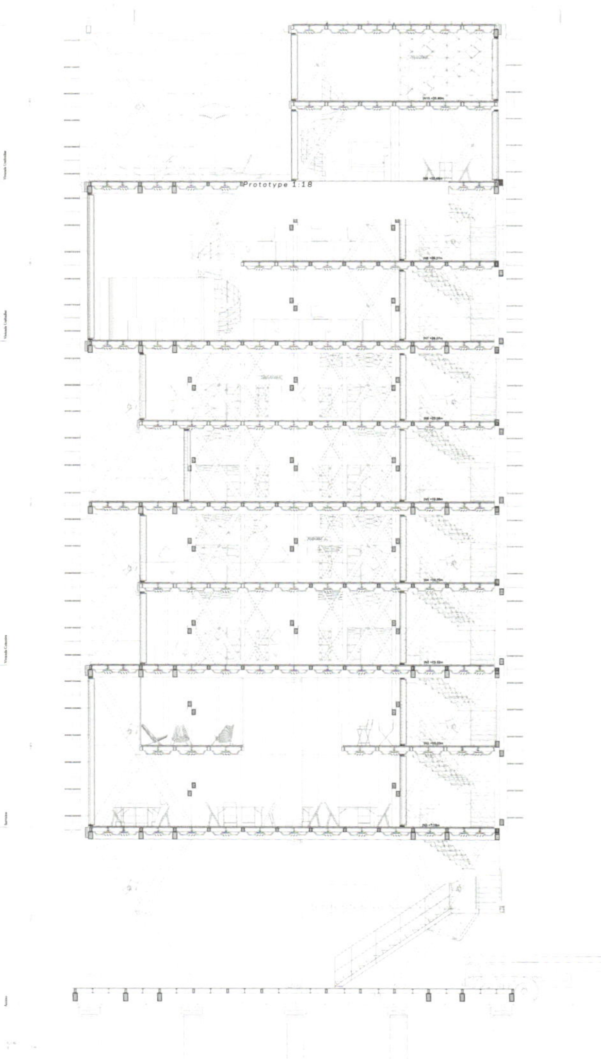

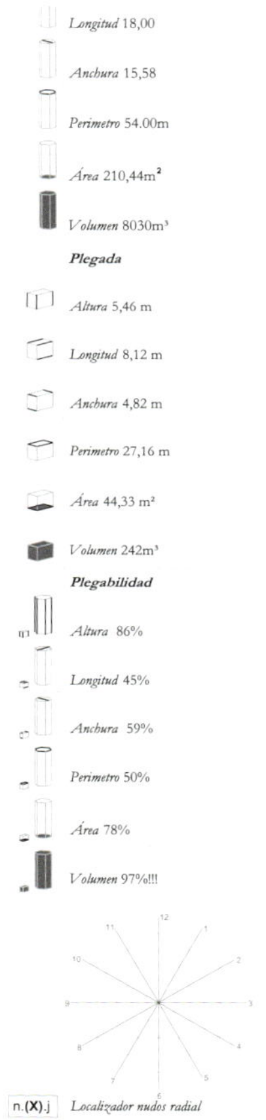

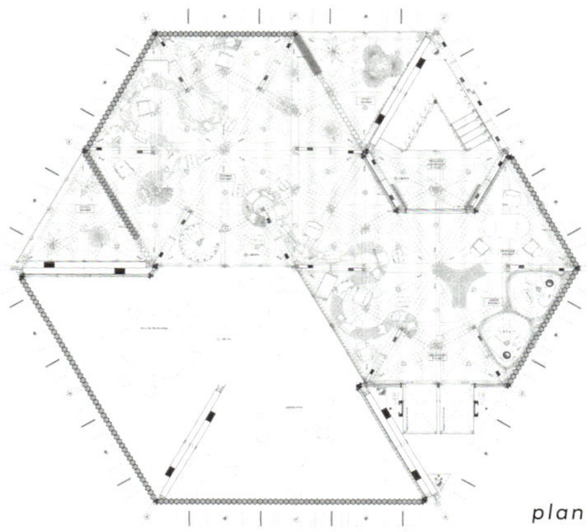

plan

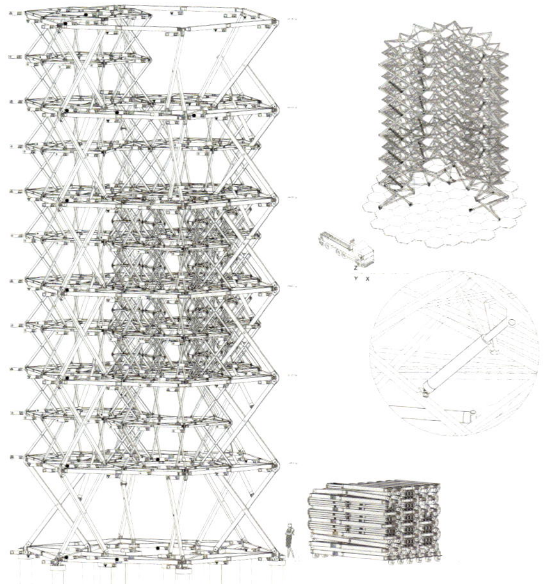

Anna Vasof EUROPE - GREECE - VOLOS

Under **construction**

A HABITATION BUILDING IN GREECE IN A STREAM NAMED KRAFSIDONAS, IN VOLOS

DISCIPLINE(S): ARCHITECTURE / TUTOR: KOSTIS PANIGIRIS / **UNIVERISTY OF THESSALY**, DEPARTMENT OF ARCHITECTURE, FACULTY OF ENGINEERING

The contemporary, mostly illegal, cheap home-building construction practices in Greece are elaborated into proper habitation models and forms to be adopted and generalized. The word "Yapi", describing an unfinished and often abandoned construction, refers to a void filled with a variety of uses and definitions in the modern Greek city. The impetus for the project arose from a fictive collapse of an existing Yapi into the "Krafsidonas" stream, traversing the city of Volos. The horizontal skeleton generated, which bridges the opposite banks of the stream, is composed of the main and the secondary structure. The main structure consists of (a) the 12 bridges, (b) the shores, as defined through peripheral ditches, (c) the terrain design (domestic cisterns, outdoor staircases) and (d) the six amphitheaters, filtering and retaining the water of the stream. The secondary structure consists of three habitation typologies located across the bridge borders. As we get closer to the center of the structure, the above-mentioned typologies advance into a state of constructional non-finito. Basic elements such as walls or floors are omitted so that the generic construction of the skeleton appears. Public space (riverbed, the theaters and the bridges) grows parallel to the non-public areas of the project. This gradual deconstruction implies the emergence of the meaning of space through the inhabitant's interference in the completion process, as opposed to a strategy of total design, leading to controlled and homogeneous completion of the construction. The whole estate is run by a public organization, regulating property prices according to the degree of completion each property would have. Access to the living areas is provided by the bridges which also function as internal corridors. The compartments of each property, with their different functions, are distributed across different floors. Therefore it is unavoidable that public area is crossed by residents moving from one space to the other. By reducing privacy, the project aims at reducing the primacy of private property in the organization of social life. The project develops a new design rationale: no gap can arise between the time of design, the period of construction and the moment of inhabitation. A continuous space transformation is proposed. The project acts not only as a filter of the riverflow, but simultaneously of the flow of all natural or urban events that are evoked. People are asked to redefine (space-) community relationships, either through cooperation or conflict.

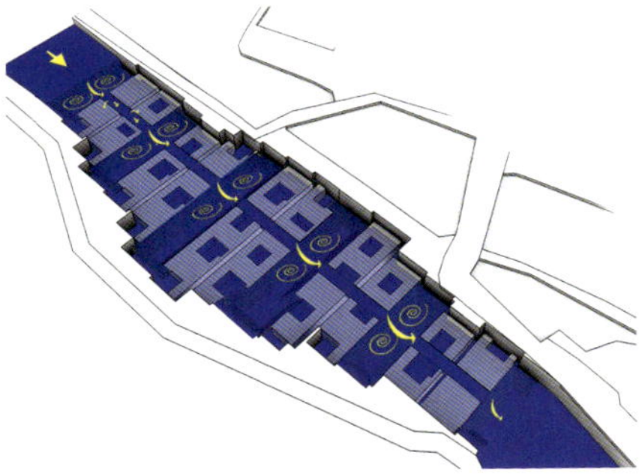

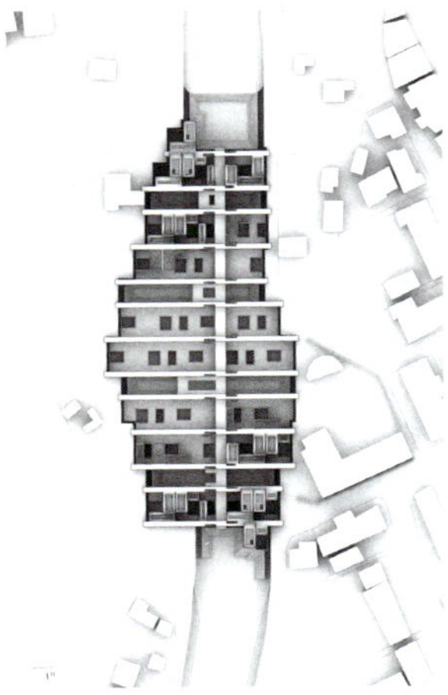

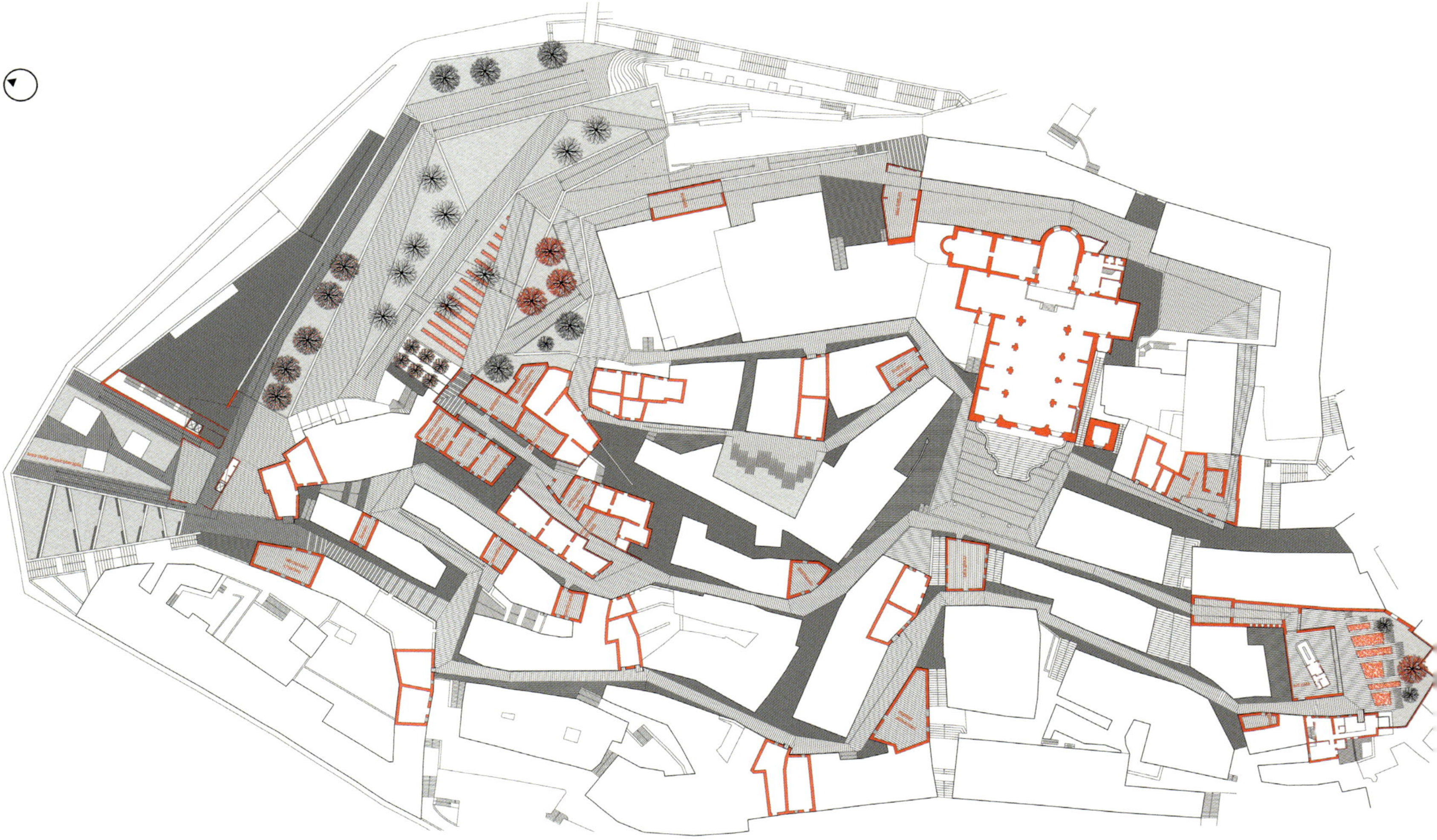

Plan of the project. The urban dimension as a new model of social integration

The site selection. The historic center of Ozieri, Italy

Giuliana Frau **EUROPE - ITALY - ALGHERO**

Fra-m-**menti**

URBAN DIMENSION AS A NEW MODEL OF SOCIAL INTEGRATION, CARE AND SUPPORT FOR ALZHEIMER'S DISEASE

DISCIPLINE(S): ARCHITECTURE, URBAN DESIGN / TUTORS: FABIO BACCHINI, ERIKA BONACUCINA, FRANCESCO SPANEDDA
UNIVERSITY OF SASSARI, FACULTY OF ARCHITECTURE / **NOMINATED**

Alzheimer's disease

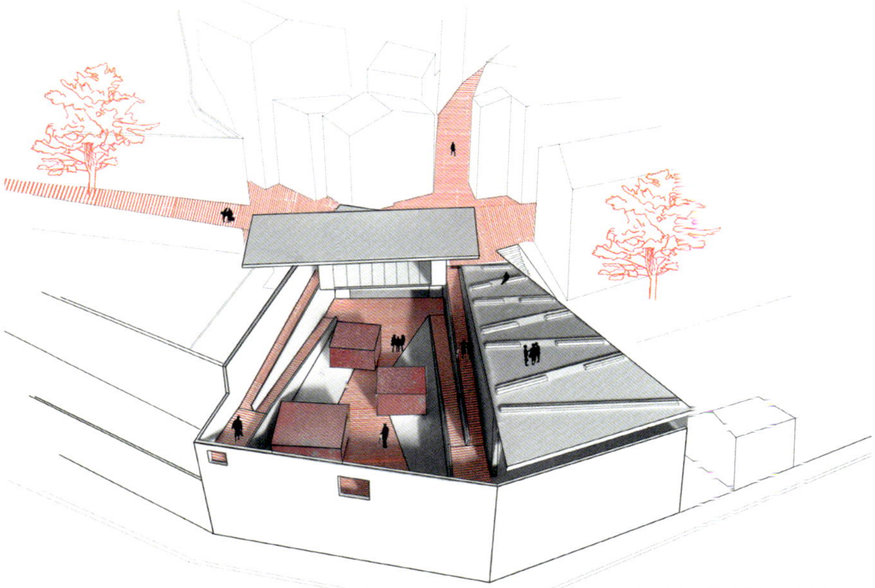

Music therapy area

This work begins with some reflections of a social nature concerning the conditions of the mentally disabled who, for genetic or other biological reasons, are no longer self-sufficient. In particular, it studies Alzheimer's disease, with the aim of creating a new model of social integration, support and care for the ill. The challenge is to go beyond the asylum model, which still exists even after the Basaglia Act of 1980, albeit on a smaller scale.

The project is located in the historic center of Ozieri (12,000 inhabitants, SS, Italy), a place rich in intermediate and interstitial spaces that shape and reflect its identity. The project is characterized by attention to the preservation and enhancement of these spaces, with the aim of creating an ideal habitat for social interaction. The key project is the identification of three pedestrian rings that help the patient to return to the starting point while he or she is out walking. Each ring displays some reference points that establish memories in the mind. None of the design interventions affects the present urban area (except for the music therapy area), but approaches or goes through it. All the other elements of the project are developed along the rings: the sensory park, music therapy area, art café, house of someone with Alzheimer's and supporting family, the Alzheimer center.

Street view historical centre

Art café and Alzheimers house

WINNER + PARTICIPANTS FAVORITE: 9 VOTES UNIVERSITÀ DI GENOVA **EUROPE, ITALY, GENOVA / YOU ARE HERE** DESIGNED BY

ORENZO TROMPETTO, VERONICA RUSCA, MAURIZIO PIZZOCRO

WORLD'S BEST GRADUATION PROJECTS - ARCHITECTURE - URBAN DESIGN - LANDSCAPE ARCHITECTURE
2011
CAMBRIDGE USA
Archiprix
INTERNATIONAL www.archiprix.org
YOU ARE HERE
Lorenzo Trompetto,
Veronica Rusca,
Maurizio Pizzocro
UNIVERSITÀ DI
GENOVA ITALY

HunterDouglas AWARD
WINNER
AWARDED JUNE 9TH 20
GUGGENHEIM - NEW YORK
WORLD'S BEST GRADUATION PROJECTS - ARCHITECTURE - URBAN DESIGN - LANDSCAPE ARCHITECTURE

Media tower

Stadium

Library

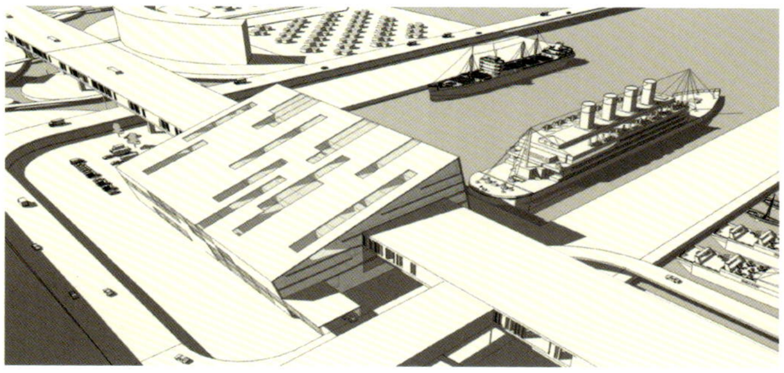

Terminal

Terminal

Cultural center

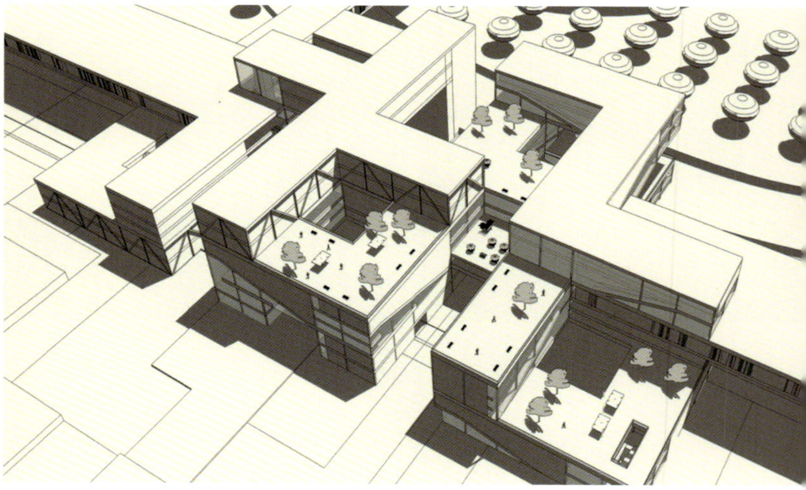

Cultural center

Lorenzo Trompetto, Veronica Rusca, Maurizio Pizzocro EUROPE - ITALY - GENOVA

You are **Here**

CRITICAL ANALYSIS OF CONTEMPORARY CITY

DISCIPLINE(S): ARCHITECTURE, URBAN DESIGN, LANDSCAPE DESIGN / TUTOR: PROF. GIOVANNI GALLI / **UNIVERSITÀ DI GENOVA** FACOLTÀ DI ARCHITETTURA / **PARTICIPANTS FAVORITE: 9 VOTES + WINNER**

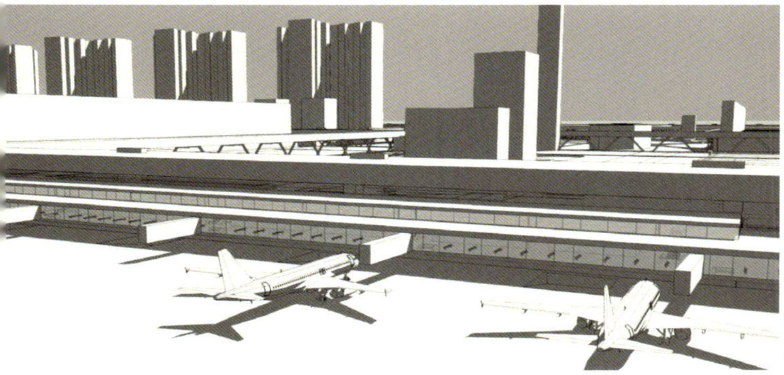

Airport

Mall of America

What does it mean to design a new city now that architecture has replaced this physical setting with a media context? How did consumerism change architecture, and fashion rules assume the role of Utopia? Our answer to these questions is an island, a city but also the largest shopping mall worldwide. This island is a juxtaposition of landscapes where 20th-century utopias are stacked in patterns, lose their ideological values, are consumed. Above, a "flying tube" contains a shopping mall, as well as means of conveyance and all the social spaces. The mall is a C-shaped ring that follows rules of serial repetition. It is an anti-iconic element, nevertheless it's the core of the island, its backbone. Where the mall infrastructure touches the ground, it generates several buildings we called "the feet". Feet are locations where the isotopic space of the mall changes in order to host social events. If "the tube" contains the streets of the city, the "feet" are its squares and its monuments. The assumption of media logic overcomes the category of "public space", turning the opposition of public/private into privacy/publicity. The construction process is not governed by soil ownership but by the visual relationship between the "outside" - where everyone can see me and I'm in the medium - and the "inside" - where I can see everything because I'm watching the medium. We trust in architecture as a medium and this project is the translation into shapes of a short book, where we try to link theories by Koolhaas, Colomina, Kuleshov, Gruen, McLuhan, Tafuri and others. Paradoxically arranging utopian projects by Leonidov, Le Corbusier, Hilberseimer, Buckminster Fuller, Cason, Wright, the Smithsons and Tange side by side and superimposing them upon the largest commercial infrastructure in the world, we find ourselves in a hyperbolic - but not unearthly - landscape that reveals the features of today's city.

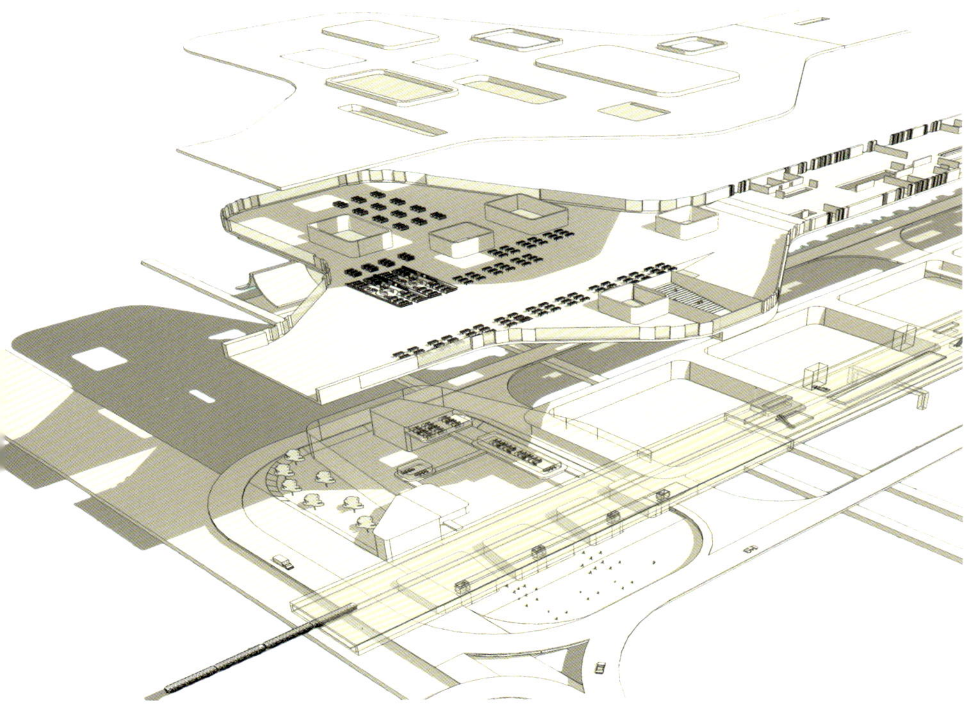

Fair

Museum, or is it an urban promenade?

Ege Özgirin EUROPE - TURKEY - ISTANBUL

Great Time Capsule

DISCIPLINE(S): ARCHITECTURE / TUTORS: PROF. DR. ARZU ERDEM, ASSIST PROF. IPEK YÜREKLI, RESEARCH ASSISTANT OZAN AVCI
ISTANBUL TECHNICAL UNIVERSITY, FACULTY OF ARCHITECTURE

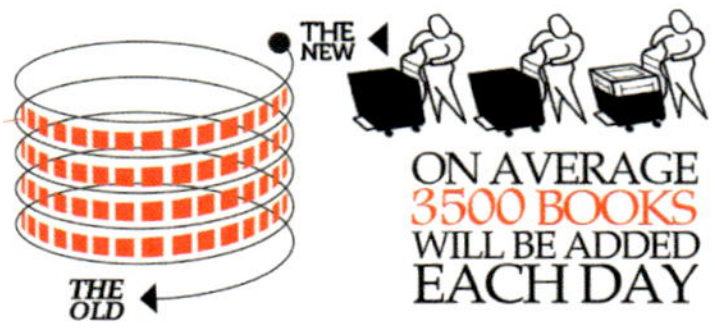

Is it possible to build a structure for collecting and protecting books containing the entire body of human knowledge?

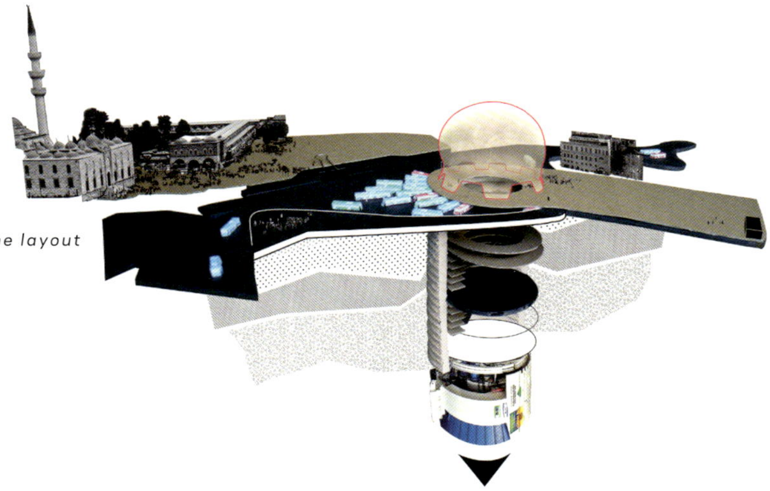

The layout

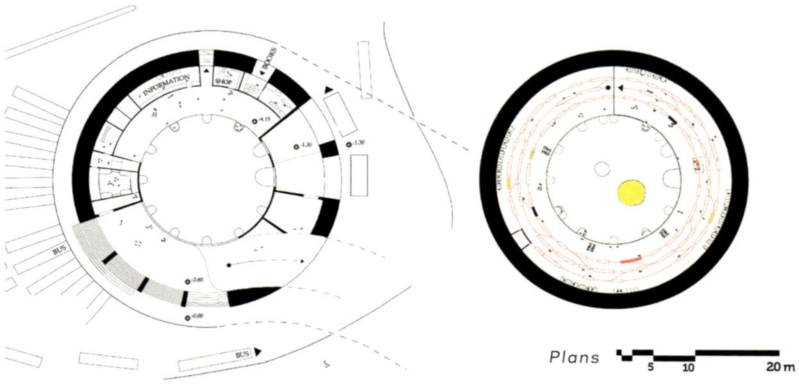

Plans

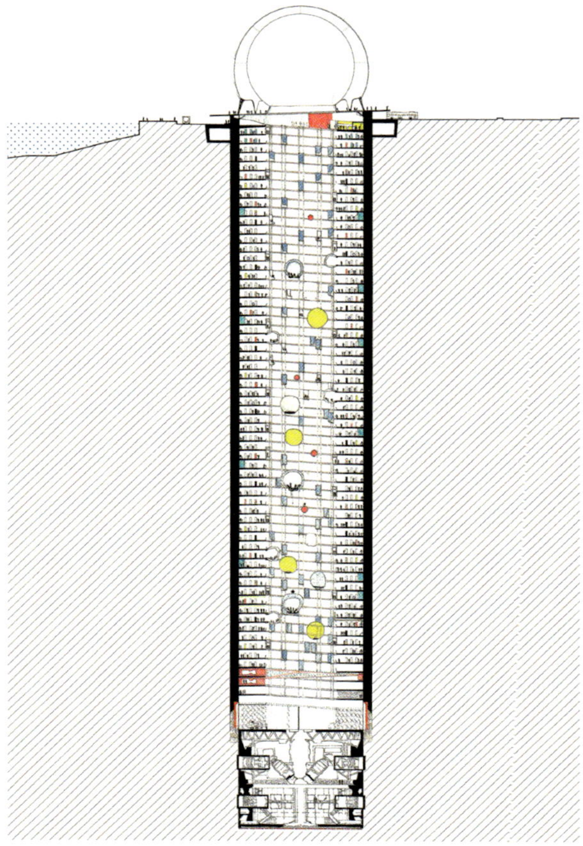

Section, year 2022

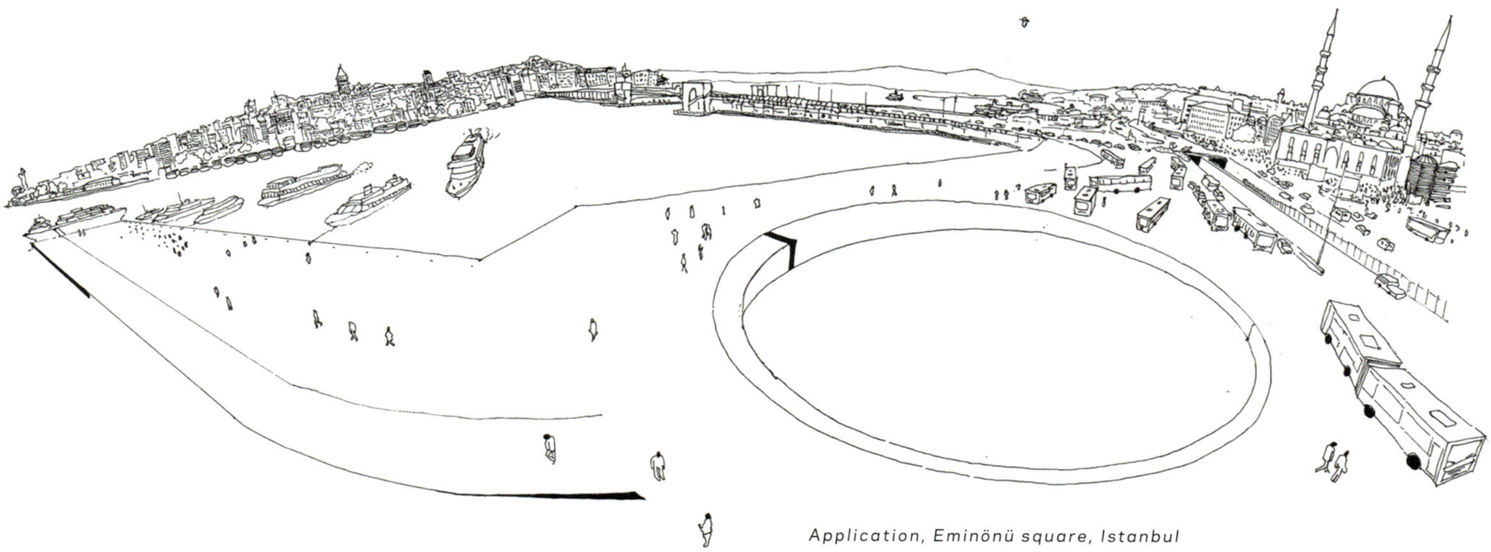

Application, Eminönü square, Istanbul

Milos Mirosavic **EUROPE - SERBIA - BELGRADE**

Hole in the Hole

SOUND AND NATURE IN THE CITY CENTER

DISCIPLINE(S): ARCHITECTURE, URBAN DESIGN / TUTOR: VLADIMIR MILENKOVIC, MSC ARCH, ASSISTANT PROFESSOR
UNIVERSITY OF BELGRADE, FACULTY OF ARCHITECTURE

The brief for this project was generated through a research-by-design approach in the field of architectural form. The program had to stress the specific qualities of a site that is bustling with life. This area is well known, not for its existing structures, but for the stories about those that have never been built. This elusive transition between appearance and disappearance can be noted as one of the characteristics of the city of Belgrade. The site for this project is known as Miticeva rupa (Mr. Mitic's Hole) after Vlada Mitic, the famous Serbian pre-war merchant. Just before the Second World War, the plot was cleared for the construction of "the biggest fashion store in the Balkans", but the site has remained empty to the present day. At the moment, it is a semi-cultivated green area in the middle of a city centre saturated by heavy infrastructure and public transport. Paradoxically, this historical, urban and ecological context has been taken as a beneficial starting point for the study. With the addition of a cultural program it has become the topic for the following design. A typological hybrid of a concert hall and a park has materialized through a void and a system of public spaces that offer diverse sojourn intensities. The structure, filled with additional functions such as cafes, terraces and vantage-point areas, has a counterpoint in a 1400-seat concert hall, located at its core. This space has been designed to hold powerful performances of the biggest performing ensembles of late-Romantic composers such as Mahler, Wagner, Stravinsky and Rachmaninoff. Delicate in design, with special dedication to quality and aesthetics of natural and artificial light, it displays the unquestionable qualities of a symbiosis of urban and natural life in contemporary architectural and cultural context.

Park structure

Main Concert Hall

Grand Terrace / Champagne Bar

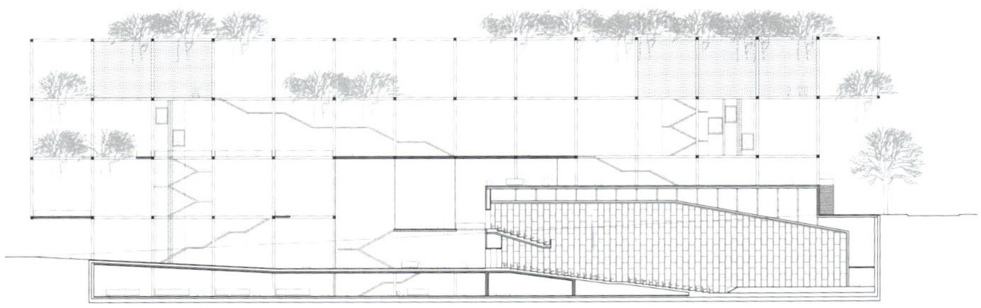

Longitudinal section

Chamber Hall

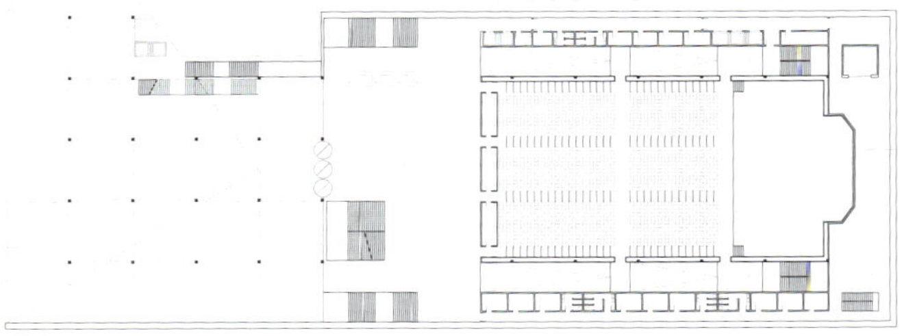

Plan - Foyer Level

Foyer

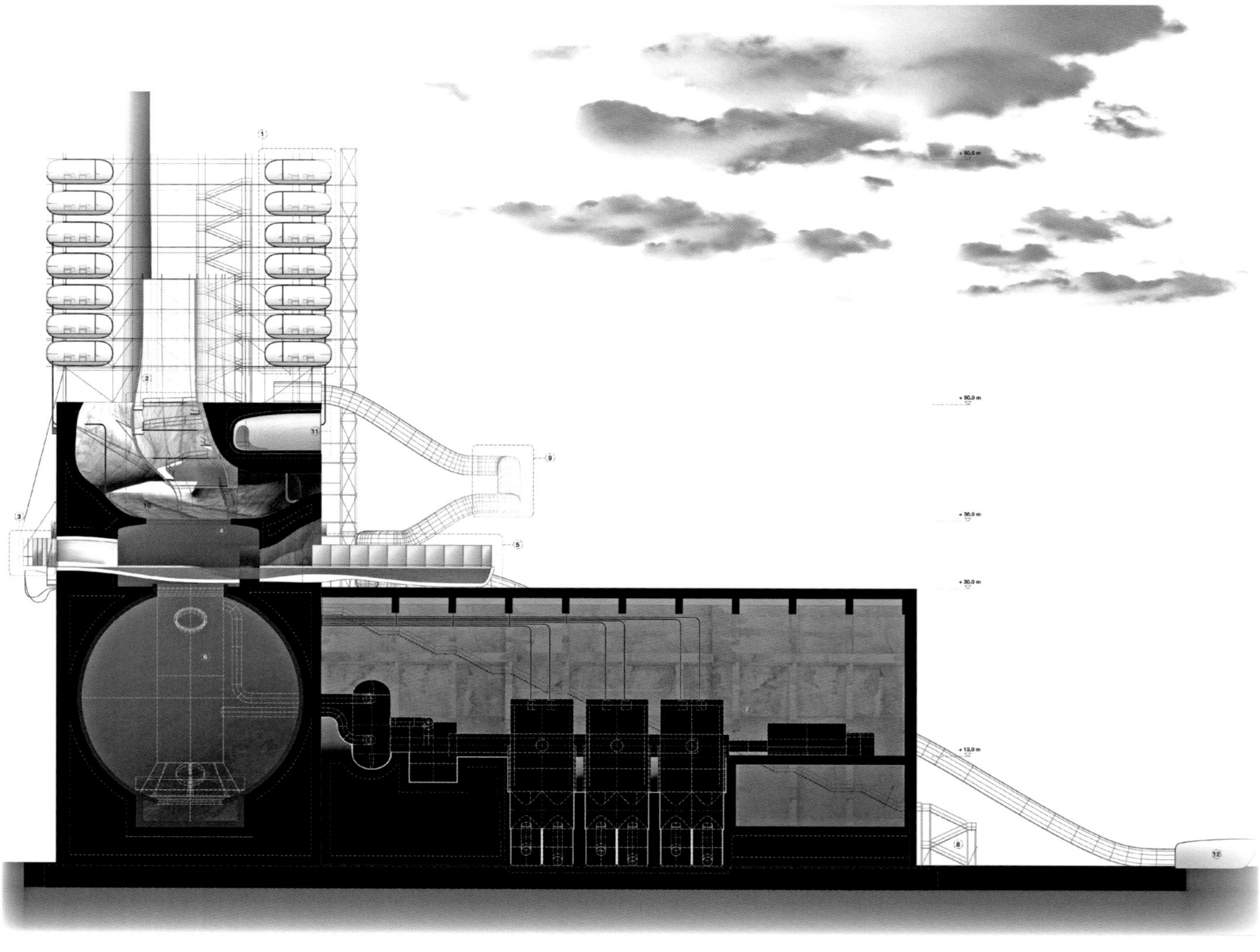

Longitudinal section

Christian Tonko **EUROPE - AUSTRIA - VIENNA**

Sana**torium**

A NEW CHAPTER IN THE PRODUCTION OF BODIES

DISCIPLINE(S): ARCHITECTURE / TUTOR: NASRINE SERAJI / **ACADEMY OF FINE ARTS VIENNA** INSTITUTE FOR ART AND ARCHITECTURE
PARTICIPANTS FAVORITE: 15 VOTES + NOMINATED

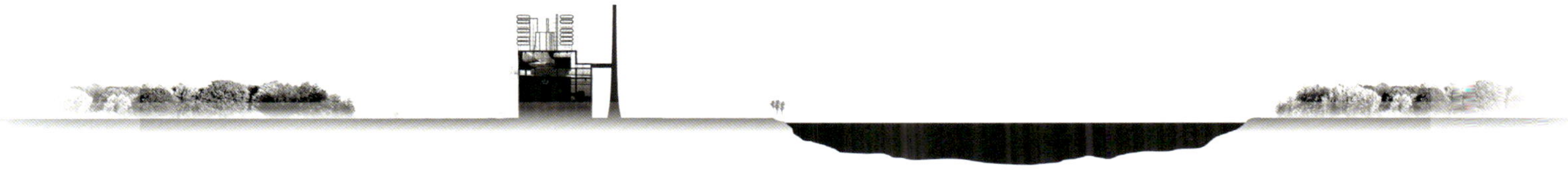

The core of my diploma thesis consists of the assumption that sustainability is just another chapter in modernism. At the threshold of modernity, the human body, in its biological reality, was identified as a valuable resource; now the climate is recognized as the decisive factor to guarantee further development of productivity and economy on a global scale. The pursuit of economic and technological progress is the main objective and the driving force shared by the discourse of classic modernity and the contemporary discourse on sustainability. My interest lies in architecture as still being essentially entangled with in the same field of primarily economic and political forces that Foucault analyzed in his theory of power. Therefore I am interested in the way architecture currently organizes bodies in relation to the given milieu in order to guarantee an increase in productivity and continued progress. In classic modernity, the organization of bodies in relation to the milieu was led by an idea of hygiene. Nowadays, bodies and climate are being organized according to the idea of energetic efficiency. The aim of my project is to question the regime of efficiency and to try to conceptualize an architecture which positions itself beyond the territory of power but is modern and sustainable nevertheless. Sanatorium proposes a haven for escapists who seek refuge from ecological panopticism and the uniformity of 'green' buildings. It aims to achieve this through creating an entirely dialectic situation. Illness and wellness, efficiency and extravagance, hygiene and filth, interiority and exteriority, heaviness and lightness come together to create something unclassifiable: a misfit that consciously acknowledges the same goals as the mechanisms of power. Sanatorium does not play by the rules but nevertheless pursues the optimization of life.

Sectional perspective - section

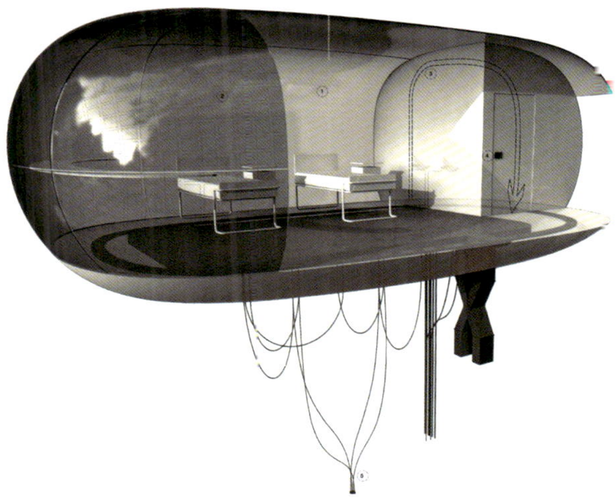

Patients room

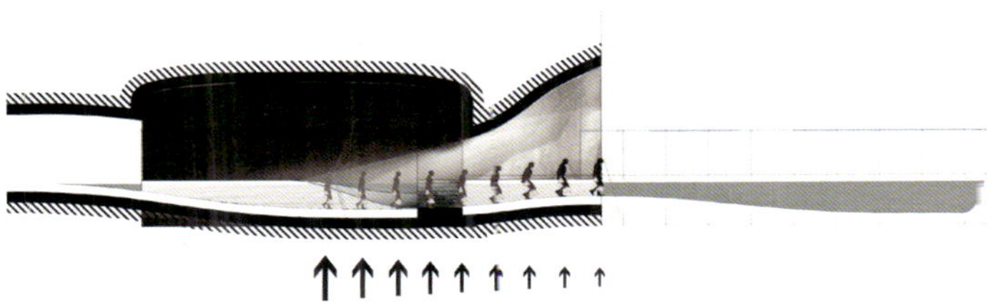

South Africa's cities top the UN list of the world's most unequal cities

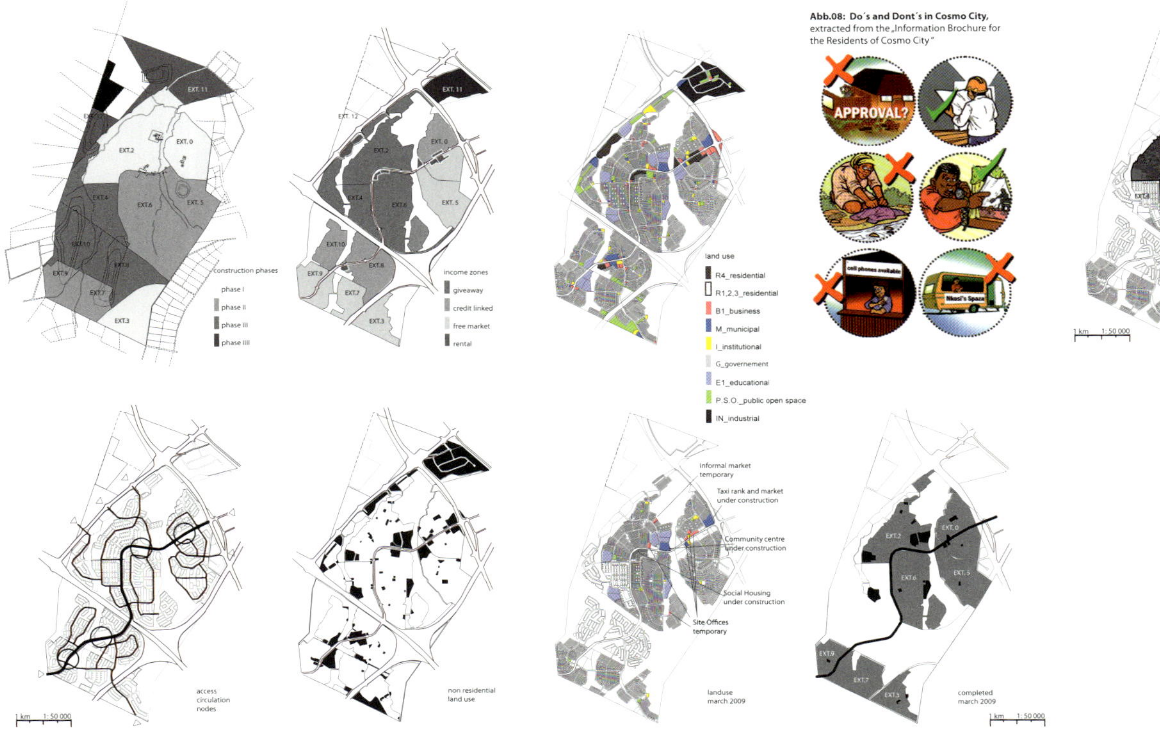

5000 RDP/give away houses
(fully subsidised) Ext. 2, 4, 6,
3000 credit linked houses
(partially subsidised) Ext. 0, 8, 10
1000 social/institutional housing
(partially subsidised) Ext. 0, 2, 4, 6, 8
3300 bonded/free market houses Ext. 3, 5, 7, 9

250 ha fenced Conservation Area
43 Parks
32 Plots for business use
(incl. 3 garages)
18 Plots for industrial use (40ha)
40 Plots for institutional use, incl.
12 Plots for social facilities
(schools, Community Centres, Taxi Rank,
4 Informal markets)

Showcase-housing project and my field of research, Cosmo City, Johannesburg

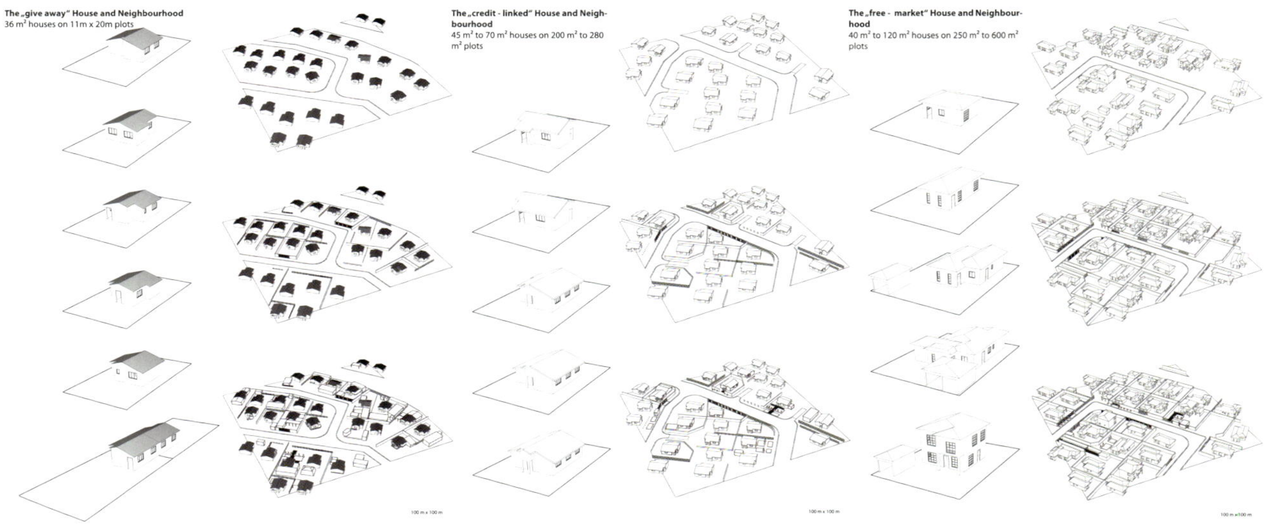

Marlene Wagner EUROPE - AUSTRIA - VIENNA

A Place under the Sun **for Everyone**

DISCIPLINE(S): ARCHITECTURE, URBAN DESIGN / TUTORS: CHRISTIAN KÜHN, HARALD TRAPP / **TECHNISCHE UNIVERSITÄT WIEN, FAKULTÄT FÜR ARCHITEKTUR UND RAUMPLANUNG** / **NOMINATED**

The core of my diploma thesis consists of the assumption that sustainability is just another chapter in modernism. At the threshold of modernity, the human body, in its biological reality, was identified as a valuable resource; now the climate is recognized as the decisive factor to guarantee further development of productivity and economy on a global scale. The pursuit of economic and technological progress is the main objective and the driving force shared by the discourse of classic modernity and the contemporary discourse on sustainability. My interest lies in architecture as still being essentially entangled within the same field of primarily economic and political forces that Foucault analyzed in his theory of power. Therefore I am interested in the way architecture currently organizes bodies in relation to the given milieu in order to guarantee an increase in productivity and continued progress. In classic modernity, the organization of bodies in relation to the milieu was led by an idea of hygiene. Nowadays, bodies and climate are being organized according to the idea of energetic efficiency. The aim of my project is to question the regime of efficiency and to try to conceptualize an architecture which positions itself beyond the territory of power but is modern and sustainable nevertheless. Sanatorium proposes a haven for escapists who seek refuge from ecological panopticism and the uniformity of 'green' buildings. It aims to achieve this through creating an entirely dialectic situation. Illness and wellness, efficiency and extravagance, hygiene and filth, interiority and exteriority, heaviness and lightness come together to create something unclassifiable: a misfit that consciously acknowledges the same goals as the mechanisms of power. Sanatorium does not play by the rules but nevertheless pursues the optimization of life.

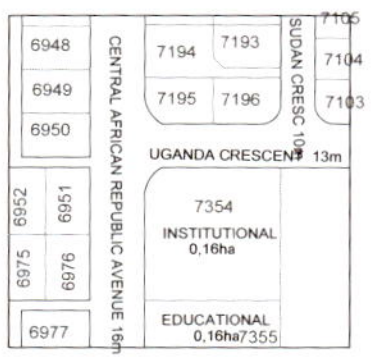

100 m x 100 m

Enormous spatial divergence between the haves and the have nots

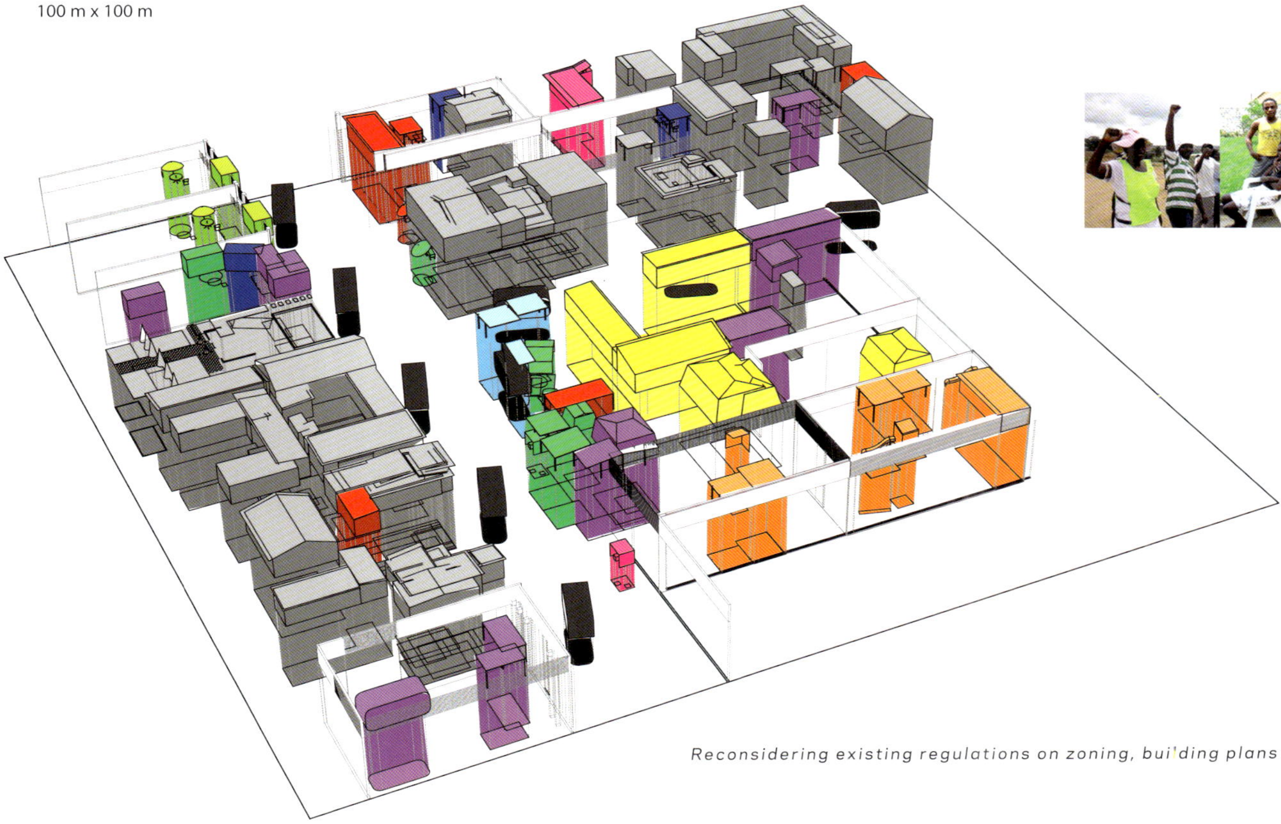

Reconsidering existing regulations on zoning, building plans and standards

Julia Koerner EUROPE - AUSTRIA - VIENNA

Superhuman **Enticement**

BIOMECHATRONIC SPORTS CENTER, NEW YORK CITY

DISCIPLINE(S): ARCHITECTURE / TUTORS: PROF. GREG LYNN / ASSISTANTS: KRISTY BALLIET, OLLIVER BERTRAM, JUSTIN DILES
UNIVERSITY FOR APPLIED ARTS VIENNA, INSTITUTE OF ARCHITECTURE / **PARTICIPANTS FAVORITE: 12 VOTES**

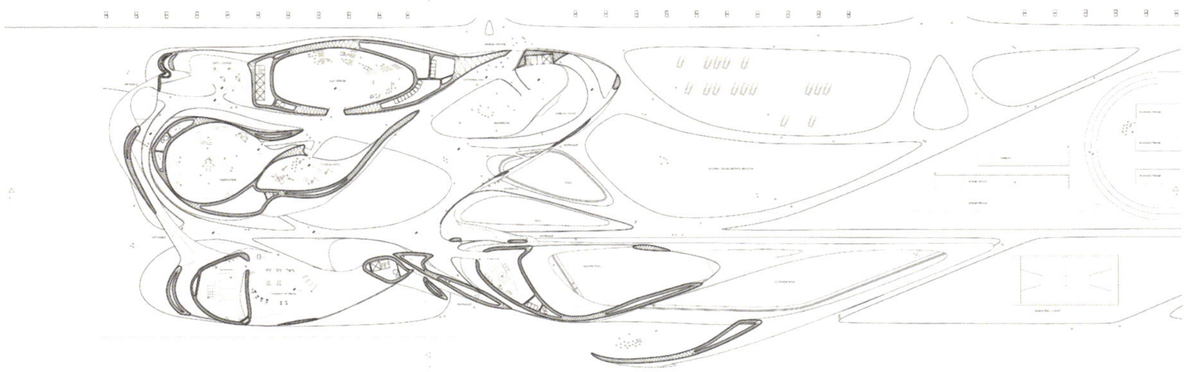

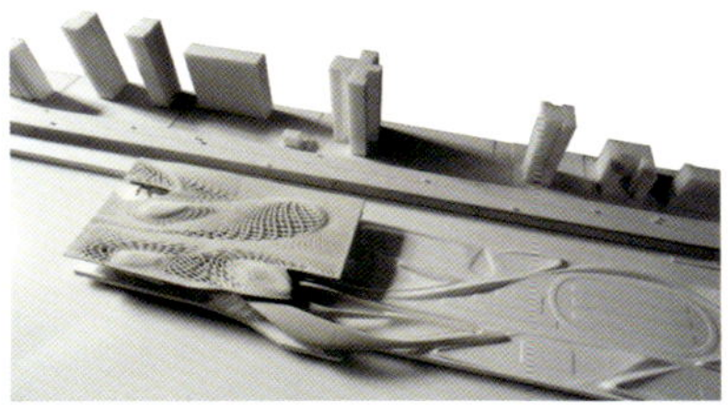

Superhuman Enticement is a new showroom, manufacturing and therapy building catering to clients of advanced prosthetic and biomechatronic devices. Located in New York City, the project occupies an existing pier on the East River near Manhattan Bridge. The project creates an architectural identity for the evolutionary, futuristic lifestyle of the contemporary amputee: a lifestyle celebrating a mysterious synthesis of organic and technological body parts. Similarly enigmatic effects are created through the fusion of landscape, highly articulated volumes and a luminous, gravity-defying roof. Synthesizing the aesthetics of humanoid robot design and a wooded forest, the project animates the smooth, clean and continuous surfaces of the volumes with constantly changing light and shadow patterns produced by a space frame roof structure. This roof - a technological magic carpet covering the entire building - actually uses the organic volumes as columns, and forms a nested roof-space poche relationship with the surface of the organic volumes where they connect. The building's three primary systems - the ground, the volumes and the roof - collaborate to control the circulation flow on the site and create the architectural language of the project. The shapes of the volumes and the flowing patterns of the roof structure and landscape create an architecture of fluid movement and speed. Walking through the building, over ramps, clients experience enigmatic spatial effects as motion is communicated through formally different geometries that are still part of a single organic family. This highly designed ambience fully fuses and transforms the therapy, factory and showroom hybrid building typologies into a continuously shifting field of sophisticated, highly-differentiated architectural moments.

View from East River

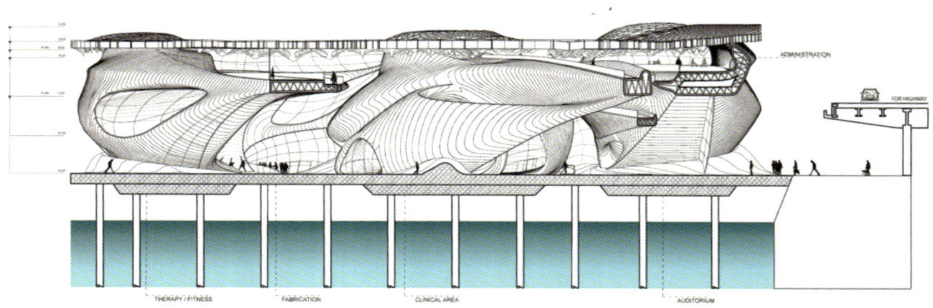

Interior views and close-up towards downtown Manhattan

Jessica Stuecklin EUROPE - SWITZERLAND - MENDRISIO

Varese Railway District

DISCIPLINE(S): ARCHITECTURE, URBAN DESIGN / TUTORS: QUINTUS MILLER, MARIO BOTTA
UNIVERSITÀ DELLA SVIZZERA ITALIANA, ACCADEMIA DI ARCHITETTURA

The old historical centre of Varese (Italy) lies adjacent to a huge void created by the intersection of two different railway lines. This makes the area an almost inaccessible wasteland as it creates a hole in the urban texture. In the near future, one of the lines will be extended all the way up to Switzerland, establishing a new connection between Northern and Southern Europe. The city's highly strategic position along this novel artery is expected to generate considerable urban growth, and requires a representative city entrance. The urban strategy suggests a densification of the district and the creation of a clear system of streets, squares and referential buildings that connect with the existing structure. The main axis is extended to the new square, which is thematized by the new market hall and station building. The railway station is placed precisely at the crossing of the two railway lines in order to profit from the minimal distance between the tracks and to unite the two stations into one representative building. In order to make the area accessible, one railway line is sunken below the surface, which opens up the site towards the centre, while the earth wall supporting the other line is provided with passages permitting entry. The station is not only conceived as a functional building but also as a new referential center for the entire city. Its massive character and the portico on the ground floor refer to the surrounding architecture. From the grand central hall you access the tracks (level +1 and -1), the bus terminal, and the upper office floors. The hall also contains numerous shops and its dimensions allow temporary public and cultural events to take place, which guarantees continuous use.

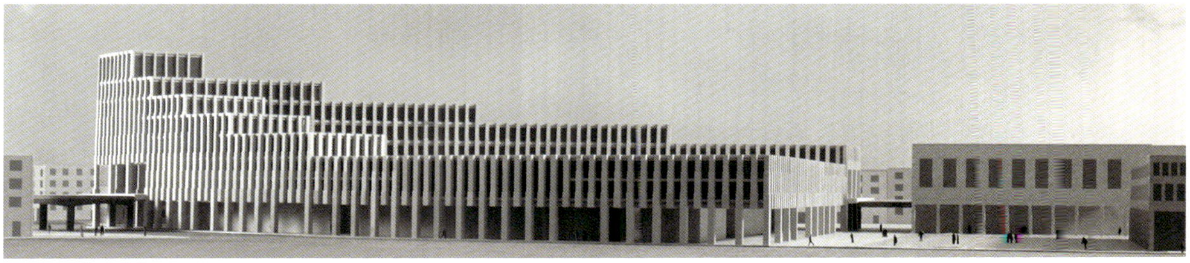

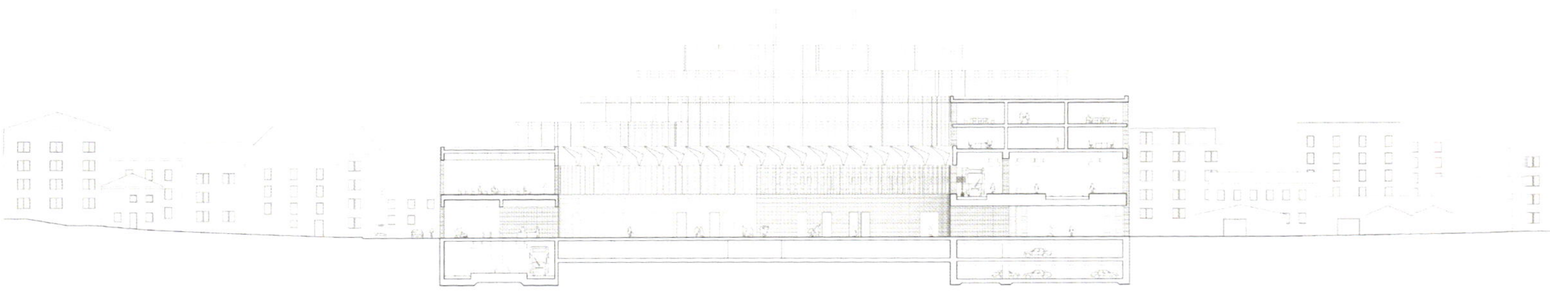

Derk Thijs EUROPE - SWITZERLAND - ZURICH

The succulent plant collection Zurich

SUSPENDING LANDSCAPES INTO THE CITY

DISCIPLINE(S): ARCHITECTURE / TUTORS: PROFESSOR GREGOR EICHINGER, ASSISTANT MARKUS JUNG
ETH ZÜRICH (SWISS FEDERAL INSTITUTE OF TECHNOLOGY), FACULTY OF ARCHITECTURE

The program is concentrated into one point, surrounded by a park that connects the Zurich lakeshore boulevard with the Rietberg and Bellevoire parks. The position, size and geometry of this concentrated volume react to the adjacent city blocks that are part of the early 19th-century development of the Zurich lakeshore. In this way the volume defines a clear reference to the history of the city and sets a landmark for its development into the 21st century. The structure itself exhibits the collection of succulent plants of the 'Sukkulentensammlung Zuerich', by suspending two 'chunks' of succulent landscape over one another. Inside these 'chunks' of landscape are offices, research and educational spaces, plus a club and a bar on the top level. The succulent landscapes are regarded as an addition to Zurich's public space. The structure's transparent lifts and escalators make the landscapes accessible twenty-four hours a day, so that people can flow uninterruptedly from a boulevard or park stroll into the exhibition. With the landscapes positioned at twenty and forty meters height, respectively, they put the succulents in front of a panoramic view of Lake Zurich and the Alps. Whilst the volume is positioned to respond to the city, the motif of suspension is used to illustrate the exoticism of these succulent landscapes. In this, I wish to give the plants the right context at the right place.

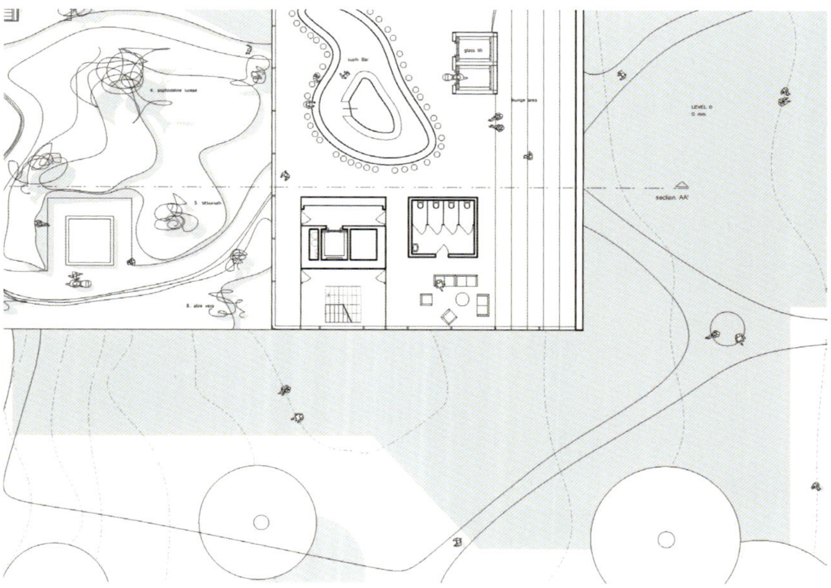

Raphaël Boursier EUROPE - FRANCE - PARIS

Level Rise City

ROOSEVELT ISLAND NEW YORK: A METROPOLITAN LABORATORY FOR FLOODING FUTURE

DISCIPLINE(S): ARCHITECTURE /TUTORS: LUCA MERLINI, JEAN PIERRE VALLIER / **ECOLE NATIONALE SUPÉRIEURE D'ARCHITECTURE PARIS-MALAQUAIS**

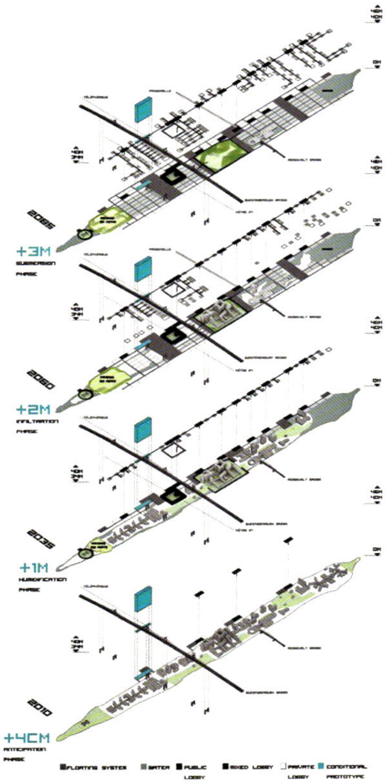

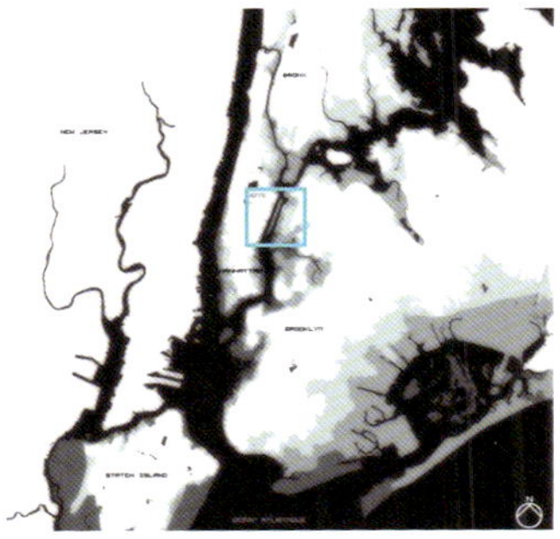

Simulation of sea-level rise in New York City / A new relationship between Queensboro Bridge and Roosevelt Island

Development strategy for Roosevelt Island, NY. / Manhattanism must be revisited with regard to sea-level rise / View from Roosevelt Island

Is Manhattan dead? Or more precisely, has Koolhaas's Manhattanism come to a dead end? Facing all the 21st century impediments, including the environmental crisis and a promised sea-level rise, this research/speculative project attempts to revisit the history of Manhattan's future. It engages a retro-prospective vision for Roosevelt Island in New York City. Depending on the PlaNYC, and on whether or not the city wishes to anticipate an additional one million inhabitants by the year 2030, it is essential to reflect upon the problem of the sea-level rise as a new factor in metropolitan congestion. Because this island is the second most densely inhabited Island of Manhattan's boroughs, and because Roosevelt Island is a vulnerable example regarding sea-level rise, the project suggests considering the area as a laboratory for a flooded future. As a first-step strategy, a conditional prototype is designed to activate the relationship between the mega-structure of Queensboro Bridge and the geographical condition that it spans and ignores. Pedestrian and bicycle access could be instantly and easily created. The bridge deck, at 40 meters elevation, becomes an alternative ground for the future island's development. Under this new reference level, we flip the skyline as a theoretical tool for (re-)thinking the many ways that skyscrapers hit the instable ground. As a possible three-dimensional urbanism detonator, the morphology of this tower claims the simultaneous urgency of the horizontal and the vertical. In fact, the building becomes less of a tower than a suspended HUB opposing what Paul Virilio calls the "impasse en altitude" concerning the skyscraper. The square elevation is the result of two logics of parceling: the building and the island itself. This project proposes a "city within the city", with many programs in declining relations to water. The skyscraper, tired of rushing up to the sky, will then inaugurate a mutation of its priorities for tomorrow in Manhattan.

Architecture, infrastructure and urbanism meeting the flooded future

WINNER + PARTICIPANTS FAVORITE: 20 VOTES THE UNIVERSITY OF WESTMINSTER **EUROPE - ENGLAND - LOND**

A DEFENSIVE ARCHITECTURE DESIGNED BY NICHOLAS ADAM SZCZEPANIAK

General reading room book wall

Front elevation

Nicholas Adam Szczepaniak EUROPE - ENGLAND - LONDON

A Defensive Architecture

DISCIPLINE(S): ARCHITECTURE / TUTORS: SUSANNE ISA, SACHA LEONG, MARKUS SEIFERMANN / **THE UNIVERSITY OF WESTMINSTER** SCHOOL OF ARCHITECTURE & BUILT ENVIRONMENT / **PARTICIPANTS FAVORITE: 20 VOTES + WINNER**

This thesis is intended to present unexpected developments in the built environment that will occur if we do not take more drastic steps to deal with climate change. The project is deliberately provocative and allegorical. Set in the Blackwater Estuary in Essex, the project envisages a set of militarized coastal defense towers that perform multiple functions. The principle role of the towers is to act as an environmental warning device. The architecture is alive, dramatizing shifts in environmental conditions: breathing, creaking, groaning, sweating and crying when stressed. Air-bags on the face of the towers expand and contract, while hundreds of tensile trunks are sporadically activated, casting water on to the heated façades to produce steam. An empty watchtower at the top of each tower gives the impression that the fragile landscape below is constantly under surveillance. Across the estuary, a bed of salt marshes provides a natural form of flood defense and habitats for wildlife. Due to rising water levels and adverse weather conditions, the salt marshes are quickly deteriorating. The proposal provides a way in which megastructures can be integrated and used to encourage the growth of natural defense mechanisms against flooding, in order to protect the erosion of fragile coastline areas and our most important cities. Over time, sand will accrete at the base of each tower, forming a spit across the mouth of the estuary and absorbing energy from the waves. Internally, the towers serve as a vast repository for mankind's most valuable asset: knowledge. The architecture is a knowledge ark, which protects books from cumulative and catastrophic deterioration.

Reverse side of book wall

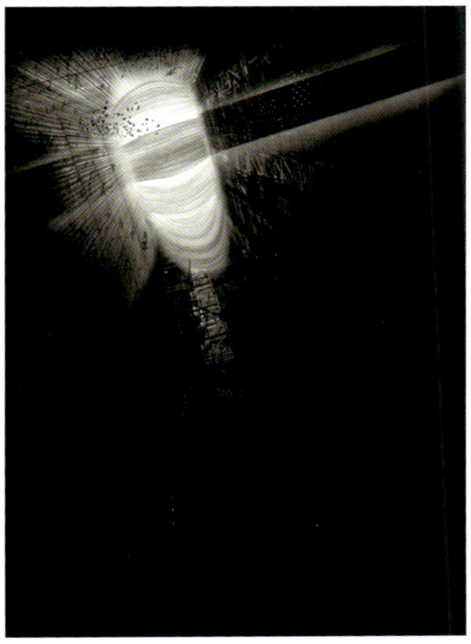

Space of inertia (looking up)

Plaza pool (internal)

View down sterile

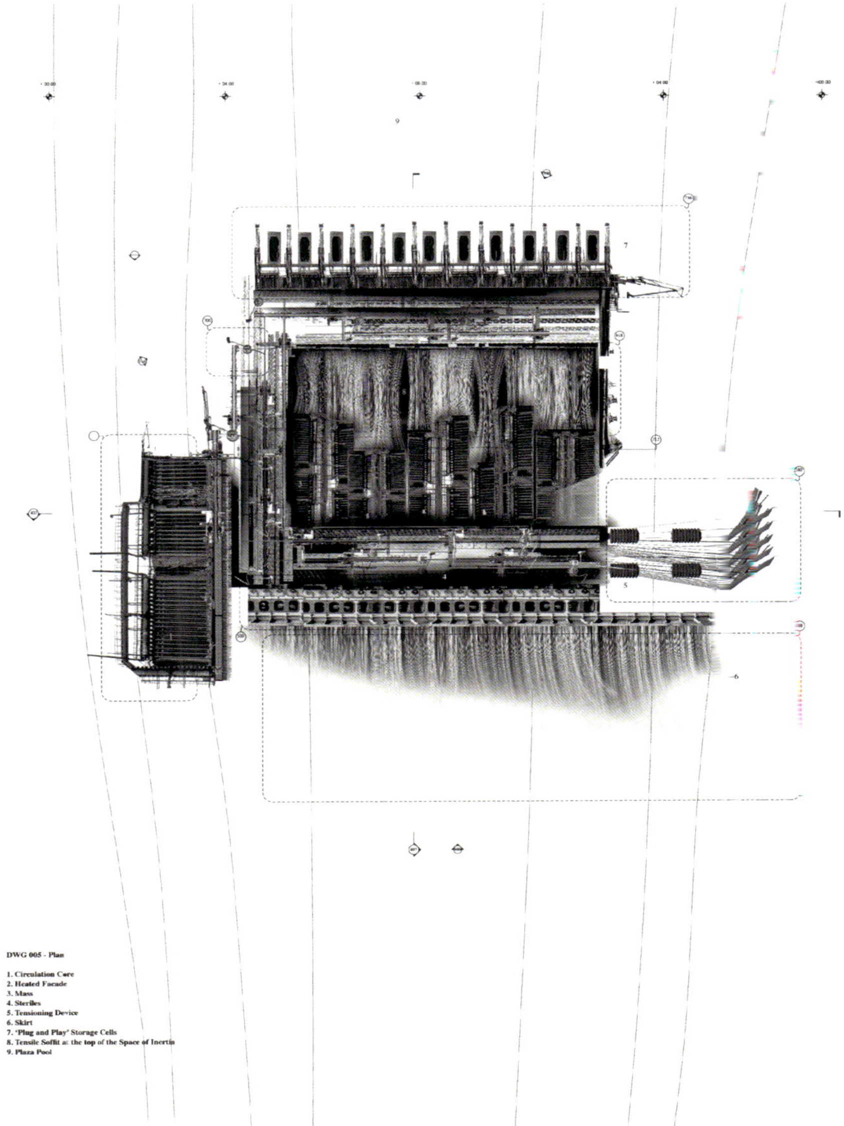

WINNER UNIVERSITY OF STRATHCLYDE **EUROPE - SCOTLAND - GLASGOW / NATIONAL APIOLOGICAL NETWOR**

WORLD'S BEST GRADUATION PROJECTS · ARCHITECTURE · URBAN DESIGN · LANDSCAPE ARCHITECTURE
2011
CAMBRIDGE USA
Archiprix
INTERNATIONAL www.archiprix.org
NATIONAL APIOLOGICAL NETWORK: AN ILLJSTRATEDHISTORY
Craig Johnston
UNIVERSITY OF STRATHCLYDE GLASGOW

LANDSCAPE ARCHITECTURE · URBAN DESIGN · ARCHITECTURE · WORLD'S BEST GRADUATION PROJECTS
HunterDouglas AWARD
WINNER
AWARDED JUNE 9TH 2011
GUGGENHEIM - NEW YORK

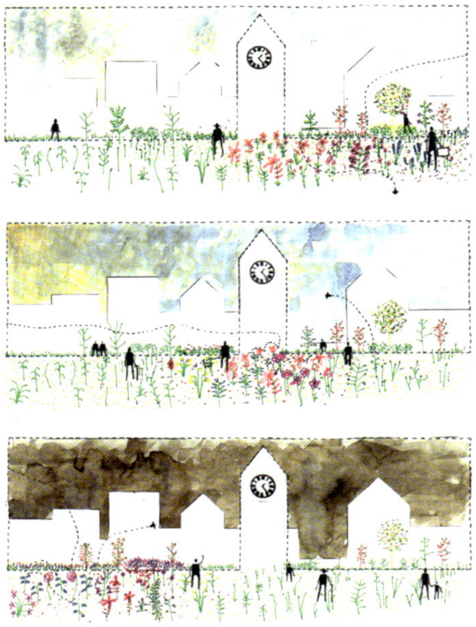

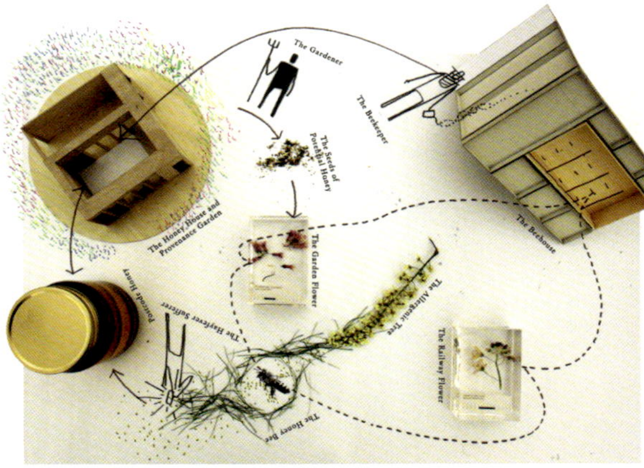

The honey bee and the garden

The honey house

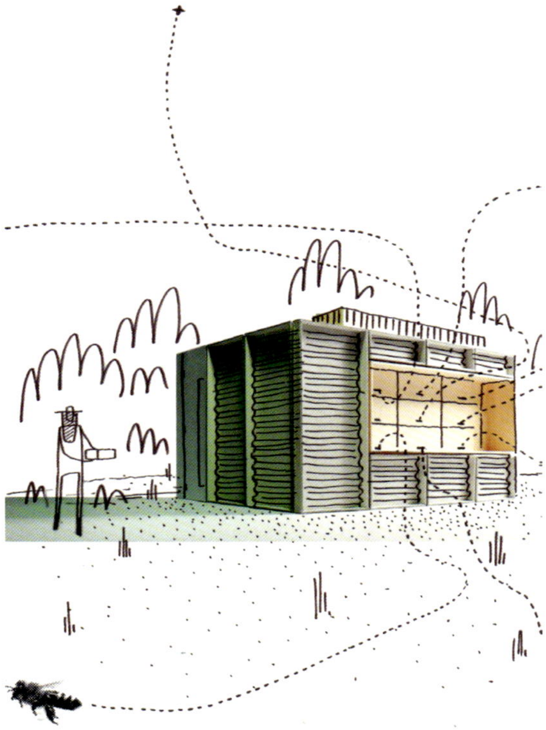

The honey bee and the neighborhood

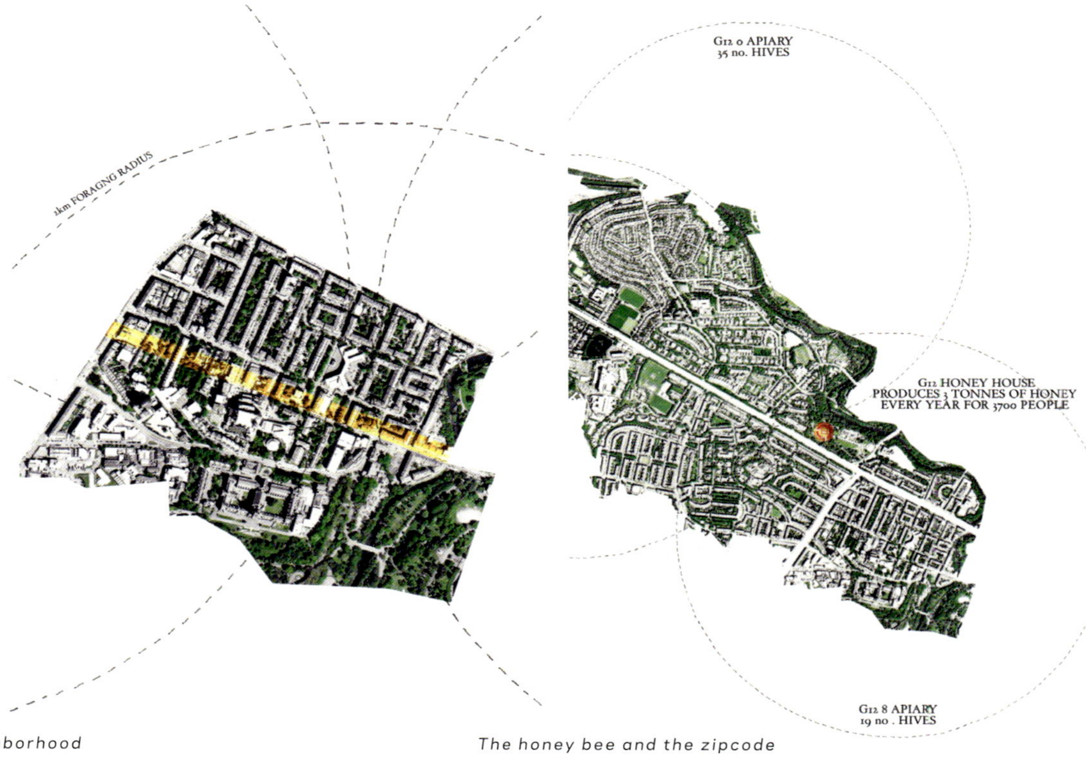

The honey bee and the zipcode

The honey bee and the zipcode

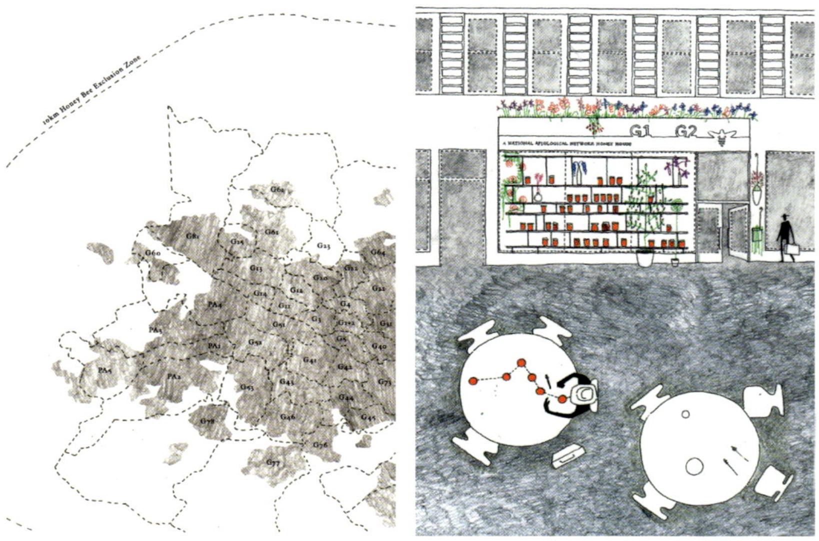

The honey bee and the city

Craig Johnston EUROPE - SCOTLAND - GLASGOW

National Apiological Network: An Illustrated History

A FICTIONAL URBAN HISTORY RECOUNTING THE RELATIONSHIP BETWEEN HUMANS, HONEY BEES, AND FLOWERS

DISCIPLINE(S): ARCHITECTURE / TUTORS: EWAN IMRIE, DAVID REAT / **UNIVERSITY OF STRATHCLYDE**, DEPT OF ARCHITECTURE / **WINNER**

It is said that one in every three mouthfuls of food we eat are due to the honey bee. Over one third of total global crop production relies on animal pollinators and honey bees make up the majority of those pollinators, at a value of around £200m to the UK agricultural industry alone. In recent years, a series of crises have threatened the honey bee and its important ecological role. In 2008, beekeepers in the UK and USA reported that one third of honey-bee colonies did not survive the winter. In response, my thesis has become a celebration of the delight, wonder and fascination with the humble honey bee and the sheer majesty of honey. Through an illustrated book and a 20-minute film, the project presents a fictional urban history recounting the relationship between humans, honey bees and flowers. Told through six chapters of increasing scale: flower, garden, neighborhood, zipcode, city and nation, the project explores historical interventions such as neighborhood apiaries, zipcode honey houses, city breeding programs, mobile laboratories, flavor-controlling gardens and planting rituals. As opposed to the toxic agricultural environments in which honey bees are commonly kept, cities are increasingly becoming the best habitats for bees. They provide many sources of food all season round and are free of pesticides. What if cities were to become areas for bee populations to recover from depopulation? What if honey bees were so ubiquitous that local 'zipcode' honey could be used to remedy hay-fever? What if bee-hives were so prevalent that each area of the city had its own flavor defined by those flowers found beside a railway, weeds in vacant lots or motorway sidings? Could the city's inhabitants alter their local honey flavor through planting different flowers? In turn, would this change not only the taste but also the look of each neighborhood?

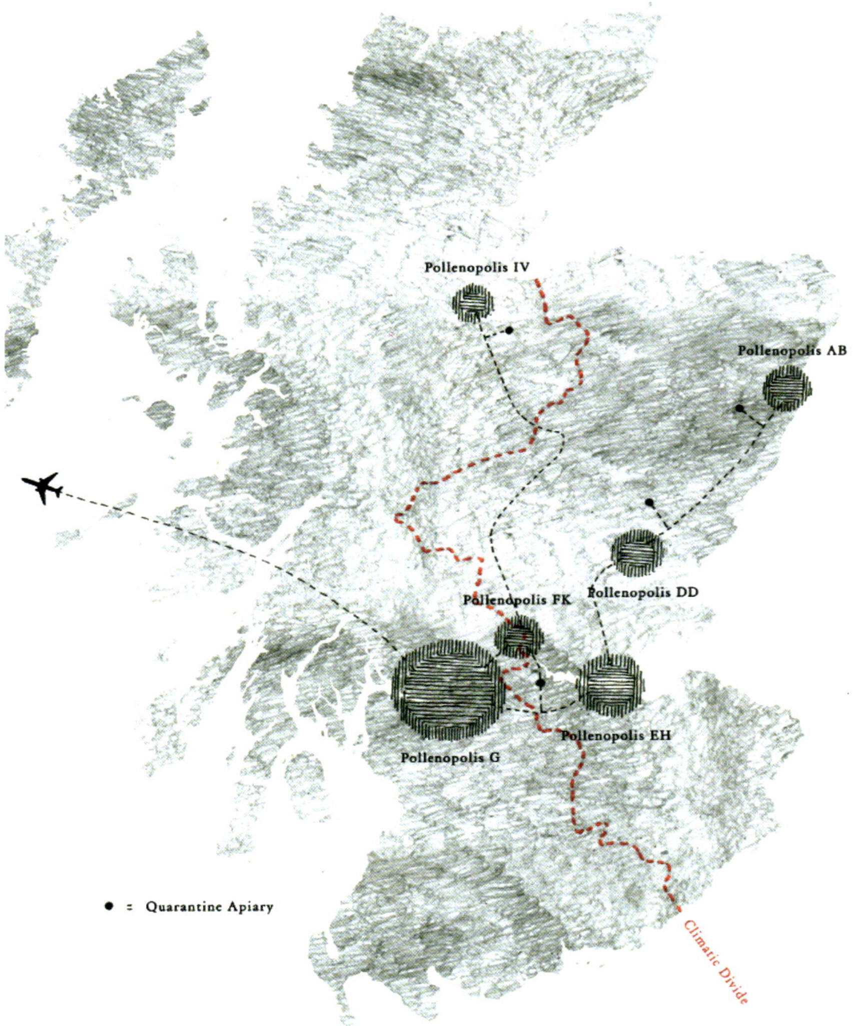

The honey bee and the nation

Zipcode honey, the taste of place

Rachel Harding EUROPE - ENGLAND - LONDON

A Crime of Passion

SYNTHETIC MURDER IN OUR MIDST

DISCIPLINE(S): ARCHITECTURE / TUTORS: NICOLA KOLLER, ROSY HEAD, GERRARD O'CARROLL / **ROYAL COLLEGE OF ART**
SCHOOL OF ARCHITECTURE & INTERIOR / **PARTICIPANTS FAVORITE: 13 VOTES**

A patient cherishes her donor's DNA in a heart-shaped frozen keep-sake / Patient and donor can enjoy the occasional romp in the love pit

Ted Bundy, America's most notorious serial killer, received 200 love letters a day. The phenomenon of genetic attraction, in which people with similar genetic codes feel attracted towards each other, is believed to affect half of all estranged adopted siblings. In 2030, the detritus of British crime scenes has become a romantic commodity. A health-obsessed public are turning to genetic miracles to cure their many ills. As our genetic blueprint has become increasingly vital to our lives, so has our aversion to donation. Criminal DNA is used to meet public demand for genes. As treatments progress, donor and patient become increasingly homozygous, and peculiar romances begin to form. In an attempt to revive readership, News International founds Gunpowder Park, a love resort providing a medical honeymoon of genetic perfection. Here, patients can receive gene therapies whilst enjoying romantic rendezvous with their criminal donors. Couples enjoy a highly controlled courtship. Criminals are kept locked in concrete structures whilst housewives enjoy their fairy-tale romance in a castle of golden mirror-glass.

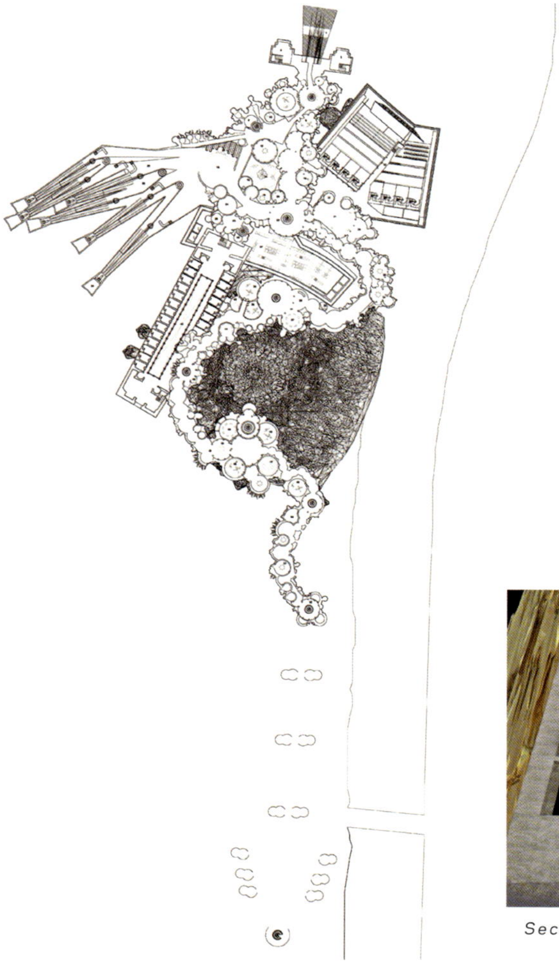

As patients progress through the park, their romantic contact is increased

Security gates: patients are subject to intensive security checks / Criminal Love Park, Enfield, 2030

Paul Michielsen **EUROPE - NETHERLANDS - ROTTERDAM**

Archi**coustics**

A SOUND(ING) ARCHITECTURE

DISCIPLINE(S): ARCHITECTURE / TUTORS: DOUWE BOONSTRA, RENÉ PIJNENBURG, PAUL PANHUYSEN, YURI LANDMAN, JEROEN VUGTS
ROTTERDAM ACADEMY OF ARCHITECTURE AND URBAN DESIGN

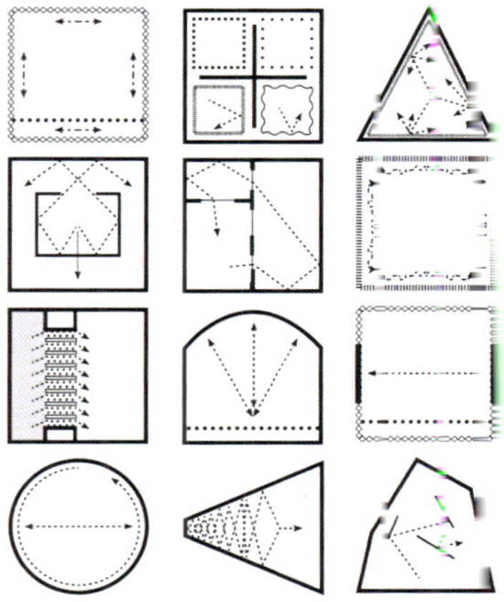

The Archicoustics soundless public plaza at dusk / Study of acoustic conditions within Archicoustics

Archicoustics gives acoustics a starring role rather than treating it as a side-effect of the design process. The term is an interpretation of the relationship between 'sound' and 'space', which can be traced to the ancient Greek auditoriums. Archicoustics studies the archetypal acoustic conditions that define new spatial assumptions. Such conditions define the basis of the form given to the various sound chambers in the building. Extreme acoustic conditions - each treated as a specific characteristic - are taken into consideration in the design of these spaces. Amidst the clamor of life in the city, Archicoustics provides a moment of silence with a public character. The sound chambers create varying accents within this - primarily underground - tranquil pause. The program is further rounded out with a foyer, a shop and archives: facilities inserted into voids between sound chambers. A 'soundless' ground-level plaza is open to the public, and here visitors find the entrance. Stairs and elevators 'leaking' sound from underground shafts make the entrance 'audible'. An existing cycle and pedestrian connection runs through this plaza, and a route begins here, where visitors find a permanent exhibition on sound. A stack of 12 sound chambers, each with a specific acoustic character, follows an increase in the spatial perception of sound inside Archicoustics. Stairs, elevators, restrooms and plazas feature small acoustic details that refer to archetypal sound chambers. Sound experience is essential while wandering through the building. All vertical walls are clad with wood. This skin is perforated to absorb sound, and built-in lighting in the cavity walls emits an attractive glow that illuminates the atrium. Ambient lighting in the atrium is dim; in this space sound is the sole focus of attention. Light entering through perforations blurs the formal expression of the spaces. Archicoustics claims an auditive moment!

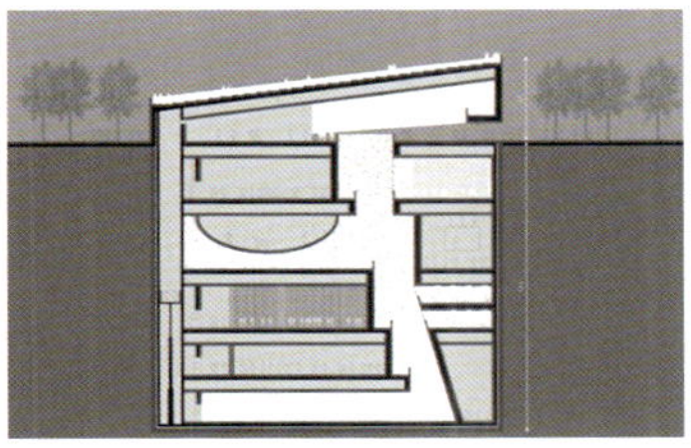

Impression of the sound room (diffusion) / Section Archicoustics

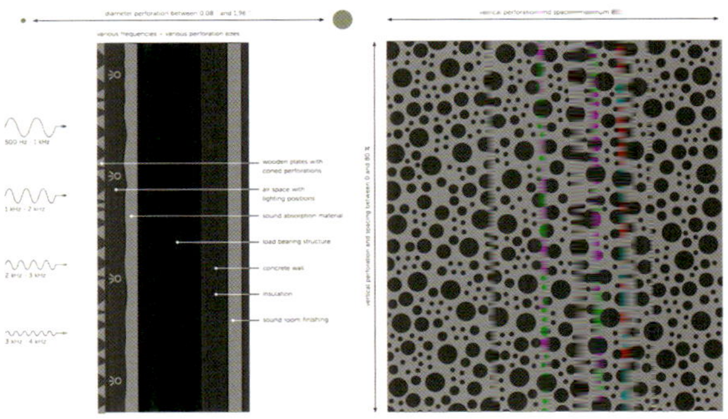

Underground auditorium, an auditive moment!

Impression of the acoustic void

WINNER + PART FAVORITE: 10 VOTES / DELFT UNIVERSITY OF TECHNOLOGY **EUROPE**

ETHERLANDS, DELFT / SPACES, POETICS AND VOIDS SIMONE PIZZAGALLI

WORLD'S BEST GRADUATION PROJECTS · ARCHITECTURE · URBAN DESIGN · LANDSCAPE ARCHITECTURE
2011
CAMBRIDGE USA
Archiprix
INTERNATIONAL www.archiprix.org
SPACES, POETICS AND VOIDS
Simone Pizzagalli
DELFT UNIVERSITY
OF TECHNOLOGY,
THE NETHERLANDS

HunterDouglas AWARD
WINNER
AWARDED JUNE 9TH 2011
GUGGENHEIM - NEW YORK
WORLD'S BEST GRADUATION PROJECTS · ARCHITECTURE · URBAN DESIGN · LANDSCAPE ARCHITECTURE

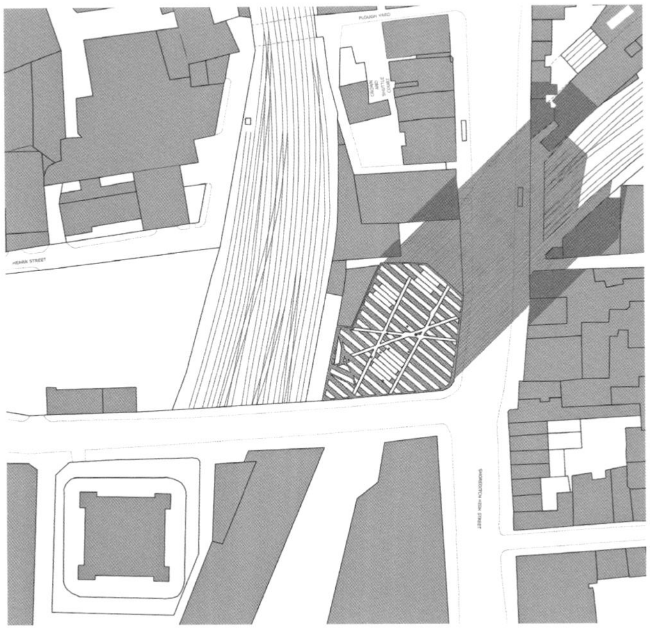

Masterplan / The building seen from Shoreditch High Street

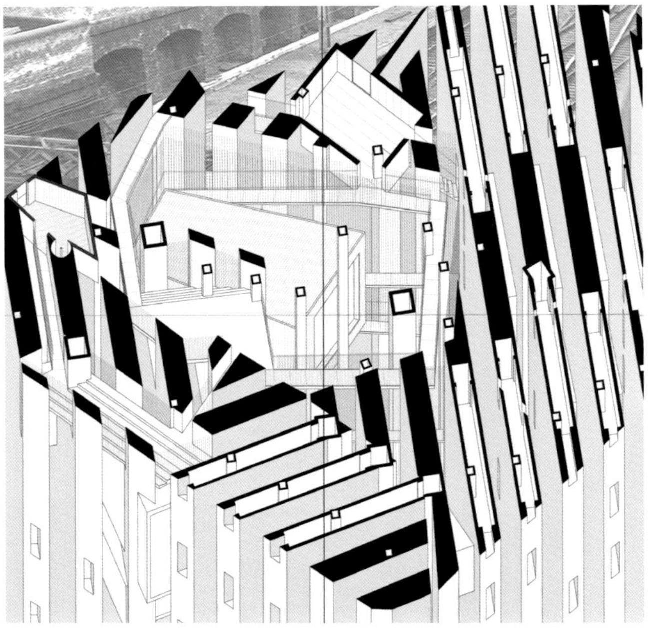

Section looking east / Isometric section through level +24: prisoners' open air activity areas

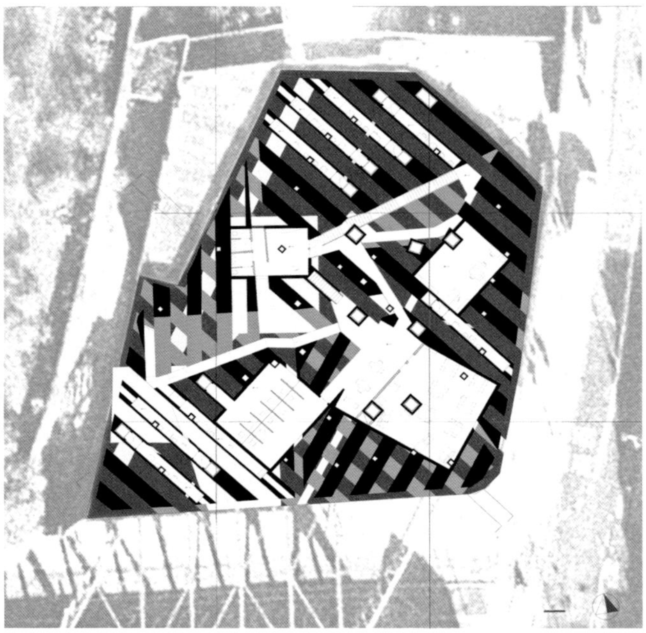

Plan of level +9, entrance and visitors' rooms / Interior of structure and prisoners' exercise yard, recreation area

Simone Pizzagalli EUROPE - NETHERLANDS - DELFT

Spaces, Poetics and Voids

THE PRISON DESIGNED FOR A VACANT LOT IN LONDON IS A MEANINGFUL PAUSE IN A CHAOTIC WORLD

DISCIPLINE(S): ARCHITECTURE / TUTOR: MARC SCHOONDERBEEK / **DELFT UNIVERSITY OF TECHNOLOGY**
FACULTY OF ARCHITECTURE / **PARTICIPANTS FAVORITE: 10 VOTES + WINNER**

The East Railway Line in London is a fascinating subject of study. It is rich in history and forms a surreal and fragmented physical presence between the City and the East End. A literary analysis of the chaotically ordered composition of this part of the metropolis involves spaces, places, voids and objects within the realm of this place of experience and imagination, with its visible elements and its ethereal body of histories and myths. The process of naming spaces and elements becomes a new way of making them exist in reality, a way of translating the complex and chaotic body of the city into some rough material capable of being rearranged and sequenced in a story or on a map: words, pauses, punctuation, rhythms. As in a text, what is not written remains the place of the active reading imagination, and similarly this applies to empty city areas, voids, unnamable places where a consistently different interpretation of the metropolis is created by the active (living) reader. From an empty plot of the city, the place of emptiness, the idea of reclusion and forced detachment from the world started to arise: a prison. It is a regular, obsessive, enclosed structure that is simultaneously open, light and transparent, with an ordered composition of elements and functions that range from diversity to repetition and rigidity. A set of different functional elements and spaces are intertwined into a repetitive structure rigid enough to be an ambiguous in-between, an inside without an outside, simultaneously present and indefinitely far away. A prison is a silent and critical element in the city, a meaningful pause in a chaotic realm of confusion. The prison is a formal interpretation of the language of the metropolis, a place where lives and stories unfold and are reconstructed into something new and different.

Section of the structure between two slabs

A cell; visitors' entrance stairs; entrance corridor

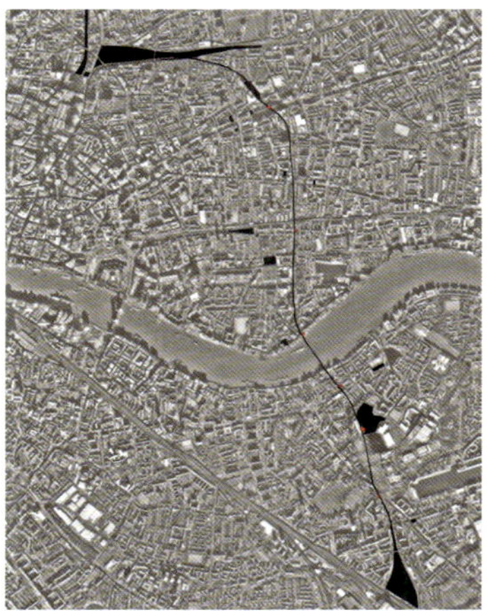

East Railway Line

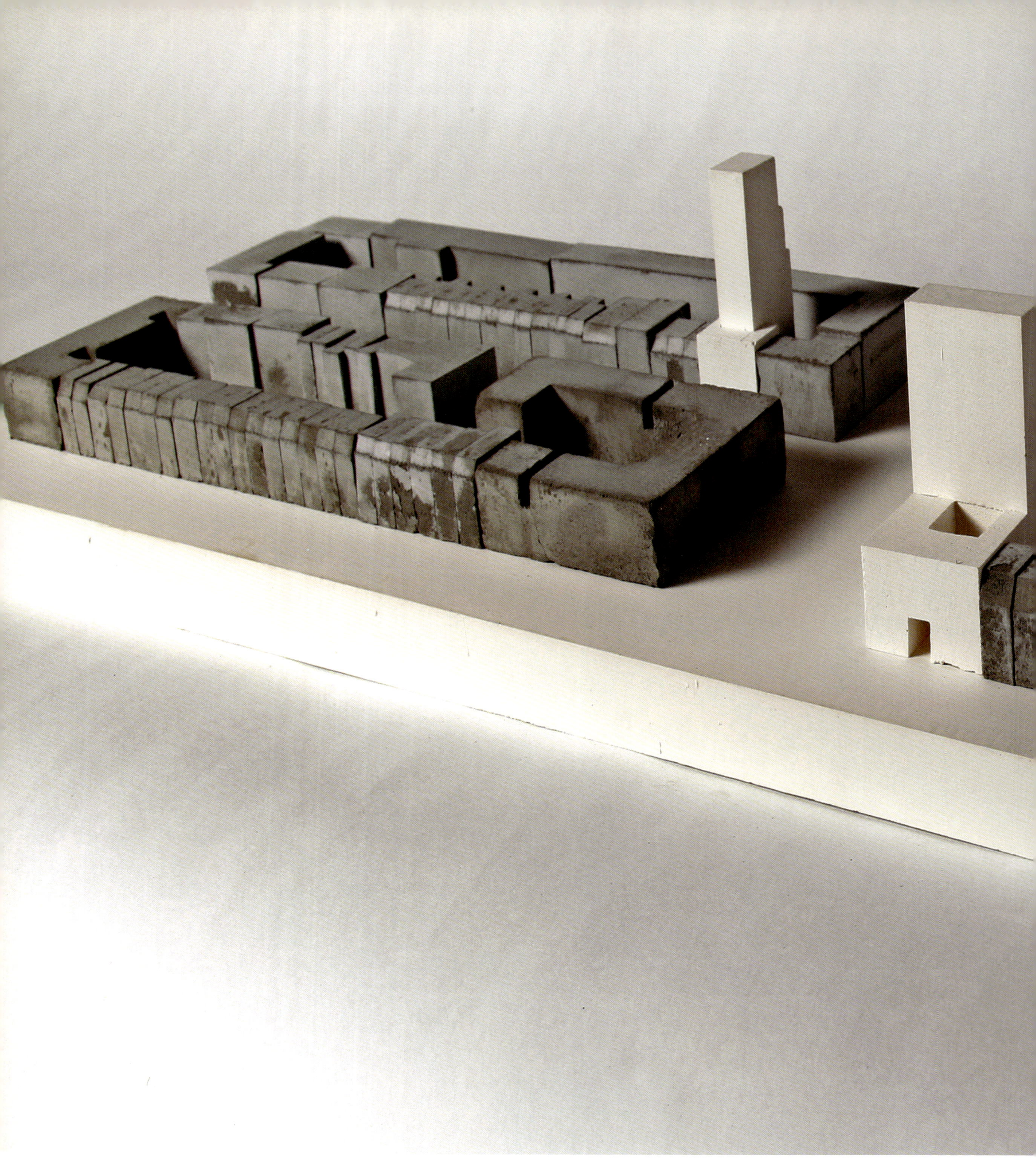

WINNER / EINDHOVEN UNIVERSITY OF TECHNOLOGY / **EUROPE, NETHERLANDS, EINDHOVEN**

AMSTERDAM ALPHABET DESIGNED BY GIJS ADRIAANSENS

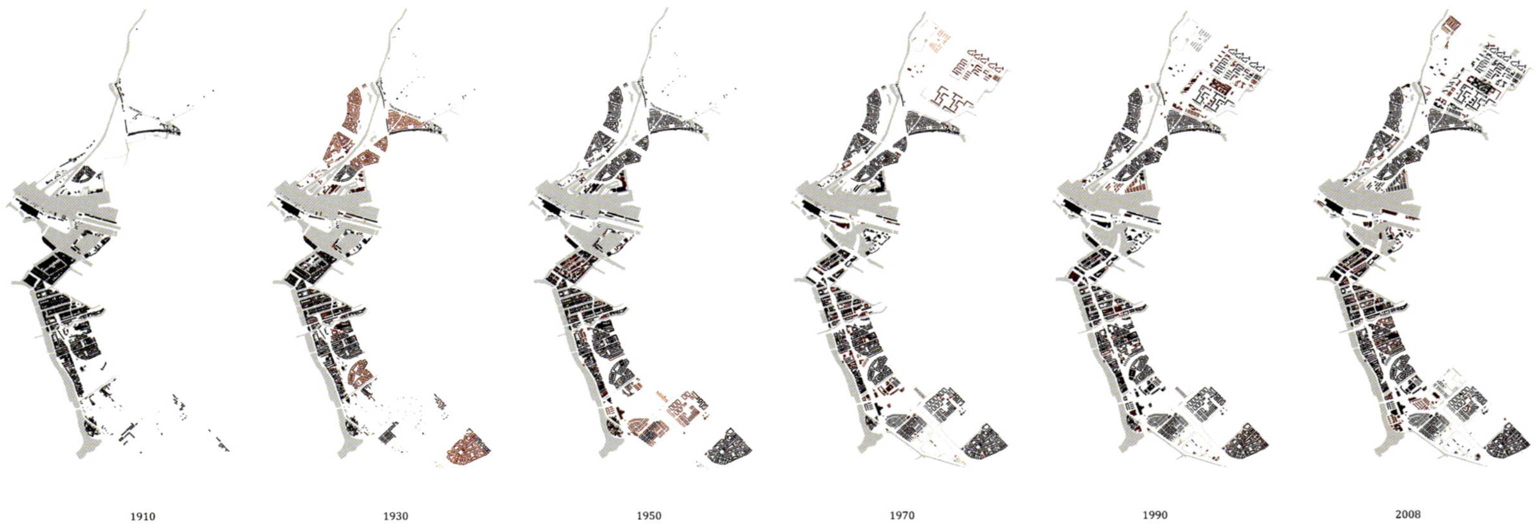

Cross-section of Amsterdam 1910-2008

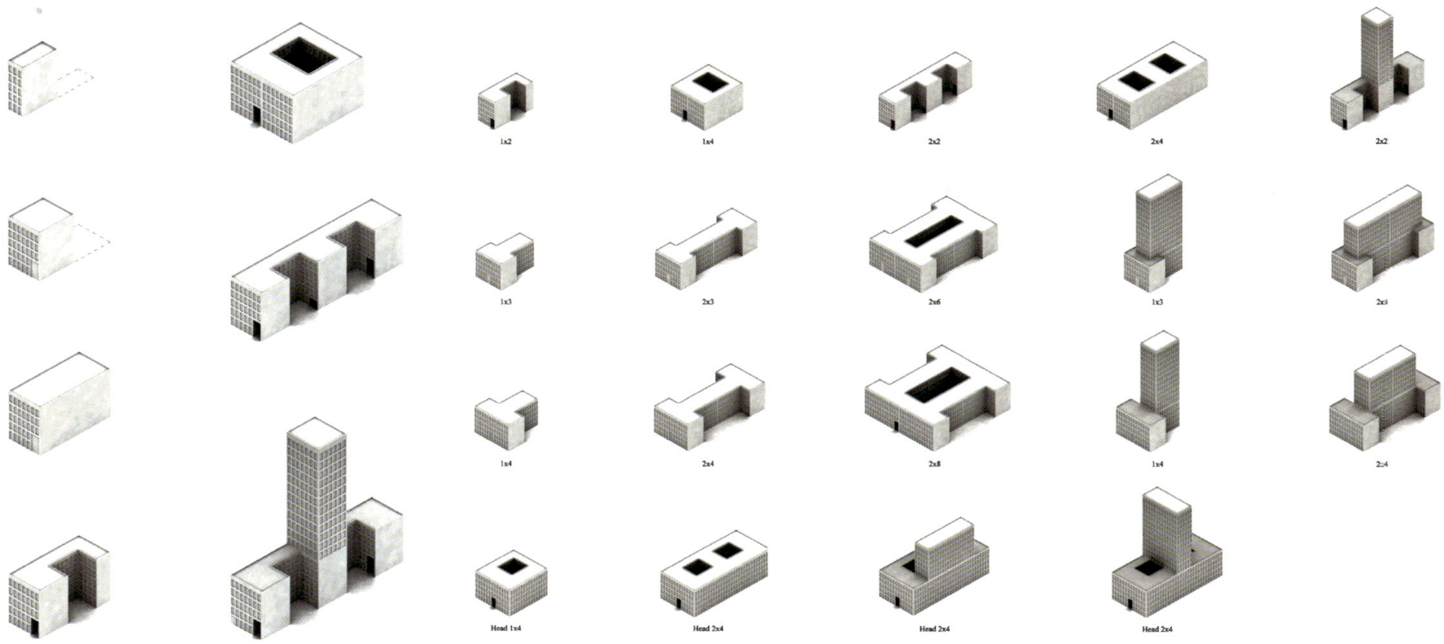

A catalogue of new types

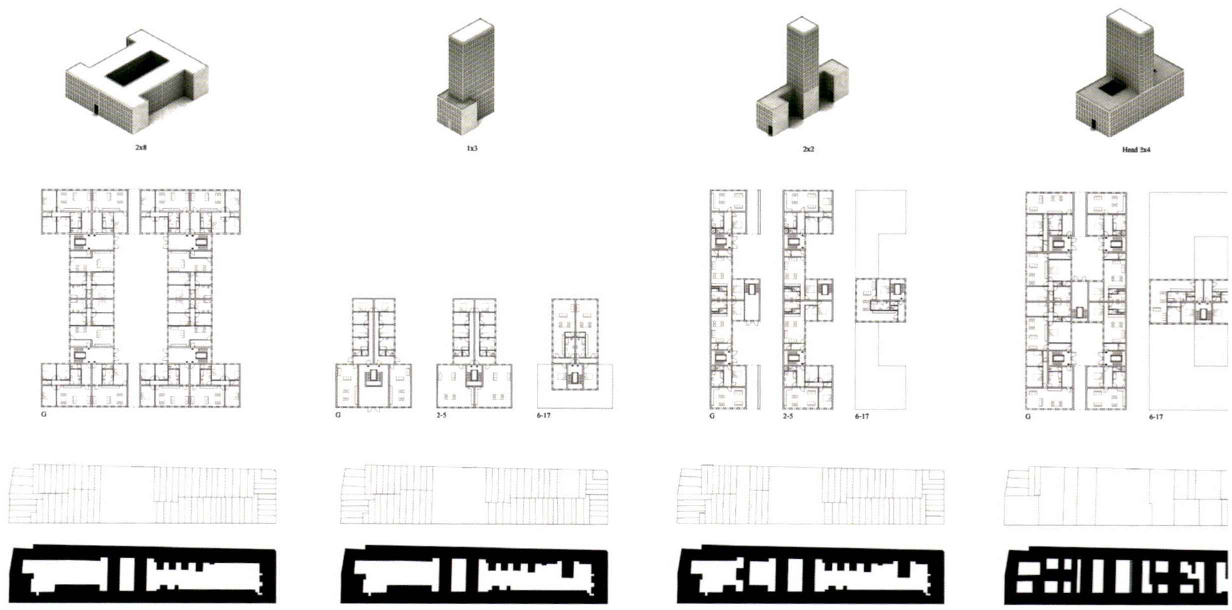

Building types and building block

Gijs Adriaansens **EUROPE - NETHERLANDS - EINDHOVEN**

Amsterdam **Alphabet**

CATALOGUE OF NEW, DENSE BUILDING TYPES BASED ON THE TYPICAL BLOCK THAT CAN BE USED ON THE WHOLE 19TH-CENTURY RING OF AMSTERDAM

DISCIPLINE(S): ARCHITECTURE, URBAN DESIGN / TUTORS: BERNARD COLENBRANDER, CHRISTIAN RAPP
EINDHOVEN UNIVERSITY OF TECHNOLOGY, FACULTY OF ARCHITECTURE, BUILDING, AND PLANNING / **WINNER**

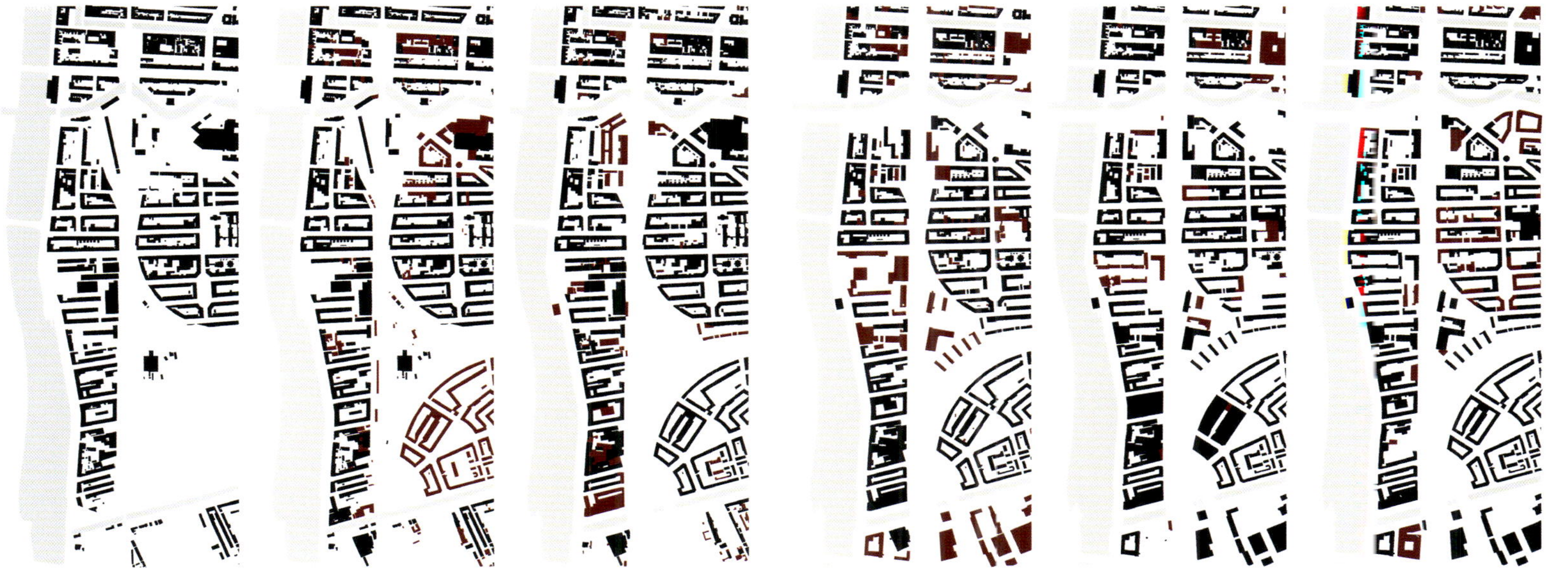

1910 1930 1950 1970 1990 2008

Wibautstraat 1910-2008

Until the nineteenth century, the growth of Amsterdam was determined by the concentric rings of urban canals. The Wibautstraat is a strange street, being fifty meters wide. It was once a railway track. The buildings on both sides are a mere fifteen meters high, like the rest of Amsterdam. A start was made on ensembles of big buildings in the mid-sixties, as a response to the width of the street, but they clashed with the building blocks of the nineteenth-century ring. As a consequence people tend to read the street as if picturesque nineteenth-century housing was demolished in favor of modern office buildings. It couldn't be further from the truth. The object of my project is to give the Wibautstraat the required height and to densify, without erasing the modern buildings. The main product of this project is a catalogue of new, dense building types based on the typical nineteenth-century building block. We start with the 5.6m.-wide and 12.5m-deep alcove house which fills half the plot. The front has a representative façade, the rear is more informal. Multiple plots are combined, and the whole plot is filled. This creates a problem because this leaves us with a 25-m.-deep space with no rear windows since it now connects to the backdoor neighbor. A cut needs to be made to allow light into the building. This is the starting point of the typology. It leaves us with a type consisting of a typical Dutch voorhuis and achterhuis ('front and back house' divided by a private courtyard). The 'L' shaped achterhuis only receives light from the courtyard and therefore is only 5 m deep, whereas the voorhuis receives light from the courtyard and the street and therefore is 10m. deep. This 'logic of light' is used for all types and generates different shapes on different sizes of plots. It becomes more interesting when the type is flipped to occupy the full width of the block. Now it's possible to take a shortcut through it. So, the typology enriches the urban fabric: to the public street and private inner court it adds a third intermediate space of the courtyard – rare in Holland. The tower, as an extension of the achterhuis, relates to the big buildings.

A specific plan for the Wibautstraat

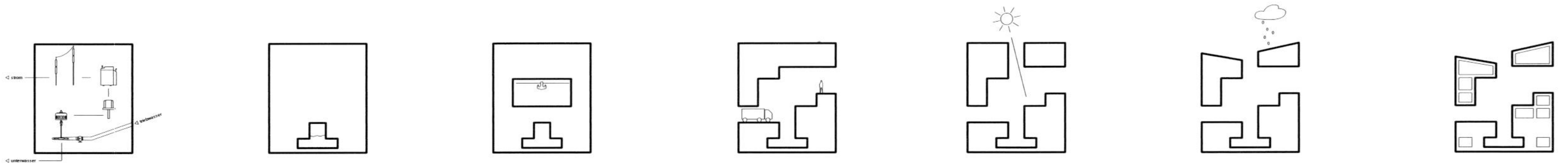

Perspective and concept

1. high voltage electricity 110kV
2. transformator
3. office
4. reception
5. batteries
6. sanitary room
7. high voltage electricity 8kV
8. workshop
9. engine hall
10. turbine technics
11. main tenance
12. hydraulic and cooling system
13. entrance access
14. process control

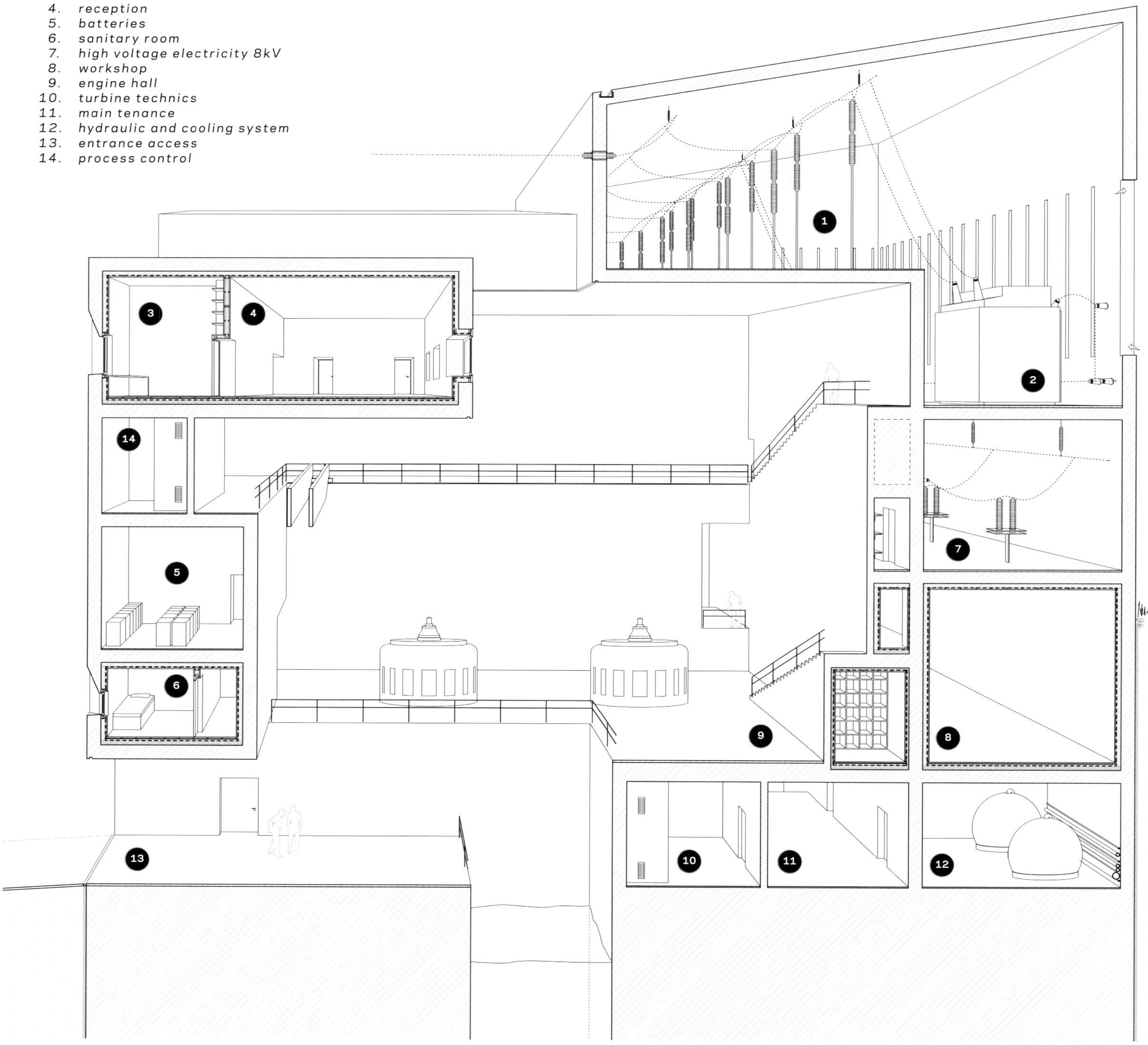

Detailed section

Marie Luise Kister **EUROPE - GERMANY - AACHEN**

About **the water's force**

'CHLUS' HYDROPOWER STATION

DISCIPLINE(S): ARCHITECTURE / TUTORS: PROF. MEINRAD MORGER, PROF. ANNE BERNHARD (DEPARTMENT FOR BUILDING TYPOLOGIES)
RHEINISCH-WESTFÄLISCHE TECHNISCHE HOCHSCHULE AACHEN / FAKULTÄT FÜR ARCHITEKTUR / **PARTICIPANTS FAVORITE: 23 VOTES**

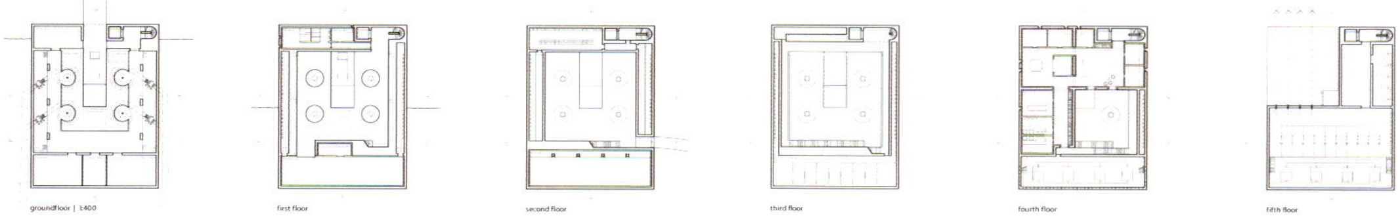

Floor plans

The new Chlus hydropower station completes the row of hydropower stations in the Davos Valley. The water is led through an underground pipeline to the cliff at the Chlus gorge. Withdrawn from this impressive canyon, the secluded building stands on the edge of the trees and at a distance from the busy main road. Surrounded by the forest, it is located in the transition between the mountain and the plane. Different landmarks are situated near one of the national hiking trails, such as ruins and rundown air-raid shelters. Within this sequence, the hydropower station becomes one of these landscape objects. The process of generating electricity from water requires a certain volume. This total volume is composed by "solids" and "hollows", which means closed and open spaces around the turbine. A huge space depends on various technical parameters, even though it is at the center of the building, and it is interfused by the outer climate. To people passing by, the building appears to be an introverted sculptural landscape object that does not merge with surrounding nature because of its red-colored concrete. Holes in the façade have been reduced to a minimum. The unique shape of the roof is due to inner, volumetric parameters and the result of a controlled water runoff. The pure, rough concrete underlines the industrial character of the building and is strong enough to keep it in place against the massive force of the hydropower. On a rather poetic level, a resemblance of water's ability to realize space by substracting material is created by showing the water in the core. The water seems to have cut into the massive volume over the years.

Site plan and hydropower stations along the Landquart river

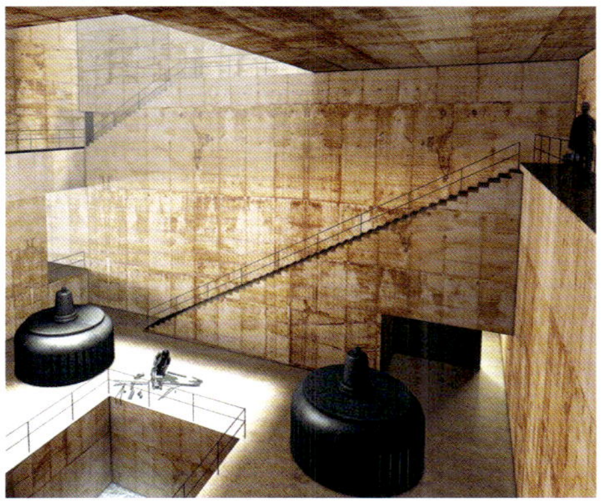

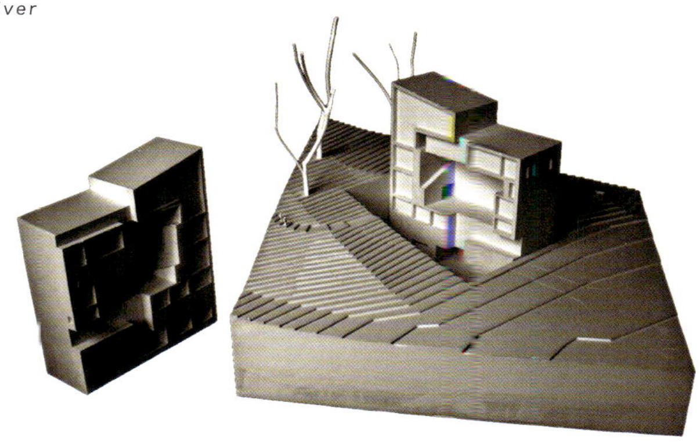

Model of the building

Sarah Wloka, Caroline Krawczyk EUROPE - GERMANY - KASSEL

The orangutan project

ORANGUTAN CARE AND RESEARCH CENTER FOR BORNEO (INDONESIA)

DISCIPLINE(S): ARCHITECTURE / TUTORS: PROF. DIPL.-ING. M.ARCH. MAYA REINER, DIPL.-ING. NATALIE HEGER, PROF. DIPL.-ING. BRIGITTE HÄNTSCH
UNIVERSITÄT KASSEL, FACHBEREICH 06 - ARCHITEKTUR, STADTPLANUNG, LANDSCHAFTSPLANUNG

Human housing

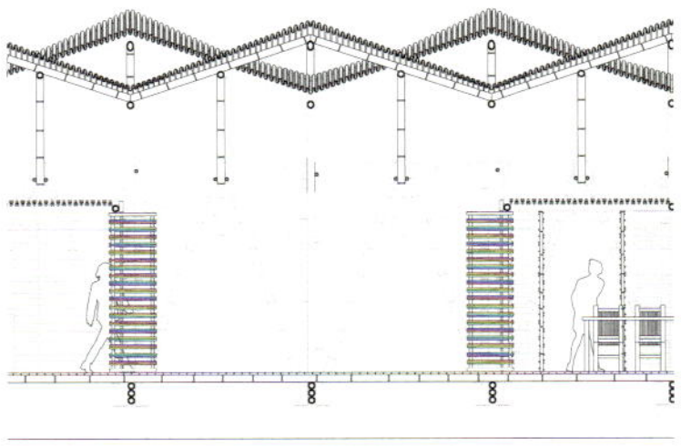

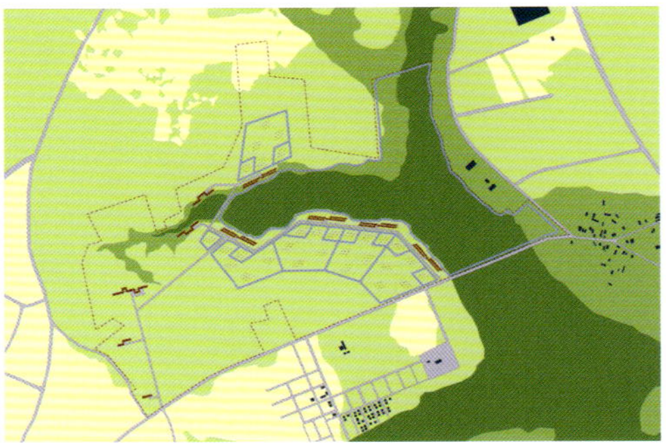

The task was to plan a new orangutan care and research center on Borneo for the Max-Planck-Institute, Leipzig. This center takes care of young orangutans that have lost their mothers as a result of illegal deforestation and poaching. The arriving apes are helpless, often traumatized, ill and undernourished. They need intensive medical care and supervision in order to survive and to function in nature. The aim is to plan an environment as close as possible to the native habitat of the orangutans, and to create ideal conditions for keepers and scientists to work with the apes. Indigenous materials, simple constructions and natural cooling are used exclusively for all buildings to achieve a reasonable and sustainable planning. All buildings are made of bamboo because of its great sustainability, low cost, and its great suitability for building in the tropics. There should be only little use of other materials. A type of housing with variable length and optimal adjustment to the climatic conditions has been planned. Its construction with pre-fabricated frames prevents faults, and native workers can easily carry out the building. Each year, about 50 orangutans arrive at the center. At first they stay in the young animals' houses, later they live in cage enclosures, as it is not possible to attend to them exclusively in outdoor enclosures. Because of illegal deforestation, it will not be possible to return the orangutans back to the wild in the future. Therefore it will be necessary to increase the number of cage enclosures. Depending on their age and gender, the orangutans live in different groups. The construction of the cage enclosure is based on a grid and so it permits great variability and different sizes. Each cage has three outdoor enclosures: two smaller single enclosures for the males and one for the females and young apes.

Uranutang housing

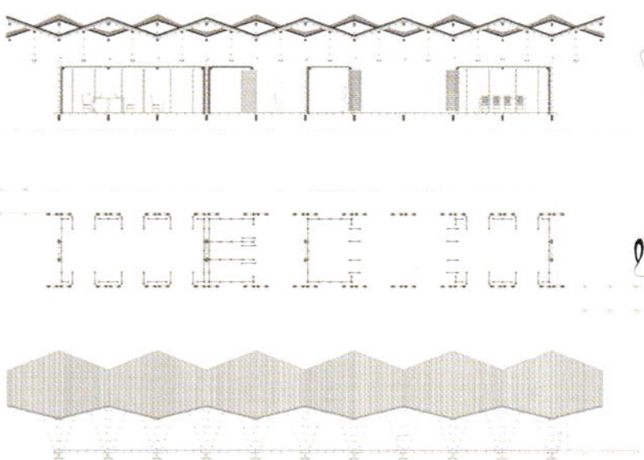

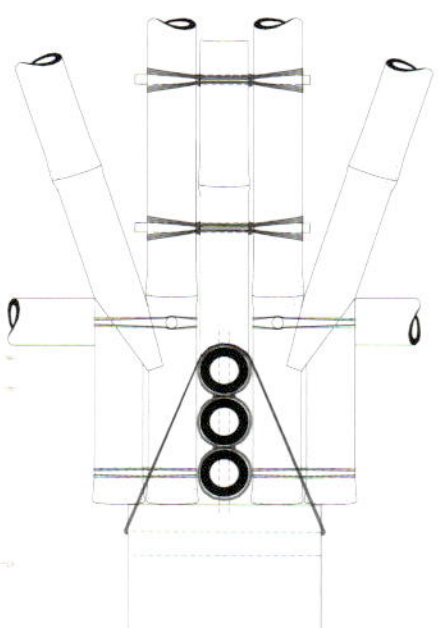

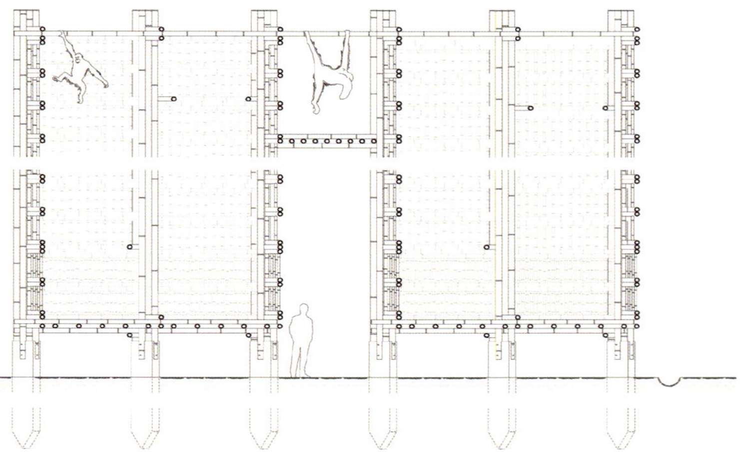

Sections and detail

Vilja Larjosto EUROPE - FINLAND - ESPOO

Urban Agriculture for Vila Brandão

SALVADOR, BRAZIL

DISCIPLINE(S): URBAN DESIGN, LANDSCAPE DESIGN / TUTOR: PROF. JYRKI SINKKILÄ, LANDSCAPE ARCHITECTURE
AALTO UNIVERSITY, SCHOOL OF SCIENCE AND TECHNOLOGY, DEPARTMENT OF ARCHITECTURE/LANDSCAPE ARCHITECTURE

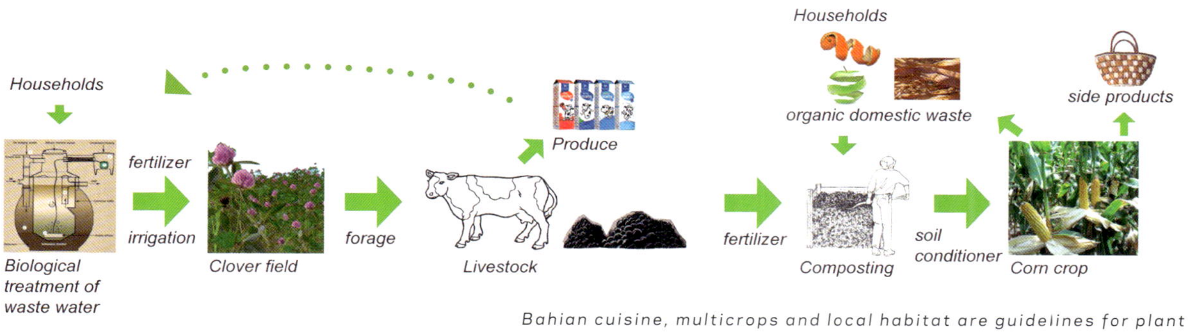

Bahian cuisine, multicrops and local habitat are guidelines for plant selection

The subject of my Master's Degree thesis is urban and peri-urban agriculture (UPA), including food production, processing and marketing in urban areas. The food crisis, along with social and environmental problems caused by rapid urban growth, makes UPA topical. Focusing on Latin America and Brazil, the thesis is divided into two parts. The first part is a literary study on urban and peri-urban agriculture. Today the growth of UPA has two main motives. In the north, appreciation of local organic food is growing and the development of world food production is necessary for the survival of poor urban dwellers. The thesis points out the importance of including UPA in environmentally and socially sustainable urban planning. The second part of the thesis is an urban horticultural proposal for Vila Brandão, a squatter settlement in Salvador da Bahia, Brazil. The plan is based on information about urban and ecological cultivation practices in tropical climates, as well as observations in Salvador including field visits to urban agriculture initiatives. Vila Brandão has approximately 300 inhabitants and it is located in the heart of a wealthy and dense neighborhood. The 60-year old squatter settlement is threatened by land speculation and the urban horticultural plan aims to strengthen its position. Vila Brandão is located by the sea and surrounded by 2 hectares of unused slopes. The steepest areas are cultivated as multi-species agroforestry. Approximately half of the planning area is less than 1:2 slope, which is shaped into terrace cultivation to control erosion. The selection of plant species is based on the local climate and diet. Ecological cultivation practices like multicropping and composting have been introduced. The urban horticultural area joins the urban fabric above the slopes through a public square with a sea view and a stall for commercializing the products.

Urban agriculture promotes environmental benefits and social integration

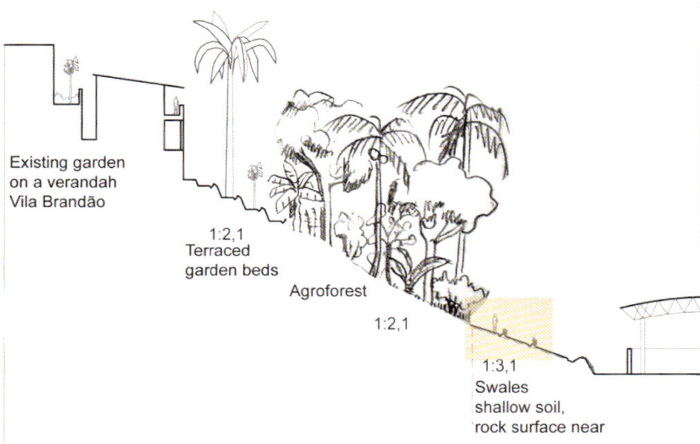

Agroforest and terracing: edible vegetation controls erosion on slopes over 1:2

Extra large

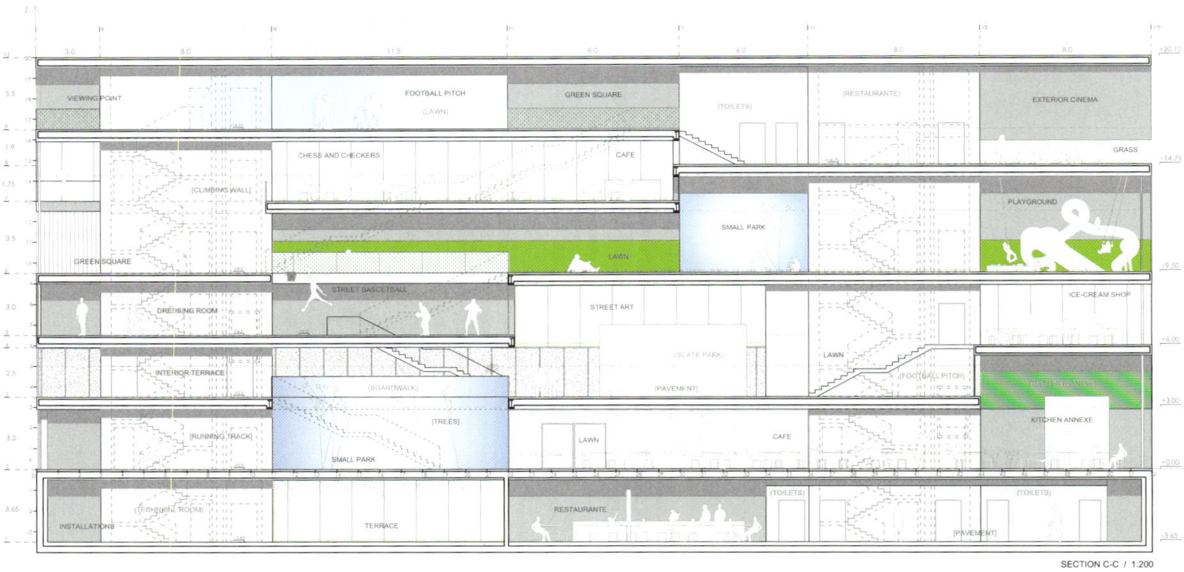
VIEWING POINT
FOOTBALL PITCH
GREEN SQUARE
EXTERIOR CINEMA
CHESS AND CHECKERS
CAFE
GRASS
PLAYGROUND
SMALL PARK
GREEN SQUARE
LAWN
STREET BASCETBALL
ICE-CREAM SHOP
DRESSING ROOM
STREET ART
INTERIOR TERRACE
LAWN
RUNNING TRACK
KITCHEN ANNEXE
SMALL PARK
CAFE
INSTALLATIONS
TERRACE
RESTAURANTE
SECTION C-C / 1:200

SECTION B-B / 1:200

Maciej Siuda EUROPE - POLAND WROCLAW

XYZ Structure

A CONCEPT FOR OVERPOPULATED CITIES, PROVIDING VARIOUS PUBLIC FUNCTIONS

DISCIPLINE(S): ARCHITECTURE / TUTOR: ADA KWIATKOWSKA / **WROCLAW UNIVERSITY OF TECHNOLOGY**, FACULTY OF ARCHITECTURE
PARTICIPANTS FAVORITE: 14 VOTES + NOMINATED

The XYZ dimensional structure is a system to design a building in the most crowded parts of densely populated cities that are deprived of public, green and people-friendly places. It can be built on any location, where the small size of the plot doesn't allow a large public square, a backyard, or a playground for kids. It is a multifunctional independent structure, which facilitates various public functions, such as cafés, restaurants, ice-cream shops, backyards, small football pitches or basketball courts, streets, footpaths, green squares, lawns or parks. An applied system of working with only one element and various incisions in different places allows us to devote every part to an independent function and, at the same time, obtain changeable sections. The result is not only an interesting architectural form, full of spaces of different proportions, measurements, heights, lengths or widths, with different quantities of light and shadow, but also something which seems to be impossible - an open and common public space, despite being limited by walls and ceilings. On the one hand, the various sections and gaps formed between stores combine them visually and, on the other, they allow all the sounds and scents to flow freely through the interior, so that one can hear the sound of children playing in playgrounds, or a ball bouncing on a basketball court in every part of the building. It can be built to every scale and size, from a small architectural intervention or house-size form to a skyscraper. It is a concept, a system, a way of thinking about architecture in extremely dense districts rather than a finished solution. The scale is less important than the concept, the space and the architecture itself.

Medium

Small

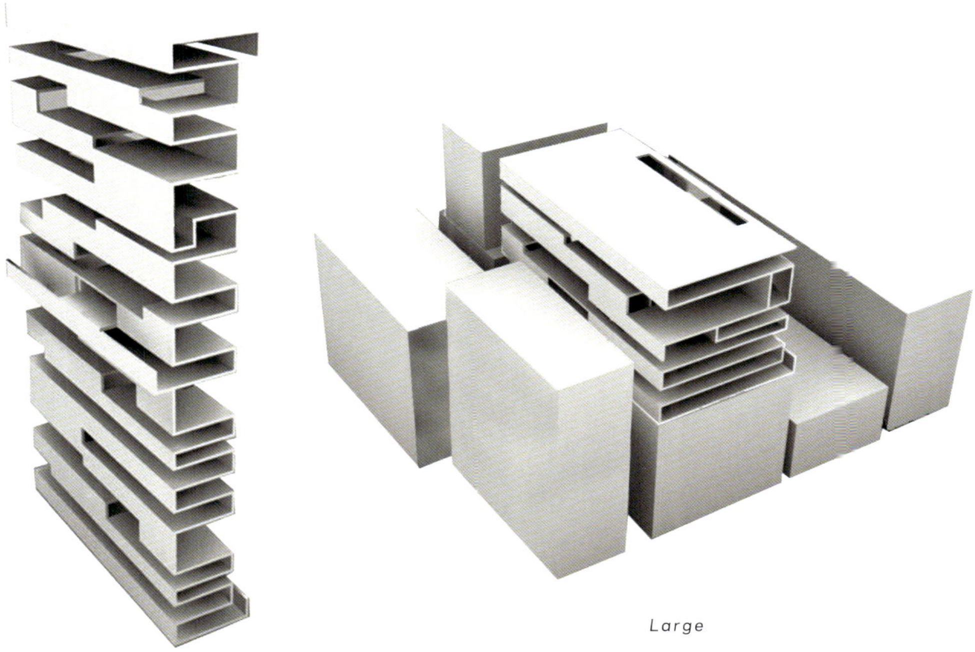

Large

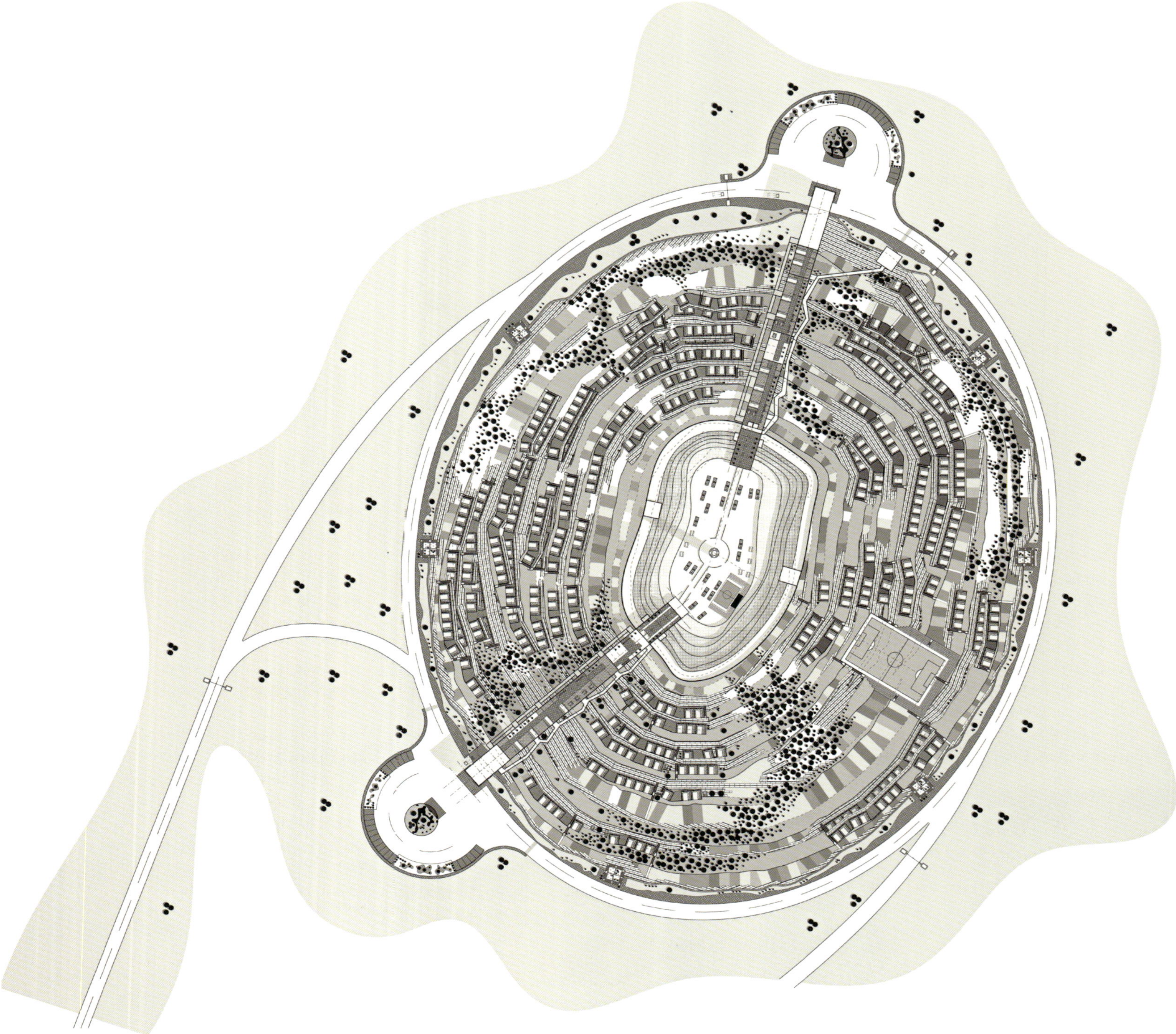

Special regime penal colony

Kristina Ishkhanova **EUROPE - RUSSIA MOSCOW**

Penal (penitentiary) **Institution**

THE PRISONER INCARCERATED IN THE MINE GETS THE OPPORTUNITY TO IMPROVE HIMSELF AND MOVES UPWARD TO REGAIN HIS FREEDOM

DISCIPLINE(S): ARCHITECTURE / TUTORS: PROFESSOR OSCAR R. MAMLEEV, ASSOCIATE PROFESSOR PAVEL V. ROMANOV
MOSCOU ARCHITECTURAL INSTITUTE STATE ACADEMY / PARTICIPANTS FAVORITE: 10 VOTES + NOMINATED

Figuratively speaking, a person who commits a crime "has fallen". By locating a penitentiary institute in an opencast mine, the process of improving the lawbreaker can easily be imagined. Incarcerated in the mine, the convict can come to terms with his mistakes and improve himself with the aim of moving upstairs to regain his freedom. The special-regime penal colony is located at the bottom of the mine. With good behavior and by complying with all demands, after 2/3 of the prison term, the prisoner is moved to the colony situated on the upper levels. This kind of system should stimulate improvement. The prisoners in penal colonies are engaged in a process of rehabilitation, which is based on a 4-stage system. First three stages are located in the special-regime penal colony, where single-person cells are situated. An enlargement of the narrow windows allows more light into the cells where the prisoners are held most of the day. 1st stage: the prisoner remains in the cell for 23 hours a day, food and books from the library are brought to the cell. 2nd stage: meals are taken in the dining room, there is education in classes, and literature reading. 3rd stage: same as the 2nd, plus socially necessary work, which can be paid; there are also sports. The 4th stage is the colony where the prisoners are free to live in their own separate condominiums, and are occupied with gardening, providing food to the institute and helping to serve the colony, as well as learning new professions. Thus, the prisoner arrives at the colony as a destroyer, but he gets an opportunity to learn to create, starting with theory and moving on to practice. After his release, the prisoner can begin a new life full of creation.

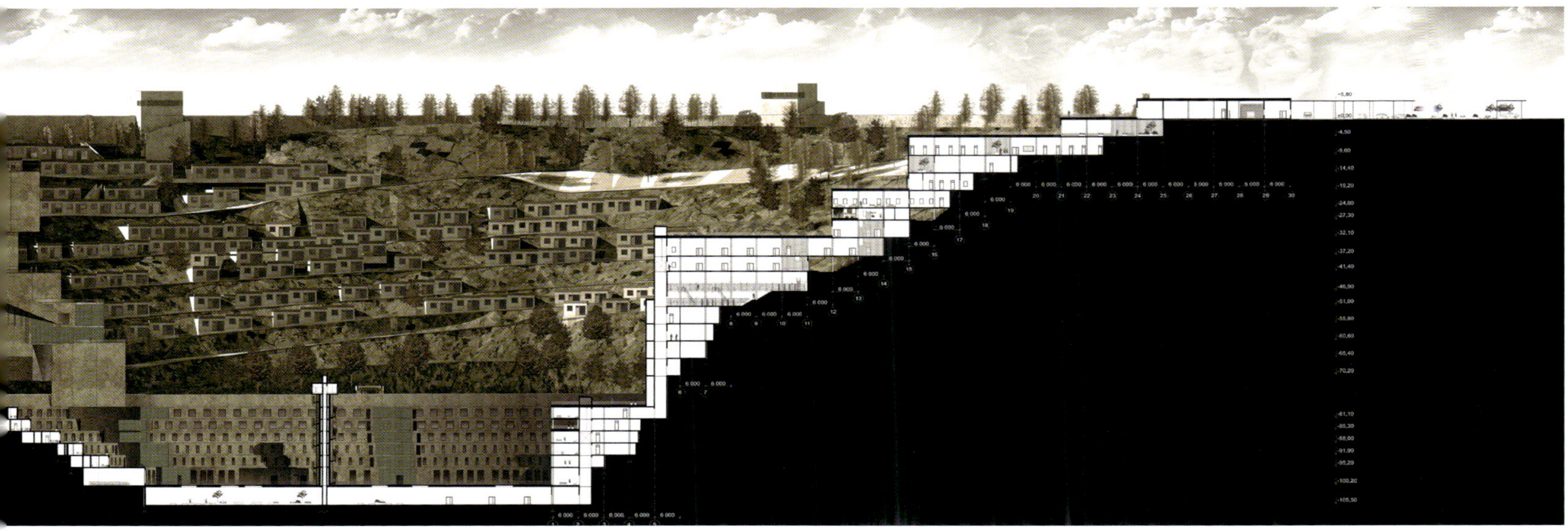

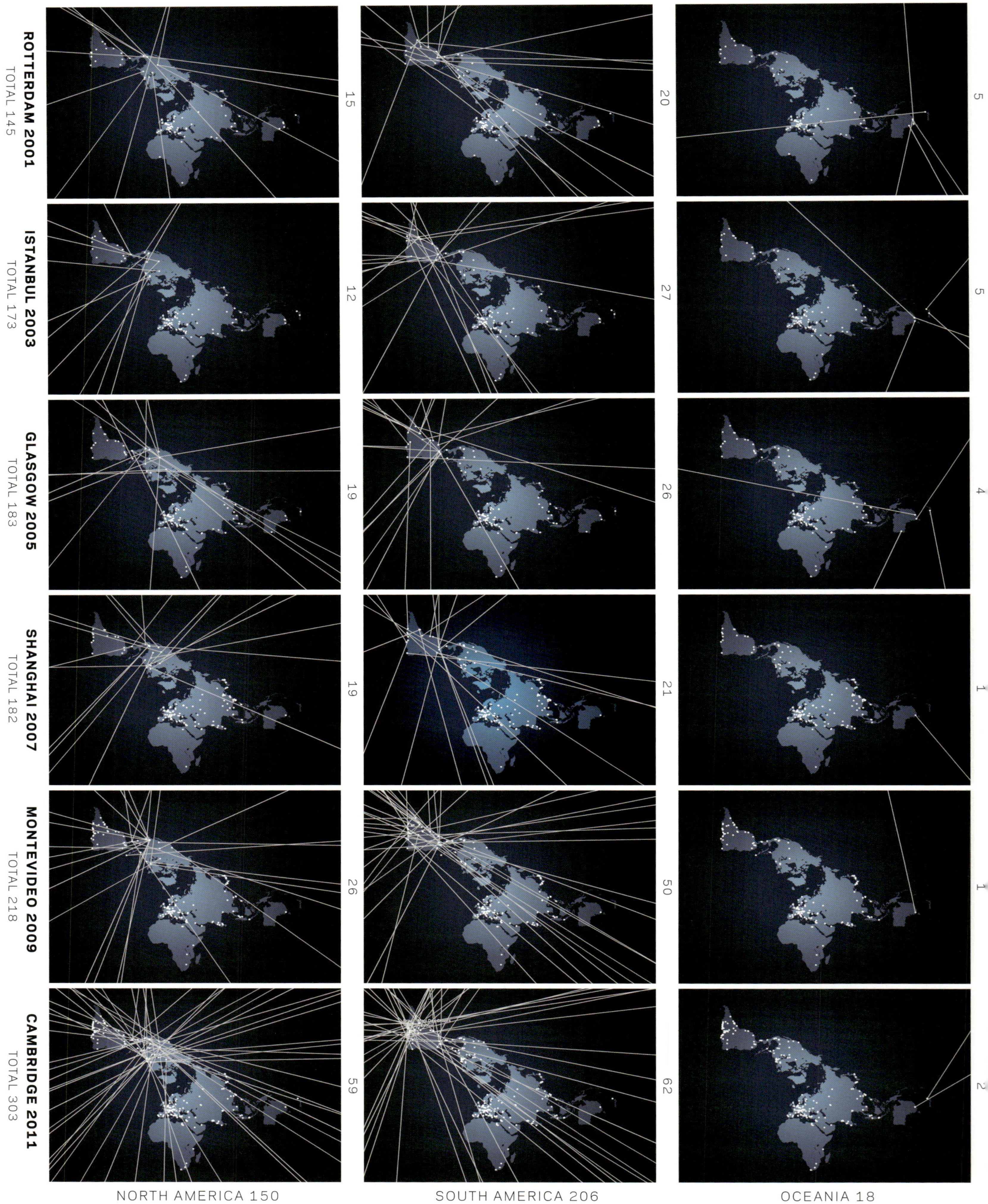
ROTTERDAM 2001
TOTAL 145
15
20
5
ISTANBUL 2003
TOTAL 173
12
27
5
GLASGOW 2005
TOTAL 183
19
26
4
SHANGHAI 2007
TOTAL 182
19
21
1
MONTEVIDEO 2009
TOTAL 218
26
50
1
CAMBRIDGE 2011
TOTAL 303
59
62
2
NORTH AMERICA 150
SOUTH AMERICA 206
OCEANIA 18

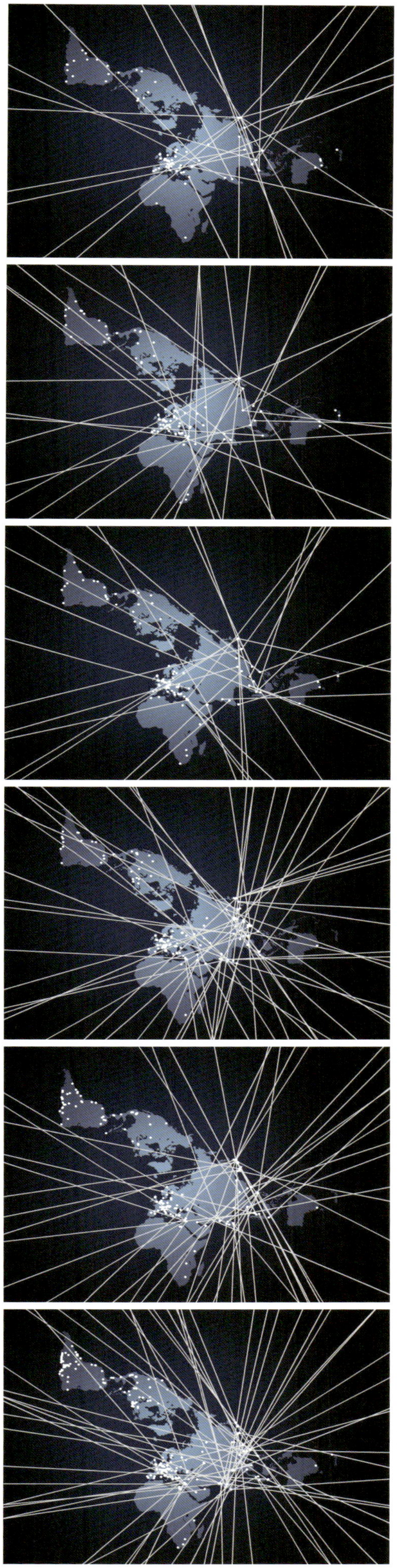

26
37
33
63
52
65

ASIA 276

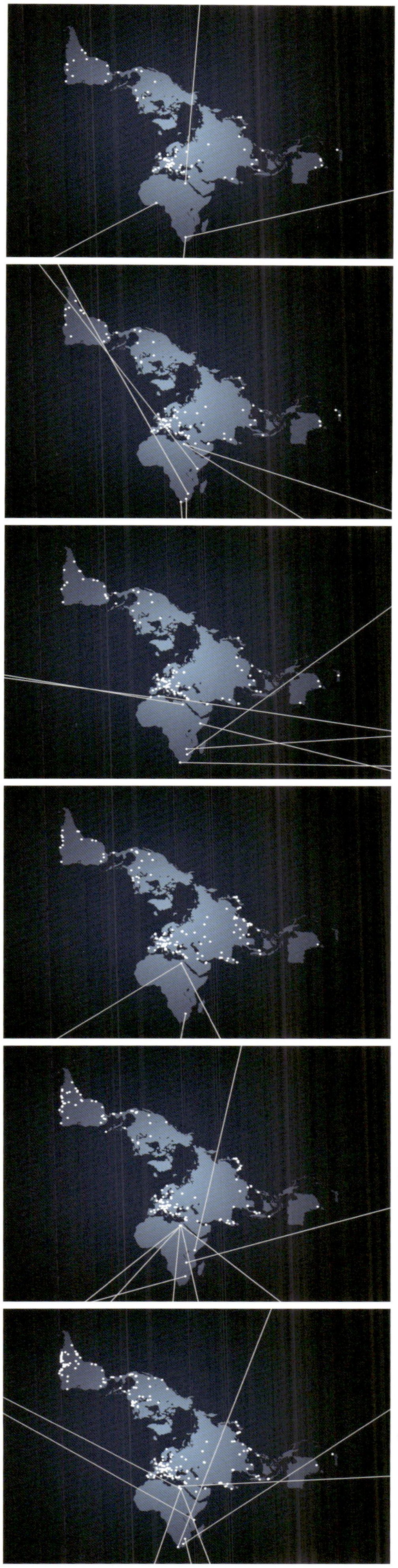

4
6
7
3
8
8

AFRIKA 36

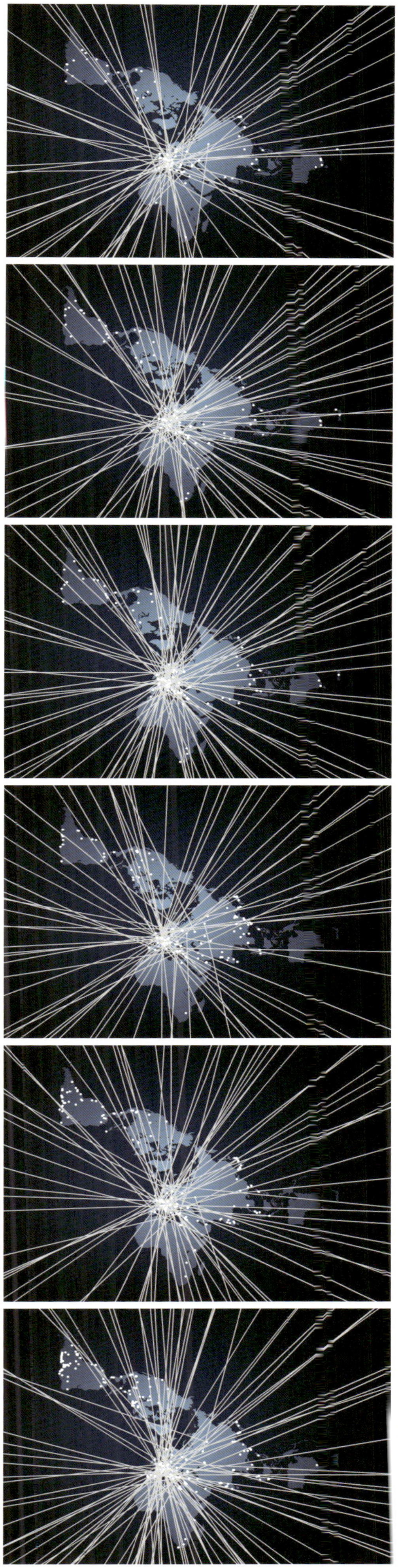

75
86
94
75
81
107

EUROPE 518

1. WHY I WANT TO BE AN ARCHITECT / 2. FAVORITE ARCHITECT / 3. FAVORITE BOOK OR MOVIE / 4. WHAT I AM DOING NOW

Ronald Bongers 1.To stimulate people to become aware of the specific context. I strive for subjective approach to concept and design, seeking alternative interpretations of modernism. The context and its conditions of the architecture are of profound importance to this thinking in addition to cultural and social concerns. 2. Alvaro Siza (B. Matosinhos, Portugal 1933) His architecture can communicate to us an extraordinary sense of freedom and freshness. 3. My favorite movie is Koyaanisqatsi: Life out of Balance - 1982 (directed by Godfrey Reggio with music composed by Philip Glass and cinematography by Ron Fricke). 4. At this moment I work as an architect at an office in Breda (Netherlands).

Nelleke Karst 1. I don't think architecture can change society, but I do believe that architecture can attribute, by creating circumstances. How do we move, what do we see, what do we do? 4. I Work as an architect/ interior architect at the Dutch design firm Aequo. [www.aequo.nl] Besides this, I teach some spatial courses, at the art academy and academy of architecture in Groningen.

José A. Gallardo del Castillo
2. Tadao Ando,
Santiago Calatrava /
4. working in a particular way, traveling

Yoshikazu Tanaka 1. Because I wanted to design my room. 2. Kengo Kuma and Zaha Hadid 3. The Night of the Milky Way Train, Kenji Miyazawa 4. Internship in Architect Office

Sarosh Mulla 1. Because I think the spaces we live in can make a positive contribution to the way we live and can create tangible changes in our quality of life as a global society. I have always known I wanted to be an architect. My parents have science and engineering backgrounds, but for most of my childhood they worked restoring sculpture in a space adjoining our home. As a result I began to appreciate design and craftsmanship as a child and wanted to be part of the creative process. I was fortunate to also have many teachers through school that exposed me to the design process, metal work, carpentry, poetry and painting alongside my interest in chemistry and physics. I have always loved the variety and challenges posed by architecture. I hope to one day be able to use architecture to make a substantial difference to people's lives. 2. Tom Kundig and Louis Kahn 3. The Godfather 4. I am currently practicing architecture at a medium size commercial firm during the day and at night I run my own studio which focuses on experimental architecture for public events.

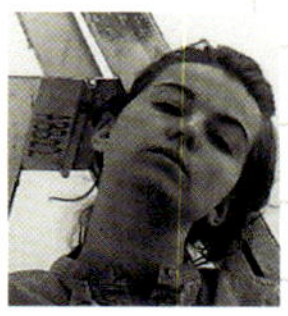

Guro Alver 1. to be able to add a structure/contribution/element/ material to a context, and with that change the way the context is understood/seen and used, and in the same time create a new context/ situation that is open for new addons/contribution/new use in the future. 4. working as a teacher 3 at Bergen School of Architecture, and working in a planning firm.

Nikita Kolbovskiy 1. An architect? I want to be a cosmonaut! 2. Aleksander Brodsky, Oscar Niemeyer

Roland Lipusz 1. to create Harmony in a disharmonic world...3. The Hitchhiker's Guide to the Galaxy 4. working as an architect in Denmark

Teimuraz Ninua 1. I'd like to be among the people , who, regarding to profession, creates an easthetic environment. 2. Emilio Ambasz 3. Gabriel García Márquez. "One Hundred Years of Solitude". 4. I'm a second year student of Master Program at The Faculty of Architecture, Urban Planning and Design, Georgian Technical University.

Paulo Plass Alvarez 1. I always wanted to be I never imagined doing anything else. 2. It's hard to choose just one, I like: Campos Baeza, Rem Koolhaas, Kazuyo Sejima, Jorge Elton, BIG. There are many more, but I remember these now. 3. I'm bad for reading, from the movies: Instinct is my favorite of the series LOST and I am a big fan of the Simpsons.4. Trabajo de forma independiente, realizando concursos y proyectos para privados.

James Richardson 3. Book: Twilight of the Idols by Friederich Nietzsche. Movie: Waking Life.

Laura Charlton 1. As a designer, my goals are to participate in the discussion and innovative design of the built urban landscape. I'm specifically interested in the blurring of lines between architecture, ecology and infrastructure, and this theme continues to be present in my professional work. 2. Many architects and designers have shaped my thinking over the years, including Peter Zumthor, Luis Barragan, and Pierre Chareau. 3. Books: Pale Fire, In the Labyrinth. Movie: Days of Heaven, The Life Aquatic 4. Upon graduation with a Masters of Architecture from Columbia University GSAPP, I relocated to San Francisco. I am currently practicing architecture with a local firm that specializes in museums and aquariums.

Annie Kurtin 1. Architecture touches people's lives in innumerable ways, everyday. Our behaviors, the way we experience space and our surroundings have a direct connection to the built environment. I am passionate about being involved in this conversation, in the translation from ephemeral concept to physical expression. I want to be an architect and have a voice in the way we interact with the world around us, thus producing new opportunities and moments for revelation, contemplation and inspiration. 2. I admire the work of so many practitioners and thinkers. A few of them include: Glenn Murcutt, Field Operations, Noero Wolff, Tadao Ando, SANAA, and Louis Kahn. 3. Anna Karenina by Leo Tolstoy is my favorite book. A few others include essays by Joan Didion, Lolita by Vladimir Nabokov, and Of Human Bondage by W. Somerset Maughm. Favorite films include The Royal Tenenbaums by Wes Anderson, Love Story, Badlands, Silent Light by Carlos Reygadas. 4. I just relocated to Tucson, Arizona from New York City where I had been living for 8 years. I am currently teaching in the School of Architecture at the University of Arizona.

Fabrizio Furiassi 2. Mies Van Der Rohe, Rem Koolhaas/OMA, Kazuyo Sejima & Ryue Nishizawa, SANAA, Toyo Ito, Renzo Piano, Steven Holl, Zaha Hadid, Herzog & De Meuron, Ben Van Berkel & Caroline Bos/UNSTUDIO, Winy Maas/MVRDV, Bjorke Ingles/BIG, Hitoshi Abe, Junya Ishigami 3. S,M,L,XL / Forrest Gump 4. Travelling from Shanghai Expo to Venice Biennale

Michael K Leung
2. Peter Zumthor, Renzo Piano, UN Studio, Diller+Scofidio, Office Da, Reiser+Umemoto

Natalia Bartolomeo 1. i can't stop creating spaces 2. Lina Bo Bardi, Eladio Dieste, Afonso Reidy, Paulo Mendes, koolhaas, Le Corbusier... 4. A small public school of literature, with space for shows on weekends, very close to the MUSIC SQUARE (100 meters), a reform of a small apartment in Botafogo and working in the studio "Progetto" (www.progetto.arq.br). I'm working 16 hrs a day!!!

Kristína Martoníková
1. because... ...I´m architect ...I was ...and I always will ...that´s my nature :) 2. Mies van der Rohe | Tadao Ando 3. ...many books about architecture...but I don´t have only one special...I love all of them 4. I´m working for CEPM and studying for the graduate degree at the Slovak University of Technology

Mauricio Mendez Wiesner
2. Rem Koolhaas, OMA / Herzog & de Meuron 3. Chronicles, Volume 1 by Bob Dylan 4. Working at Daniel Bonilla Arquitectos

Marlene Wagner 4. building a community centre in magagula heights with our own NPO build-Collective. check out www.build-Collective.net

Kim Jungmin 1. Just I like it. It's not nature. But I will change better than bad environment. Environment have urban, society, human, build, and so on.Finally, I am doing architecture for our country & education & identity. 2. Peter Zumthor, MVRDV, NL'Architects 3. Books, Le citta invisibili, Les Oiseaux vont mourir au P rou, Ornament and Crime, (Architectural symbols of the reason), Movies: TaeGukGi: Brotherhood Of War, Transformer, P.S. I love you, One piece Animantions 4. Other projects. Never Ending _ Dream

1. WHY I WANT TO BE AN ARCHITECT / 2. FAVORITE ARCHITECT / 3. FAVORITE BOOK OR MOVIE / 4. WHAT I AM DOING NOW

Gustavo 'LeSclamb' Vilches 1. 'The world is not good if it's not good to everyone.' That phrase was written in a card I've received as a kid, and as utopian as it is, got stuck in my brain ever since. I've been lucky enough to travel over 35 countries, working in all sort of jobs and places, and during that time I came to learn in the skin that the human dilemmas and aspirations are the same all over the planet. Regardless of religion, language or history.I've decided to work for those human aspirations ever since. To directly engage in the development of tools, systems and new 'ways of living' that will effectively improve the life of communities in times to come. I prefer to see this from a global perspective, that is to say, completely regardless of the land where I can perform my work, since people in China, USA, Germany or Chile share the same challenges. 2. I can think of too many to list (old and contemporary) But here's a clue:The common factor on Architects I admire is certainly not a style, because there's no style over another. The reason why I admire an architect (And even more deeply, a collective of architects) is their capacity to be consequent. The will to define a line of search and stick to it, finding new answers in every project. Coop Himmelb(l)au, Tadao Ando, Zaha Hadid, Renzo Piano, Hundertwasser, Gaudi... just to randomly name some of the best. 3. "The Taiko" by Eiji Yoshikawa for the long days. "Le Petit Prince" by Antoine de Saint-Exupéry for the short days and "Papelucho" by Marcela Paz for every day 4. Working and living in Munich, researching about a possible MSc or investigation program, I'm thinking about maybe coming back to school.

Ada Kołodziejczyk 1. I want to be an architect and landscape architect to create the space where people can feel good and pleased.2. Le Corbusier (Charles-Édouard Jeanneret-Gris), Antonio Gaudí (Antoni Plàcid Guillem i Cornet) 3. Under the dome by Stephen Edwin King/ Corpse Bride by Tim Burton and Mike Johnson 4. Now I am working as an architect assistant in a small privat company

---

Alissa Bankovskaya 1. There is an opinion that the form influences contents also as well as contents influence the form. For me the architecture is that form which influences people, cooperating with them. For this reason I want to be the architect to bear to people the harmony embodied in architecture. 2. Santiago Calatrava 3. "The master and Margarita" Michael Bulgakov 4. Now I'm creating my life's base founded on knowledge, experience and statement of the purposes.

Nicholas Adam Szczepaniak1. My motivation comes from the ability to capture peoples imagination and allow them to experience a piece of work whether it's a drawing, piece of text, building or installation in a unique way. Architecture allows me to draw/ design/ think about places, spaces, devices, systems, procedures, materials, furniture, light fittings, door handles, door hinges - everything from the macro to the micro. It has the ability to delight, provoke and most importantly inspire people. 2. I find it very difficult to name a single architect as my favourite architect. There are aspects of many architects that inspire me. I love the tectonics of Richard Rogers Buildings and his attitude towards creating public space. In particular The Pompidou Centre in Paris and The Lloyds Building in London. Buildings which are machnic or expose there working parts excite me. OMA for their bold, uncompromising form and politically/ socially charged projects. The early work of Zaha and her use of speculative drawing to generate concepts and inform the execution of an architectural spectacle. 3. Manufactured Landscapes by Edward Burtynsky, His work has the ability to take scenes that are often considered ugly and worthless by most and then shoot them in a way, which seduces the viewer and really provokes them to think in new ways. Appliance House by Ben Nicholson. Here I enjoy his drawing practice as a tool for finding out about ideas, places and spaces as well as it being a prescribed method for describing them. 4. I'm currently working for a small firm of architects in London who specialize in environmentally friendly residential projects. After work hours I am undertaking freelance work in Malaysia designing flat Interiors for a new development in Kuala Lumpur. I am also a founding member of the experimental architecture collaborative called E.R.I.C based in London where we produce speculative works and have recently completed an installation titled a 'House for Sue Real' at the Barbican Centre in London. Other freelance work has included producing a concept design for the 'Cloudscape' pavilion at the Venice Biennale 2010.

Samuel Bernier-Lavigne 4. PhD in architecture. Working for UNStudio, in Amsterdam. (Sept'10)

Melanie Hammer 1. I want to be an architect to add value to planning and building of all kinds of architecture that serve society and people.4. freelancer **Waschma Sahin** 4. freelancer

---

Bagriy Ksenia Ya 1. I want to be an architect because it is a wonderful profession and I can't imagine my life without it 2. Daniel Libeskind, Norman Foster, Alexander Asadov 3. Doctor Zhivago by Boris Pasternak 4. I'm working in the architectural studio "Griff" in Vladikavkaz

---

Damien Antoni 1. To understand both science and art 2. Jose Plecnik 3. Pi, Darren Aronofsky 4. www.smallinfrastructures.blogspot.com

---

Willem Steenkamp1. I love the challenge of solving design problems and improving lives through architecture, especially in a country where a large part of the population is "homeless". 2. Will Bruder, Renzo Piano, Glenn Murcutt 3. Little Prince, Nacho Libre, Big Fish 4. I am currently living and working in Windhoek; Namibia doing architecture throughout Southern Africa.

Loc Huu Pham 1. At the beginning, I think it's just for fun. At the moment, I think it's just for money. In the future, I think it's just for fun again. 2. Tadao Ando, Frank Lloyd Wright, Toyo Ito. 3. The World Is Flat. 4. Professor Assistant.

Maria Luisa Pineda 1. I wanted to be an architect because architects can transform the world and make it beautiful. 2. Frank Gehry, Zaha Hadid, Tadao Ando, Luis Barragán 3. Brave New World 4. I'm a full time teacher at Universidad Peruana de Ciencias Aplicadas and also have my studio.

Marcus Calhoun 1. I want to be an architect so I can design affordable, sustainable architecture to improve the quality of life for all people. 2. Cameron Sinclair 3. Ten Commandments for the Environment: Pope Benedict XVI Speaks Out for Creation and Justice/Julie and Julia 4. I am currently serving as an AmeriCorps VISTA at YouthBuild Providence. I have developed the curriculum for an affordable home design project among other capacity building efforts for the program. **Laura Thomas** 1. To have my ideas and concepts realized in the physical world. 2. Richard Meier 3. The Holy Bible | Inception 4. I am currently an Intern Architect at Barron Heinberg & Brocato Architects and Engineers. **Craig Jirak** 1. To have a circuitous, impact on peoples lives. 2. Alvar Aalto / Kevin Stevens 3. Of Mice and Men / Band of Brothers **Lance Mathews** 1. I've wanted to become an architect since I was a child but now it is for different reasons, I want to be responsible for improving inhabiters quality of life and bringing social justice to people through architecture 2. One of my favorite architects is Eero Saarinen because to me he was ahead of his time with some of his organic and abstract building types; he had faith in his work and pushed the profession to new levels. 3. My favorite book is Atmospheres by Peter Zumthor. 4. Currently I 'am working for a small firm in Staten Island, designing in many different areas of the profession.

Paulius Vaitiekunas 2. Bernard Khoury, Paisajes Emergentes, Darius Ciuta, OMA. 3. A Clockwork Orange. 4. Working for 'Dvieju Grupe' in Kaunas, LT.

Haosheng Zhang 1. To provide a better choice for other people and expand the boundary of beauty. 2. Kengo Kuma, Peter Zumthor 3. Thinking Architecture Peter Zumthor) 4. Enrich my knowledge in order to receive higher education abroad.

Maria Yandulova 1. Because I want to make the world more beautiful 2. Calatrava 3. Baraka 4. working in Italy

---

Manuel Felipe Woodcock 1. Because living architecture makes me happy, because studying architecture makes me happy, because doing architecture make me happy. Because I feel that making architecture is the way that I can contribute more to my society and grow up as a person. 2. Rogelio Salmona, Peter Zumthor, Alvar Aalto. 3. The Story of Art, E. Gombrich. The modulor, leCorbusier. The Seven Spiritual Laws, D.Chopra. 4. Studying Master in architecture and working as assistant in the university.

Edgar Nonato Mr Cusi 1. Even in my childhood, I have shown much interest in creating things graphically. This skill was fostered by my Mother who taught me the basics of drawing, and by my late Father who inspired me in understanding how those tall, giant buildings were built. My family as whole helped me be more sensitive to the situation of the people around me and how helping the unfortunate is an advocacy that we should all work for. These and many other life experiences have given me the dream of building good, strong homes for families, complexes that would feature the diversity and rich culture of my country, and most of all, architectural designs that carry on the legacy and vision of my father who is also my mentor. 2. In addition to my late Father who mentored me in architectural designs, the following people have also inspired my work: 1 - Jose Maria V. Zaragoza (Author of "Architect for God and Man", designed many of the Philippines' landmark Churches) 2 - Francisco Manosa (Designed the famous Coconut Palace of the Philippines) 3. In highschool, we were asked to read Pilipino Writer Stevan Javellana's only novel in English "Without Seeing the Dawn" as part of our summer book list. It has become my most favorite novel.The book has two main sections, Day and Night. "Day" tells the story of a pre-war town and its people, illustrating their colorful traditions and simple ways of life. "Night" begins with the start of World War II in both the U.S. and the Philippines. It retells the story of the resistance movement against the occupying Japanese military forces of the same barrio people. It narrates the people's grim experiences during the war" and how their strength of will and faith helped them survive. 4. I worked as a Junior designer at Newtrends International Corporation at Makati, Philippines. Since my Father's passing last June 2010, I have chosen to focus on helping with our family business. I specifically manage the construction for our small commercial building. I am also currently preparing for the Architectural Board Exams.

Gergely Szacsvay 2. Eduardo Souto de Moura, Gion Antoni Caminada 3. Pierre Boulle: The Bridge On The River Kwai, Géza Ottlik: School at the Frontier, Brian G. Hutton: Kelly's Heroes

Aya Fujimoto 1. Recently, buildings are cruelty. I think that it is dangerous for future. I'd like to design a space where the atmosphere says everything,and tell him/her it's a space for you. I'm glad if many people feel something good from the space I proposed.2. Alvar Aalto, Yoshio Taniguchi 3. "Kamome Shokudo(Dining room)"It's a Japanese movie.But It's made in Finland. They teach me something good. 4. I'm a student of graduate school.Now, I'm working for Internship in Paris.

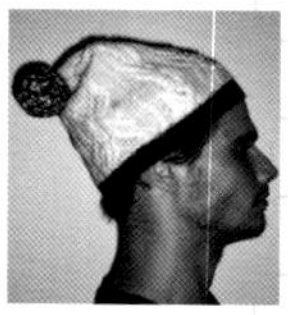

Coll Swann 1. Change my way of life. 2. International: Daniel Libeskind, O.M.A, B.I.G R.C.R arquitectos, M.V.R.D.V, Michel Desvignes (landscape); National: Portzamparc (Open blocks), Ricciotti, Corajoud (landscape) Regional (Languedoc-Roussillon), Pierre Tourre, N+B, Lauriol 3. movie: "Le Mèpris" de Jean-Luc Godard, book: "Cent ans de Solitude" de Gabriel Garcia Marquez 4. I'm searching agencies to make my HMONP.

Timothee Boitouzet 1. To build a house for my mum 2. Toyo Ito, SANAA, Tokujin Yoshioka 3. Eternal Sunshine of the Spotless Mind 4. Student at Harvard University School of Design, MArch II Program

Anna Plekhanova 1. it is the way to make life better 2. Zaha Hadid architects, MVRDV, Eisenman, Kas Oosterhuis... 3. Gabriel Garcia Marquez - One Hundred Years Of Solitude 4. I'am an architector at the architecture studio in my city

Gerrell Wilson 1. I love good living environment and would like to be one part that helps making that. 2. Zaha Hadid Architects 3. Spirited away 4. Working with Skidmore, Owings and Merrill LLP in San Francisco, USA.

Linde Van Reeth1. I want to make a valuable contribution to the cities' layout and landscape on a large and small scale. 3. book: Kafka on the shore, Haruki Murakami. movie: Bin Jip, Kim Ki Duk, Clockwork Orange, Stanley Kubrick 4. working for Edouard François, Paris, France

José Vidalón 2. Cedric Price + Manuel Piqueras Cotolí 3. Travels in Hyperreality by Umberto Eco The Nature of the Universe by Lucretius 4. Working @ Diller Scofidio + Renfro

André C. B. Soares 1. To help contribute to the understanding of society and to express spacial possibilities that improve general life quality. 2. BIG - Bjarke Ingels Group has the most interesting design process that I'm familiar with. John Habraken because of its theories. 3. This is a relative matter - It depends of my mood. 4. I'm studying to get my masters degree and working at my own architecture firm, Umma Arquitetos.

Jimenez Fernandez-Palacios Luz 1. Because is what I dream to be. 2. Peter Zumthor, Mendes da Rocha, Souto de Moura, Siza Viera, Aires Mateus, Elias Torres 4. working in Lisbon with Aires Mateus

Huub Donkers 1. For me, architecture is like an opportunity. Creating conditions that affect and support everyday life. 2. Constructivism, Adolf Loos, Situationists, Richard Price, Smithsons, Steven Holl... 3. All our yesterdays, Natalia Ginzburg, 1952. Naked Lunch, Directed by David Cronenberg, 1991 4. Working at A2O architects, Hasselt, Belgium Collaborator of BRAT

Tatyana Khaissundinova 1. It is my chance to change the world for the better 2. N. Foster, F. Hundertwasser, S. Calatrava, Z. Hadid and of course L. Savina - thanx for supporting and inspiring me! 3. S.R. Covey "The 7 habits" 4. enjoying my new status - The Bachelor of Architecture

Daniella Molina 1. I believe in the harmony between Nature and Society that can be achieve through Architectural Spaces 2. Frank Lloyd Wright - Lois Kahn - Tadao Ando - Herzog & de Meuron - Frank Gehry - Alvaro Siza - Rafael Moneo 3. Gattaca - Pulp Fiction - Fight Club - Meet Joe Black. Books & magazines: El Croquis - the trial - The Metamorphosis, Franz kafka. 4. Architect & Designer at Espacio 154, Caracas - Venezuela

Andri Klausen 1. I believe in the power of creative design in creating beautiful environments that inspire everyone by acting as a frame for culture and society. 2. Barcelona is the home of my favorite architects, Antoni Gaudi and Enric Miralles - Benedetta Tagliabue 3. The Motorcycle Diaries 4. Currently I am working as a 3D designer at RAA NY.

Kristina Ishkhanova 1. I am an aesthete, that's why it's crucial for me that people should live in beauty. I dream them to want to leave in the environment that i'am creating. Atmosphere at whole, not just single part of the street is important for me. I want to create functional spaces, beauty and purity of solution is concentrated in the functionality. Architecture should be in harmony with the life of the city and people. 2. Tadao Ando, MVRDV, JDS Architects, BIG 3. book: Dostoyevskiy F. M. "The Brothers Karamazov". movie: "Gone With The Wind" directed by Victor Fleming. "The Godfather I, II, III" directed by Francis Ford Coppola. "The Pokrovsky Gate" directed by Mikhail Kozakov 4. Now I'm working in architectural bureau, studng English language, going in for sports, looking for an apportunity to obtain masters degree in Europe or in USA.

Nguyen Bao Thang 1. I love simple things, so I choose a complicated one, being an architect. 2. Buonarroti Michelangelo, Santiago Calatrava, Renzo Piano. 3. Books: Romance of Three Kingdom, God Father, Fountain Head. Movies: Minority Report, Wall-E, Up.

Jose Fernando Pérez Alcobé 2. Burle Marx landscape architect 4. project designer at NM+A, (Nestor Medina Architecture) project designer at Jardineros (landcape design).

Tim Nørlund Jensen 1. I want to be able to influence the future of our build environment, and do what little I can to push things in the right directing in terms of how we live on the planet. I think that architecture is the perfect combination of vision and reality as well as arts and crafts, and that makes it exciting, fulfilling and challenging work. 2. Foster+Partners, Grimshaw Architects, Tadao Ando, Herzog & de Meuron... 3. Movie: Inception 4. Working at my own practice, based in Denmark.

Rodrigo Mathias 4. working at gmp architekten - rio office http://www.gmp-architekten.de/ 2. Renzo Piano, Peter Zumthor, Tadoa Ando. Rem Koolhaas,Daniel Libeskind, Toyo Ito 4. I just graduated with a BArch, and I'm applying for a master's program

Christian Tonko 1. The moment of awareness that the struggle was somehow worth it is quite rewarding. 2. I prefer not to name someone in particular. 3. I prefer not to name something in particular. 4. Trying to get a building permit for a project in western Austria.

Mauricio Manning Zerón 1. because I like creating spaces to upgrade peoples lives 2. architect Luis Barragan Morfin 3. Lord of the Rings 4. working in a Construction Office dedicated to housing for low-income people

Maya-Maria Joannides 2. Frank Lloyd Wright, Paulo Mendes da Rocha, Shigeru Ban 4. Currently pursuing a Master of Science in Building Construction at the University of Florida and working as a teaching assistant.

Mohamed Fawzy Abdelkarim 1. "Firmness, Commodity & delight "by Vitruvius. Transferring those trios through architectural level becoming the main aim of an architect towards the society's architectural quality. This is the task for whom caring about his community future, an architect is one of the main players in the community who can navigate to a sustainable city. Firmness, which means the strength of the structure, commodity is the useful space the user can benefit from and eventually the word delight, which is the beauty of the architecture. One of the main challenges of an architect is to achieve the Vitruvius trios towards the society in a perfect manner. This objective is faced with further challenges, when it meets reality. The reality of designing where aesthetics appreciation is quite varied, and highly linked to contrasting economic and social factors. Appreciation of simple and true architecture, like that of Hassan Fathy's concept design, is met with Kitsch appeal and it becomes even more challenging to an architect to set out a design that blends into such a contrasting environment and providing almost free shelter for the poor.I think I got the motivate to help my environment to face political, environmental and economical challenges through architecture, delivering variable solutions to the surrounding community. 2. Imhotep, Hassan Fathy, Abdel Halim Ibrahim, Norman Foster, Jean Nouvel, Michael Graves, and many others........ 3. Book: Alchemist, Movies: Ocean 11 & 13,The Italian Job & Phone Booth, 45 Youm (EGYPTIAN) 4. Working in Engineering-Architecture firm, "DAR AL-HANDASAH" ......

Danielle Reimers 1. to make a positive change in our surroundings 2. too many to mention 3. Flatland by Edwin A. Abbott 4. working for RPBW

Rafael Alcantara 1. Architecture is my expression of art. 3. "Ten Little Niggers" by Agatha Christie / movies by David Lynch. 4. Growing.

Alena Vanshulina 1. I think that should try to make this world better those ways which are accessible to me. I find interest and necessity in any area of designing. 2. I find interesting ideas at different architects. 3. I prefer to read those books which I need at present lives for which I feel requirement and interest 4. I try to type more experience in that area in which I am engaged at present. My class now - town-planning and territorial planning.

Christian Garcia Arreguin 1. I want to be an architect to be able to design something from nothing, to get free my imagination and then be able to see it becoming real and that present and future generation get to live it. 2. Frank Lloyd Wright 3. The Phantom of the Opera 4. I am currently studying a Master Programme in Sustainable Architecture and Computer Aided Environmental Design at the Department of Architecture in the University of Sheffield in the UK.

Sigi Atteneder 1. because architecture in all its aspects meets best with my interests. I like the german term "gestaltung", which has no real equivalent in english, to describe the variety and power of thinking "architecturally". 2. no rankings - PLEASE! 3. see above! 4. work as research assistant at the university of art and design, linz, austria; prepare for my PhD

Luis Enrique Carrazana González 1. because architecture is all the surrounding physical environment of human life: I can not leave her while part of civilization. 2. Santiago Calatrava 3. Neufert, El Arte de Proyectar 4. I am pursuing a Master Title. · Restoration and Rehabilitation in buildings ".

Kang bok Wee 1. All people use buildings because of specific purposes. I want to be an architect considering people using every kind of building. 2. Peter D. Eisenman, Louis Kahn, Louis barragan 3. The Spiriting Away Of Sen And Chihiro 4. I am preparing jobinterview of architectural design office.

Emily Arden Wells 1. I love the process of making something out of nothing. 2. Le Corbusier Brodsky & Utkin 3. Titus. Amadeus..

Haonan LU 1. About fifteen years ago, I was really interested in how things are made and how do they work. Years later, after a very old doctor cured my serious fever by just one bottle of herb tea, I really lost in the philosophy of ancient Chinese medicine. It's interesting that the two kinds of thinking drove me to opposite directions. Sometimes I found it amazing to think systematically and mechanically. Here "systematical" means much more like "can not be divided at the very first beginning", it has structures but cannot be simply understood or analyzed. This contradictory way of thinking really helps when I meet some complicated problems. As for urban planning, it is not easy (impossible?) to analyze or calculate something very precisely. But it is really needed to penetrate into the way it works for improvement. It feels like struggling to the truth that may never get. But I have to say, I really like it when I'm on the way. 3. a one and a two 4. Running a small social investigation.

Vit Svoboda 1. I did not know what to do, I wanted to contribute reasonably to change the surroundings and architecture were among the few things that affects me and creating 2. Karel Prager , Melnikov , Lissitzky ,Jean Nouvel 3. subway art / style wars 4. love my girl and follow life

Gabriela Costa de Castro 2. Daniel Libeskind, Zaha Hadid 3. Cidade de Deus 4. After graduation I've worked for one and a half year with urbanization, especially with Rio de Janeiro slums. Now I'm working at SuperUber office.

Karen Matos 1. I chose to be an architect to realize my dreams. But I'm learning that the shelter needs of others building me myself. 2. Antonio Gaudi, B. Fuller. Frei Otto, Shigeru Ban, Cecil Balmond, Javier Senosain. 3. "The Power of limits", "Eupalinos o el Arquitecto"/ The fifth element. 4. I am researching in the area of light weight structures and proposing new technologies in sustainable materials like bamboo, for temporary shelter (the case of earthquakes) and extremely poor housing. **Roxana Garrido** 1. The power of been an architect made my ideas become reality and the best of all is that my imagination has no limits.2. Frei Otto,Shigeru Ban, Antonio Gaudi, Santiago Calatrava, Toyo Ito. 3. BOOKS: Blindness, Divina Commedia, The Pigeon, Sangre, El Tunel, La Peste, El Hombre Duplicado, The Cave, Faust. MOVIES: Amelie, The Final Cut, 50 First Dates, The Butterfly Effect, Mare Dentro,Forrest Gump. 4. I am currently working in an architectural office dedicated to the development of torism projects

Luiza Campana 1. Because I just love it 2. Zaha Hadid 3. The Art of Happiness 4. I have my own office

Gabriel Lara García Rojas 1. It's very complex to explain this, not only the social commitment that this profession implies, but i also like the humanistic side, refered to culture, antropology, art, that makes you dive into humanity. 4. I'am working at LAR+FR in the Soumaya museum

Rita Helayel 1. Honestly I find that architecture allows freedom in expressing oneself, imagination, creativity, and inspiration. Although you can be taught the basics in architecture but no one has the ability to teach you the above mentioned. Having these qualifications, I find myself in no place other than architecture. 2. Zaha Hadid!!! 4. Freelancing- Self Employment!

Luis Eduardo Guísar Benítez 2. Luis Barragán. Wang Shu. Reem Kollhaas. Enrique Norten. Kokkugia Studio, BIG. SANAA.

Grete Soosalu 1. I like the so-called architects' approach towards.. anything. 2. I preffer not to have one or few favourites. 3. Border State by Emil Tode - I guess most spellbinding book I've read as it is describing the viewpoint of a citizen of a "border state" (i.e. from Eastern-Europe, like Estonia) in West after the fall of the Iron Curtain. 4. This summer I have participated in a few architectural competitions with my friends. The next step would be applying for a job, probably outside of Estonia for an international experience.

Claudio Palavecino Llanos 1. To turn abstract ideas into real things which improve how we live. 2. I don't have a favorite architect; maybe i don´t like to have a favorite architect, because I prefer make my own knowldge from many sources, not only architects or buildings. 3. Citizen Kane 4. Thinking - Doing - Working!

Simionescu Oana Alexandra 1. because the architect is the coolest fusion between scientist and artist!..or so it seamed when i was 10 :) 2. BIG, HERZOG&DeMEURON, SANAA, etc. 3. can't decide on a favourite book/studio ghibli movies 4. just finished school...on my way to win some competitions :)

Carlos M. Mena Porras 1. I think that Architecture can help people to get in a deeper contact with their sorroundings, with themselves and others, with the Earth, can help to acknowledge our living in the world, and how can people be better human beings, and by that help in the preservation of Earth. I believe in the good of people and how it can reflect in Architecture and by that in a better and more balanced dwelling environments. 2. dont have a favourite, but if I have to answer Alvaro Siza, and Peter Zumthor. 3. book, "In praise of shadows" by Jun Ichiro Tanizaki 4. Working as an architect

Dulce Adriana Luna Hernández 1. I want to be an architect because I want to make a difference in the way we experience how we feel spaces. I want to make a better way of life, because I think that no matter your social condition, to create a really nice desing and way of living. 2. My favourite architect is Zaha Hadid, because she is capable to make her ideas turn into reality. 3. My favourite book is "Ensayo sobre la ceguera" by Jose Saramago, and my favourite movie is "Le fabuleux destin d'Amélie Poulain" by Jean-Pierre Jeunet. 4. I am starting my own office with some friends. We have small projects but it is 100% satisfactory to do all by ourselves. We also organize some art visits in our town, we would like to make an art installation in a museum or somewhere in the city. And also we are interested in sustainable architecture and how to solve city common problems. specially living in such a big city.

Tiago Castelo Branco Lourenço 1. To actually participate in the construction of the world 2. Bernard Tschumi, Carlos Nelson Ferreira dos Santos, Éolo Maia, Jô Vasconcellos, Rem Koolhaas, Sylvio de Podestá. 3. Apologia da História de Marc Bloch, Sétimo Selo de Ingmar Bergman 4. Project Manager in a company of models, technical adviser with low-income communities, a professor in architecture school, Maíra's husband and father of Arthur

Dongchoul Park 1. nothing. Just I enjoy it It make me happy 2. BIG 3. secret / forrest gump 4. portfolio

Molly Hunker 1. Molly believes in design and it's ability to easily and immediately change a person's spatial and visual experience of a place. It's not elitist, it's not esoteric - it's an everyday experience for everyone, or should be. She is most interested in architecture fusion – how various art and body design fields (fashion design, product design, urban street art, advertising, etc) can cross-pollinate to produce something fresher, weirder, more curious, and more beautiful than any individual discipline. 4. Molly has just finished an installation for SPORTS, her design practice / collaboration with Gregory Corso. She is also working with the artist / designer Doug Aitken in Venice, California and is teaching an architecture studio at Woodbury University in Burbank, California.

Pedro Câmara 1. I hope onde day i can inspire and touch people through my design. this will make me a happy person. 2. Lina Bo Bardi | Paulo Mendes da Rocha | Tadao Ando | Álvaro Siza | Louis Kahn 3. book: 1984, George Orwell. movie: You and me and everyone we know, Miranda July | Jogos de Cena, Eduardo Coutinho 4. working at the office Architectus

Gunnar Ploner 1. We all live in space. But this space articulates itself in a very sophisticated way and shows topologically different characteristics and qualities. On the one hand architecture gives me the chance to unfold complex spatial configurations and to recognize inherent processes, hierarchies and organizing structures. That is the learning facet of architecture. On the other side I am really fascinated by the fact that it is possible to immediately influence space and environment. With the tools and instruments of architecture you can create conditions for the emergence of new spatial configurations and patterns. 4. As I am really motivated and interested in further urban research, I am putting much energy an effort in the further development of the Lagos Urban Research Group LURG.ORG. Beside this activity a couple of friends and I are working together as a design consultancy for architecture offices. In fall this year I am planning to go on a surfing boat trip to Indonesia.

Steven Schenk 2. Phidias, Sir John Soane, Sigurd Lewerentz 3. David Lynch movies 4. Studying at the Accademia di Architettura in Mendrisio, and doing an internship in Miller Maranta Architekten in Basel.

Julia Koerner 1. I enjoy exploring enigmatic spacial effects inspired by nature and biology. 2. Greg Lynn, Hani Rashid, Heran Diaz Alonso, Ross Lovegrove 3. Elecroma by Daft Punk, Avatar by James Cameron, Cremaster Cycle by Mephew Barney and animation videos by Lynn Fox, Chris Cunningham, Devein 4. Currently Senior Designer at Ross Lovegrove Studio in London,UK, as well as teaching workshops at LTH Lund, Sweden, at the Department of theoretical and applied Aesthetics and previously teaching assistant at the University of applied Arts Vienna, Austria, at the postgraduate program of Hernan Diaz Alonso. From oct 2010 onwards Architect in residency at MAK Los Angeles, US, Schindler Scolarship together with Adam Vukmanov. (www.sub-d.com)

Andrew Laufenberg 1. It is just something I have always loved to do. 2. Le Corbusier, Louis Kahn, Sevrre Fehn, it's an on going list. 4. Currently I am working at a small firm located in Milwaukee, Wisconsin.

Nazar V. Ratushynskyj 1. ... to try to create the ideal world ... 2. Antonio Sant'Elia, Frank Owen Gehry 3. Book's: John Twelve Hawks: "The Traveller", "The Dark River"; Carlos Ruiz Zafon "La Sombra Del Viento"; Albert Camus "The Plague" (La Peste). Movie's: The Godfather, Bella mafia, Prison Break. 4. I'm working on my doctoral studies now.

Fagner Marçal 1. As many other people all around the world, I believe I can contribute to build a better future. 4. Currently, I´m finishing my Master´s Thesis in Urban Planning having as object of study the relationships established between ephemeral artistic activities and public space. The methodology developed is being applied at Copacabana´s Beach as case study.

Rodrigo García González 1. I don't know yet if I want to be an architect 2. Alejandro Aravena, Gernot Minke, Shigeru Ban, Balkrishna Doshi 3. Noviembre (Achero Mañas) 4. Traveling

Meenakshi Chauhan 2. Tadao Ando, Richard Rogers, Behnisch Architects, Le Corbusier, Toyo Ito, Herzog & de Meuron 3. City of Djinns by William Dalrymple, SMLXL by Rem koolahs & Bruce Mau, Indian Summer by Alex Von Tunzelmann

Alberto Andres Herrera Salas 1. I'm an architect because as a humanist profession, it allows the knowledge af all, providing the chance to make better desicions to guide the contruction of social identities. 2. Herzog & de meuron y Mansilla &Tuñon, are studios where architecture is an evolution and investigation process in which ideas are taken to the imaginary limit. 3. Phylogenesis, Foa's Ark and "La Clave Gaudi", books that show each in their own way, since architects througout years build pasions by means of reason. 4. I work as an architect in MGP Architecture and Town planning, a recognized architecture studio, with relevant projects national and international.

1. WHY I WANT TO BE AN ARCHITECT / 2. FAVORITE ARCHITECT / 3. FAVORITE BOOK OR MOVIE / 4. WHAT I AM DOING NOW

Diana Carolina Rojas Galan 1. I'm an architect because the posibility to build legitímate societies is in architects' hands and minds. 2. Herzog & de Meuron y Diller & Scofidio + Renfro, because I like the way in which they develop projects, since the beginning until the end. 3. 10x10, the opportunity to look at the different sides of architecture, affirming the idea of no absolute true about a project's resolution. 4. I am exercising my work at a company dedicated to construction, design and consulting.

Mateusz Lesniak 1. to experience the delight of creation 2. Sverre Fehn 3. The Picture of Dorian Gray by Oscar Wilde 4. working as an architect assistant

Jessica Stuecklin 1. I want my passion for architectural design to contribute to a pleasant environment. 2. Sigurd Lewerentz 3. Bertold Brecht: The good Woman of Setzuan, Lars von Trier: Dancer in the Dark 4. I am working for Bearth & Deplazes Architekten (CH).

Ulla Prami 1. To improve my skills of making decisions 2. Édouard Francois, Clenn Murcutt 3. Astanga Yoga by Gregor Maehle, El cine de Pedro Almodóvar by Nuria Vidal 4. Expecting a baby

Ethem Ovunc Tar 1. I want to have fun while working and work while having fun. 2. Zumthor, Nouvel, Perrault, Herzog, De Meuron 3. Le Petit Prince.

Piyas Choudhuri 1. Architecture and urbanism have started a process of learning for me. Understanding the process of formation of cities, buildings,psychology of people and an idea to build. I have realized that man is known only and only for the work he does. One needs to understand that a city or a building is like a seed that we sow and we have to nurture it, take care of it at every stage for the rest of our life. 2. Rem Koolhaas, BV Doshi, Tado Ando, Corbusier 3. When rivers run dry, Jalyatra, We are like that only, Water urbanism, Thet fable book of utopias 4. Currently working as an urban design under the guidance of Prof. BV Doshi and Prof. Rajeev Kathpalia at Vasta Shilpa Consultants, Sangath, Ahmedabad.

Chuchu Wei 1. I love, therefore I am. Just do it! 2. Le Corbusier /Rem Koolhaas /Jiakun Liu 3. BOOK:The Image of the City/Gone With The Wind MOVIE:The Shawshank Redemption 4. I'm studying for the graduate degree in Huazhong university of science and technology (HUST) **Yiqiao Li** 1. Because I love architecture,tying to put my minds becoming buildings with all of my emotion. 2. Norman Foster 3. Pearl Harbor 4. I am an architect at China Southwest Architectural Design & Research Institute Corp.Ltd.

Elizabeth López Romero 1. Being an architect to me, means to get our hands to make dreams come true; be able to create: spaces, times, and different sensations. How?... with a volume, a shadow a texture, mixing colors, etc. 2. Well, actually I don't have only one... Some of my favorites are: Enrique Norten, Bernardo Gómez Pimienta, Javier Sordo Madaleno, Renzo Piano, Santiago Calatrava, Cesar Pelli, Peter Zumthor, Richard Meier & Tadao Ando. 4. I'm working at ACFHEL company in Mexico City.

Aezad Alam 1. Architects make extraordinary contributions to the built environment. And as a result their designs positively affect the social and cultural issues. Therefore I want to offer my skills and knowledge to this prestigious field. 2. Thom Mayne - Morphosis 3. Fight Club - Chuck Palahniuk 4. With a team of student architects, I am designing a primary school in remote village of Umbissa in Cameroon, Cenral-West Africa.

Wijaya Suryanegara Yapeter 1. I want to create a design that can give an advantages for people and for the environment. I love to draw, design and travelling so it makes me love architecture. I have a passion in architecture and i have a plan to continuing my education to the higher level, i'm planning to take a postgraduate degree major in urban planning and design. I really have a curiousity about urban design, to designing a better city for my country, Indonesia 2. Tadao Ando, Bjarke Ingels, Frank Gehry, Fumihiko Maki, Renzo Piano 3. Books: BIG:Yes is More; Gehry; The Space of Encounter; Bernard Tschumi: Tschumi Event Cities 2 & 3. Movie: Sketches of Frank Gehry Star Wars, Inception. 4. Now i work as a freelance architect, designing a couple private residence in Surabaya, Indonesia. Also i frequently participating in design competition, either it's national and international competition.

Indira Sari Asima Naibaho 1. I want to be an architect because I love travelling and I am intrigued by buildings, architecture and their environment. I like to create, design, and construct the fabulous buildings that are an integral part of our lives. I want to be a person that not only have a large amount of creativity and imagination, but a tremendous amount of technical knowledge as well. Training as an architect is a long process requiring extensive education but the results are well worth it. :) I also want to built my own country, Indonesia, to be a better living environment. :) 2. Kisho Kurokawa - because of his symbiosis architecture theory. Tadao Ando - has brilliant idea upgrading his own country with his green design. Bjarke Ingels Group (BIG) - has the most interesting design process that I'm familiar with. 3. I love Science-fiction and Fantasy in every their form. For me they represent the highest & free expression of power of the mind to imagine the future and make dreams come true. My favourite movies/books are Lord of the Rings, Avatar, Harry Potter, Inception (only to mention a few) and also The Philosophy of Symbiosis book (by Kisho Kurokawa) 4. I am currently working as a junior architect freelancer in capital city Jakarta, Indonesia. And I also work as a classic piano teacher. Music and architecture are along together so well.. :D

Manasseri Ezequiel 1. I wanted to be an architect because I always had a love of creating, drawing, game volume, the diversity of form ... inventing new things. And I found a career in architecture in the mix of all those things. 2. I appreciate many architects, and I admire those who seek innovation, the new search, and the needs of today's world. I like the complete architect, one who can express any idea or thought through the paper, a model, a painting, or text. I have no one in particular, but I appreciate those legendary architects and those who remain in day to day. Koolhaas, Miralles / Tagliabue, Zaha, and many more. 3. I have no favorite book. My favorite movie is Gladiator and The Departed.

Ruann van der Westhuizen 1. Architecture and urban design has the potential to dramatically influence our environment. 2. Renzo Piano 3. Atlas Shrugged 4. Working as an architect.

Demostenez Mori Pelaez 1. I think things on my country and the world can be better, i hope to be an architect is a way to do. 2. Glenn Murcutt 3. Art History (E. H. Gombrich) 4. a magister of infraestructure and landscape on Santiago of Chile

Godchance Gamaliel 1. Why! as a matter of fact I'm in love with the entire design issue, cars, furniture, fashion etc. By being an Architect, I see it as the only way that I can put my stamp on the ground that can stick there for decades, that people live in, look at and talk about. I consider myself very lucky to have fallen into this. Given the environment that raised me, Architecture is really not a a famous field of study, even my close relative and friends still call me "Engineer"! I cant picture myself doing any other business with this same passion. I believe this to be a blessing, having the talent and getting the chance to exercise it. 2. Renzo Piano, I. M. Pei 3. The Matrix 4. I'm hired in one of the registered local Architectural firm called PSM Architects Co Ltd, of which i started working as part time since my forth year of study 2008. I started working as a full time since January this year. By now I have been exposed to various projects among them being, Office building - Under construction, housing project - under construction - AIC church building - Proposal, Mosque building - Proposal and more recently an Orthopedic hospital building still in design stages. My role in the office is to design and prepare presentations. I also regularly go to the construction sites during inspections. I have gained a great deal of experience and trust and now I work with very minimum supervision. I wish to go for further studies in master programs in a year or two when the opportunity comes. I want to add more technological advanced construction techniques in terms of structure and materials into my thinking and the cheaper ways of doing them. I also want to learn more on how other architects perform outside my country.

Rakan Ayyoub 1. urban designer 3. favorite movie : Amelie Favorite Book :war-Sebastian Junger

1. WHY I WANT TO BE AN ARCHITECT / 2. FAVORITE ARCHITECT / 3. FAVORITE BOOK OR MOVIE / 4. WHAT I AM DOING NOW

Huang Zhexuan 1. Architects offer people a better condition of living 2. SANAA, Peter Zumthor 3. the Fountainhead/Lock,Stock and two smoking barrels 4. Doing my master program at KTH

Cheng Wei Lo 1. I want to be an architect because I believe that architecture is a great career. Furthermore, not only provides people with basic shelter, but also architecture have to consider what kind of impact on this community. 2. My favourite architect is Neil Leach who is an architect and theorist. has taught at a number of institutions worldwide, including the Architectural Association in London, the Dessau Institute Dessau, Germany, and Columbia University. 3. my favourite book is THE Architecture of the city ,the author is Aldo Rossi. 4. I attend school with my master's degree. And now, I pay attention with processing , a visualize software for design, with java language.

Noorain A Ahmed 1. There are many aspects to architecture, while on one hand we can strive to achieve the most difficult of feats, build the tallest towers, and longest bridges, on the other hand we can choose to respond to the need of humanity and earth-which is as challenging a task and an important one too. I believe that design has the ability to make a difference in people's lives and I believe that as architects we must do our bit to give back to earth... to humanity. 2. Architecture for Humanity, Michael Reynolds, Laurie Baker, Louis Khan 3. Catcher in the Rye, Eragon series, Design like you give a damn! 4. Currently i'm looking for opportunities where I can learn and explore the possibilities of 'Building with Earth', and also want to be involved in Humanitarian works. Also very eager to do some hands on work, get some real experience, build something - put the academic knowledge to test!!!

Autthawut Kruethongsri 1. because i want to make the city more beautiful. 2. Zaha Hadid, Rem Koolhaas 3. Three Kingdoms 4. work at "Tandem Architecture 2001." office in Bangkok.

Monon bin Yunus 1. To create an impact, even if it's the slightest, in the architectural world. 2. Louis I. Khan, Peter Zumthor, Carlo Scarpa, Geoffrey Bawa. 3. Movie: Perfume, Stardust, 300, Forrest gump, 3 Idiots, Tare zameen par. 4. I am currently working under architect Kashef mahaboob chowdhury in his architecture studio- " URBANA".

Sahar Nivi 1. I want to be an architect because I can show my ideas and imaginations. I can create new things. I like designing and innovations; also I can be useful for our society by designing well & improving its features 2. Santiago Calaterava 4. I am graduated & work on architectural projects includes: designing, searching & investigating. Also I attend the project management courses.

Aly Ahmed kamal Soliman 1. To form a new life with a new unique way of use , Building people dreams , Sketching a new world 2. Hassan Fathy, Norman Foster, Daniel Libeskind, Zaha Hadid, BIG 3. books: A Tale Of Two Cities Concept Annual book. movies: National treasure, Ocean 11, The League Of Extra-Ordinary Men, Omar Al-Mokhtar 4. I have just graduated and i am studying for M.Sc working as a teacher assistant in ocotber 6 university

Rory Felix 1. Architecture is everything is my life. The drug experience is to design, design is lost in our own confusion. The architecture is a preface of events that we do not determine the accuracy of the universe. That is architecture. 2. Los arquitectos que influyeron en mi son: Thom Mayne, Zaha Hadid, Wolf Prix, Le Corbusier, DJ Tiësto. 3. The Apology of Socrates, A Beautiful Mind. 4. Design a house and now I'm teaching assistantship at the university.

Luis Estuardo Flores Hernández 1. solo quiero ser un arquitecto diseñador de cualquier proyecto, en participación con otros colegas, aunque los proyectos que mas me apasionan son los de vivienda. 2. Richard Neutra y Louis Kahn y contemporáneo, Luis Respreto 3. mi película favorita es el caso Thomas Crown, y mis libros favoritos son los de historia tanto de arquitectura como de la vida cotidiana de mi país. 4. diseño un café bar en una vivienda que posee una cabaña, y un jardín grande.

Andrè Geoffroy 1. I would like to design hightech estructures that responds to different condition. It´s very important to me to contribute to Architecture´s evolution. 2. I don´t have a favorite one. I don´t think I can admire just one because I admire different aspects of each one. I like the process and the approach to developing projects. of MVRDV, the research method and the final forms of Greg Lynn and the greats constructions that Rem Koolhaas is able to take from theory to reality. 3. when I was a child amazed me Robotech series, how human beings were able to adapt and live in other space in these great design spaceships capable to change their shapes. 4. I improve my skills as an Architect and I am seeking ways for to continue my studies and investigation in another countries.

Mehbuba Tune Uzra 2. Louis I Kahn 3. Matir Moina, Scent of a woman, Brave Heart, 3 Idiots 4. I am working as an architect at Tania Karim N.R. Khan & Associates in Dhaka www.tknrk.com/

Stephanie Monieca 1. I want to be an architect because I love art and architecture. For me, architecture is a special form of art combined with logical thoughts and relationship between architects and the client or a society. Then it's a real happiness to see a design becomes real especially if it can satisfy people... 2. Louis I. Kahn... :) Local one : Y. B. Mangunwijaya 3. Book : Dan Brown and Kahlil Gibran's. Movie : Forrest Gump, Ice Age. 4. Freelance designer... Learn and experience as much as I can. Prepare myself to reach my dream to have a design studio with my friends and travel to many countries, see the world...

Yinghua Wen 1. Space is more interesting than the others. 2. Sou Fujimoto. 3. Star Wars, Mulholland Drive... 4. A master student of TUDelft, the Netherlands.

Josh Gothard 1. I have always appreciated good design and find a lot of enjoyment in working to create it myself. I never stop asking myself why something was designed a certain way and could I have done it better. 4. I am currently about to spend a year sailing and traveling around the world. My concentration will be on the architecture of the many port cities and villages around the worlds oceans.

Alejandra de la Rosa 1. I want to be an interior architect because I believe that spaces express a lifestyle. We are in constant interaction with different environments and as a consequence are affected by them. Designing is a way of expression and it contributes to better living experiences. As a designer you have the opportunity to create different atmospheres that express individuality and contribute to the balance of the human interventions. 2. My favorite architect's are Jacques Herzog and Pierre de Meuron. I find it interesting how they find balance between architecture and nature by combining texture and natural materials in a very unique way. 3. My favorite book is The Shadow of the Wind by Carlos Ruiz Safón. My favorite movie is The Fifth Element, 1997, Luc Besson. Director. 4. I am currently living in New York City continuing my studies in Interior Design at Parsons, The New School of Design and at NYU. I am interested in retail design and showrooms, and with no doubt this city has shown me very creative and innovative designs. I've also kept learning about designing childcare environments, which relates to my undergraduate project, complementing it with some theory at NYU. I plan to return to Mexico City this December, and look forward to applying this new knowledge at work.

Medina Spahiu 2. Richard Meier, Tadao Ando. Herzog & de Meuron 3. Peter Zumthor / Thinking Architecture, History of Architecture 4. I work in an architectural studio, and studying interior design.

Anna Vasof 1. Because i like to compose 2. Eisenman 3. 100 year loneliness / spring autumn winter summer and spring 4. I try to study further

Charles Rudi 1. Because I want to make my environment to be a better living. Create a good quality of space and make the urban more sustainable. 2. Renzo Piano, Glenn Murcutt 3. 'Into the wild' 4. looking for an ideal job beside designing home to my sister.

Omar Arshad Al Hafith 1. Building my country 2. Rasem Badran 3. Courtyard house : Past, Present and future 4. studying Master

Dustin Willis 1. I want to be an architect because it allows multiple creative outlets that can influence and affect society. I would like to use these outlets as a way to improve interaction with the urban environment as well as with other members of society. 2. My favorite architect is Peter Zumthor. 3. My favorite book is House of Leaves by Mark Z. Danielewski. My favorite movie is A Clockwork Orange. 4. After graduating in May 2010, I moved to Green River, Utah to work as an AmeriCorps VISTA for the summer. While there, I worked for the Economic Progress Instigation Center (EPIcenter) on affordable housing and renovation projects. I am currently back in Atlanta, and seeking my next employment opportunity.

Caio Calafate 2. Paulo mendes da Rocha, Alvaro Siza Vieira, Rem Koolhaas 3. SMLXL - Rem Koolhas, Helvetica 4. Working at the office Fabrica Arquitetura http://fabricaarquiteturario.com/ Editor of Noz Magazine, www.revistanoz.com

---

Erick Capeleti Carbone 1. It's a real pleasure designing spaces that are not only 'appropriated', but specials.2. The Nature. 3. Book: 1984 Movie: Rear Window 4. Senarezi arquitetos

---

Paula Ibarrondo 2. Rem Koolhaas, Enric Miralles, Coop Himmelblau, Morphosis, Libeskind, Eisenman.

Miguel Angel Quispe Mamani 1. Para sorprenderme como niño, para enamorarme perdidamente como adolescente, para disfrutar los sueños de juventud, para sentir la plenitud de de la vida como adulto, para tener recuerdos bohemios de anciano, y es que el arquitecto debe tener presente la atemporalidad de la vida al momento de recrear contenedores espaciales en medios naturales y urbanos. 2. Enric Miralles definitivamente. Jorge Urquidi gran urbanista de la ciudad que habito Cochabamba. Edwin Santragens Buro Sant en Co por los paisajes recreados. 3. Estambul, ciudad y recuerdos, de Orhan Pamuk por el arraigo de un arquitecto a su ciudad desde la infancia. Metropolis dirigida por Fritz Lang. 4. Trabajo en la firma Zeballos Bialet, como adjunto al arquitecto Enrique Zeballos en el diseño supervisión del edificio Torre Lafayette en Cochabamba. Además de estar ejerciendo la auxiliatura de docencia en el Taller 5° de la LINEA A de la Facultad de Arquitectura de la Universidad Mayor de San Simón.

Richard Nelson Mamani Callisaya 1. Porque, Ahí encontre un refugio perfecto, ahí encontre un mundo único para soñar y diseñar el futuro mejor, ahí encontré para plasmar mis ideas, mis creaciones...y más, tengo una tarea un proyecto inacabado de mi ciudad que se llama Cochabamba.2. La primera mujer ganadora del Premio de Pritzker para la Arquitectura en la historia de sus 26 años, Zaha Hadid (1950-) ha definido un radical nuevo acercamiento a la arquitectura por crear edificios, como el Centro de Rosenthal para el Contemporáneo Art en Cincinnati, con múltiples puntos de la perspectiva y se ha fragmentado la geometría para evocar el caos de vida moderna. Arquitectura; Carlos Villagómez Paredes, Licenciatura en Arquitectura: Facultad de Arquitectura y Arte. Universidad Mayor de San Andrés. La Paz, Diseñador Urbano, 3. Croquis, porque tiene un perfil más alto y publicaciones prestigiosas en el mundo arquitectónico. Avatar, porque me encanta la ciencia ficción. 4. Desde el despacho de mi casa Quillacollo-Cochabamba, diseño una casa colonial privada para la empresa y contructora "GUERRA". Fui encomendado para el siseño de una vivienda minimalista para la familia Quiroz. Soy asesor de un anteproyecto academico. Otorgo diseños cretivos de muebles en 3D para la empresa "Muebles Cofort" Hago diseños meritorios para mi sociedad y las personas de escasos recursos.

Lucio Riccobono 1. It is fasciating to shape Space, Time, Light, and with them human emotions and perception of reality but, above all, it is an ethical act. This difficult Art and Science at human service have no given facts. Proportion, Order, Balance, Control, Measure, Consistency are all continuous achievements. Being an architect is to accept this challenge. 2. I believe in the values of History and Memory. Only through the awareness and strength of being part of a stream, of being rooted in the material and building culture of our land, it will be possible to build the Future with socially legitimate transformations. Every architect has left his mark of continuity or innovation. Each personal path of growth is fundamental for all of those who want to pursue this profession. Masters like Mies van der Rohe, Wrights, Loos, Kahn, Le Courbusier are certainly in my personal Top Five Hit. 3. I love Science-fiction and Fantasy in every their form. For me they represent the highest and free expression of power of the mind to imagine the Future and make dreams come true. My favourite movies/books are Blade Runner, Star Trek Sagas, The Fifth Element, Aliens, Dune, Brazil, Lord of the rings, Avatar, only to mention a few. 4. I am working as an architect and engineer in Bari, Italy. My preference would be to work in a large International Studio to grow my experience.

Giuliana Frau 1. because I love architecture and I love designing spaces that improve the lives of men 2. http://www.stevenholl.com/ 4. I am preparing for competitions

---

Rafael Campos Rangel 1. To modify the ignorance of the people. 2. Marcelo Ferraz, Francisco Fanucci, OMA (Rem Koolhaas), Daniel Libeskind, Paulo Mendes da Rocha, BIG, Solano Benitez, Triptyque... 4. own office: ATO4 Arquitetura

---

Anand Sonecha 1. To serve the Race 2. B.V.Doshi,Tadao Ando, Luis Barragan. 4. I am working as an Architect in Sangath, Ahmedabad with Prof B.V.Doshi

Alina Turekulova 1. To share my ideas and fantasies with people in order to make them a little bit happier 2. Yakov Chernihov, El Lissitzky, Rem Koolhaas, Frank Gehry, Paolo Soleri 3. Woman in the Dunes (Kabo Abe), Le Spleen de Paris (Charles Baudelaire) 4. Enjoying every moment...

David Cremer 1. Someone once asked me how I felt about being in school for a profession that depends on the continued growth of the rich. I had no response. It's true that architects have traditionally relied on providing sensuous forms for those with money, designing skyscrapers for commercial districts or building second homes for the well traveled. It's ironic that those who need the shelter most are often ignored. It is also ironic that many of the most famous modern buildings are those that are essentially unnecessary: summer homes, modern art museums, high-end residential skyscrapers. I am a firm believer in the power of architecture for all. I do not want my skills wasted on the unnecessary. After five years of school, I now have a response: Architecture is altruistic. It's easy to design a trendy sculpture that will be dated within ten years, just as it is easy to only read the stocks column in the newspaper. But it is far more difficult to work within social implications and design for the ignored minority. I want to use my training for the betterment of society, I want to prove that architecture does not depend on the growth of the upper class. 2. Peter Zumthor is currently my favorite designer though David Adjaye holds a close second. Both have a mastery of light and form that I hope to someday emulate. 3. Of the literature I've read, my favorite novel is To Kill a Mockingbird; my favorite movie is Eternal Sunshine of the Spotless mind. 4. I am currently living in Connecticut, working with Habitat for Humanity and Americorps as a construction coordinator. I work with the many daily volunteers, as well as the future homeowners, and train them in the varied tasks required to fully erect a home. I'm currently overseeing the construction of three different houses, as well as providing secondary architectural services to the in-house architect when needed.

Ma. Teresa Vera Ramirez 1. Ya me he titulado. 2. Lopez guerra. 3. Arquitectura, ciudad y medio ambiente 4. Buscando donde estudiar un posgrado

---

YoungJoon Choi 2. Adriaan Geuze, Peter Walker, Michel Desvigne, PARKKIM 3. The Royal Tenenbaums, The Darjeeling Limited by Wes Anderson 4. SWA LA

FAVORITE ARCHITECTS MENTIONED BY THE PARTICIPANTS OF ARCHIPRIX INTERNATIONAL

Rem Koolhaas (50)
Zaha Hadid (42)
Herzog & De Meuron (34)
Tadao Ando (32)
Renzo Piano (30)
Peter Zumthor (28)
Le Corbusier (27)
Louis I. Kahn (24)
Santiago Calatrava (23)
BIG (20)
MVRDV (20)
Toyo Ito (18)
Norman Foster (15)
Jean Nouvel (15)
Luis Barragán (14)
SANAA (14)
Alvaro Siza (12)
Alvar Aalto (11)
Frank Gehry (11)
Mies van der Rohe (11)
Frank Lloyd Wright (11)
EMBT (10)
Antonio Gaudí (10)
Daniel Liebeskind (10)
Glenn Murcutt (9)
Steven Holl (9)
Paulo Mendes da Rocha (8)
Richard Rogers (8)
Peter Eisenman (7)
Archigram (6)
Foreign Office Architects (6)
Thom Mayne (6)
Oscar Niemeyer (6)
Lina Bo Bardi (5)
Adriaan Geuze (5)
Greg Lynn (5)
Richard Meier (5)
Rogelio Salmona (5)
Kenzo Tange (5)
Shigeru Ban (4)
David Chipperfield (4)
Charles Correa (4)
Hassan Fathy (4)
Sou Fujimoto (4)
Massimiliano Fuksas (4)
Carlo Scarpa (4)
Eduardo Souto de Moura (4)
Bernard Tschumi (4)
David Adjaye (3)
Architecture for Humanity (3)
Mario Botta (3)
Alberto Campo Baeza (3)
Yung Ho Chang (3)
Coop Himmelb(l)au (3)
Diller & Scofidio (3)
Balkrishna Doshi (3)
Kengo Kuma (3)
El Lissitzky (3)
Adolf Loos (3)
Gordon Matta-Clark (3)
Rafael Moneo (3)
Nox (3)
I.M. Pei (3)
Dominique Perrault (3)
Aldo Rossi (3)
UN Studio (3)
Rasem Badran (2)
Laurie Baker (2)
Geoffrey Bawa (2)
Behnisch Architects (2)
Bolles&Wilson (2)
Yves Brunier (2)
Roberto Burle Marx (2)
Gerardo Caballero (2)
Pierre Chareau (2)
Michel Desvignes (2)
Fuksas (2)
Sevrre Fehn (2)
Buckminster Fuller (2)
Future Systems (2)
Hundertwasser (2)
Imhotep (2)
JDS Architects (2)
Kulka (2)
Sigurd Lewerentz (2)
Edwin Lutyens (2)
Fumihiko Maki (2)
Richard Neutra (2)
Enrique Norten (2)
Frei Otto (2)
Cedric Price (2)
Wolf Prix (2)
R.C.R arquitectos (2)
Reiser+Umemoto (2)
Wang Shu (2)
Giuseppe Terragni (2)
DJ Tiësto (2)
URBANUS Architects (2)
Simón Vélez (2)
Ken Yeang (2)
Zhang YongHe (2)
Abalos & Herreros (1)
Hitoshi Abe (1)
William Alsop (1)
Emilio Ambasz (1)
Jun Aoki (1)
Alejandro Aravena (1)
Vilanova Artigas (1)
Alexander Asadov (1)
Asymptote (1)
Atelier Van Lieshout (1)
Campos Baeza (1)
Jaap Bakema (1)
Cecil Balmond (1)
b-architecten (1)
Carlos Barjas Milan (1)
Barney and Jaime Cardenas (1)
Sergusson Bates (1)
baumschlager & eberle (1)
Jaime Beltran (1)
Solano Benitez (1)
Guilermo Bermudez (1)
Jaap van den Bout (1)
Bow Wow (1)
Marcel Breuer (1)
Aleksander Brodsky (1)
Brodsky (1)
Will Bruder (1)
Fillippo Bruneleschi (1)
Erik Bryggman (1)
Angelo Bucci (1)
Gion Antoni Caminada (1)
Caruso St John (1)
Yakov Chernihov (1)
Darius Ciuta (1)
Constructivism (1)
Hafeez Contractor (1)
Ricciotti Corajoud (1)
Neil Denari (1)
Heran Diaz Alonso (1)
Eladio Dieste (1)
Hans Dollgast (1)
Dutch pragmatism and irony (1)
Jorge Elton (1)
Wilkinson Eyre (1)
Francisco Fanucci (1)
Carlos Ferrater (1)
Marcelo Ferraz (1)
Carlos Nelson Ferreira dos Santos (1)
Édouard Francois (1)
Yona Friedman (1)
Mahatma Gandhi (1)
God (1)
Bruce Goff (1)
Bernardo Gómez Pimienta (1)
Michael Graves (1)
Grimshaw Architects (1)
Lopez Guerra (1)
John Habraken (1)
Itsuko Hasegawa (1)
Anna Heringer (1)
Ludwig Hilberseimer (1)
Raymond Hood (1)
Sauerbruch Hutton (1)
Seung Hyo-Sang (1)
Rafael Iglesia (1)
H. Imawan (1)
Junya Ishigami (1)
Mazharul Islam (1)
Arata Isozaki (1)
Jensen & Skodvin (1)
Philip Johnson (1)
Bernard Khoury (1)
Waro Kishi (1)
Klein Dythham Architecture (1)
Marcio Kogan (1)
Kokkugia Studio (1)
John Körmeling (1)
Tom Kundig (1)
Kisho Kurokawa (1)
L. L.Savina (1)
Lacaton & Vassal (1)
Peter Latz (1)
Bernard Lauriol (1)
John Lautner (1)
Neil Leach (1)
Leeser (1)
Francisco Leiva Iborra (1)
Lelé (1)
Leonidov (1)
CJ Lim (1)
Jiakun Liu (1)
Leandro V. Locsin (1)
Michelangelo di Lodovico (1)
Ross Lovegrove (1)
Kevin Lynch (1)
Neil M (1)
Éolo Maia (1)
Y. B. Mangunwijaya (1)
Francisco Manosa (1)
Mansilla & Tuñon (1)
Takasaki Masaharu (1)
Aires Mateus (1)
Mayalin (1)
Melnikov (1)
Buonarroti Michelangelo (1)
Gernot Minke (1)
Sanjay Mohe (1)
Morphosis (1)
Mother Nature (1)
Michael Mussotter (1)
MUST (1)
N+B Architectes (1)
Edward Ng (1)
NL Architects (1)
Juan O´Gorman (1)
Off the Road/103,8MHz (1)
Office Da (1)
Valerio Olgiati (1)
Kas Oosterhuis (1)
Field Operations (1)
Paisajes Emergentes (1)
Frits Palmboom (1)
Mario Pani (1)
Fabio Páramo (1)
PARKKIM (1)
John Pawson (1)
Pawson (1)
Cesar Pelli (1)
Phidias (1)
Walter Pichler (1)
Reima Pietilä (1)
Manuel Piqueras Cotolí (1)
Jose Plecnik (1)
Sylvio de Podestá (1)
Ricardo Porro (1)
Christian de Portzamparc (1)
Karel Prager (1)
Madhura Prematilleke (1)
Richard Price (1)
Franco Purini (1)
S. Radic (1)
Pedro Ramirez Vazquez (1)
Hani Rashid (1)
Afonso Reidy (1)
Renfro (1)
Luis Respreto (1)
Michael Reynolds (1)
Michael Rojkind (1)
Eero Saarinen (1)
Antonio Sant'Elia (1)
Edwin Santragens (1)
Y. Saputra (1)
Karl F. Schinkel (1)
Javier Senosain (1)
Ho-Sang Seung (1)
Buonarroti Simoni (1)
Situationists (1)
Smithsons (1)
John Soane (1)
Paolo Soleri (1)
Javier Sordo Madaleno (1)
Kevin Stevens (1)
Virgilio Suárez (1)
SungYong (1)
Marina Tabassum (1)
Yoshio Taniguchi (1)
Bruno Taut (1)
Pierre Tourre (1)
Enrique Triana (1)
Triptyque... (1)
Tschernichow (1)
Han Tümertekin (1)
Felipe Uribe de Bedout (1)
Jorge Urquidi (1)
Utkin (1)
Livio Vacchini (1)
Jô Vasconcellos (1)
Topy Vasquez (1)
Carlos Villagómez Paredes (1)
Carlos Raul Villanueva (1)
Peter Walker (1)
Noero Wolff (1)
Lebbeus Woods (1)
Tokujin Yoshioka (1)
Jose Maria V. Zaragoza (1)
Cino Zucchi (1)